The Management of Non-Governmental Development Organizations

International and local NGOs have moved centre stage in the fight against poverty and are now seen as an important element of 'civil society', a concept which has been given increasing importance by global policy makers.

Drawing upon current research in non-profit management, development management and management theory, this new edition of a highly successful textbook explores the activities, relationships and internal structure of the NGO. David Lewis develops a composite approach to NGO management that makes it possible to analyse the distinctive, complex challenges these organizations face. Key issues and debates include:

- the challenging global context of development cooperation
- trends in international development assistance
- the issues of NGO accountability, governance and participation
- the role of partnership between NGOs and the government and business sectors
- the changing concepts and practices that NGOs work with
- judging the effectiveness of NGO work
- organizational culture and organizational learning in NGOs
- dealing with complexity and uncertainty.

With up-to-date case studies throughout, a throughly revised page design and website with student and lecturer resources to support the text this fully updated edition of *The Management of Non-Governmental Development Organizations* is essential reading for all students, academics and professionals concerned with NGO management.

David Lewis is reader in Social Policy at the London School of Economics. An anthropologist by training, he undertakes research on development policy issues mainly in South Asia, and has been a consultant for a range of NGOs including Save the Children Fund, Oxfam and the Bangladesh Rural Advancement Committee (BRAC).

The Management of Non-Governmental Development Organizations

Second edition

David Lewis

Routledge
Taylor & Francis Group

LONDON AND NEW YORK

First edition published 2001
by Routledge
2 Park Square, Milton Park, Abingdon, Oxon OX14 4RN

Simultaneously published in the USA and Canada
by Routledge
270 Madison Ave, New York, NY 10016

Second edition published 2007

Routledge is an imprint of the Taylor & Francis Group, an informa business

Typeset in Perpetua and Bell Gothic by
Florence Production Ltd, Stoodleigh, Devon
Printed and bound in Great Britain by
TJ International Ltd, Padstow, Cornwall

British Library Cataloguing in Publication Data
A catalogue record for this book is available from the British Library

Library of Congress Cataloging in Publication Data
 Lewis, David
   The management of non-governmental development organizations/
 David Lewis. – 2nd ed.
      p. cm.
   Includes bibliographical references and index.
   1. Non-governmental organizations – Management.   I. Title.
   HD62.6.L49 2006
   338.90068–dc22   2006024243

ISBN10: 0–415–37092–2 (hbk)
ISBN10: 0–415–37093–0 (pbk)

ISBN13: 978–0–415–37092–9 (hbk)
ISBN13: 978–0–415–37093–6 (pbk)

Contents

List of illustrations   viii
Preface to the second edition   xi
Acknowledgements   xii
List of abbreviations   xiii

Introduction   1

1   The NGO management debate   6
     Introduction   7
     Concept of management   17
     Synthesizing an approach to NGO management   30
     Conclusion   32

Part I   THE THEORY OF NGO MANAGEMENT   35

2   Contexts, histories and concepts   37
     Introduction   38
     The rise of NGOs in development   38
     The changing policy context   41
     Terminological muddles   43
     Problems of defining NGOs   46
     The histories of NGOs   49
     NGOs and 'civil society'   53
     From civil society to the 'third sector'   67
     Conclusion   71

3   NGOs and development   73
     Introduction   74
     NGOs and the 'aid industry'   74

CONTENTS

The changing face of development aid   *78*
NGOs and the contexts of 'development' and 'relief'   *84*
Analysing NGO roles: implementers, catalysts and partners   *88*
Effectiveness: are NGOs any good at what they do?   *95*
Conclusion   *100*

4   Culture, ambiguity and NGO management   102
Introduction   *103*
NGO cultural attitudes to management   *103*
Organization theory   *105*
Anthropological perspectives   *121*
Conclusion   *125*

PART II   THE PRACTICE OF NGO MANAGEMENT   127

5   Advocacy and Service delivery   129
Introduction   *130*
Relationships between service delivery and advocacy   *130*
Service delivery: means or end?   *131*
NGOs and advocacy: strategies for structural change   *143*
Role of innovation in NGO management   *153*
Evaluation, impact and 'scaling up'   *158*
Conclusion   *161*

6   NGOs and the management of relationships   163
Introduction   *164*
A framework for managing relationships   *165*
NGO relations with communities   *170*
NGO relations with government   *172*
NGOs and the business sector   *177*
NGOs and international development agencies   *182*
The discourse of 'partnership'   *185*
Conclusion   *188*

7   The dynamics of internal management   189
Introduction   *190*
Third sector management research   *192*
Internal management   *198*
Capacity building   *205*
Organizational change and NGOs   *209*
NGOs and information management   *213*
Conclusion   *215*

8   Conclusion: Understanding NGO management   216
     Introduction   217
     Three approaches to NGO management   217
     The composite model   218
     Muddying the waters: hybridity and ambiguity   221
     Growth of organizational and policy complexity   224
     Looking forward   227
     Conclusion   228

Appendix: Some useful NGO management websites   230
Glossary   232
Notes   235
Bibliography   243
Index   272

Illustrations

FIGURES

Chart 1   Chapter map   2
Chart 2   NGOs as a subcategory of third sector organizations and 'NGDOs' as a subcategory of NGOs   4

1.1   A conceptual framework: four interrelated areas of the NGO management challenge   16
6.1   A framework for strategic NGO management   165

TABLES

2.1   The myriad of NGO acronyms and labels   45
5.1   A framework for assessing NGO campaign impacts   153
6.1   Contrasting characteristics of 'active' and 'dependent' partnerships   186
8.1   A composite framework for understanding NGO management   219
8.2   The sectoral origins of selected concepts relevant to NGO management   220

BOXES: NGOs IN ACTION

1.1   The 'business of helping'?: NGO management in the headlines   12
2.1   NGOs and the 'strengthening of civil society'   57
2.2   Informal social services, NGOs and social capital   59
2.3   How relevant is the concept of civil society to non-Western contexts?   62
2.4   NGOs and the context of post-socialism   64
2.5   NGOs and internal governance: crisis at the Kenya NGO Council   65
3.1   Official development assistance flows to NGOs   76
3.2   Some implications of the rights-based approach for NGO practice   80
3.3   New donor approaches with NGO funding: Manusher Jonno, Bangladesh   82
3.4   From emergency to development – building partner capacity in post-tsunami Sri Lanka   85

3.5	The Turkish earthquake and the NGO sector	87
3.6	Afghanistan: recent concerns about performance-based health partnerships	94
3.7	Lack of agreement and evidence about the effectiveness of NGOs	97
3.8	The 1997 DAC donor evaluation of NGO impact	97
4.1	Research traditions in organization theory	106
4.2	Gender and organizational culture	114
4.3	Learning and information management	118
4.4	NGOs and organizational development (OD) in Malawi	123
5.1	Growth of non-state actors in health service delivery in Africa	132
5.2	NGOs and international advocacy roles	144
5.3	The work of PDI in the Philippines: An SNGO combining advocacy and service delivery	148
5.4	An NGO innovates a post-harvest processing system for small-scale Indian hill farmers	155
5.5	The rise of participatory monitoring and evaluation (PM&E)	160
6.1	Improving accountability through self-regulation: complaint and redress mechanisms for NGOs	170
6.2	Confronting corruption: an NGO uses the Delhi Right to Information Act	175
6.3	Projeto Bagagem: NGOs and community-based tourism in Brazil	178
6.4	NGOs and corporate coffee partnerships	179
6.5	International and local private sector support to an NGO in Nepal through 'fair trade'	181
6.6	The pursuit of partnership by NNGOs: power, funding and the dilemmas of 'agency creation'	187
7.1	Contrasting organizational characteristics of two NGOs in South Asia	200
7.2	Issues in the 'internationalization' of NGO management	204
7.3	Challenging the North/South conventions of 'capacity building'	207
7.4	Government-sponsored NGO capacity building in Mexico	208
7.5	Internal processes and participation: learning within IIED	210

Preface to the second edition

When this book was first published in 2001, I had no idea that five years later I would have the opportunity to revise and expand it in order to meet increasing interest in the field of NGO management. It has been an enjoyable, if daunting task. I have chosen to maintain the same basic structure for this second edition, but I have updated the text and included new readings wherever I have judged it appropriate. When an older reference still seems relevant, or makes its point effectively, my policy has been to leave it alone. Aside from a selective updating of the text, then, the main addition to this second edition has been to draw upon the knowledge of a range of colleagues (some of them former students) working in the NGO sector around the world who have kindly provided me with material for additional and up-to-date information for text box examples of NGO management issues. Here I am particularly grateful to Markus Ketola, Alisha Myers, Mónica Tapia, Yaaminey Mubayi, Agnes Kithikii, Stephan Judge and Armine Ishkanian. I have also benefited greatly from useful feedback on the first edition of the book provided by colleagues who have used the book. These include Daniel D'Esposito, Alnoor Ebrahim, Jo Beall, Nidhi Srivinas, Diana Mitlin, Simon Batterbury, Paul Opoku-Mensah and Tony Bebbington. I particularly thank Ann Marie Thomson for her detailed feedback, and an anonymous referee. I'm also grateful for comments from students of Ann Marie's NGO course at the University of Indiana, including Shanna Dietz, Hansell Bourdon, Megan Hershey, Bobae Park and Rana DeBey and other anonymous contributors to my informal survey. I wish to thank Francesca Heslop and Emma Joyes at Routledge for their commitment to and encouragement with this second edition. Finally, I could not have written this book without the love, patience and support of my partner, Nazneen Kanji.

June 2006

Acknowledgements

There are a great many people who have helped me during the long, slow period of this book's emergence. At the London School of Economics (LSE), I would like to thank David Billis and Margaret Harris, former colleagues at the erstwhile Centre for Voluntary Organization (CVO) who first set me the challenge of writing about the management of NGOs; and Howard Glennerster, who encouraged me to write a book based on my NGO lectures. I would also like to thank Helmut Anheier, who in 1999 steered the CVO into a new phase at the LSE as the Centre for Civil Society (CCS), and more recently Jude Howell, director of the CCS since 2003, for her valuable advice and support. I owe a very large debt of gratitude to all the students who have taken the LSE Management of NGOs Masters course since 1995. I have learned a great deal from the perspectives of a diverse and experienced group from Asia, Africa, Latin America, North America, Europe and the Caribbean. I also learned a lot from co-teaching the course at various times with Arti Sinha, Nina Bowen, Hakan Seckinelgin, Jo de Berry and Nuno Themudo. Many of the comments of these NGO practitioners and researchers are, I hope, reflected or addressed in these pages, although the gaps, shortcomings and limitations are of course entirely my own.

Many visiting speakers and researchers at the LSE, in particular Harry Blair, Bruce Britton, John Clark, Mike Edwards, John Farrington, Marie-Claude Foster, John Hailey, David Hulme, Jacqui MacDonald, Allister McGregor, Roger Riddell, Salil Shetty, Graham Thom, Tina Wallace and Geof Wood, have over the years discussed many of these themes with me. I have also benefited from a lively group of PhD students over the years at the LSE, including Mônica Mazzer Barroso, Preecha Dechalert, Nandita Dogra, Paola Grenier, Marit Haug, Hammad Hundal, Sarah Lister, Nisrine Mansour, Tasneem Mowjee, Alejandro Martinez Natal, Ebenezer Obadare, Salma Shawa and Nuno Themudo. I would also like to thank many people in the NGO world who have given me the opportunity to observe or to work with NGOs in the field: F. H. Abed, Q. F. Ahmed, Shaheen Anam, Keiko Asato, A. M. R. Chowdhury, Aine Fay, Rick James, Mahbubul Karim, Aurea G. Miclat-Teves, 'Nibi Oloniyo and Md Shahabuddin are just a few. Finally, I would like to thank Nazneen Kanji for her encouragement and support throughout the writing process, and Kamil Kanji for his help with the bibliography.

David Lewis
Department of Social Policy
London School of Economics

Abbreviations

AEI	American Enterprise Institute
ASEAN	Association of South East Asian Nations
ASSEFA	Association of Sarva Seva Farms (India)
BAIF	Bharatiya Agro-Industries Foundation (India)
BRAC	Bangladesh Rural Advancement Committee
BRLC	Baptist Rural Life Centre (Philippines)
CAFOD	Catholic Agency for Overseas Development
CBO	community-based organization
CIVICUS	World Alliance for Citizen Participation
CSCF	Civil Society Challenge Fund (UK)
CSO	civil society organization
DAC	Development Assistance Committee (OECD)
DEC	Development Emergency Committee
DFID	Department for International Development (UK)
DOD	development organization development
ECOSOC	Economic and Social Council (UN)
EU	European Union
GM	genetically modified
GONGO	government-organized NGO
GSO	grassroots support organization
ICVA	International Council for Voluntary Agencies
ID	institutional development
IDR	Institute of Development Research (USA)
IIED	International Institute for Environment and Development
ILO	International Labour Organization
IMF	International Monetary Fund
INGO	international NGO
INTRAC	International NGO Training and Research Centre
LFA	logical framework analysis
MBO	management by objectives
MBRLC	Mindanao Baptist Rural Life Centre (Philippines)
MDG	Millenium development goal
MJ	Manusher Jonno ('for the people') (Bangladesh)

MKSS	Mazdoor Kisan Shakti Sangathan (India)
MOD	managerialist organization development
MSO	Membership support organization
MYRADA	Mysore Relief and Development Agency (India)
NFAZ	National Farmers' Association of Zimbabwe
NGDO	non-governmental development organization
NGO	non-governmental organization
NNGO	Northern NGO
NPM	new public management
OD	organizational development
ODI	Overseas Development Institute (UK)
OECD	Organization for Economic Cooperation and Development
ORAP	Organization of Rural Associations for Progress (Zimbabwe)
PDI	Project Development Institute (Philippines)
PIA	Philippines Irrigation Authority
PLA	participatory learning and action
PO	people's organization
PPA	programme partnership agreement
PRA	participatory rural appraisal
PROTERRA	Instituto Tecnologico Agrario Proterra (Peru)
PRSP	poverty reduction strategy paper
PSC	public service contractor
PVO	private voluntary organization
QUANGO	quasi non-governmental organization
SALT	sloping agricultural land technology
SCF	Save the Children Fund (UK)
SDM	Savings Development Movement (Zimbabwe)
SEWA	Self-Employed Women's Association (India)
SIDA	Swedish Agency for International Development Cooperation
SIT	School for International Training (USA)
SNGO	Southern NGO
SWAP	sector-wide approach
TINA	there is no alternative
TQM	total quality management
TSO	third sector organization
UNCED	United Nations Conference on Environment and Development
UNDP	United Nations Development Programme
UNESCO	United Nations Educational, Scientific and Cultural Organization
USAID	United States Agency for International Development
VADA	Voluntary Agencies Development Assistance (Kenya)
VO	voluntary organization
VSO	Voluntary Service Overseas (UK)
WHO	World Health Organization
WTO	World Trade Organization

Introduction

This book is about non-governmental organizations, better known as 'NGOs' or sometimes more specifically as 'NGDOs'. NGDOs – non-governmental development organizations – are usually understood to be not-for-profit or 'third sector' organizations concerned with addressing problems of poverty and social justice, and working primarily in the developing world. They do this either directly through the provision of services to people themselves or indirectly through campaigning and policy advocacy to bring about wider structural change that will improve the position of people who are poor. NGO management is an important emerging topic, since NGOs are growing in numbers and increasing their profile around the world.

NGO management is a specialized field that warrants its own text because it requires new creative thinking that goes beyond existing mainstream business management or public sector administration science. This is because NGOs have distinctive organizational characteristics and face complex multifaceted challenges in their work. Many people argue that organizations of the third sector are a distinctive type of organization that is different in important ways from the more familiar forms of private sector business or public sector government organization.

Although there are many types of NGO, this book is primarily concerned with NGO management from the perspective of organizations working in the field of development and poverty reduction in the various and different contexts of Africa, Asia, Latin America and the Caribbean, as well as in the 'post-socialist' or 'transition' areas of the former Soviet bloc. An effort has been made in the text wherever possible to present material and examples from across all of these regions. However, readers will notice that there is more material drawn from the context of South Asia than from elsewhere, reflecting the author's own first-hand experience which is mainly from that part of the world.

PARTS AND CHAPTERS

The chapter map (Chart 1) provides the overall structure of the book. Chapter 1 sets the scene with a short overview of the rise of NGOs, discusses the history and the growth of interest in NGO management and presents a basic conceptual framework.

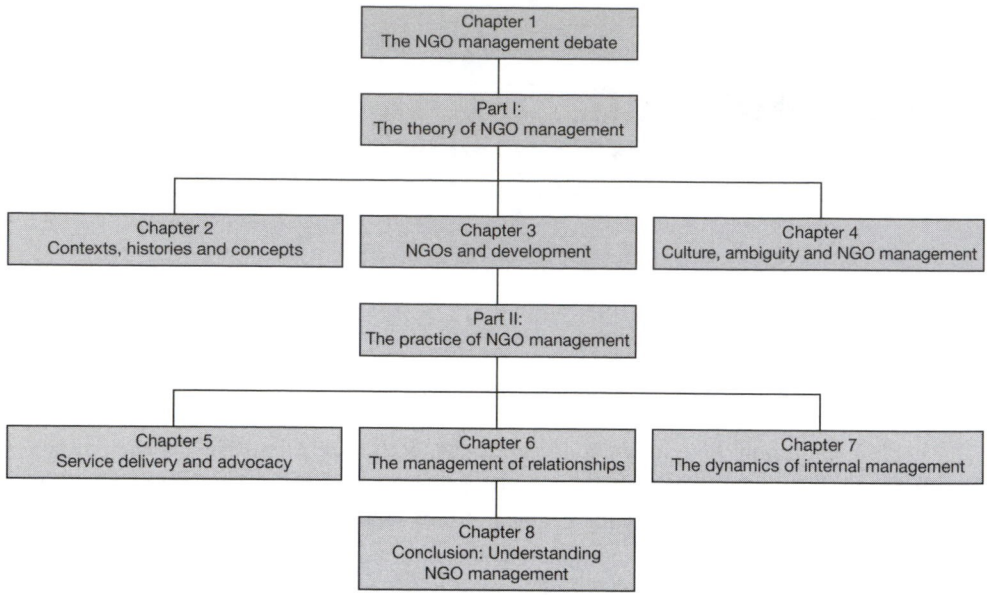

Chart 1 *Chapter map*

After this, the book is divided into two parts. In Part I, we examine the theory of NGO management. It explains how NGOs have come to be seen as important actors in development work, and the approaches that can be used to understand the management challenges that they face. This task is covered in three chapters.

NGOs are found all over the world and work within very different environments. Chapter 2 explores some of these different contexts and histories and shows the ways in which development NGOs have evolved as a diverse family of organizations. While all NGOs share some common characteristics, their different histories in Europe, North America, Asia, Latin America, Africa and elsewhere mean that there are also distinctive variations within and between contexts.

Chapter 3 goes on to discuss the relationship between NGOs and the wider 'development industry' that has emerged since the Second World War, made up of multilateral funders such as the World Bank and bilateral donors such as the US Agency for International Development (USAID) or the Department for International Development (DFID) in the UK. Many NGOs receive useful resources from the broader world of development agencies, but the relationships that emerge between NGOs and their donors bring several challenges, not least of which is the struggle for NGOs to keep up with and negotiate within the rapidly changing framework of international aid.

Chapter 4 moves on to discuss in general terms how the concept of management might relate distinctively to development NGOs as specific kinds of organization. While mainstream business management, public sector management and non-profit management are all shown to have relevance, a 'composite' model is identified as the most appropriate way forward for NGOs.

Part II is concerned with the 'practice of NGO management' and contains three chapters, each of which focuses on a key area of activity. These are broken down into the three interlocking circles of organization, activities and relationships (outlined in the conceptual framework in Figure 1.1).

Chapter 5 covers the main activities undertaken by development NGOs, which largely fall under the two headings of service delivery and advocacy. It examines how these activities can be understood in relation to the ways in which NGOs relate to the policy process and select roles within it as 'policy entrepreneurs'. The key management challenge for NGOs is to learn how both to participate effectively and to seek pro-poor influence within the policy process.

In Chapter 6, NGO relationships are considered in relation to communities, state, business and other development agencies. The complex task of managing multiple accountabilities is seen to be at the heart of the management of all these relationships. The increasingly common but often problematic idea of 'partnership' is analysed.

Chapter 7 brings us to the dynamics of internal management within NGOs. It focuses on the complex organizational issues that are faced by development NGOs, and draws on a range of emerging issues from the field of non-profit or third sector management research and explores their relevance to NGOs. It then moves on to discuss the small but growing literature on the internal organization of NGOs, and reflects on capacity building and organizational learning.

Chapter 8 concludes by drawing the themes of the book together and considering the overall theme of 'NGO management', its changing forms and its future.

CHAPTER FEATURES

Each chapter begins with generally three 'Learning Objectives'. These are the main objectives that should be focused upon as you consider the material that is introduced in each chapter. In the same way, the list of 'Key Terms' is designed to provide a ready-made checklist of the terms that you will need to be able to define and understand by the end of each chapter. Each chapter, with the exception of Chapters 1 and 8, contains several case study boxes 'NGOs in Action' embedded within the text. These boxes illustrate up-to-date examples of NGO management ideas and approaches in practice. There are also shorter examples integrated within the chapter text itself. At the end of each chapter, there are 'Review Questions' that might be considered individually or debated in small groups in a class or seminar. These are designed to clarify understanding of the ground covered in each chapter, to compare different points of view discussed in the text, and to allow opportunities for the application of the material presented to specific organizational or geographical contexts that may be of particular interest to readers.

The end-of-book materials include the notes that are used in each of the chapters, and a comprehensive set of bibliographic references that brings together relevant classic and contemporary academic research on NGO management, alongside many 'grey literature' references to agency reports, NGO evaluations and other official documents. This second edition includes many new references from the literature that reflect the changing landscape of NGO management in the period since 2001. However, I have also avoided the gratuitous novelty of scattering contemporary references throughout the text when an older source or example still remains the best illustration of a point or an idea. In my view, many policy debates on development and management thrive on promises of delivering 'the next big thing' at the expense of learning from even the recent past. My policy is therefore intended as a small contribution to the need to maintain a sense of historical perspective in thinking about development work.

A list of websites is also provided for readers who wish to pursue their research further online, and, wherever possible, website references are provided in the text for particular organizations that are referred to. Additional websites and other materials can be found on the website designed for this book (www.routledge.com/textbooks/9780415370936).

Finally, the subject and author index gives the reader a systematic way to access further information about each of the topics covered in this book, and the means to follow up in more detail on the authors whose work has been drawn upon in the writing of this textbook.

TERMINOLOGY

The study of NGOs is a field in which there are an unusually large number of complex and confusing terms and acronyms. A glossary is provided at the end of the book to help guide the reader through this complexity. The problem of terminological confusion in relation to NGOs is discussed at some length in Chapter 2.

There are many different types of NGOs and these organizations work not just in the development field but also in human rights or environment, as well as in other less related spheres such as arts, sport and recreation. Most researchers and policy makers tend to stick to the term 'NGO' in common usage whether they are referring to development NGOs, human rights NGOs or any other type. The use of the acronym 'NGDO' is used by a few authors in their texts (e.g. Fowler 1997) but it is not widely deployed, and is to my mind a rather clumsy acronym. In the first edition of this book, the attempt was therefore made to try to keep things simple by using the generic term 'NGO' throughout, rather than deploying the additional acronym 'NGDO'. Feedback from some readers suggested that this was sometimes confusing. In this second edition, I therefore try to provide more clarity by explaining the different subcategories of NGO more clearly (Chart 2).

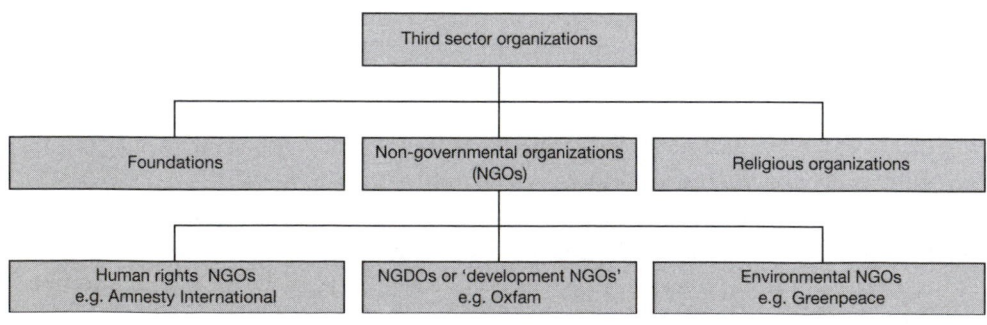

Chart 2 NGOs as a subcategory of third sector organizations and 'NGDOs' as a subcategory of NGOs

However, I have again resisted the term 'NGDO' and prefer to use 'NGO' or 'development NGO'. This is for two reasons. The first is that I think it better to try to stick to the terms most people use themselves in organizations 'on the ground'. The second is that the majority of texts on development NGOs on which I draw – and from which I frequently quote – predominantly use the term 'NGO', and it would probably confuse matters even further to have both acronyms used side by side in the text.

Having negotiated these somewhat tedious but necessary formalities around terms, it suffices to say that the term NGO that is employed here is a broad one. It includes both national and international organizations, those from both 'industrialized' and 'developing' country contexts, organizations that are funded from the development industry and those that are not, and finally both membership and non-membership organizations.

Chapter 1

The NGO management debate

LEARNING OBJECTIVES

After considering this chapter, the reader will be able to describe and analyse:

- The diversity of NGO types
- A conceptual framework for understanding the principal NGO management challenges
- The history of NGO management as an idea
- The composite model of NGO management that draws on ideas from
  - Mainstream management
  - Development management
  - Third sector management

KEY TERMS

- NGO
- Management
- Managerialism
- Third sector
- Development

INTRODUCTION

The past decade or so has witnessed a spectacular growth in the numbers and scope of 'third sector organizations' around the world – organizations which are active in a vast spectrum of activities from welfare services to leisure pursuits, from political pressure groups to arts and hobby groups (Salamon and Anheier 1999). Salamon (1994) writes of a 'global associational revolution' in which third sector organizations, so called because they form an important arena of social, cultural, economic and political activity alongside the state and the market, have come to play increased roles in public policy. Whether providing services, promoting particular values, forming the basis for community self-help initiatives or campaigning on public issues, different types of third sector organizations now have an increasingly high profile.

An important subgroup of the third sector organizational family is that of the 'nongovernmental organizations', commonly termed NGOs. The term NGO originated after the Second World War in the context of the United Nations, where there was provision made for certain international citizen organizations, that were independent from UN member governments, to observe and participate in UN affairs. These citizen organizations were concerned with a range of issues that included human rights, peace, the environment and, of course, development. Many of these were not new organizations – the Red Cross for example had existed since the nineteenth century – but through being designated as 'NGOs' these agencies gained a new status and profile. While NGOs can be understood as a subgroup of organizations within this wider third sector, it is also the case that NGOs themselves form a highly diverse organizational category (Chart 2). The primary focus of this book is on nongovernmental *development* organizations (sometimes known as NGDOs), as opposed to other forms of NGO whose focus may lie more squarely within the fields of the environment, human rights, peace building, the arts or a range of other less-related specialized activities.[1]

NGOs then are a group of third sector organizations that are engaged in development and poverty reduction work at local, national and global levels around the world.[2] The profile of NGOs has increased steadily among development policy makers, activists and researchers in both the rich industrialized countries of the 'North' and among the low-income, aid recipient countries of the 'South'. NGOs now feature prominently in efforts to secure social and economic change in favour of marginalized populations by the agencies which make up the international 'aid industry', in the growing number of public interest groups seeking alternative approaches to poverty reduction through better service delivery and through advocacy and campaigning work, and in the self-help efforts of organized local communities to improve their conditions of life (Korten 1990; Clark 1991; Edwards and Hulme 1992, 1995; Farrington and Bebbington 1993; Hulme and Edwards 1997; Tembo 2004). NGOs have come to be seen by many as part of an emerging 'civil society' in many countries which may serve as a counterweight to the excesses of the state and the market (Hadenius and Uggla 1996; Van Rooy 1998; Howell and Pearce 2001; Glasius *et al.* 2004). For Mitlin *et al.* (2005), the attraction of NGOs is the role that they may play in constructing and demonstrating 'alternatives' to the status quo:

> NGOs exist as alternatives. In being 'not governmental' they constitute vehicles
> for people to participate in development and social change in ways that would not

7

> be possible through government programmes. In being 'not governmental' they constitute a 'space' in which it is possible to think about development and social change in ways that would not be likely through government programmes . . . they constitute instruments for turning these alternative ideas into, and alternative forms of participation, into alternative practices and hard outcomes.

As we have seen, the category of 'NGO' covers a wide range of organizations and activities that go beyond narrow definitions of 'development' or 'poverty alleviation'. For example, Deacon *et al.* (1997) draw attention to the ways in which international non-state actors are increasingly contributing to transnational social policy under processes of economic, technological and cultural change which have together become loosely referred to as 'globalization', and the potential role of NGOs in working to link poor people with the benefits of globalization is argued for by Tembo (2004). In the field of international relations and politics, there is a new interest in the growth of increasingly active non-governmental networks of environmental, gender and human rights campaigning organizations (Keck and Sikkink 1998; DeMars 2005). Related to this is the emerging concept of 'global civil society'. Social scientists and activists have begun deploying this concept in relation to a wide range of public action undertaken by different non-state actors, including protests about genetically modified (GM) food, policy activism on climate change and opposition to current international trade rules (Anheier *et al.* 2001). For example, the G8 Gleneagles summit held in the summer of 2005 generated discussion, demonstrations and policy advocacy initiatives among a wide range of non-governmental actors and social movements at the international level (Glasius *et al.* 2006).

NGOs are also important in relation to their roles within international humanitarian relief in the context of wars and natural disasters (Bennett 1995). Many NGOs are active in long-term humanitarian work in locations characterized by what has come to be termed 'complex political emergencies', such as Sudan or Somalia. From post-conflict reconstruction roles in the wars in Iraq and Afghanistan – as well as strong criticism of Western policies from some sections of the NGO community – to natural disasters such as the 2003 Iran earthquake and the 2005 floods in New Orleans, the global profile of NGOs has never been higher. The growth of non-state actors is increasingly linked to the broader ways in which the economic and social ordering of modern societies are constructed. For example, some social scientists have begun to take an interest in the ways in which NGOs play a role in mediating relationships between global processes and local lives (Fisher 1997; Hilhorst 2003). Although many of these wider NGO roles and types will be touched upon in this book, the kinds of NGOs with which we will be principally concerned are those Fowler (1997) defines as 'non-governmental development organizations', which are third sector organizations whose presence is 'legitimised by the existence of poverty'.

Literature on NGOs

The 1990s witnessed a large growth of writing about development NGOs. Much of this work presented a positive picture of the work NGOs were doing, and was often written by people directly involved with or very sympathetic to NGO work. However, while some of this material was of a high quality and served to highlight the new importance of NGO work in development, in retrospect it is possible to see that in other respects it had some important limitations. This was a literature that tended towards the descriptive rather than the analytical, tended to focus on individual organizational cases rather than the broader picture, and the work frequently carried a strongly prescriptive or normative tone (Clarke 1998; Stewart 1997; Najam 1999; Lewis 2005; Lewis and Opoku-Mensah 2006; Tvedt 2006).

Furthermore, very little of this literature was concerned with the structure and management of development NGOs. Instead, the focus was on the roles played by NGOs in development processes and the potential of NGOs to challenge existing policy and practice (Lewis 1999a).[3] Only in 2002 did broader acknowledgement of the field of NGO management begin to move forward with the publication of a 'reader' that drew together a collection of writings on the topic (Fowler and Edwards 2002). This relative lack of attention given to management remains an important gap, because 'Management capacity is the lifeblood of all organizations, irrespective of whether they are private entities, public agencies, not-for-profit concerns or non-governmental varieties.' (Udoh James 1998: 229). Where there has been research carried out on the internal management and organization development of NGOs, this work has, as Stewart (1997) points out, tended to be at the expense of wider context and politics.

By contrast, considerable attention has been given to understanding management issues in the worlds of business and government. Today, management is a diverse field of academic study and practice, encompassing approaches laden with high theory as well as, at the other end of the spectrum, those which take a 'hands-on' training approach. There is also a rapidly changing succession of popular management fads and management 'gurus' all seeking to deliver the latest ideas and techniques to managers, a phenomenon that has itself become a lucrative business (Micklethwait and Wooldridge 1996; Bate 1997). In the public sector, what used to be called 'public administration' has now gradually metamorphosed into 'public management', reflecting the elevation of the idea of management into a dominant force across all levels and corners of society. Much has been made of the emergence of the 'new public management' in the public sector during the past decade or two, which has drawn further on principles derived from the private sector, discussed in more detail later in this chapter (Ferlie *et al.* 1996; Minogue *et al.* 1998).

This book argues that there is an emerging field of NGO management. It examines the key management challenges faced by development NGOs, by focusing on both internal and contextual issues. These NGO management challenges follow from the types of roles and strategies being undertaken by different kinds of NGOs in the struggle against poverty, and these can be summarized in general terms as:

- the delivery of new or improved services to sections of communities which are in need,
- efforts to catalyse social, economic and political change processes at the level of group or individual action, and
- the attempt to create 'synergies' among different agencies and initiatives through the building of 'partnerships'.

As many people who have studied NGOs or worked within them will know, there is much discussion and debate about the various types of roles that NGOs play in development, but relatively little attention generally is given to the ways in which these roles can be managed. A key objective of this book is therefore to build a conceptual framework in which the distinctive challenges of the management of NGOs might be better understood and analysed. In a modest way, it is hoped that this approach can cast some new light on the subject of NGOs and offer some critical perspectives on the concept of 'management'.

NGOs' critics and supporters

For many years, the dominant view of NGOs was one of essentially heroic organizations seeking to 'do good' for others in difficult circumstances. However, there are many voices that are critical of NGOs. Criticisms have been wide-ranging and made from different political viewpoints. Some people have criticized the shift away from donor support to state institutions towards a more privatized – and potentially less accountable – form of development intervention involving NGOs (Hanlon 1991; Tvedt 1998). Indeed critics on the left have long seen NGOs as broadly supporting or facilitating neo-liberal policy orthodoxies, clearing up the mess left by what they see as destructive policies such as structural adjustment, and as sapping the potential of more radical grassroots action from social movements or organized political oppositions. For example, Yash Tandon (1996) is a long-standing critic of the ways in which NGOs play a role in sustaining and extending neocolonial relations in Africa. There have also long been criticisms of NGO roles in humanitarian and emergency work – particularly in African contexts. Many of the earliest criticisms came from those observing NGO work that did not live up to expectations in the context of humanitarian assistance in emergency situations (e.g. Abdel Ati 1993; de Waal and Omaar 1993).

These critiques of NGOs are not confined to the 'developing' world. Critics on the neo-conservative US right have seen NGOs as potentially harmful to US foreign policy and business interests. For example, the American Enterprise Institute (AEI), a think tank close to the current US Republican administration, made headlines in June 2003 when it outlined its critique of international NGOs. The AEI and others have set up an NGO 'watchdog' website (www.ngowatch.org). It lists a set of grievances in relation to NGOs that includes their support of 'global governance' agendas, their efforts to restrict US room for manoeuvre in foreign policy and their attempts to influence the power of corporations and, by extension, the 'free market'. The increase of this anti-NGO ideology in the USA may in the future narrow the 'room for manoeuvre' of Northern NGOs, which may have to defend their right to undertake campaigning and advocacy work more vigorously. There have been related moves by the US administration to use private contractors in place of NGOs in Afghanistan and Iraq for reconstruction and relief work, and reports of tighter regulations governing contracting between USAID and NGOs in order to reduce the latter's independence. One report suggested that Andrew Natsios, head of USAID, was unhappy that NGOs were not giving sufficient credit to the US government as the source of their funds. Another quotes Jeremy Rabkin, a Cornell University government professor, who suggests that NGO influence over corporations is a form of 'protection racket' and that the global governance agenda is 'anti-national' and essentially a 'left-wing programme'. The fact that NGOs have now become the focus of criticism from many different political perspectives is also of course a reflection of the wide diversity of NGO types and roles.

But one general consequence of this trend is the need for NGOs to protect their own credibility against a growing number of criticisms. Some criticisms are ungrounded and based on misinformation, others may be primarily ideological in nature. However, many of the criticisms made of development NGOs are quite reasonable. Even long-term pro-NGO writers such as Edwards *et al.* (2000) conclude a general paper on NGO trends with:

> few NGOs have developed structures that genuinely respond to grassroots demands. Although NGOs talk of 'partnership', control over funds and decision-making remains highly unequal. . . . The legitimacy of NGOs (especially those based in the North) is now an accepted topic of public debate . . . NGOs must be leaders in cultivating a global moral order that finds poverty and violence un-acceptable. They must be exemplars of the societies they want to create, and work much harder to mainstream civic values into the arenas of economic, social and political power.

Long gone are the days when NGOs could simply rely on the 'moral high ground' to give them legitimacy and justify their work. This is entirely as it should be.

NGOs have not continued to be as openly 'flavour of the month' in mainstream development circles as they once were in the 1990s.[4] The idea of NGOs as a 'magic bullet' that can easily solve development problems is one that has now passed. In some quarters of the media NGOs have become 'fair game', variously criticized as ineffectual do-gooders, over-professionalized large humanitarian business corporations or self-serving interest groups (see Box 1.1 for some examples). At the same time, international donors are a little more shy about NGOs than they were in the 1990s. It is more common these days to hear donors and governments speak more indirectly about NGOs, in terms of 'civil society', 'citizen organizations', 'community associations' or 'faith-based groups'. There is a faint sense in which NGOs are thought to have disappointed in some way, or that they were overrated in the past. These changes of language and emphasis nevertheless continue to reflect the fact that non-state actors play increasingly important roles across developing, transitional and developed societies. The amount of international assistance going to NGOs in development, humanitarian and post-conflict reconstruction contexts is still very high. The *Newsweek* article referred to in Box 1.1 has figures that indicate that official development assistance channelled through NGOs increased from 4.6 per cent in 1995 to 13 per cent in 2004, and that the total volume of international aid increased from US$59 billion in 1995 to US$78.6 billion in 2004. These significant figures, along with the fact that NGOs receive a less easy ride these days than perhaps they did in the 1990s, speaks to the continuing importance of understanding their management strategies and challenges more clearly and systematically.

11

The 'business of helping'?: NGO management in the headlines

'*Sins of the secular Missionaries*' (*The Economist*, 29 January 2000)

In particularly florid journalistic style, this article argues that NGOs, 'once little more than ragged charities', increasingly act as large-scale private contractors for Western governments. It also suggests that in many developing countries NGOs have become vehicles for unscrupulous individuals to connect opportunistically with aid resources. The article then goes on to chart the increasing scale of NGO operations, and argues that 'non-governmental' is often a misnomer because many NGOs increasingly depend on public funds. Overall, the article is critical of this new 'business of helping' and while it acknowledges that many NGOs 'do achieve great things' it hints darkly that NGOs 'can also get into bad ways because they are not accountable to anyone'.

'*Alliances between companies and non-governmental organizations attracts varying degrees of enthusiasm*' (*Financial Times*, 29 November 2002)

Charting the increasing relations between NGOs and the world of business, this article suggests that NGO profiles are increasing as they experiment more with working with private companies, citing as examples the diamond, mining and clothing industries. Around the issue of child labour, for example, the article describes one UK NGO which seeks to pursue multiple strategies with the private sector, by talking informally with companies to address problems 'quietly' (and perhaps protect the vulnerable livelihoods of children) while simultaneously undertaking high-profile campaigning on child rights.

'*Hearts and minds at any cost*' (*The Guardian*, 13 July 2004)

This article argues that humanitarian efforts have been increasingly co-opted into the 'war on terror'. It illustrates the ways that boundaries between public and private agencies in Iraq and Afghanistan have been eroded, making it difficult for NGOs to exist in an independent and critical 'civic space' away from both US government policy and the terrorists. The article to some extent blames many of the NGOs themselves for having outgrown their 'charitable' origins and become largely funded by governments.

'*The $1.6 trillion non-profit sector behaves (or misbehaves) more and more like big business*' (*Newsweek*, 5 September 2005)

This story covers the growth and scale of the NGO sector and argues that greater regulation is needed. It begins by describing Oxfam GB's Director Barbara Stocking, referring to her 'no-nonsense manner' and 'power broker's schedule'. It suggests many NGOs 'are dropping their image as anti-capitalist do-gooders and adopting the look of the Fortune 500 companies that they have been known to criticise'. But the article also comments on the search by many NGOs for more independent non-governmental sources of income from private giving and fair trade activities, citing the Iraq conflict as a wake-up call to some NGOs. While Oxfam GB with more than half a million individual donor supporters was able to take a clear position against the war, the article points out, CARE USA, which receives approximately half its income from the US government, had to 'tread softly'. In Iraq, the US government has compelled US NGOs to display American logos on aid deliveries and has required that discussions with the press are officially cleared first.

The diverse organizational universe of development NGOs: brief examples

One of the main challenges faced in writing a book such as this is the sheer diversity of organizations that fall into the general category of 'NGO'. NGOs can be large or small, formal or informal, externally funded or driven by volunteers, charitable and paternalistic or radical and 'empowerment'-based. One NGO might combine several of these different elements at any one time. It may be constantly dealing with change, locked into an unpredictable context in which it alternates between periods of fashionable affluence (in which it is favoured by donors who provide extensive funding and leave it with problems of rapid growth and formalization) and periods in which resources can suddenly dry up. There are many NGOs that live a 'hand-to-mouth' existence, ever more concerned with the need to secure their own organizational survival in the face of donor or public apathy, or struggling to exist in the context of political oppression and government or private sector suspicion.

Some brief organizational examples can be used to illustrate this point. The Bangladesh Rural Advancement Committee (BRAC) is a formal, bureaucratically structured NGO which works closely with government in the delivery of a wide range of services in urban and rural areas, and it is now one of the largest NGOs in the world (Lovell 1992), employing more than 97,000 people and working in 78 per cent of Bangladesh's villages (BRAC 2004).[5] In its organizational structure and behaviour it mirrors aspects of government and private sector in its large scale and formal bureaucracy, but it also challenges some of the prevailing public and business orthodoxy. A visit to the BRAC office in Dhaka presents a picture of a hierarchical organization that is structured rather like a government department or a big corporation, with clear roles, job descriptions and routines. It is highly professionalized, yet a second look reveals innovations and adaptations in its structure and organization that can often challenge the norm, and BRAC seeks ways to introduce a more participatory style into the administrative hierarchy. For example, the executive director makes it possible for any staff member, no matter how junior, to gain direct access for a face-to-face discussion through a regular daily 'surgery' in the event of either an idea or an unsolved problem, thereby bypassing the many rigid strata of bureaucracy which typify most government offices. The successful handicraft store chain Aarong, which BRAC operates, sells many of the products made by its mostly female group members and is highly profitable, but profits are ploughed back into the NGO's own development programmes, challenging some of the prevailing rules of the commercial business game as well.

By contrast, Jute Works is an NGO which provides a marketing outlet for low-income women handicraft producers in Bangladesh (Norton 1996). Following its establishment in the 1970s, it sold relatively simple handicrafts to a largely solidarity-based Northern market of NGOs and their supporters, but the 1990s saw a steady growth in the competitiveness of the handicraft market and the rise of a new ethically driven 'fair trade' movement. This has presented Jute Works with something of a dilemma, since it cannot stand still and remain as an NGO which is used to operating along essentially charitable lines, because its income has begun to decline steadily in recent years. If it is to survive, the organization must design and market its handicrafts more effectively in order to attract new customers and to ensure that the rural women with whom it works can maintain their livelihoods. As a result, this NGO is now looking to the private sector for new skills in product design, quality control and marketing that will ensure that it provides a better service to the community it serves. Although Jute Works remains driven by its commitment to the values of fair trade and the needs of its users, it is increasingly choosing from a portfolio of business sector management tools which it hopes will allow it to engage more successfully with market forces (Lewis 1998a).

A third example illustrates how fast the NGO world is changing at the international level. Vetwork UK was set up by activists interested in improving animal health in low-income farming communities in poor countries, and began as an information network on the Internet, run by a small but dedicated group of professionals volunteering their time and specialized skills.[6] Within a year, a similar organization had formed in Sudan and the plan is now to catalyse a network that will support initiatives of this kind across the world. This is a value-driven, 'virtual organization' (in Handy's 1995 phrase) at the cutting edge of thinking about the third sector, using emerging information technologies and the more familiar principles of international solidarity to steer a course through new ground. It is also an organization that is beginning to challenge the conventional distinction between a 'Northern' NGO which works in a developing country through country offices and a 'Southern' NGO partner organization from that country, since Vetwork is a network of people exchanging ideas and information with no particular geographical base. Very few NGOs are able to stand still for long, and in a sense all three of the NGOs which have been briefly reviewed here are moving towards hybridity as they combine management approaches and tools from the private, public and third sectors in order to remain effective in a changing environment.

Since the heyday of the 1990s, interest in NGOs has begun to take on a more critical, reflective tone as the emphasis has shifted away from the notion of NGOs as a 'magic bullet' for poverty reduction (Hulme and Edwards 1997). There is more serious thought being given to questions of efficiency, accountability and effectiveness within NGO work (Fowler 1997, 2000). Some commentators have spoken of a 'backlash' against NGOs by those disappointed at NGOs' own lack of accountability and standards of governance (e.g. Bond 2000). Others increasingly simply see NGOs as just one type of development actor within a wider institutional landscape which includes broader civil society, the state and the market. Ideas about how to promote better synergy between NGOs and these different actors are gradually taking precedent over the ideas of 'comparative advantage' of NGOs over the state which held sway in the 1990s (e.g. Tendler 1997). Perhaps there is now a more realistic view among policy makers about what NGOs can and cannot achieve. However, it remains the case that relatively little consideration has been given, in either the development or the management literature, to the question of NGO management issues and, in particular, to the question of whether a set of distinctive management challenges exists for these organizations.[7] Such concerns, and the increasing media interest and public scrutiny of NGOs and their work, makes it more important than ever before for NGO management as a subject to move up the agenda and be taken more seriously.

There has been a growth of academic research on third sector organizations working within industrialized country contexts (where they are often termed 'voluntary' and 'non-profit' organizations). This is a largely unexplored area for researchers familiar only with the world of NGOs and development. Some of this literature engages with questions of organization and management in more depth than the NGO literature, and this book tries to make the case for linking insights from both literatures. However, as might be expected, there are important limitations in the fact that such work rarely moves beyond the United States or Britain in its geographical focus (Lewis 1999a; Hailey 2006).

A conceptual framework for NGO management

The aims of a book such as this one must remain modest if it is to stand any chance of being taken seriously, because its subject is one that defies simple generalization. The intention is therefore to present a conceptual framework and selective review of the main issues of NGO management from my own perspective, based on research and consultancy work in the NGO and development field over the past fifteen years, and drawing on more than ten years of teaching postgraduate courses on NGO management and social development to reflective practitioner students.[8] As we have seen, there are as many different types of NGOs as there are organizational forms, and there are as many different areas of work which concern NGOs as there are sides to debates about what 'development' means and how problems of poverty and social justice can be addressed. And not all NGOs are necessarily concerned with support for pro-poor change. As Morris-Suzuki (2000: 68) points out: 'NGOs may pursue change, but they can equally work to maintain existing social and political systems.' There can be no rigid definition or understanding of 'NGO management', but instead a range of important themes and debates can be uncovered and analysed. In undertaking such an exercise, more can be learned about the ways NGOs work as organizations and their potential roles and contributions within development activities.

Figure 1.1 sets out the four interrelated areas of the NGO management challenge and provides a basic conceptual framework for thinking about NGO management. Despite their diversity, all NGOs need to manage in three main areas: the organizational domain of their internal structures and processes; their development activities, which may be in the form of projects or programmes, campaigns or services; and finally their management of relationships with other institutional actors – the state, the private sector, other NGOs and organized components of the communities in which NGOs operate. These can be portrayed as overlapping circles, since while each is a distinctive sphere of activity, all three are clearly interrelated.

All three are located within the broader environment in which NGOs work. This is the crucial variable of 'context', against which an analysis of any NGO must be placed, and which has political, historical and cultural dimensions. It varies over both time and space. For example, when a change of government in a particular country takes place it may open new doors for NGO activity or conversely it may bring a new set of restrictions on NGOs. The geographical contexts of NGO activity are also diverse. This makes it difficult to draw NGO management lessons from a specific country such as Bangladesh – where NGOs have been shaped by distinctive processes of culture, history and politics – and then unthinkingly apply them to other countries in Europe, Africa or Latin America. This book is structured around this conceptual framework as follows: Chapters 2 and 3 relate primarily to context,

Figure 1.1 *A conceptual framework: four interrelated areas of the NGO management challenge*

Chapter 5 to activities, Chapter 6 to relationships and Chapter 7 to organization. Chapters 4 and 8 are bridging chapters which seek to draw connections between each of the different spheres of NGO management activity.

Some further information and a few caveats will clearly be needed. First, the focus of this book is primarily on development NGOs, as opposed to those working in humanitarian relief, human rights, conflict resolution or environmental campaigning. Yet there is much that is relevant here to these other types of NGO, as we shall see. Second, the primary emphasis is on Southern NGOs rather than Northern ones, although the latter do receive considerable attention. Third, there is a geographical bias, since my own experience is drawn mainly from work in South Asia and from Bangladesh in particular. However, wherever possible, an attempt has been made to illustrate the text with examples from all over the world. In addition to Africa, Asia and Latin America, some effort has also been made to include examples from the 'transitional' or post-socialist countries. Fourth, this is not a book about 'how to manage an NGO'. Other people would be far more qualified than I am to write such a book, although I have my doubts, given the diversity of organizations, approaches and contexts, whether such a book could be written with any degree of usefulness. The tone of this book is intended to be discursive rather than prescriptive. It is hoped that by reviewing the relevant literature, a preliminary understanding of our subject can be achieved, and that through further action, debate and research, this understanding can be taken forward.

In addition to setting out a conceptual framework for thinking about NGO management, the book includes short case studies in each of the chapters that follow that are intended to highlight 'real-world' examples and generate issues for further discussion. It is hoped that the main audience for this book will be students of development policy and non-profit management, at either graduate or undergraduate level; and that those interested in managing development organizations and people working 'on the ground' in NGOs might also find parts of the book useful.

CONCEPT OF MANAGEMENT

We turn now to the concept of management, in order to consider its various meanings and the ways in which it might be applied to NGOs. There is a distinct academic field of management studies with diverse themes and debates, as well as a bewildering range of popular 'self-help' books on management. NGOs of course face a set of management problems which they share, at least in part, with all other kinds of organizations. It therefore follows that NGO management can in part be understood by exploring relevant ideas from within the wider world of management. However, we must bear in mind that there are two strong elements of bias in the wider management literature. The first is the fact that management studies has usually been concerned with the management of commercial businesses, while most NGOs see themselves as not-for-profit organizations. The second is that there has been a tendency for mainstream management to focus on Western ideas and models, while NGOs work predominantly in non-Western cultures and contexts. There will therefore be considerable areas of NGO management where such ideas may not apply.

Management studies has become a vast research field with a range of different approaches and paradigms and, like that of development, is characterized by tensions between academics and practitioners.[9] The study of management has been characterized as 'a mysterious thing in so far as the more research that is undertaken the less we seem to be able to understand' (Grint 1995: 3). Modernist management writers such as Taylor and Fayol, who laid the early foundations of the field, based their analyses on an understanding of organizations as logical machines which required systemic maintenance and fine-tuning. Management was seen as a rational science in which improvements in efficiency could be produced by the 'right' changes to structure and process. These classical management theorists drew to some extent on principles which came from military and engineering thinking, and saw management in terms of 'planning, organization, command, coordination and control' (Morgan 1997: 18).

In stark contrast, other theorists such as Stacey *et al.* (2000) prefer to argue in postmodern terms that chaos and complexity theory is a more appropriate conceptual framework with which to understand management dynamics, because there is little real scope for predicting how managers and organizations will behave. In this view, there is always both order and disorder existing side by side, and organizational success is seen to come from an ability to manage the 'chaotic edge' between disintegration and ossification. Writers on management informed by the 'chaos and complexity' approach argue that an understanding of ambiguity and paradox gives important clues to understanding how organizations work and has the potential to unleash creativity. The concept of 'self-organization' is a key idea within the complexity approach to management because it implies analysis of a process in which: 'the power, politics and conflict of everyday life are at the centre of cooperative and competitive organizational processes through which joint action is taken' (Stacey *et al.* 2000: 8). There is now a noticeable lack of confidence among management theorists, as earlier modern, rational paradigms of controlled organized activity have gradually given way to views which place a heavy emphasis on uncertainty, rapid change and an absence of measurable, objective practice.

Also relevant to NGOs is the loose set of approaches which has emerged since the 1990s as 'critical management studies' (Grey and Willmott 2005). Contributions to this tradition are varied and diverse, but most share a critical stance to the dominance within management of ideas from the New Right and the tyranny of 'managerialism' (discussed at the end of this section), an interest in moving beyond a preoccupation with Western management ideas in an era of globalization, and an interest in opening up a set of reflexive methodological alternatives to scientific, positivist management research in management studies. The three common threads of critical management studies – de-naturalization, anti-performativity and reflexivity (Grey and Willmott 2005) are all of potential interest to NGO managers. *De-naturalization* refers to the need to challenge assertions about the existing order and its set of assumptions about 'how things are' in order to avoid the kind of closed thinking sometimes termed There Is No Alternative (TINA). *Anti-performativity* refers to the idea of challenging the assumption that management relationships – and other social relationships – are simply concerned with maximizing outputs from inputs, and seeks to bring more in-depth discussions of values, politics and ethics into management debates. Finally, *reflexivity* draws on thinking within the social sciences that seeks to understand the role of the observer or the position of researcher in the way in which knowledge is produced, rather than simply taking accounts of management and organization as objective or fixed.

What is management? Definitions of management range from those that emphasize 'control and authority' to others which speak of 'enablement and participation', and from the functional definition of 'getting the work done by the best means available' to the more diffuse idea of 'reducing anxiety'. The analysis of management has tended to distinguish two main groups of approaches to the concept (Thomas 1996). The first is 'blueprint' or 'scientific' management which stresses control, hierarchy and instrumentality, and this approach is often stigmatized as being 'top down' by development people. The second is 'people-centred' or 'enabling' management, which by contrast emphasizes process, flexibility and participation, and which has found favour with writers on development management such as Chambers (1994) and Friedmann (1992). The 'command and control' side of management has tended to alienate some senior staff in NGOs, who may instead choose to see themselves as 'facilitators', 'organizers' or 'coordinators'. In a survey of the directors of US NGOs undertaken by Stark Biddle (1984), there was a clear reluctance among most of these managers to accept that their organizations could be run like other organizations because of a sense of 'difference', which these managers saw as stemming from staff values which prioritized community participation, the closeness of the NGO to the poor and the need for overall organizational flexibility. These managers seemed to feel worried that they would become 'contaminated' by the 'mainstream' values of hierarchy and authority. Nevertheless, the evidence gathered by Stark Biddle pointed to a set of common basic management weaknesses among these organizations which had apparently not been addressed through these NGOs' 'alternative' stance in relation to management.

A second area of management which is important to NGOs is the distinction made between values and action – between the 'instrumental' and 'expressive' elements of the management process. In the context of the British voluntary sector, Paton (1991), for example, has argued that the *functions* of management (such as controlling, planning, motivating, directing or monitoring) can be distinguished from the *style* of this management (such as consultative, participatory, cooperative or top down). In other words, the fact that something 'gets done' is only one aspect of management, because it may also be important to consider the *way* in which it is done. This dichotomy is particularly important for thinking about third sector organizations, because most third sector organizations tend to assert the primacy of 'values' in their organizational set-up. Some NGOs have been observed going so far as to suggest that the fact that they are trying to do something about a problem is more important than worrying about whether what they are doing is effective or adequate (Riddell and Robinson 1995). An issue of current concern for NGOs is the idea that as third sector organizations engage in closer relationships with states and donors in contractual service delivery roles, they may take on more and more of the characteristics of private sector or public sector organizations and lose this distinctive, value-driven character (Edwards 1996; Fowler 1997).

The dangers of managerialism (an unwarranted and often ideological reliance on technical problem solving) familiar from debates in the public sector, are also implicit in aspects of the new NGO management agenda discussed in this chapter. For example, Pollitt's (1993) reflections on public sector management demonstrate the potential pitfalls for NGOs of taking on board management ideas uncritically. Pollitt defines managerialism as an apparently self-evident – though in practice seldom tested – truth that 'if things are better organized they will improve', an assumption which brings controversial and even contradictory implications. For example, it tends to create a type of thinking that decrees that when new challenges or problems arise solutions can always be found from within the status quo, a perspective which can easily become oppressive and exploitative to staff. It can also suggest, with more idealistic overtones, that answers to problems can be found 'to hand' and solutions can be built with the help of creative thinking and leadership. Nevertheless, Pollitt argues that at the core of managerialism is the implication that progress is subject to increases in economically defined productivity and the application of increasingly sophisticated technologies, and that managers – as distinct from other elements of the organization – hold the key to positive change. Managerialism also tends to see the private sector as the leading exponent of practice from which others must learn, and identifies an opposition between itself and its 'enemies' among the public sector and civil society in the form of bureaucrats and trade unions.

Managerialist approaches have the obvious danger for NGOs that other kinds of organizational values such as friendship, voluntary cooperation or politics can become 'squeezed out' and undervalued. Wallace *et al.* (2006: 165) found that NGOs in Uganda and South Africa feel pressure to use whatever training resources they have available to ensure that their managers can complete donor documentation 'to a satisfactory level' instead of using those resources to train front-line staff on issues such as recognizing gender inequality, building communication and listening skills, or facilitating the inclusion of marginalized people. On the other hand, a rejection of managerialism cannot be confused with a rejection of management itself. For example, research by Stark Biddle (1984) and Dichter (1989a) indicates that there are NGOs out there that lack even the basic common-sense management structures and principles, and that a more rational application of management means to ends would be a worthwhile endeavour. However, within an organization driven primarily by development values, one of the key management challenges is the need to pursue the expressive aspect while maintaining or increasing effectiveness. We will return to these issues in Chapter 4. In the following section, we link the concept of management with the world of development NGOs.

NGOs and management

We have yet to see the evolution of a clear set of ideas about the management challenges of NGOs or the emergence of a distinctive field of 'NGO management'. Part of the reason for this lies with the fact that for many years NGOs have not taken management very seriously. At times, parts of the third sector have expressed hostility towards the whole idea of management, which it has seen as belonging to another, alien, set of ideologies and concerns. While people in NGOs have often been committed activists, they have been reluctant managers. There are at least five sets of reasons for the reluctance with which management has been associated with development NGOs.

The first is that many NGOs are characterized by a 'culture of action' in which NGO leaders and staff are reluctant to devote significant amounts of time to thinking about organizational questions, because such a prioritization might interfere with the primary task of 'getting out there and doing something'. This may, as Korten suggests, be particularly true of NGOs in their early stages of evolution, since the origins of many NGOs lie in the efforts of key individuals to mobilize action based on altruism:

> They have relied upon high moral purpose, good will, hard work, and common sense to make them successful. Until recently the application of effective professional management techniques, and in some instances even the acquisition of technical competence, has not been seen as relevant to their purposes.
>
> (Korten 1987: 155)

A second reason is the widespread view, particularly among the public and donors, that NGOs should use almost all their funds for working with poor people and should not spend money on administrative overheads or waste too much time on administrative questions. As Smillie (1995: 151) suggests, there is a 'powerful public myth that development should be cheap', which has led in some quarters to a tendency to take low NGO administrative overheads as one of the main criteria for judging success. A third reason is the fact that development NGOs may be established by people consciously searching for 'alternatives' to mainstream thinking, and that the subjects of management and administration, with their strong associations with the business and the public sectors, are 'tainted ground' for these kinds of organization. The reluctance of some NGOs to take management seriously has sometimes been based on a fear of what Chambers (1994) has called 'normal professionalism', which negates many of the stated values and priorities of NGOs in their work. Normal professionalism, in Chambers's view, gives preference to rich over poor, 'blueprints' over adaptation, things over people, quantity over quality, and the powerful over the weak. This has led Korten to point out that

> Some NGOs actively espouse an ideological disdain for management of any kind, identifying with it the values and practices of normal professionalism, and placing it in a class with exploitation, oppression and racism.
>
> (Korten 1990: 156)

The rapid growth and change which many NGOs have experienced means that NGOs are always 'one step behind' in thinking and taking action around organizational responses. This brings a fourth set of possible reasons into the frame. NGOs that have started out as small, informal structures in which management issues can be dealt with on an ad hoc, informal basis may rapidly grow in size if they find favour with donor agencies. In this case they may find themselves developing more complex, multidimensional projects and programmes but will not immediately realize that they need new ideas, systems and procedures with which to cope.

A fifth reason for reluctance relates to the power of external forces and pressures. As some NGOs have grown closer to donor agencies, they have been required to develop new systems of accountability, and their efficiency and effectiveness may be questioned and challenged. This has led to the feeling – which is not altogether false – among some NGO staff that much of the impetus for thinking about 'NGO management' is being driven from outside and is therefore suspicious. Management agendas have at times taken the form of an imposed 'managerialism', rather than emerging organically as part of an NGO's own agenda. A good example of this is the ongoing debate about efforts by Northern NGOs to bring about the 'capacity building' of Southern NGOs – at least until recently, capacity building was widely seen as something that Northern NGOs 'did' to Southern NGOs rather than as a two-way, exploratory learning process (Lewis 1998c; Simbi and Thom 2000). Another is the popularity of logical framework analysis with development donors, which can make its adoption a requirement for NGOs wishing to secure funds and implement donor-funded projects, and has therefore created strong 'professionalizing' pressures on NGOs (Smillie 1995).

In spite of these complex pressures, and processes of action and reaction, there has in recent decades been a small but evolving history of initiatives dealing with NGO management issues, which arguably signify the potential importance of NGO management as a field. Interest in management and organizational issues in the North started to appear in the mid-1980s when the 'NGO Management' newsletter was produced from the International Council for Voluntary Agencies (ICVA) in Geneva. This newsletter laid the groundwork for discussing the concept of NGO management, and carried some lively debates, but it had ceased publication by the early 1990s, though it is not clear whether this was because it had already served its purpose of putting the subject on the agenda or whether its members ran out of funding or enthusiasm. The International NGO Training and Research Centre (INTRAC) was established in the UK in 1991 and has grown steadily since that time.[10] In the USA, the Institute of Development Research (IDR) in Boston has for many years worked on organizational issues for NGOs, while in the South, among other organizations, the Society of Participatory Research in India (PRIA) and El Taller in Tunisia have also pursued NGO organizational training and research agendas.

The subject of NGO management has also become popular again as renewed interest in 'civil society' has led to the creation of global citizen organizations such as CIVICUS. The issue of NGO staff management training has been addressed by multi-agency initiatives such as the Global Partnership Program for NGO Studies, Education and Training jointly organized by the Organization of Rural Associations for Progress (ORAP) in Zimbabwe, the Bangladesh Rural Advancement Committee (BRAC) and the School for International Training (SIT) in the United States which operated from 1995 until 2004. For some organizations, there is a realization that NGO staff may have focused a disproportionate amount of attention on 'where they want to go' and less on 'how they might get there'.

The preoccupation with NGO 'capacity building' which arose in the 1990s was a reflection of many things, such as the search for new useful roles by Northern NGOs. No longer wishing to implement their own projects directly in low-income countries, and bypassed in some cases by bilateral donors eager to work directly with third sectors in these countries, many turned instead to the challenge of 'building the capacity' of their local 'partner' third sector organizations (Smillie 1994; Lewis 1998c).

The increased attention being paid to the management of NGOs therefore has both a positive and a less benign side. But the capacity-building issue also indicated a concern that NGOs in developing countries could, with the right kind of organizational support, strengthen their roles as development actors in providing services, building democratic political processes and advocating for policy change and development rights. However, capacity building has remained an area of conflict and confusion, embodying both the risk of managerialist tendencies in the training agendas it has spawned (witness the many NGO training consultancy businesses and websites which have emerged) and the debates over power and autonomy which have led many to question Northern assumptions about Southern organizations, and to numerous attempts to re-evaluate the concept of 'partnership' so readily deployed in discourses of development policy and practice (Lewis 1998b; Bebbington 2005; Hoksbergen 2005; Ridde 2006).

It is possible to identify two contradictory trends within the world of development NGOs, in which some organizations continue to see management issues as being 'in the way' of their work and at best a remnant of a previously undesirable mainstream, while others rush headlong towards the solutions promised by the 'management gurus', who emerged in the private sector but have begun to appear in other kinds of organization (e.g. Drucker 1990). A similar, and at times parallel, debate has been under way in the British voluntary sector about the nature and roles of management. The weakness of many radical voluntary sector initiatives in the 1970s and 1980s was sometimes attributed to 'a serious misunderstanding of how management works' based on factors such as ideological rejectionism, cultural snobbery and a short-sighted inability to see management in terms other than 'command and control' (Landry *et al.* 1985). It has been argued that after this period of neglect and disdain, and in an effort to embrace the idea of management more fully, some British voluntary organizations went on to overreact in the other direction:

> What is interesting is not merely that the voluntary sector developed a self-conscious concern with management but also that when the voluntary sector took up management it did not look for knowledge and best practice within its own ranks, but rather turned to the private sector for its concepts and practices.
>
> (Leat 1995: 7)

On the other hand, there are more positive examples from the wider third sector which illustrate how some organizations have approached management issues more successfully. Debates about management and organization have a long history in the world of 'alternative' organizations in the third sector. In the women's movement in the United States, for example, the experience of seeking to reject formal organizational forms in favour of experimental collectivism famously led to Freeman's (1973) critique of 'the tyranny of structurelessness', in which it was found that the lack of organizational structures merely allowed charismatic leadership and individualism to run riot, subordinating organizational aims to personal agendas. Later work on women's third sector organizations in New York has shown that some of the most effective organizations were those which managed to combine elements of traditional bureaucracy and hierarchy with informal or 'collectivist' structures which reflected the alternative values of the organization (Bordt 1997).

Nevertheless, some development NGOs revised their opinions about management and rushed headlong into trying to import the latest management techniques from the private sector, in an attempt at quick-fix solutions to perceived management weaknesses. For example, many Northern NGOs during the 1990s began implementing systems for strategic planning, which had been a popular business management technique in the 1970s and 1980s, just at the time when some private sector management theorists (such as Mintzberg (1994), who earlier had been one of the originators of the whole idea) were becoming more aware of its limitations.

There is, however, a strong interest among development NGOs in striving to improve management practices both within their agencies, in terms of their programmes and projects, and in the relationships which they pursue with other development actors. Both internal and external factors are influencing this process. The disillusionment among many development donors accustomed to working only with governments in many parts of the world, and the growing evidence of poor results of government projects and programmes, motivated a search for alternative channels for development assistance (Edwards and Hulme 1995). Having brought NGOs more fully into the mainstream development policy processes, pressures of accountability then led some aid donors and policy makers to examine more closely whether NGOs are properly equipped to play these new high-profile roles. Studies undertaken by or for aid donors such as those by Tendler (1982), Stark Biddle (1984) and Riddell (1999) were frequently less than flattering about the realities of the claims made by and on behalf of development NGOs. These studies found that many of the taken-for-granted advantages and achievements attributed to NGOs could not be uncritically assumed, and showed that the positive press which NGOs often received was in some cases based more on wishful thinking than on hard facts.

Not all of the pressure for management thinking was driven from the outside. As NGOs have grown in scale and ambition, some have themselves recognized limits to their own effectiveness and begun to examine management and organization issues in more depth, recognizing that idealism and alternative ideas require a sound organizational framework if they are to make any impact on long-standing and complex problems of poverty and inequality. There may also be signs that things are moving too far the other way among some development NGOs, as the development industry becomes more professionalized. One critic of this trend is Dichter (2003), who reflects, after thirty years of experience, on an increasingly professionalized but largely ineffective international development effort. He argues that development has become a professional field rather than simply a calling or an amateur pursuit, and that newer concerns with career and salary among development professionals way outweigh the benefits of improved effectiveness.

What types of management problems have been identified in relation to development NGOs? These inevitably vary from organization to organization and context to context, but some patterns emerge and there are many quite predictable common problems. For example, Sahley (1995) highlights recurring areas of organizational weaknesses for NGOs. These will be familiar to many who work with or observe these organizations, and form a useful starting point. For many NGOs, management is not an explicit priority, and NGOs may be preoccupied with a focus on short-term details rather than on longer-term horizons and strategy. There is often a wish for NGOs to respond immediately, with little time for learning or reflection, and NGO responses are frequently 'over-committed and emotional' rather than achievable. There may be an inability to decentralize decision making, and it is rare to find true collaboration or partnership with other agencies. Individual agendas are often imposed on the overall NGO organizational remit, and there is an insecure funding climate which inhibits planning, and this ultimately produces a tendency for NGOs to maintain a 'grant mentality' rather than seeking to mobilize resources more widely.

There is no doubt a 'managerialist' edge to some of this new interest in the organization and management of NGOs, which may overemphasize financial accountability and advocate the wholesale importation of private sector 'quick-fix' management techniques and solutions. However, the central argument of this book is that the management of development NGOs is a legitimate area for concern and study because it promotes discussion and debate about improving the ways in which NGOs go about their work. Not only does it seem that many NGOs may have paid more attention to the 'what' rather than the 'how', there is increasing concern that NGOs may be in danger of being promoted beyond their levels of competence – that having raised their profile they may be seen as having overreached themselves (Edwards and Hulme 1992). In one critique, Mallaby (2004) suggested that some campaigning NGOs have simply become self-interested 'professional agitators' and have grown out of touch with the ordinary people they claim to represent. In the next section, we turn to the issue of development management, a broad sphere of thinking within development that includes ideas and strategies for both NGOs and a range of other development agencies.

Development management

There has been increasing disillusion with purely state-centred efforts to solve development problems through public action, and there has been a corresponding decline in the tradition of 'development administration', which was once a vibrant sub-field within the wider field of public administration. Policy was previously seen in 'prescriptive' terms, in which governments took action to promote development. At the level of practice, early approaches to development projects were generally 'top-down', in that they were based on the logic that 'development' was needed in a particular place, that the technical, spatial and administrative boundaries of its operation could be determined and that outcomes could be measured in what became known as the 'blueprint' approach (Gardner and Lewis 1996).

There is now greater acknowledgement that policy is best seen as 'process', referring to the actions of public institutions, both governmental and non-governmental, within a long-term historical perspective (Mackintosh 1992: 1). There has been a growth of research on the area of 'development management', which is intended to reflect the principle that both public and private efforts at bringing about development are increasingly relevant, and that 'management', rather than simply 'administration', is the matter at hand.

What makes development management a distinctive form of management in this new paradigm is that, broadly speaking, it is focused on the achievement of social goals outside the organization rather than on internal objectives such as making a profit (Thomas 1996). In the context of NGOs, the interest in development management is fertile ground which needs to be explored for possible clarification and new thinking. If NGOs are understood as third sector organizations concerned with the promotion of development objectives, then NGO management arguably forms a subset of wider development management. The problem is that there is no clear agreement about how to define the management of development, because efforts to combine ideas about the concepts of 'management' and those of 'development' are far from straightforward.

Development itself is in many ways one of the most slippery concepts of the late twentieth century, with very little agreement as to its meaning. It is generally used to mean positive change or progress, but can also be used to imply natural metaphors of organic growth and evolution, and the *Oxford English Dictionary* gives its meaning as 'a stage of growth or advancement'. Thomas (1996) points out neatly that development can refer to both deliberate attempts at progress through intervention, or to the efforts of people to improve their quality of life through their own efforts. As a verb it refers to the activities required to bring these changes about; as an adjective, it implies a value judgement, a standard against which things are compared – the implication being that the South is undeveloped or being developed, while the North has already reached a state of development.

Until relatively recently, development was debated primarily in economic terms, with a concentration on growth rather than distribution, and on statistics rather than actual people. At the level of theory, the previous polarization between the concepts of 'modernization' (the idea that to develop, poor societies need to achieve economic take-off and free themselves of 'traditional' social and cultural impediments, and that the benefits would eventually 'trickle down') and 'underdevelopment' (the idea that poor countries had been actively underdeveloped by direct colonization and unequal terms of trade, and that development was not possible without large-scale structural change) gave way to an 'impasse' (Booth 1994). The resulting vacuum has been gradually filled by a variety of ideas, among which action by NGOs has occupied a central position. The concept of 'human development' devised by the United Nations Development Programme (UNDP) provides the means to assess development using non-material measures, and draws upon Sen's (1983) 'capability approach', which sees development in terms of the capacity of individuals to make choices which allow them to expand quality of life. Quality of life in this approach includes non-material benefits such as political freedoms, equal opportunities and improved environmental and institutional sustainability.[11]

Postmodern ideas about development have emphasized diversity, the primacy of local-ized experience and the colonial roots of discourses (Escobar 1995). It has been suggested that there are no generalized answers and solutions, and that emphasis be on strategies rather than solutions. This has brought a focus on 'actor-oriented' accounts of social change (a term coined by Long and Long (1992), drawing in part on Anthony Giddens's writings on the relationships between individuals and structure), on local action, indigenous knowledge, participation, sustainability, empowerment, popular movements, and a range of other areas of development policy and practice concepts – i.e. on 'bottom-up' rather than 'top-down' approaches. These positions see development practice and research as non-linear, unpre-dictable and with complex and 'open' systems. They set great store by participation of the subjects of enquiry in the research process, and seek explicitly to bridge the gap between research and practice and between different academic disciplines and theories. For example, Chambers has been influential in developing a set of ideas about changing personal behav-iour and attitudes within organizations ('reversals'), arguing that what is needed is to stem and reverse trends of dominance and deception, through personal changes and action by the individuals in power who determine policies, procedures and organizational cultures (Chambers 1983, 1994, 2005).

In the wake of grand theory, the 'development as empowerment' approach (e.g. Black 1991; Friedmann 1992) emerged as the means to link theory and practice and avoid the pitfalls of the top-down paradigms. Psychologically and organizationally, grassroots capacity is built through experience of collective self-help to assert greater control over the envi-ronments in which people live. For example, the World Bank's (2002) 'sourcebook' on empowerment lists the four key elements of empowerment as access to information, inclu-sion within decision making, accountability of organizations to people, and local organizing capacity to resolve problems of common interest. Within these types of ideas, NGOs are seen as being able to play a role in linking local action back into processes of national and structural change. For example, Korten (1987) argued that NGOs could contribute to empowerment within political processes which link grassroots initiatives, broader social movements and political organizations to build what he termed 'people-centred develop-ment'. More recently the concept of 'social capital' (e.g. Putnam 1993; Bebbington 2004; Bebbington et al. 2004) has been brought into development policy debates (see Chapter 2). Here also NGOs and the third sector are seen as contributing to the creation of cross-cutting social ties and networks which might form the basis for collective action and increased levels of democratic participation.

In two influential articles, Thomas (1996, 1999) has tried to explore the ways in which the concepts of development and management are related. Thomas shows that while the term 'development management' refers crucially to people, it nevertheless also expresses ideas about authority and power. It cannot therefore be detached from the political discourse which links development as an idea with institutions and communities around the world. As Staudt writes in her introduction to a book on this subject:

> development management . . . involves more than adopting some bag of tricks from, say, western corporations, assuming techniques work the same way every-where. Development management is inherently political and the text stresses the diagnosis of political contexts and organizational politics more than techniques.
>
> (Staudt 1991: 3)

Development management debates have therefore centred on the need to decide what the nature is of the development tasks and activities which need to be managed. These of course cannot easily be defined, because development tasks and activities cover a wide-ranging, highly contested territory which includes economic growth, social welfare, resource redistribution, political process, empowerment and human rights. As we have seen, 'development' is a contested concept which is associated with a range of different, sometimes contradictory, approaches to reducing poverty, building capacity and providing social welfare. For some NGOs the delivery of services will doubtless require a set of practices and techniques which could usefully draw upon public and private sector approaches. For NGOs involved in campaigning and networking, perhaps less of this material will be of value, and new approaches are needed.

Thomas (1996) suggests that development tasks involve four distinctive elements: the directing of efforts towards external goals as well as internal organizational ones; an emphasis on influence and intervention in social processes rather than simply using resources to meet goals directly; a lack of agreement on exactly what needs to be done leading to values-based debate and conflict; and the centrality of process and continuity and not just task. Thomas goes on to suggest that the two views of management discussed earlier (top-down, instrumentalist as opposed to participatory, unpredictable) are not in the end mutually exclusive. There may also be circumstances, as in the cooperative case already discussed, when the 'command and control' variant of management is an appropriate one. Thomas suggests three ways of approaching development management. The first is termed 'management in development', which is simply management in the context of long-term historical change. The second is 'management of development', which is management of the deliberate efforts at progress undertaken within more formal development initiatives. The third is 'management for development', and this third type, which is management with a specific development orientation, is not the same as just good management, as his 1999 article goes on to show, because it is important to evaluate how well development tasks have been undertaken. In this way, both the instrumental and the expressive elements of management can be combined.

NGO management can therefore be seen as an area of 'development management', but this realization does not in the end get us very far, since there is no broad agreement on what are the tasks to be managed in development – merely a range of complex choices based on ideology, analysis and objective.[12] We turn in the following section to the field of third sector management, which constitutes another fertile area of enquiry from which to continue building our conceptual overview of NGO management.

Third sector management

As we saw earlier, NGOs are organizations with two distinct sides to their identity – as well as being development organizations, they are also part of the larger family of so-called 'third sector' organizations. This larger family includes a wide range of organizations which are neither part of the government sector, nor for-profit businesses whose *raison d'être* is the making of money. The third sector includes education establishments, pressure groups, religious organizations, trade unions, recreational clubs, community self-help initiatives and charitable welfare societies.

Within the growing body of academic research specializing in the third sectors of Europe and North America (e.g. Powell 1987; Salamon and Anheier 1994) and more internationally (Salamon *et al.* 2003) we can identify a growing section concerned with organization and management issues (e.g. Batsleer *et al.* 1992; Billis 1993a; Harris 1999; Hudson 1995; Anheier 2005). Such research has obvious implications for understanding NGO management, since almost all third sector organizations will arguably have at least some types of management issues in common.

Researchers working on the third sector have investigated organization and management issues in far more depth than their development NGO colleagues. A group of third sector scholars have set about developing a body of new theory, concepts and models which would reflect the distinctiveness of many of the management challenges of the third sector, based on research into these organizations. For example, Billis and Harris (1996: 6) stated, in a discussion of the application of knowledge to organizational issues in the British voluntary sector, that 'existing theories developed for other sectors went so far, but not far enough', and much of their work has been concerned with explaining this distinctiveness. Such work therefore draws on – but also challenges – areas of 'mainstream' organization theory (most of which has been developed with reference to the commercial and government sectors). An example is Billis's ideas about organizational choice, which assert that theories about the inevitability of organizational change based on resource dependency and ecological perspectives have only a weak application to some third sector contexts.

Little of this work has been systematically explored in terms of its relevance (or otherwise) to NGO management issues, despite the rather obvious possibilities such a comparison would appear to offer. For example, the large quantity of research on the organizational implications of the growth of contracting relationships between voluntary agencies and local government in the provision of social services – the so-called 'mixed economy of care' – which took place over the past decade or so in Britain and the United States (e.g. Smith and Lipsky 1993; Kramer 1994) could carry lessons for those interested in the ways in which, in countries such as Bangladesh, large local NGOs are increasingly taking over responsibilities for delivering services which were previously the responsibility of the state (Wood 1997), and as NGOs more widely become embroiled in 'partnerships' between the government and international donors (Lewis 1998b).

Since this third sector research literature is primarily concerned with Northern contexts, and with organizations engaged in welfare work and social service delivery, there will be significant differences among third sector organizations in Northern and Southern contexts. At the organizational level, cultural norms and rules mediate organizational forms, while at the level of the environment no one would want to pretend that working in Britain is in any way comparable with the context NGOs face in Somalia. Nevertheless, there may be areas of basic similarity between third sector organizations, and third sector scholars argue that we might expect them to face a common range of distinctive organizational and management challenges that are qualitatively different to those in either the public or the for-profit sectors. In his work, Gaventa (1999) makes the case that under the current global economic changes it is increasingly becoming possible to talk of 'Norths in the South' and 'Souths in the North', because islands of 'Third World-like poverty' exist in parts of otherwise rich countries and wealthy minority communities are common in many otherwise poor countries. The hurricane which led to the disastrous flooding of the city of New Orleans in August 2005, and the inability of large numbers of its poorest residents to take action following evacuation warnings, provide a sobering example of the way in which the contextual challenges of NGO work do not fit neatly into distinctions between 'developing' and 'developed', or 'North' and 'South'.

Alongside the generic organizational issues discussed in the previous section, we now turn to a brief discussion of some of these distinctive issues, which draws upon the emerging field of non-profit theory. At a very basic level, Handy (1988) suggests that third sector organizations are essentially 'value-driven' organizations and that this poses distinctive management challenges, because people work in these voluntary organizations from a variety of public and private motivations: a sense of altruism, an escape route from dominant ideologies, or increasing public status from being a member of an NGO board. This may not *always* be true in the NGO sector, of course, because in some societies NGO posts are highly prized since a job in a foreign-funded organization may bring significantly higher material rewards than many other forms of employment. In addition, third sector organizations differ from the other two sectors in that there is no clear link between the providers of funds and the users of the services (Hudson 1995). In the private sector customers pay for goods and services at a market price; in the public sector people can vote officials in or out of office. These elements of third sector distinctiveness generate distinctive management challenges such as difficulties in monitoring organizational performance, problems of managing multiple accountabilities, the need for intricate management structures in order to balance multiple stakeholders, conflicts between voluntarism and professionalism, the need to maintain sight of the organization's founding values and the tendency for third sector organizations to set vague organizational objectives.

Research on NGO accountability, the role of boards of governors and the organization of staffing and volunteering, are all areas of management from which models and concepts developed in the wider third sector might be applied to development NGOs. There are, of course, obvious dangers to the idea of importing and imposing yet more Western models in the name of development. As Baig (1999) shows in a review of the role of NGO boards in Pakistan, using concepts developed by Harris (1999) in the UK, there is only so far that one can go with such an approach, but it is nevertheless demonstrated to be a potentially fruitful one.

SYNTHESIZING AN APPROACH TO NGO MANAGEMENT

NGO management will clearly be a diverse and diffuse field for study and action, requiring a complex mix of concepts and skills which draws upon a combination of generic management ideas and more specialized solutions which reflect the distinctive characteristics and activities of NGOs as 'third sector' organizations. In addition to the organizational diversity of NGOs, a key problem is the nature of the work that NGOs do. There is, as we have seen, no clear agreement on what 'development' really means, and this problem therefore makes it difficult to discuss how development should be 'managed'. Many NGOs may not see themselves as doing 'development' at all, particularly those in the campaigning field or those which do not choose to work with the international development industry. A second problem is whether NGOs as groups can really be distinguished from other kinds of third sector organizations, because it is not enough to make a simple distinction between 'developed' and 'developing' country contexts, or 'welfare' or 'development' approaches – in the end, these are questions of labelling and judgement rather than indisputable fact. For example, the Highlander Institute in the United States described by Gaventa (1999) works locally with Appalachian communities but has a wide range of contacts and initiatives with NGOs in developing countries, and effectively dissolves the conceptual distinction between the US 'non-profit sector' and the world of development NGOs.

Despite these issues, and the overall lack of research attention which NGO management has so far received, there has been the emergence of what Stewart (1997) terms 'a school of NGO management science'. This can be traced to the late 1980s and early 1990s when a series of short articles appeared in the pages of the ICVA's *NGO Management* newsletter and later in some of the academic development journals, and I have termed this the 'NGO management debate'. It took the form of a discussion between writers on NGOs and development, some of whom were excited by the new emphasis on 'alternative' management practices – such as empowerment, participation and other bottom-up approaches – while others were frustrated at the ways in which the idealism of NGOs, along with the growing expectations of funders and policy makers, often seemed to outstrip NGOs' own understanding and practice of basic management skills.

From this first perspective, Korten had written in 1987 that a new management paradigm was emerging among development NGOs, which was being influenced by, among others, the work of Robert Chambers, which embodied a set of emerging 'alternative management approaches' designed to address the problems which had become apparent within top-down, professionalized development management approaches. Korten spoke of a 'new development professionalism', in which

> Rather than supporting central control, [these NGOs] . . . support self-assessment and self-correction driven by a strong orientation to client service and a well-defined sense of mission. Highly developed management systems provide rich flows of information to facilitate these self-management processes.
>
> (Korten 1987: 156)

An example of this was the evolution of the existing concept of 'strategic planning', in which a specialized planning unit developed a blueprint which is often then resisted by other staff at different levels of the organization into the newer idea of 'strategic management', which, if undertaken properly, becomes a more inclusive, consultative process that brings staff at all levels of the organization into the identification and implementation of organizational choices.

Dichter's (1989a: 387) counter-argument was that development NGOs need to be able 'to walk before they can run'. In one short case study, for example, Dichter described an organization in which leaders and staff were given courses in participatory leadership training by a well-meaning development organization when they really needed to learn far more basic practical management skills such as 'how to set up and keep administrative, accounting, book-keeping, and record-keeping systems for the co-op'. In another case, Dichter related how a Northern NGO, planning to establish a presence in West Africa, provided preliminary state-of-the-art 'development management' training to its expatriate executive director, who then went to set up the local country office and proceeded to make two basic management mistakes. First, the director did not pay attention to the need to make sure that the right person was carefully recruited for the job, and without any feel for local culture or job markets appointed a person too quickly who turned out to be unsuitable. Second, he neglected to make sure that basic information systems were established, selected an office in an inappropriate area of town, and neglected the practical matter of setting up a proper vehicle maintenance programme. Very soon these somewhat prosaic management shortcomings undermined the NGO's efforts to carry out its work successfully. Such problems have not necessarily gone away. Edwards (1999a and see Box 7.1) also found in a study of NGO work in South Asia that lack of attention to 'the basics' of management was an important contributory factor in the failure of NGO initiatives, such as selecting appropriate staff and local partners, maintaining a clear sense of purpose and goals, and maintaining good communications with clients and constituents.

Dichter (1989a) argued therefore that thinking about NGO management needs to start 'plain' rather than 'fancy', and that in his cases the preoccupation with experimental, participatory development management styles was frequently found to be at the expense of more basic management tasks. NGOs needed to understand budgeting and personnel issues; they needed to analyse the markets, legal framework and policy environment within which they operated; and they required a knowledge of how to maintain relationships, information systems and assets. Dichter's case was close to the 'management is management' idea – the argument that no matter what kind of organization we are talking about, generic management rules apply – at least in the early years of a development NGO. Rejecting simple North/South, business/voluntary or top-down/bottom-up dualisms, he suggested that basic management principles:

> are not that different for North and South, or for business and the not-for-profit sector. . . . Indeed, if 'good' management in a generic sense exists, it encompasses task, people, process and organization. What makes for salient differences are context and the ends of management. These cannot be ignored, any more than we can forget that different theories of management are themselves contextual.
>
> (Dichter 1989a: 385)

31

Both Western and non-Western NGOs have been drawn to people-centred participatory management ideas, and these may fit well with the NGOs' overall ideologies and objectives. But such ideas have usually originated in stable, strongly defined organizations in the context of strong supporting structures and institutions. These conditions, Dichter argued, were unlikely to exist in many of the Southern contexts in which NGOs tend to be active. Dichter's assumptions were perhaps oversimplified in assuming that, as opposed to the North, the South is 'under-organized' because such dualist thinking can be misleading. But his analysis finds more favour if it is applied to third sector organizations in general, which as we have seen are sometimes too quick to rush headlong towards management approaches which may not always be appropriate.

CONCLUSION

In summary, it is clear that development NGOs can vary very significantly in their structure and in the nature of their operations. This is one of the factors that makes NGO management a complex topic. NGOs include large, bureaucratic organizations with multi-million dollar budgets as well as small, informal local initiatives. Some NGOs are engaged in long-term community development work, while others are primarily campaigning organizations seeking to influence policy. Others provide short-term emergency relief in response to natural disasters or human calamities created by conflict. Some find that emergency relief work becomes a longer-term challenge, as violent conflict and instability becomes chronic and remains unresolved, as in Somalia or Sri Lanka. How then can we best approach the subject of NGO management? As this introduction has shown, there is no clearly defined body of literature to which we can turn. Instead, we will need to work across subject boundaries and synthesize ideas from quite different fields of research and practice.

This introductory chapter has raised a set of important questions that need to be borne in mind by the reader for the rest of the book. Should NGOs take management more seriously, and if so, what kind of management models should they be interested in? Do NGOs pay enough attention to the basic 'nuts and bolts' of mainstream business practice? Most NGOs need to be able to keep accounts, assign roles to their staff and make strategic decisions. Certain more innovative techniques from the private sector, such as 'management by objectives' and the social audit, are increasingly part of the world of development organizations. Will such techniques move NGOs from being primarily value-driven and voluntaristic towards a more professionalized approach to their work?

Should NGOs look to the public sector, where new management ideas have arguably provided a range of new concepts and practices for development? For example, the development of approaches such as 'participatory learning and action' (PLA)[13] – despite its strong popular association with NGOs – actually has its roots in the more forward-thinking sections of the public sector in certain parts of South Asia (Biggs and Smith 1998). What used to be termed public administration has been transformed into the 'new public management', which emphasizes the use of private sector management techniques, downsizing and privatization (Polidano and Hulme 1999). As new technologies have begun to restructure some of the relationships between citizens and governments, and the limitations of new public management ideas have become more apparent, some argue that we are entering a new phase of 'digital-era governance' (Dunleavy *et al.* 2005). How might these changes and trends impact on NGOs?

Should NGOs turn instead to the growing field of what is termed 'non-profit management', a growth area particularly in the United States where the non-profit sector, it has been argued, now requires a new set of specialized models and concepts to assist these distinctive kinds of organizations to improve their management (Bryson 1994)? Or should development NGOs — as a diverse and increasingly multicultural group of organizations — seek to develop their own distinctive new management models, perhaps by exploring the possibilities offered by experimenting beyond the boundaries of existing practices, and outside primarily Western templates of organization?[14] These are not merely conceptual questions, and they have important implications for policy and practice.

REVIEW QUESTIONS

■ Review the reasons for the growth of interest in NGO management with reference to an organization or a context with which you are familiar.

■ Discuss the extent to which the various different management approaches discussed in this chapter might each highlight different aspects of NGO management.

■ Identify a particular NGO management challenge that you have encountered and explore how it might fit within the conceptual framework presented in the chapter.

Part I

The theory of NGO management

Chapter 2

Contexts, histories and concepts

LEARNING OBJECTIVES

After considering this chapter, the reader will be able to describe and analyse:

- Historical and structural factors which contribute to the wide diversity of different contexts in which development NGOs operate
- Different approaches to the classification of NGOs, along with the range of different terms that are used
- A conceptual understanding of the terms 'third sector' and civil society

KEY TERMS

- Structural-operational definition of non-profit organizations
- Third sector
- Civil society
- New policy agenda
- Citizenship

INTRODUCTION

Before returning to the question of NGO management per se, the following two chapters explore the background to the current policy interests in development NGOs, and the concepts which are now being used to understand and analyse them. In our conceptual framework (Figure 1.1), we need to begin understanding the context in which NGO management can be located.

During the past two decades, there has been a dramatic change in the way in which we see the institutional processes of development. Before the mid-1980s, there was little or no mention of NGOs in the academic research of the policy literature, save for brief discussion of 'humanitarian' organizations such as Oxfam whose work was seen as somehow separate, different or peripheral to mainstream development. A search of the major development textbooks from the 1960s through to the 1980s for mention of NGOs or voluntary organizations yields little or no references at all (Lewis 2005). Yet the 1990s saw a veritable explosion of writings on the subject, as NGOs moved into a mainstream position in development policy. NGOs have appealed both to activists and those interested in development alternatives, as well as to the 'establishment'. By the mid-1990s, NGOs had become the 'favoured child' of the official development donors (Edwards and Hulme 1995). NGOs became 'catapulted into international respectability' such that governments and multilateral institutions suddenly saw NGOs as important actors in development (Brodhead 1987: 1). While NGO fortunes have waxed and waned according to rapidly changing development donor fashions since this time, there is no doubt that NGOs continue to play a central role in development and relief work at the start of the twenty-first century (Lewis and Opoku-Mensah 2006; Wallace *et al.* 2006).

THE RISE OF NGOs IN DEVELOPMENT

What explained the dramatic entry of NGOs into the development mainstream during the 1990s? On one level, the rise of the NGOs was something of an illusion, because NGOs, or 'NGO-like organizations', were in fact far from new. The concept of 'philanthropy', which can be defined in general terms as 'the ethical notions of giving and serving to those beyond one's immediate family', has existed in different forms in most cultures throughout history, often driven by religious tradition (Ilchman *et al.* 1998). Local third sector organizations of various kinds worked relatively unnoticed in most societies for generations in the form of religious organizations, community groups and organized self-help ventures in villages and towns (Anheier 2005). For example, the social and cultural anthropological literature of West Africa in the 1950s and 1960s contains accounts of the adaptive role of local 'voluntary associations' in helping to integrate urban migrants into their new social and economic surroundings (Lewis 1999b).

At the same time, the colonization by European powers of large areas of what we now call the South included the participation of missionary groups whose activities can now arguably be seen as a diverse set of prototypical NGO ventures into the fields of education, health service provision and agricultural development, and included both 'welfarist' and 'empowerment' approaches to community work (Fernando and Heston 1997). Some of the more well-established Northern NGOs also have origins which go back far longer than the current period of NGO fashionability. The Save the Children Fund was founded by Eglantyne Jebb in 1919 after the trauma of the First World War. Oxfam – originally known as the Oxford Committee Against the Famine – dates from 1942, when it was established in order to provide famine relief to victims of the Greek Civil War. The US agency CARE has its origins in sending US food packages to Europe in 1946. We will briefly discuss the varied roots and 'hidden histories' of NGOs later in this chapter.

Why do we find that NGOs have risen to prominence in the development field in recent years? There are perhaps at least four main interrelated clusters of reasons. The first can be linked to the emergence of what has been termed the theoretical 'impasse' within development thinking (Booth 1994). It was argued that macro-theories of both mainstream 'modernization' and radical 'dependency' which had dominated development ideas for two decades had lost their appeal, and a search was on for alternative ideas and by extension different organizational actors in development processes (particularly in relation to the state), and NGOs 'fitted the bill'. For example, the work of Korten (1990) illustrates the way in which theorists and practitioners on both the left and right, disillusioned with conventional ideas about development, were attracted by new ideas about 'people-centred' approaches. NGOs in both the North and South came to be seen as crucial to this new bundle of ideas.

The second set of reasons is related to the perceptions of many development agencies that governments of both the North and South had performed poorly in the fight against poverty. A search for alternatives to public sector action and 'government to government' aid became a priority. The simple transfers of aid resources between governments were felt to have yielded poor results in terms of impact on poverty, and to have contributed to growing levels of bureaucracy and corruption. A pervasive argument gathered force that in general development work, policy makers had overestimated the capacity of the state to initiate, implement and monitor appropriate development activities. Brodhead (1987) consequently suggested that the new policy interest in NGOs had little to do with any real understanding of the capacities or the potential of NGOs, but was instead driven primarily by a sense of disillusionment that more than twenty years of official overseas development assistance had apparently generated little in the way of measurable results. Many of those who wrote about NGOs were highly critical of the state, such as Fisher (1998: 2), who in her book *Nongovernments* speaks of the 'increasing inability of the nation-state to muddle through as it confronts the long-term consequences of its own ignorance, corruption and lack of accountability'. While some were undoubtedly driven by an anti-statist ideology, for others there was a more opportunistic sense in which people concerned with official aid 'discovered' NGOs and then proceeded to invest them with a set of roles within an agenda for improved aid effectiveness.

The two reasons discussed above for the rise of NGOs focus on their 'discovery' by outside agencies, but this is not the whole story. A third set of reasons centres on the ways in which NGOs themselves have contributed to this new profile in both the North and South. As the traditional economic and political concerns of development shifted in the 1990s to include debates about the importance of environment, gender and social development, a growing NGO presence and policy 'voice' became apparent. NGOs began to gain increased access to policy makers, and demanded that their ideas, views and models should be taken seriously. This was achieved through a combination of activism, campaigning and policy dialogue. For example, it seems unlikely that the influential UK 1997 White Paper on International Development would have placed so much emphasis on poverty reduction had not the NGO community advocated for a greater poverty focus in the British aid programme for many years (Gardner and Lewis 2000). Today there is still a view of NGOs that sees them primarily as sources of development 'alternatives' in terms of both ideas and practices (Mitlin *et al.* 2005).

At the international level there are other reasons which might explain the rise to prominence of NGOs in international governance. Charnovitz (1997) lists four sets of reasons: the growth of inter-governmental negotiation around domestic policy brought about by integration of the world economy; the end of the Cold War, which removed the polarization of global politics around the two superpowers; the emergence of a global media system which provides a platform for NGOs to express their views; and the spread of democratic norms which may have increased public expectations about participation and transparency in decision making. In both the North and South, current policy interests in the roles of 'faith-based organizations' – which represent one of the latest ways of thinking about NGOs and civil society – have also served to maintain policy attention on the world of NGOs. Smith (2002) traces this new policy trend to the discourse of 'compassionate conservatism' in the USA which is associated with the ideas of US academic Marvin Olasky, and the subsequent establishment of US$30-million Compassion Capital fund in January 2002 by President George W. Bush (to whom Olasky has been a close adviser) to provide contracts for services from local faith-based welfare initiatives.

It is possibly the fact that NGOs mean all things to all people that may explain their current ubiquity. As DeMars (2005: 2) puts it: 'The NGO organization form has become so irresistible that a broad assortment of notables, missionaries, and miscreants are creating their own NGOs.' Indeed, NGOs appeal to all sides of the political spectrum. For liberals, NGOs help to balance state and business interests and prevent abuses of the power these sectors hold. For neo-liberals, NGOs are part of the private sector and provide vehicles for increasing market roles and advancing the cause of privatization through private 'not-for-profit' action. Finally, for the left NGOs promise a 'new politics' which offers the chance of social transformation but presents an alternative to earlier radical strategies for capturing state power and centralization (Clarke 1998).

NGOs in short have come to be seen as highly ambiguous organizations within the moral and political frameworks of development policy and practice. They can sometimes display a dual character, as they alternate between theoretical and activist discourses, between identities of public and private, professionalism and amateurishness, market and non-market values, radicalism and pluralism, modernity and tradition, and ultimately perhaps (as in the case of the review into the Rwanda genocide) good and evil. Turner and Hulme (1997) refer to the 'Janus-like' quality of organizations which can combine the rhetoric of Freirean transformative ideology for radical supporters at one moment, and the market rhetoric of enterprise culture for government, business and donors the next. Other critics such as Temple (1997) see NGOs in more negative terms as merely a continuation of the missionary tradition and as handmaidens of capitalist change. In this view, NGOs are modernizers and destroyers of local economies which were once based on age-old systems of reciprocity, into which NGOs introduce Western values to local communities and bring about a process of 'economicide'. For Velloso de Santisteban (2005: 208) NGOs are merely an inadequate response to complex, long-standing problems: 'NGOs are simply the form in which people of goodwill organise . . . the poor will always be with us. And so will NGOs, for all the difference that will make.'

THE CHANGING POLICY CONTEXT

The emergence in the 1990s of what Robinson (1993) called the 'new policy agenda' heralded a period of heightened profile for NGOs. NGOs were identified as suitable vehicles for two new related areas of policy impetus within development policy: the idea of 'good governance', in which NGOs were viewed as public actors with a key role in supporting democratic processes in the political sphere; and the priority of 'economic liberalization', in which the 'private' aspect of NGOs was emphasized, and NGOs were seen as important new market-based actors with the potential to deliver services more efficiently than the state (Edwards and Hulme 1995). At the same time, after the end of the Cold War, there was a related set of policy agendas which saw NGOs as useful policy instruments not for 'development' as such, but for containing disorder in troubled regions of the world such as the former Yugoslavia and the Horn of Africa. NGOs had always been concerned with humanitarian relief and assistance work, but in some quarters NGOs became seen – in Fowler's (1994) apt phrase – as 'ladles for the global soup kitchen' within the process of what Deacon et al. (1997) have termed the 'residualisation of welfare'.

These two trends have continued and intensified. The good governance agenda has evolved into a more tightly coordinated and 'upstream' effort by development donors to influence recipient governments and build greater ownership of policy reforms and development interventions through mechanisms such as direct budget support and partnership agreements (Mosse 2005). The new policy agenda has evolved into what Maxwell (2003) has termed a 'new "New Poverty Agenda"', which brings developing country governments back to the centre of poverty reduction while arguably seeking to increase external influence over them.[1] This has generated a new set of policy instruments for aid delivery in the form of the collaborative poverty reduction strategy papers (PRSPs), underpinned by an emphasis on results-based management in the form of the millennium development goals (MDGs) with eight poverty reduction goals and eighteen targets, with the ultimate aim of reducing by half the number of people living on less than US$1 per day by 2015. Despite a trend of 'regovernmentalization' of aid processes that is implied by budget support and PRSPs, these newer forms of global governance continue to envisage important roles for NGOs in service delivery and advocacy. The humanitarian agenda has also advanced further as new areas of conflict and crisis have led to the widening and deepening of NGO roles in countries such as Afghanistan, Iraq and Sudan, along with increases in official funding to NGOs. Yet this has also brought concerns that humanitarian aid is becoming more instrumentalized as a more radical, intrusive and politicized tool of governance to resolve conflict and secure order in troubled areas of the world (Duffield 2002). This process has intensified since the 9/11 attacks in 2001, as donors have increasingly linked development assistance with fighting terrorism in what has been termed the 'securitization' of aid (Harmer and Macrae 2003).

The emergence of NGOs is not only linked with the increasing level of resources which have been made available to NGOs in the South by aid agencies and Northern NGOs, but by the new interest among Southern governments in working with NGOs, particularly in service delivery (Clarke 1998). The bundle of ideas loosely termed the 'new public management' (NPM) approach to administrative reform, which has dominated public policy in the industrialized world since the 1980s, has also been influential in many developing country contexts and has informed conditions imposed by the World Bank and the International Monetary Fund (IMF). These ideas and prescriptions, which generally refer to changes in public management practice that include the purchaser/provider split in public service provision, the use of agency contracting in order to link performance and incentives, and efforts to improve accounting transparency based on quantifiable output indicators, have contributed to a changing policy climate. New roles were opened up for NGOs to become involved in service provision as government structure and roles have been redefined and reduced (Turner and Hulme 1997). For example, as more aid has been provided to developing country governments directly, these governments have contracted out service provision to local NGOs more extensively in a new NGO contracting culture.

More recently, the processes of desegregation, competition and incentivization that were central to the new public management agenda have been found increasingly to produce problems of institutional and policy complexity. According to Dunleavy *et al.* (2005: 1), NPM in seven Organization for Economic Cooperation and Development (OECD) countries has impacted negatively on citizens' abilities to address and solve problems because of these associated problems of increased complexity brought about by the proliferation of multiple agency partnerships, excessive user choice and intricate targeting incentives. At the same time, public management is becoming increasingly transformed, particularly but not exclusively in the North, by information technologies. As a result, the emerging post-NPM scenario is characterized by Dunleavy *et al.* (2005) as one of 'digital-era governance'. This may bring the potential of a more integrated set of governance functions within the government sphere, bringing better access to information for citizens and the need and greater potential for increased scrutiny of governance processes by civil society organizations.

Such changes have affected NGOs engaged in service provision as well as those seeking to influence government efficiency and accountability. NGOs are generally highly dependent for 'room for manoeuvre' on the type of government they find themselves dealing with at the national or local level. Clark's (1991) view that 'NGOs can oppose, complement or reform the state but they cannot ignore it' is still a useful summary of the NGOs' basic options. In the public interest the government can legitimately claim the need for financial control of NGOs to ensure probity, and to coordinate the different types of development services which are being provided by different state and non-state actors. NGOs are likely to favour as an operating environment or as a development goal what Chambers (1994) calls an 'enabling environment', in which the state provides sound management of the economy, provides basic infrastructure and services, and maintains peace and the democratic rule of law.

Government attitudes to NGOs nevertheless still vary considerably from place to place, and period to period. These range from active hostility in which governments may seek to interfere in the affairs of or even dissolve NGOs (with or without good reason) through to periods of active courtship, 'co-optation' or 'partnership', through which governments – and donors – seek to bring NGOs into policy processes, usually at the level of implementation. Within the changing frameworks of international aid, NGOs have become important components of the new forms of international governance that have become 'dispersed' beyond the nation-state within a shifting transnational framework of actors, aid flows, policy prescriptions and institutional relationships (Mosse 2005). In this sense, NGOs have been seen as de facto extensions of the neo-liberal state and crucial to the way in which such a state can operate. One interesting phenomenon which has emerged is the exchange of personnel between NGOs and government, which appears to be becoming more common in some countries. For example, the government of President Luis Inácio Lula da Silva in Brazil is sometimes known as the 'NGO government' because of the numbers of activists it contains.

But it is also the case that NGOs may continue to pose a dilemma – or even a threat – to the state, because by putting forward alternative visions of social and economic development they can expose the limitations of the status quo (Bratton 1989). While government may sometimes be able to take some of the credit for successful NGO work which brings increases in living standards to the sections of the population untouched by government-run services, the state may also easily be threatened if its legitimacy is brought into question through the exposure by NGOs of its inability to deliver. NGOs which actively campaign for democratic and other rights may threaten entrenched interests, and their activities may quickly be seen by the state as subversive. In 2005, for example, this scenario became starkly apparent in Russia, where the government – mindful of civil society-led political activities in neighbouring states such as Ukraine, and of the funding of local NGOs by Western and other interests – began setting in place tough new laws which aimed to curtail the rise of NGOs in the post-Soviet era.[2]

TERMINOLOGICAL MUDDLES

Research on the so-called 'third sector' – a concept reviewed in more detail later in this chapter – has generated a substantial level of debate and discussion on the variety of NGO terms and labels. Organizations which might be called 'non-governmental organizations' in one country are termed 'voluntary organizations' or 'non-profit organizations' in another, for little or no apparent reason. There is no straightforward way through the terminological mire of the world's third sector organizations, although each of the above terms can be seen to be culturally generated, and its usage can be historically traced back to specific social, economic and political contexts. This is more than just a semantic problem, because labelling has important resource and policy implications in terms of 'who is in and who is out'.

'Voluntary organization' or 'charity' are terms widely used in Britain, where there is a rich tradition of voluntary work and volunteering and a history of charity law which emphasizes Christian, sometimes paternalistic, values. 'Non-profit organization' is commonly used in the United States, where the market has long been dominant and alternative forms of organization receive fiscal benefits if they can demonstrate that they are not commercial, profit-making entities. Finally, as we saw in Chapter 1, the term 'non-governmental organization', which tends to be applied mainly (though not exclusively) either to third sector organizations which work internationally or to those which belong to developing country contexts, has its roots in the United Nations system established after the Second World War. The designation 'non-governmental organization' was awarded to international non-state organizations given consultative status in UN activities. In order to illustrate the terminological problem, Najam (1996b: 206) drew up a list of over forty different acronyms used for various kinds of NGO by practitioners and researchers all over the world, and even this list, as the author states, is far from exhaustive! I have added a few more in Table 2.1.

If each of these terms were used logically and consistently, then they might prove useful in providing a way of categorizing the different types of third sector organization which exist. But they are rarely used with any level of consistent logic. In Britain, the term 'voluntary organization' might typically be employed to refer to an organization working with the homeless in London, while a similar organization working with the homeless in Bangladesh is likely to be termed a 'non-governmental organization'. In the United States, the term 'non-profit organization' covers many of the third sector organizations working domestically, but for some reason the term 'private voluntary organization' has traditionally been used within the United States government's Agency for International Development (USAID) to refer to non-profit organizations which work overseas in development work. Some non-governmental organizations in 'developing' countries resent the label 'voluntary' because they feel it detracts from the professionalized character of many organizations which may not use volunteers, while others dislike 'non-profit' because it makes them sound too business-like. It is frequently argued that the 'non-governmental' tag lacks precision and meaning because it describes organizations by what they are *not* instead of by what they *are*.

The difficulties experienced in finding a workable and consistent terminology is complicated further by the enormous diversity of third sector organizations around the world. Some are small self-help groups or informal associations working at the community level with a membership which barely reaches double figures and no paid staff, drawing instead on volunteers and supporters who may be motivated by politics, religion or some form of altruism. Others are large, highly bureaucratized service-providing organizations with a corporate identity and thousands of staff who see their work primarily in terms of a career. Some see themselves as part of the world of development agencies and institutions working to eliminate poverty and injustice, while others are recreational societies or religious organizations with specialized purposes. Some take a 'modernization' approach to social change, others attempt more radical empowerment. Some receive funding from outside bodies and depend on such resources for their existence, while others mobilize their resources locally through their own fund-raising initiatives or through membership fees and subscriptions. Some organizations are private member benefit in orientation, while others are public benefit.[3]

It is therefore common for the authors of many texts on NGOs to begin their writing with their own sets of definitions of different terms and types of organization. For example, Clark (1991) sets out a range of six broad categories of NGO types based on the types of activities they carry out: 'relief and welfare agencies' (e.g. Catholic Relief Services and various missionary societies); 'technical innovation organizations' (e.g. Grameen Bank with its work with credit in Bangladesh); 'public service contractors' which work closely with Southern governments and official aid agencies (e.g. the US agency CARE); 'popular

Table 2.1 *The myriad of NGO acronyms and labels*

AGNs	advocacy groups and networks
BINGOs	big international NGOs
BONGOs	business-organized NGOs
CBMS	community-based management systems
CBOS	community-based organizations
COME'n'Gos	the idea of temporary NGOs following funds!
DONGOs	donor-oriented/organized NGOs
Dotcause	civil society networks mobilizing support through the Internet
ENGOs	environmental NGOs
GDOs	grassroots development organizations
GONGOs	government-organized NGOs
GRINGOs	government-run international NGOs
GROs	grassroots organizations
GRSOs	grassroots support organizations
GSCOs	global social change organizations
GSOs	grassroots support organizations
IAs	interest associations
IDCIs	international development cooperation institutions
IOs	intermediate organizations
IPOs	international/indigenous people's organizations
LDAs	local development associations
LINGOs	little international NGOs
LOs	local organizations
MOs	membership organizations
MSOs	membership support organizations
NGDOs	non-governmental development organizations
NGIs	non-governmental individuals
NGIS	non-governmental interests
NGO	next government official
NNGOs	Northern NGOs
NPOs	non-profit or not-for-profit organizations
PDAs	popular development associations
POs	people's organizations
PSCs	public service contractors
PSNPOs	paid staff NPOs
PVDOs	private voluntary development organizations
PVOs	private voluntary organizations
QUANGOs	quasi-governmental organizations
RWAs	relief and welfare associations
SHOs	self-help organizations
TIOs	technical innovation organizations
TNGOs	transnational NGOs
VDAs	village development associations
VIs	village institutions
VNPOs	volunteer non-profit organizations
VOs	village organizations
VOs	volunteer organizations

Source: adapted from Najam 1996

development agencies' which work with grassroots groups on self-help, social development and building grassroots democracy (e.g. Bangladesh Rural Advancement Committee); 'grass-roots development organizations' which are membership organizations which may receive support from other organizations or may operate without external assistance (e.g. Self-Employed Women's Association, SEWA, in India); and 'advocacy groups or networks' which are NGOs with no operational field projects but which primarily exist to carry out education and lobbying (e.g. the World Development Movement in Britain). A functional definition such as this one, however, runs into problems because many organizations increasingly carry out a range of different types of activities.

Korten (1990) divides the third sector into four main categories of organization: 'voluntary organizations' (VOs) that pursue a social mission driven by a commitment to shared values; 'public service contractors' (PSCs) that function as market-oriented non-profit businesses serving public purposes; 'people's organizations' (POs) that represent their members' interests, have member-accountable leadership and are substantially self-reliant; and 'government-organized NGOs' (GONGOs) that are creations of government and serve primarily as instruments of public policy. These definitions are useful, because they tell us something about the origins and orientation of an NGO, but they are not in the end very precise. The Johns Hopkins University Nonprofit Research Project in its research project on global civil society has broken down NGOs into twelve different types.[4] As Vakil (1997) argues in a detailed article, which seeks to analyse the range of different NGO taxonomies that currently exist, the lack of agreement on NGO terms is more than a 'mere nuisance'. The confusion creates difficulties for researchers attempting to develop theoretical work in relation to NGOs, particularly as it prevents comparative analysis of empirical work on NGOs drawn from different country contexts. In practical terms, the lack of agreement may confuse the relationship between potential funders and recipients, it may make the task of government regulation more difficult, and it may reduce the potential for NGOs to transfer knowledge and learn experientially.

PROBLEMS OF DEFINING NGOs

We have established the conceptual framework of the third sector as both a group of organizations and a social space which embodies a wide range of organizations concerned with a bewildering variety of human interests. Within this framework, NGOs have come to be seen as a specific subset of this wider family of third sector organizations. There are two main strands to the attempts by scholars to define non-governmental organizations. The first, such as the following one from the international law literature, is a general legal definition which takes a very general view that 'NGOs are groups of individuals organized for the myriad of reasons that engage human imagination and aspiration' (Charnovitz 1997: 185). It goes on to suggest that the term is usually left to refer to organizations which play an international role in environment, human rights or disaster relief, and this might therefore be termed 'the international relations' definition of NGOs. Writers such as Charnovitz document the emergence of NGOs as actors on the international stage from anti-slave trade movements to peace groups in the League of Nations era and the growth of the formal NGO role as recognized by the United Nations Charter.

The second type of definition is focused more broadly on the idea that NGOs are organizations concerned in some sense with social or economic change – an agenda normally associated with the concept of 'development'. This emphasizes the term 'NGO' as an agency engaged in development or relief work at local, national and international levels. Here NGOs may be contrasted with other types of third sector or non-governmental entities such as those engaged in sports, leisure or arts activities, or those which represent associations of business or professional persons. For example, Vakil (1997: 2060), in one of the most comprehensive and useful definitional discussions of NGOs to be found in the literature, suggests that NGOs are best understood as 'self-governing, private, not-for-profit organizations that are geared to improving the quality of life for disadvantaged people'.

This set of definitions often situates NGOs in the context of what has been termed the 'aid industry' (discussed in Chapter 3), the configuration of international institutions and transnational resource flows which emerged after the Second World War and which aims to address problems of poverty and development. For example, Fowler's (1997) discussion of NGOs is linked closely to the world of international development assistance, and he sees the future of development NGOs in terms of their ability to break free of these links and gain more room for manoeuvre and independence. For some Southern writers too NGOs are seen in very specific terms. For example, Diaz-Albertini (1991) argues from Peru that Southern development NGOs should be seen as private, non-profit Third World organizations that implement development projects and programmes with the poor in their respective countries, as organizations predominantly formed and staffed by middle-class progressive professionals, and which receive most of their resources from North American and Western European non-government funding agencies.

Is there a way out of this muddle? In response to the terminological confusion which exists within wider third sector research, Salamon and Anheier (1992) show that most definitions of non-profit organizations (their terminology and unit of analysis) have been either legal (focusing on the type of formal registration and status of organizations in different country contexts), economic (in terms of the source of the organization's resources) or functional (based on the type of activities undertaken by the organization). In place of these types of definition, Salamon and Anheier (1992) have developed what they term the 'structural/operational' definition for the non-profit sector, which they base on the observable features of an organization. As the first third sector organizational definition to attempt a measure of cross-cultural rigour (it has been 'tested' in a range of countries around the world), this work forms a useful starting point for attempting to define the organizations with which we are concerned in this book. The definition proposes that a non-profit organization has the following five key characteristics: it is *formal*, that is the organization is institutionalized in that it has regular meetings, office bearers and some organizational permanence; it is *private* in that it is institutionally separate from government, though it may receive some support from government; it is *non-profit distributing*, and if a financial surplus is generated it does not accrue to owners or directors (often termed the 'non-distribution constraint'); it is *self-governing* and therefore able to control and manage its own affairs; and finally it is *voluntary* and, even if it does not use volunteer staff as such, there is at least some degree of voluntary participation in the conduct or management of the organization, such as in the form of a voluntary board of directors.

This definition, it is argued, fits quite well in general terms with the various types of organizations accorded non-profit status in different country contexts around the world (Salamon and Anheier 1997). I tend to agree with Vakil (1997: 2059) that out of all the definitions found in the literature, the structural/operational definition 'would probably be most useful in defining NGOs as well', and that although her assertion that NGOs are a subset of non-profit organizations concerned with 'social and economic development' is ambiguous, this definition can usefully be applied to the organizations we are broadly terming NGOs. The structural/operational definition is also useful in that it allows representation of broad voluntarist values which normally exist even in the most professionalized NGOs which retain a trace of this ethos in the voluntary participation of governing body members, as Levitt points out:[5]

> The fact that a Third Sector institution may have a formal administrative structure and a paid headquarters staff whose operating style is indistinguishable from that of business or government bureau does not disqualify it from Third Sector status.
>
> (Levitt 1975: 63)

The definition allows that an NGO might generate income through profit-making activities while still stopping short of becoming a commercial business, and it illustrates the fact that NGOs cannot be part of or organized by the government – although they must of course abide by the law and may register with government – and finally it shows that NGOs are autonomous in that they attempt to manage themselves through their own structures and bodies.

An important limitation of the structural/operational definition is its insistence on a level of formality that might exclude some of the small-scale community associations or mutual benefit organizations.[6] Similarly, by excluding cooperatives and mutual societies it can be argued that the definition excludes important areas of social entrepreneurship which have characterized important moments in the history of the third sector, such as friendly societies in Victorian Britain in the development of social housing (Morris 1999). The definition is also therefore somewhat limited by its tendency to present a static picture; many NGOs have their roots in small-scale informal initiatives but, like all organizations, tend to change over time, frequently drifting towards more formal or bureaucratic organizational forms (Billis 1993a).

Throughout this book the term 'non-governmental organization' is therefore used to describe a subset of third sector organizations concerned with development, human rights and social change. 'Northern NGO' (NNGO) will be used to refer to organizations whose origins lie in the industrialized countries, while 'Southern NGO' (SNGO) refers to organizations from the 'less developed' areas of the world. The broad definition of NGO used here includes organizations which are formally part of the 'development industry' (which consists of the world of bilateral and multilateral aid donors, the United Nations system and the Bretton Woods institutions) as well as those which are not and choose to work outside these structures. It includes those organizations sometimes termed community-based organizations (CBOs) or 'people's organizations' (POs) as well as those NGOs outside communities sometimes termed grassroots support organizations (GSOs), or intermediary organizations which seek to link and work with these community-level organizations. It includes organizations which, in Tandon's (1996) distinction, are functional NGOs which are 'conveying palliatives' as well as those which he terms 'thinking NGOs' which 'reflect on alternatives'. Finally, the term includes organizations with their roots in one country (usually an industrialized one) but which work in another country (usually a 'developing' country) as well as NGOs which have developed autonomously in Africa, Asia and Latin America. When necessary, different categories of NGO will be specified in the text which follows on the basis of their characteristics relevant to the discussion.

Levitt (1975) reminds us that there are many different roles played by third sector organizations: they may be campaigning or service providing; they may be membership or non-membership; they may be voluntarist or professionalized; and they may be charitable or non-charitable in nature. He also reminds us that third sector organizations constantly change and evolve. For example, they may evolve from temporary initiatives into 'social movements', e.g. slave abolitionist movements of the mid-nineteenth century. In a widely quoted piece of work, Korten (1990) outlines the ways in which NGOs may evolve through a series of 'generations', from the relief agency which meets immediate needs in its early days, to the more mature networked social movement organization which works to address wider structural concerns. In the 'first generation', the priority is to meet immediate needs through relief and welfare work, but in the second, a growing awareness of 'development' ideas and the influence of outside agencies such as aid donors promote a new set of objectives to build small-scale, self-reliant local development. This leads to a preoccupation with sustainability in the 'third-generation' organization, and a desire to seek changes in the wider institutional and policy context, while the 'fourth-generation' NGO aims to support wider social movements for action on a national or global level to bring about wider change on issues such as gender, environment and conflict resolution.

Korten's schema is useful because it shows that NGOs, like most other organizations, rarely stand still, and it illustrates how organizations may combine several roles or activities at any one time. Distinctions drawn by some third sector researchers between service delivery organizations and campaigning organizations (such as Knight's 1993 report on the British voluntary sector) rarely reflect the complex realities of these organizations' changing agendas and priorities. Korten's generation theory should not be taken to imply that all NGOs pass through these stages. The theory also carries an Asian bias, which means that while it may fit with, say, BRAC's history in Bangladesh, it may not fit with the life history of an NGO in the more politicized contexts of Palestine or South Africa.

THE HISTORIES OF NGOs

Currently NGOs are receiving unprecedented levels of attention, but NGOs are not new. Despite the relatively recent arrival of NGOs on the stage of development, there is a long history of NGO-related activity at international, regional, national and local levels:

> Although some observers seem to perceive NGO involvement as a late-twentieth-century phenomenon, in fact it has occurred for over 200 years. Advocates of a

more extensive role for NGOs weaken their cause by neglecting this history because it shows a long time custom of governmental interaction with NGOs in the making of international policy.

(Charnovitz 1997: 185)

Charnovitz traces seven stages to the evolution of NGO roles in international affairs, from 'emergence' in 1775–1918 through to 'empowerment' from 1992 onwards. This history begins with the rise of national-level issue-based organizations in the eighteenth century, focused on the abolition of the slave trade and peace movements. By 1900 there were 425 peace societies active in different parts of the world, and the issues of labour rights and free trade were generating new forms of interest groups which were the forerunners of what we would now term NGOs. For example, in the USA the first national labour union was the International Federation of Tobacco Workers, founded in 1876, and in the UK the Anti-Corn Law League campaigned for free trade against the system of tariffs between 1838 and 1846. By the early twentieth century, NGOs had generated associations to promote their own identities at national and international levels, so that at the World Congress of International Associations in 1910 there were 132 international associations present, and these were concerned with issues as varied as transportation, intellectual property rights, narcotics control, public health issues, agriculture and the protection of nature.

A growing level of involvement of NGOs continued during the League of Nations period during the 1920s and 1930s, a period Charnovitz terms 'engagement'. When the International Labour Organization (ILO) was set up in 1919 as part of the League of Nations, each member country sent four representatives: two from government, one from employers and one from worker organizations, which created a forum in which the three sectors – government, business and community – could each begin to influence international conventions on labour rights and standards. NGOs began to move from being outsiders bringing issues to the international agenda to insiders working with governments on international problems. After 1935, there was a routinization of activities within the League, and the growing hostilities which resulted in the Second World War contributed to the inhibiting of NGO participation and a period of 'disengagement' which lasted until the period of post-war 'formalization'.

In the post-war period, Article 71 of the United Nations Charter provided for NGO involvement in UN activities, and NGOs were active in the drafting of the Charter itself. Among the UN agencies, UNESCO and WHO both provided for NGO involvement in their charters. However, the reality was that Article 71 merely codified 'the custom of NGO participation', and 'The opportunities afforded to NGOs in the early years of the United Nations were no better than those afforded to NGOs in the early years of the League' (Charnovitz 1997: 258). The period after the War was therefore one of 'underachievement' in which, though active, NGOs did not contribute much more than 'nuisance value', hampered by Cold War tensions and the institutional weakness of the UN Economic and Social Council (ECOSOC), the body liaising with NGOs as set out in Article 71. It was not until the 1970s that there was an increased 'intensification' of NGO strength and activities, as shown by their growing presence at UN conferences such as the Stockholm Environment Conference in 1972 and the World Population Conference in Bucharest in 1974. NGOs played a key role in the drafting of the UN Convention on the Rights of the Child. Since 1992, NGO influence at international level has continued to grow, as shown by the UN Conference on Environment and Development (UNCED) which saw NGOs active both in its preparation and at the conference itself, which approved policy statements about the role of NGOs and suggested that the UN system should 'draw on the expertise and views of non-governmental organizations in policy and programme design, implementation and evaluation' (Agenda 21, quoted in Charnovitz 1997: 265). From only occasional mentions of the role of NGOs in the documentation produced by the Brandt Commission in 1980, we have now moved to a position in which the Commission on Global Governance in 1995 recommended that a Forum of Civil Society should be convened and consulted by the UN every year. Charnovitz has characterized this period since 1992 as that of NGO 'empowerment'. Indeed, Martens (2006) argues that NGOs now form an integral part of the UN system.

Charnovitz's framework has been discussed at some length because it provides a much-needed historical depth to the discussion of the NGO context, a perspective often lost within current, fashion-driven debates. However, it focuses exclusively on European and North American contexts and therefore tells only part of the story. Such 'NGO history' could be written about many other parts of the world. In Latin America, the growth of NGOs has been influenced by the Catholic Church and the growth of 'liberation theology' in the 1960s, signalled by the Church's commitment to the poor, and to some extent by the growth of popular Protestantism (Escobar 1997). The philosophy of the Brazilian educator Paulo Freire, with its radical ideas about 'education for critical consciousness' and organized community action, has also been influential (Blackburn 2000). Freire believed that illiterate people possessed a 'culture of silence' which could be challenged by a form of education which, rather than simply imposing the world view of the elite, could motivate the poor to question and build new liberating structures and processes for change. Freire's ideas continue to inspire and inform current approaches, such as the well-known participatory planning reforms that have been taking place in the city of Porto Alegre, Brazil (Guareschi and Jovchelovitch 2004). Freire's ideas have informed the philosophies and strategies of many NGOs in Latin America and beyond, such as Proshika in Bangladesh. At the same time, the tradition of peasant movements seeking improved rights to land and the role of political radicals working towards more open democratic societies have contributed to the rise of NGOs (Bebbington and Thiele 1993). Despite the radical origins of one key strand in the Latin American NGO community in the 1960s, the 1990s saw the crystallization of an increasingly heterogeneous NGO sector containing different approaches, which included professionalized careerist organizations close to donors and governments as well as organizations seeking radical alternatives (Pearce 1997).

Moving to the context of South Asia, Sen's (1992) work on the background to the rise of NGOs in India highlights the influence of Christian missionaries, the Indian reformist middle classes and the ideas of Mahatma Gandhi, who emphasized the role of voluntary action in strengthening Indian development. Gandhi's campaign for village self-reliance has inspired local Indian organizations such as the Association of Sarva Seva Farms (ASSEFA). Many of these NGOs have strong local cultural and historical roots which lie outside the Western 'aid industry'. Gandhi's ideas have also contributed to the 'appropriate technology' movement more widely in the North as well as the South (Thomas 1992). There are also long traditions of self-help in South Asia, such as the traditional rotating credit groups which can be found in countries such as Nepal, where they are known as *dhikuri*, in which households as a survival strategy pool resources into a central fund and take turns in borrowing from and repaying the communal pot (Chhetri 1995).

Africa shares aspects of the missionary histories of Asia, where external organizations have interacted with local 'third sector' structures and ideologies. For example, Anheier's (1987) work on Africa highlights the wealth of associational activity which underpins many African societies, while work by Honey and Okafor (1998) on hometown associations in Nigeria shows how community organizations are increasingly important for mediating resources and relationships between local communities and global labour markets, educational opportunities and village resources. In Kenya, the *harambee* movement of mutual self-help groups was a system based on kinship and neighbourhood ties, and was incorporated by President Kenyatta as part of a modernization campaign to build a new infrastructure after independence (Moore 1988). It was seen as an alternative to top-down planning and as a way of sharing costs with local communities; while briefly successful, its initial spirit of voluntarism was gradually sapped by bureaucratization.

These examples are intended to provide a snapshot of the diverse origins and influences on the third sector in different parts of the world, but of course they represent only a small key into vast and diverse strands of cultural, political and religious influences which contribute to different kinds of NGOs around the world. Within each country context, there are multiple and often contradictory influences in the third sector. In Britain, for example, the so-called voluntary sector is rooted both in traditions of Christian 'charity', which some sections of the community criticize as being demeaning to the poor and encouraging dependency on service providers, as well as in the radical activism of the 1960s, which emphasizes instead the 'empowerment' of disadvantaged groups and individuals. One of the key problems facing any attempt to discuss any aspect of NGOs is therefore that of the impossibility of generalization. The history and origins of NGOs are diverse and can be traced back to a range of complex historical, cultural and political factors in different parts of the world. As Carroll (1992: 38) has pointed out, 'all NGOs operate within a contextual matrix derived from specific locational and historic circumstances that change over time'.

As well as being characterized by a high level of cultural and ideological diversity, trends in the third sector are difficult to compare due to the problem of gaining access to accurate data. Hulme (1994) suggested that more NGO growth is believed to be taking place in Asia and Latin America than in Africa, and that Latin American NGOs have been more prepared to take part in political action, organizing and lobbying for reform and social change, than those in Asia. In Latin America there are many women-led, small-scale, networked organizations (Lehmann 1990), while in Africa relief operations have tended to dominate the NGO landscape, with the presence of Northern NGOs to some extent inhibiting the emergence of large formal indigenous organizations (Anheier 1987). This is now changing as local organizations in some African countries are developing their own agendas and making their presence felt more strongly in development work (Kanji *et al.* 2000; Simbi and Thom 2000).And yet there are many common characteristics in the patterns of organization which emerge in third sectors around the world and in the activities undertaken. Annis (1987) describes key similarities in the ways in which people organize themselves voluntarily in order to help themselves or others. Patterns of organizational growth tend to be based on needs, such as raising incomes, securing rights, or demanding or providing services, as well as on opportunities, such as contact with new ideas, links with outside organizations with finance, or political change which allows new space for organizing. The drive amongst people to organize themselves therefore centres on both needs and opportunities. People need credit in order to undertake productive activities, roads for marketing, medical and educational services for their families, jobs for the under- and unemployed; urban squatters want rights for their land and amenities for their communities; indigenous minorities want collective legal rights and recognition of pluralism within educational systems. Annis shows that people tend to organize in response to perceived opportunities, such as the landless labourers who see uncultivated areas of land and therefore begin to explore the possibilities of how to get it, forming committees, putting forward leaders, weighing the collective against individual risks of occupation. Similarly, if someone in a village knows a powerful person in a government ministry, they may form a self-help group to explore what such a connection might bring them. There may be common purposes to taking organizational action on behalf of oneself or on behalf of others, but, as this section has attempted to show, the actual form of the third sector across different communities has varied considerably.

NGOs AND 'CIVIL SOCIETY'

During the past two decades, the concept of 'civil society' has been revived from its eighteenth-century roots in the work of political scientists and philosophers searching for an understanding of what happens in the organized 'associational realm' which lies between the family and the state (Van Rooy 1997; Hadenius and Uggla 1996; Keane 1998; Glasius *et al.* 2004). This revival of the idea of civil society has taken place not only within the development industry, but also as part of wider debates about politics and democratization, public participation and welfare, service delivery, as well as in connection with campaigning and advocacy at the international level. It is a revival which has often placed NGOs at its centre, because for some policy makers and activists, NGOs have been taken as a shorthand for civil society itself. As we shall see, civil society is a much broader concept than one that refers simply to NGOs. Another difficulty has been a tendency for some NGOs to claim to speak on behalf of civil society, which has caused some to question the accountability and legitimacy of NGOs themselves.

There are many factors which have led to the rediscovery of the concept of civil society. The term was reintroduced into political discourse by the democratic opposition to communist states in Eastern Europe during the 1970s (Keane 1998) and at the same time was deployed in the 1970s by Latin American activists and academics in the context of resisting military dictatorship (Fisher 1998). After the end of the Cold War, the former superpowers reduced their support to client states, which often had authoritarian regimes, and this released demands by citizens to challenge existing power structures. The concept of civil society was then taken up by development agencies in the early 1990s as part of the 'good governance' agenda (Van Rooy 1997; Lewis 2002a).

53

The idea of civil society is one with long roots that go back to the writings of the Scottish enlightenment thinkers such as Hume and Ferguson and the German philosopher Hegel. The French commentator de Tocqueville talked about the richness of associational life in the United States, and saw this activity as a source of democratic strength and economic power. Later in his *Prison Notebooks*, Gramsci wrote at length about civil society as a site for resistance to the exercise of hegemonic power in capitalist societies. Each of these thinkers presented different ideas about what the concept of civil society means, the ways in which it emerged in different parts of Europe and the analytical uses to which the concept might be put. Since 'civil society' is a theoretical concept rather than an empirical one, the recent challenge amongst many development agencies and NGOs has been to try to apply it. As Van Rooy (1998) has shown, the concept of civil society easily becomes an 'analytical hat stand' on which many different arguments are opportunistically placed. There has been a tendency among development policy makers to pick and choose among the many different understandings of civil society in order to operationalize the concept, with the result that 'a simplified set of arguments has been imported into Northern aid policy'.

Civil society is usually taken to mean a realm or space in which there exists a set of organizational actors which are not part of the household, the state or the market. These organizations form a wide-ranging group, including associations, people's movements, citizens' groups, consumer associations, small producer associations and cooperatives, women's organizations, indigenous peoples' organizations – and of course the groups which we are calling NGOs. For NGO managers, the long philosophical roots of the concept are less important than the fact that there are perhaps two basic approaches to civil society, which can be termed the 'liberal' and the 'radical'. In the liberal view, which is the one which has been most popular with governments and donors (and follows chiefly from de Tocqueville), civil society is seen as an arena of organized citizens and a collection of organizations that acts as a balance on state and market, as a place where civic democratic values can be upheld. In a normative sense, civil society is considered on the whole in this view to be a 'good thing'. In the radical view, which is drawn mainly from Gramsci's work, rather than harmony there is an emphasis on negotiation and conflict based on struggles for power, and on blurred boundaries with the state. Civil society contains many different competing ideas and interests, not all of which contribute positively to development.

Much of the writing on NGOs and development which has been influential has been shaped by the liberal view. Bratton's (1994b: 2) definition provides a useful starting point. He sees civil society as:

> a sphere of social interaction between the household and the state which is manifest in norms of community co-operation (trust, tolerance, inclusion, joining), structures of voluntary association (citizens coming together into voluntary associations both local/national, formal/informal) and networks of public communication (pluralist media, personal access to communication technology etc.).

This view sees civil society as a source of civic responsibility and public virtue, and as a place where organized citizens – including NGOs – can make a contribution to the public good. The liberal tradition emphasizes the socializing effects of association, which help to build 'better citizens'. The concept of civil society to which development agencies have been drawn is based upon the idea of an interdependent organic relationship between market economy, state and civil society (Archer 1994). In this model, there is a 'virtuous circle' between all three sets of institutions – a productive economy and a well-run government will sustain a vigorous civil society, a well-run government and a vigorous civil society will support economic growth, and a well-managed economy and a strong civil society will produce efficient government. This logic was embraced during the so-called 'good government' policies embodied within French and British foreign policy statements during the early 1990s, and it was made clear to developing countries that a continuation of aid, particularly to Africa, would depend on new forms of conditionality. These conditionalities required a competitive, largely privatized market economy, a well-managed state (with good education and healthcare, just laws and protected human rights, and sound macro-economic planning) and a democratic 'civil society' in which citizens had rights as voters and consumers so that they could hold their institutions accountable. The conditions also required a free press, regular changes of government by free election and a set of legally encoded human rights (Archer 1994).

Within this good government discourse, the vision of civil society featured a strong overlap with the market. This has been evident particularly in the case of donor assistance given during the 1990s to the former Eastern bloc countries, where the creation of capitalist market relations and the construction of a civil society were seen as being very closely linked. But there were also strong political elements in the new discussion of civil society. According to White (1994), the growth of civil society is seen to have the potential to make an important contribution to building more democratic governance processes, because it shifts the balance of power between state and society in favour of the latter. It can also enforce standards of morality, performance and accountability in public life, and act as a channel for the demands of organized citizen groups by creating an alternative 'space' – outside formal political structures such as political parties – for political representation and action. A good example of this can be seen in the Right to Information movement in India (see Box 6.2).

The liberal view of civil society implies a critique of state domination of public life, advocates reform rather than revolution, and would bring about political change through election and negotiation rather than conflict. Many NGO writers and activists, such as Clark (1991), have therefore argued that NGOs, both Northern and Southern, have a key role in supporting the emergence of democratic organizations and institutions in 'civil society'. USAID has been a leading donor in supporting NGOs as vehicles for strengthening democratization processes through advocacy and voter education.

Covey's work on NGO policy alliances suggests ways in which NGOs can strengthen democratic processes through working as 'civil society organizations'. In many parts of the world, political struggles are drawing NGOs towards a more active policy-influencing role as political space opens up for people's voices in public affairs:

> The promise of democracy becomes a reality however when groups (especially marginalized sectors of society) effectively participate in the marketplace of competing interests. Inclusion in political systems long dominated by elites depends,

in part, on the institutional strengths of policy newcomers and, in part, on the perceived legitimacy of their participation itself.

(Covey 1995: 866)

It is only by forming 'multilayered alliances' that NGOs can seek effective, poverty-focused change by brokering relationships between the poor, the middle classes and elites, bringing the potential to both build civil society and enhance policy outcomes. This is perhaps the greatest challenge for NGOs, but offers the best promise for gaining policy benefits for the poor. NGOs can play this role of 'intersectoral problem solving' (Brown 1994) by controlling important resources and shaping participants' awareness through a 'bridging role'. Diaz-Albertini (1993) shows how this bridging role might function. Writing about the context of Peru, he outlines the twin need for NGOs both to strengthen civil society through grassroots empowerment work and to seek to ensure the viability of the state as an apparatus which is capable of processing people's political demands and claims. He examines three ways in which NGOs have tried to institutionalize political practices and build bridges between the state and civil society in terms of welfare issues, each of which has distinctive advantages and disadvantages which need to be balanced and linked across three levels simultaneously. In the first, NGOs temporarily substitute for the state as service provider, creating higher quality services but leading to little sustainability. In the second, NGOs work to 'represent' the grassroots through lobbying work and political action, but this level of activity often tends to lead NGOs into becoming professional advocacy groups which gradually lose touch with real people at community level. At the third level, NGOs work with providing local community organizations with technical assistance, services and organizational support, but since few channels exist for presenting local demands to the state, NGOs can easily end up merely 'administering poverty' rather than working for structural change.

Some writers have emphasized the importance for NGOs to gain a better understanding of the concept of citizenship:

> Citizenship is accorded a key role in political theory because it provides the critical link between the geopolitical formation of the nation state with the polity that comprises it. Citizenship is a form of social contract made unique by its equal applicability to the vast majority of individuals by reason of birth.
>
> (Fowler 1993: 335)

For this to work, people must identify with the state as a legitimate entity, and from this stems the justification for demanding rights. Bratton (1989) illustrates the ways in which the legacy of colonialism has contributed to the creation of weak states in Africa, where ethnicity now continues to function as an important factor which helps to shape identities. Bratton describes how the NGO Silveira House in Zimbabwe attempted to work on citizenship issues by training elected civil officials in their responsibilities to meet citizen rights, and by seeking to raise public awareness about their rights.

For many donors, 'strengthening civil society' has become a specific policy objective. According to Brown and Tandon (1994), the strengthening of civil society requires attempts

---

NGOs and the 'strengthening of civil society'

Part of the new interest in civil society revolves around the argument that for development to take place, efforts are needed to build common purposes and supportive interaction among the diverse sets of organizational actors in civil society. For many activists and policy makers, the aim is to strengthen the engagement of civil society with the state and the market. There are three levels for this work. The first is the *organizational level* (individual NGOs) where there is a need to clarify organizational values, identity and strategies (linking longer-term vision and project activities, learning from experience), build organizational capacities for governance, decision making and conflict management, and developing human resources (mobilizing skilled staff without undermining social commitment) and organizational learning (building systems to avoid losing experience in the day-to-day demands on time). A second is the *sectoral level* (viewing civil society as a sector) where NGOs and other actors need to create opportunities for building shared perspectives and joint action, such as through coordinated networks and campaigns. They may also promote mechanisms to represent key sectoral issues, such as alliances to ensure that land reform or minority rights remain on the policy agenda. A third is the *societal level* where NGOs can create institutions to establish and safeguard the independence of the civil society sector, such as legislation which gives voice to NGOs in policy dialogue, and consultations with civil society over the reform of policy.

Source: Brown and Tandon 1994.

---

to improve the intellectual, material and organizational bases of the various actors within civil society. Although organizational development (OD) has long been directed at strengthening the *performance* of organizations working in the public or the private sectors, new approaches are needed to support 'mission-oriented social change organizations' (Box 2.1). NGOs are expected to play a part, and some analysts have termed this broader process 'institutional development' (ID).

Some policy researchers have therefore focused on the ways in which donors can work with NGOs in order to support democratic processes. One of the most influential of these is Blair (1997), who presents a clear working model for 'operationalizing' donor support to NGOs in the context of civil society by suggesting that only NGOs which emphasize public goals (such as those third sector organizations concerned with influencing state policy) can be seen as true civil society actors. This excludes business enterprises since their main goal is to make a profit, political parties since their main goal is to take over state power (not to influence it), and self-help groups or service delivery NGOs. A 'civil society organization' (CSO) is the characteristic institution of 'civil society' and can be defined as 'an NGO that has as one of its primary purposes influencing public policy. This means that while all "CSOs" are NGOs, by no means are all NGOs "CSOs"' (Blair 1997: 24–5).

For example, if a purely service delivery NGO in the health sector then also began to advocate reform of the health system, it would become a 'civil society organization'. Blair

(1997) argues that there have been two main types of donor approaches to working with civil society: the first is reforming the system through working on the creation of an 'enabling environment' by improving the rules of the game under which civil society operates. The second is through support to sectoral agendas through working within the existing civil society environment by supporting specific organizations directly. Blair argues that donors such as USAID have tended to go for the latter, and suggests that without having put into place conditions for the enabling environment, such a strategy does not make much sense. Cold War strategic concerns and US geopolitical considerations made such sectoral agendas typical in the 1980s, when the USA often supported military regimes, and an apolitical model of development based on technology transfer was prevalent. More recently, donors have begun to focus on the enabling environment as well as sectoral agendas, as DFID's late 1990s work in Uganda illustrated (Kanji *et al.* 2000). As the trend has moved towards increasingly 'upstream' forms of development support, such as poverty reduction strategy papers (PRSPs) and government budget support, more and more attention has been focused on the 'big picture' in which NGOs operate rather than on individual projects.

According to Blair (1997), a strong civil society can also strengthen democracy by educating citizens to exercise their right to participate in public life, by encouraging marginalized groups to become more active in the political arena, and by helping to build overlapping networks – in the sense of Putnam's (1993) idea of cross-cutting 'social capital' – which can reduce the destabilizing effect of single-interest religious or ethnic groups within a culturally diverse context. The idea of social capital has become influential in relation to development and democracy, and NGOs have been seen as organizations which can contribute to its creation and its maintenance. It is an ambiguous concept which has been understood differently by various theorists.[7] Putnam (1993: 167) argues that social capital represents the relationships of trust and civic responsibility that are built up between members of a community over a relatively long period of time: 'Social capital . . . refers to features of social organization, such as trust, norms [of reciprocity] and networks [of civic engagement], that can improve the efficiency of society by facilitating co-ordinated actions.' For Putnam, social capital is the opposite of what Banfield (1958) called 'amoral familism', which was famously observed in rural communities where the self-interest of kin-based groups dominated social life at the expense of wider norms of trust and cooperation. By taking part in formal groups and informal networks, an awareness of the greater good develops, and the observed difference in the levels of social capital is used by Putnam to explain why local democracy took deeper root in northern Italy than in southern Italy. Other theorists have included kinship structures within their definitions of social capital:

> Social capital is the set of resources that inhere in family relations and in community social organization and that are useful for the cognitive or social development of a child or young person . . . it is not a single entity, but a variety of different entities having two characteristics in common: they all consist of some aspect of social structure, and they facilitate certain actions of the individuals who are within the structure . . . social capital is productive, making possible the attainment of certain ends that would not be attainable in its absence.
>
> (Coleman 1990: 300–2)

Social capital can therefore be seen in terms of the connections between people which help to facilitate participation in civil society, either through direct and focused action towards political change, or through membership of welfare, cultural or leisure associations which help focus people further towards public responsibility. Indeed, the concept of social capital widens the issue of participation in civil society, beyond political participation and towards other forms of social participation — such as in welfare support networks — as Box 2.2 shows in the case of informal social services in Uganda. At the same time, the concept of social capital is not without its critics, since, despite being taken up enthusiastically by agencies such as the World Bank, it may overplay the potential of local organization at the expense of the importance wider structural political and economic change (Bebbington *et al.* 2004).

The more radical Gramscian view sees civil society as the location for independent resistance to the state. Rather than the focus on balance and harmony embodied in the liberal view, MacDonald's work (1994) shows that civil society is in fact a zone of conflict, and draws attention to the constraints of class and gender on people's actions, to the tensions between the state and civil society (and those which exist within civil society itself), and finally highlights the international political economy dimensions of the discourse of civil society in developing countries. In such a view, in addition to using formal state institutions, the state also uses civil society institutions such as the media and the church to maintain its authority.

NGOs IN ACTION 2.2

2.2 Informal social services, NGOs and social capital

In the south-west of Uganda, where communities have been severely affected by the HIV/AIDS virus, many international NGOs have set up programmes designed to raise awareness about preventive health, to address the social and economic consequences of the disease through support to orphans to prevent them dropping out of school, and to give small loans to households to assist with income-generation activities. At the same time, local rural communities were also seeking ways to adapt their own organizational structures and systems in order to deal with the problems. In some villages there was a tradition of *munno mukabi*, a form of self-help in which older village women clubbed together on an informal basis to help to arrange funerals for poorer households. With the spread of HIV/AIDS, the result had been an increase in the numbers of funerals and greater pressure on this informal system. It was also the case that many households now had family members who were sick, or with adult household members who were entirely bedridden. This arrangement was then adapted into a type of home-visiting service, which made sure that people who were unwell did not lose touch with the rest of the village, and received food. This was a case of evolving local community self-help structures — a form of social capital — as an adaptive response to social welfare needs, and it was supported by an international NGO which began providing small amounts of credit to the *munno mukabi* women — which was to be repaid via a profitable sideline providing catering to weddings and parties — which helped them to scale up their activities in the face of increasing need.

Source: author's own field notes.

Power, conflict and diversity therefore need to be acknowledged in discussion of civil society. Shaw (1994: 647) sees civil society not as a development 'actor' but as a 'context', within which a wide range of collectivities are formed and interact, including formal organizations of a representative kind such as parties, churches, trade unions and, professional bodies; formal organizations of a functional kind such as schools, universities and mass media; and informal networks and groups such as voluntary organizations, ad hoc activist coalitions and social movements. Civil society institutions are simultaneously located on the outer edges of the system through which state power is legitimized in society, but at the same time civil society is an arena in which various social groups can organize in order to contest state power. In Gramscian terms, civil society can therefore be seen as the site of struggle between hegemonic and counter-hegemonic forces (MacDonald 1994).

One of the criticisms which has been made of this approach is that it is often deployed in a rather 'apolitical' sense. The radical view of civil society recognizes that the conflicts over power and politics which take place in civil society may be important for formal political processes and cannot easily be separated from them. The capacity of NGOs to play a civil society role is contingent on the specific character and power of the state, and, for developing countries in particular, on the international political environment. In many countries, individuals may move between NGOs, the government and opposition political parties as the vehicles for political change. After the change of government in the Philippines in 1986 which ended the authoritarian Marcos regime, there were many activists from the NGO sector who accepted jobs in the new administration because they saw government as a potentially more effective base for putting ideas into action.

Donor support to civil society strengthening has often been through the funding of NGOs, though this has led in practice to support for service delivery NGOs rather than for more militant advocacy NGOs, which might challenge the policies of the government and the donors keen to maintain the 'new policy agenda' (Kanji et al. 2000). At the same time, when NGOs have become involved in political movements they have been criticized. For example, the participation of NGOs and other civil society actors in political struggles in Bangladesh during the 1990s led to criticisms that NGOs were getting 'too involved' in politics, but their supporters have argued that such involvements are not only legitimate, but form an essential part of NGOs' development role (Karim 2000). When some of the main NGOs joined the opposition political party and other groups to demand that a caretaker government be installed to preside over national elections in 1996, NGO leaders defended their actions by arguing that civil society organizations could not avoid involvement in vital political actions which had major implications for all citizens, and particularly the poor.

Another set of radical criticisms of the liberal view of civil society is its normative character, which assumes that civil society is a 'good thing'. Much has been made of the fact that civil society can include organized groups of many kinds and may include religious fundamentalists and political bigots as well as developmental or progressive organizations. Najam (1996b) points out that the racist Ku Klux Klan organization in the United States is an organization of civil society, while Putzel (1997) has argued in a similar vein about the 'dark side of social capital'. In Latin America, Avritzer (2004) points to the existence of uncivil society in countries such as Peru and Colombia which he contrasts with liberal civil societies existing in Argentina and Chile. It is not logical therefore to conceptualize civil society as always being positive in terms of social justice and development.

The problems of competing interests and groups is acknowledged by some proponents of the liberal view. The struggle between different interest groups can sometimes create a kind of paralysis. Blair (1997: 37) points out that it is possible to have 'too much of a good thing' in terms of civil society action in the USA: 'too much interest group influence over the state over too long a period may well lead to immobilism and a hardening of the democratic arteries or "gridlock" rather than to a rich and vibrant democratic polity.' The direct action taken by a range of civil society actors against the World Trade Organization (WTO) meeting in Seattle in 1999, or those actions against the attempts by private corporations such as Monsanto to introduce genetically modified crops in Europe, were highly visible and arguably successful engagements, but for many people such actions raised as many questions about the accountability of the civil society actors involved as about the activities of the WTO and Monsanto. But these events also showed the emergence of a global civil society (which is discussed in more detail at the end of this section) acting from a plurality of positions to challenge what is perceived as a hegemony of US economic and political interests.

Alongside the liberal and the radical views of civil society, there is also what might be termed the 'relativist' critique (Box 2.3). Anthropologists have viewed the revival of the Western concept of civil society and its application to widely different cultures and contexts in different parts of the world with suspicion, pointing out the dangers of a new post-Cold War 'universalism' (Hann and Dunn 1996). Comaroff and Comaroff (2000) have also discussed the ways in which the construction of a 'civil society' was used as an instrument of exclusion by colonial rulers in Africa.

Clearly, civil society and its institutions may take different forms in non-Western contexts, as Brown (1994) has shown in Africa. Within this view, Africa is presented as being rich in cultural and religious institutions which express collective identities, while new forms of third sector association have been created in response to adapting to urbanization and resisting colonization. In some countries, efforts by ruling elites to extend the state have sometimes met with resistance by groups such as lawyers and journalist associations in Nigeria, Christian church organizations in Kenya, and mineworkers' unions in Zambia. The concept of a national conference in Africa is a distinctive contribution to civil society. These conferences have been convened in more than a dozen francophone states, in which national elites and representatives of all major sections of society have come together, often chaired by a church leader, to discuss pressing political matters of the day. In both Benin and Congo, such assemblies met to demand the right to impeach a corrupt leader.

In some of the countries of the former Soviet Union, problems have arisen when development donors have tried to support the emergence of civil society through funding local NGOs. For example, in Uzbekistan, the introduction of the concept of civil society has in fact become simply an instrument for local Russian-speaking anti-Islamic elites to construct a new power base far from the Western liberal civil society ideal. In the attempt to bypass corrupt government officials, there was a subsequent growth of new NGOs – many of which were controlled by the same elites as controlled the government – which merely led to the

How relevant is the concept of civil society to non-Western contexts?

There has been a lively debate in recent years concerning the relevance of the civil society concept to societies beyond the West. Some argue that building civil society is a precondition for progress anywhere in the world, while others point out that efforts to build a civil society often run up against local cultural obstacles. In relation to Africa, for example, four different possible answers can be identified to the question 'is the concept of civil society relevant?' These can be summarized as follows:

Prescriptive universalism: civil society is a good thing, and needs to be built everywhere. This answer takes a positive, universalist view of the desirability of civil society as part of the political project of building and strengthening democracy around the world. There are many organizations and activists that explicitly embrace this view. For example, the global civil society network CIVICUS aims to 'help advance regional, national and international initiatives to strengthen the capacity of civil society' (see CIVICUS website: www.civicus.org).

Western exceptionalism: civil society is a specific product of Western history and culture and does not easily 'fit' with other contexts. The second possible answer is a clear 'no', based on the argument that a concept which emerged at a distinctive moment in European history can have little meaning within such different cultural and political settings. From this perspective 'civil society' is just another in a long line of attempts at misguided policy transfer from the West.

Adaptive prescription: a qualified 'yes', since the concept of civil society is very flexible, but it may not look the same or play exactly the same roles in non-Western contexts. For example, certain African kingship institutions may be included as a means of articulating relations between citizens and state. The concept will take on local, different meanings and should not therefore be applied too rigidly, either at the level of analysis or in the implementation of policy, where it cannot be deployed instrumentally in search of 'predictable' policy outcomes.

It's probably the wrong question to ask: it is more useful to focus on broader questions of democracy, politics and organization in any given context and leave the concept of civil society behind, especially since even in the West there are major disagreements about its meaning and relevance. In any case, the idea of civil society – whether explicitly recognized as such or not – has long been implicated in Africa's colonial histories of both domination and resistance, and in decisions over who is and who is not a 'citizen'. This view takes a broader perspective on social and political changes, and analyses these in historical and cultural context, whether or not there is explicit reference made to 'civil society' concepts.

Source: Lewis 2002a.

reproduction of corrupt and inefficient structures in the non-state sector. The attempt by donors to operationalize the concept of civil society arguably fails to address the pressing political and economic reforms which are needed to bring positive change (Abramson 1999). The problems of civil society building in Armenia and other former Soviet 'transition' countries (Box 2.4) highlight the special issues facing NGO managers in these areas. There are dangers in applying practical lessons on one context that have been learned elsewhere, since NGO management challenges always need to be addressed in context.

The debates about NGO roles in 'strengthening' civil society are only one aspect of the ways in which the concepts of NGO and civil society have become intertwined. An important issue for NGO management is the extent to which NGOs as organizations display characteristics of civil society within their structures and processes. In other words, the very existence of NGOs with internal democratic processes is sometimes taken to be an indicator of civil society, since the values of participation, cooperation, trust and internal democracy may help to foster wider political processes by example. Writing about the US context, Abzug and Forbes (1997: 12) suggest that leaders within third sector organizations are not only 'guardians' of civil society with civic responsibilities outside their organizations, but are also 'responsible for expressions of civil society within their organizations'. For example, the level of trade union membership among employees of NGOs is one dimension of this internal civil society dimension. Another important dimension is the gendered nature of staff structures and relationships (Goetz 1997). Howell and Pearce (2000) show that in Central America, one of the criticisms which can be made of donor preoccupations with supporting NGOs in order to 'build civil society' is that many such NGOs exhibit strongly hierarchical, non-participatory internal structures and processes. In Bangladesh, Wood (1997) has also described the ways in which NGOs tend to reflect within their own structures and processes, the social and cultural norms of patron–clientelism, hierarchy and gender subordination which predominate more widely in society. The recent tensions within a national NGO umbrella organization in Kenya (Box 2.5) highlights the fact that the ways NGOs manage *themselves* has important implications both for NGO legitimacy and wider public confidence in the idea of civil society.

This brings us back to the critique of Western visions of civil society, because there may be civil society organizations based on traditional values of kinship and ethnicity in some contexts which, while not necessarily fitting the standard definition, may nevertheless carry out many of the other functions of a civil society organization. For example, the Somali clan system simultaneously provides for the needs of the members of its communities, but at the same time contributes to the violence and hostilities which exist between different clans and factions (Edwards 1998). Perhaps Van Rooy (1998) offers a realistic view in seeing the idea of civil society as both an *observable reality* in terms of an arena of conflicting organizations and interests, and a *normative goal* in that 'having a civil society, warts and all, is better than not'.

Both liberal and radical conceptions of civil society provide different perspectives on the roles of NGOs in political processes, as Clarke (1998) has argued. In the Philippines, the liberal or de Tocquevillian view shows the ways in which NGOs have moved into territories previously occupied by political parties which found it difficult to adapt to the changing realities of human rights, the environment, minorities and gender interests. But in the radical

NGOs and the context of post-socialism

It was only in the 1980s, during the period of *glasnost* (freedom) and *perestroika* (restructuring) that independent civil society groups and social movements began emerging in Russia, Eastern Europe and Central Asia. Following the collapse of the socialist regimes, democracy promotion was a central part of Western aid programmes and civil society was seen as critical for democratization and successful transition to a market economy. The expectation was that NGOs would take over most service provision from the state and build democratic norms and values. But civil society promotion was usually a top-down, donor-driven effort which led to an artificial but phenomenal growth in numbers of NGOs. In 1994 there were only forty four local NGOs working in Armenia, but by 2004 there were over 3,500 NGOs registered with the Armenian Ministry of Justice.

Some post-socialist countries, such as the Czech Republic, Slovakia and Poland, made a transition to democracy and capitalism and went on to join the European Union. But further east, former Soviet republics such as those in Central Asia and the Caucasus experienced a serious decline in living standards and poverty, social exclusion and social polarization. Rapid impoverishment followed the 'shock therapy' policies that were supposed to kick-start market economies and reduce the state services which had previously guaranteed – however imperfectly – access to education, healthcare and housing. Many are now identified as 'developing' countries, though poverty here has features which distinguish it from that in other developing regions. There is near universal literacy, high education levels and modern (albeit non-functioning) industries and social welfare systems.

For NGOs, there are distinctive challenges. NGO capacity remains weak and service provision fragmented. Many citizens still expect the state to provide services. Foreign development workers lack local knowledge since these countries were long closed to Westerners. Local knowledge may be devalued and seen as 'tainted' by communism. Projects and policies have frequently drawn too heavily on experiences from Africa or Asia, ignoring high local levels of education and urbanization. Few NGOs are membership-based or supported by wider citizenry, and the concept and role of civil society is poorly understood by governments. Without strong local roots, and highly dependent on foreign support, NGOs in these contexts have often faced delegitimization.

In the second decade after independence, NGOs are becoming more established and confident. Relationships with donors and Western experts, while still unequal, are improving. But relations with the state remains tense. Following the Rose and Orange revolutions in Georgia and Ukraine respectively, wary governments are attempting to further curtail NGO advocacy and public activism. Much remains to be done to make NGOs more locally legitimate, accountable and sustainable, but NGOs in the former Soviet Union have come a long way since the 1990s and are now beginning to assert their rights to participate in their countries' development and transformation.

Source: Armine Ishkanian, LSE, personal communication.

NGOs and internal governance: crisis at the Kenya NGO Council

The Kenyan National NGO Council was established in August 1993 as a non-partisan body comprising all the international, regional and national NGOs operating in Kenya. A range of international donors supported it. The council has a threefold mandate: self-regulation of the NGO sector, capacity building and policy intervention. The council's purpose is to promote voluntary action in support of a more equitable society, and it operates through the decisions of an annual general assembly. A key role for the Council is to provide overall leadership to the NGO sector, championing and demonstrating the key values of probity, transparency, accountability, justice and good governance.

However, the council became the focus of disputes within the NGO sector. There had been a high turnover of senior management staff through forced resignations and irregular dismissals. Complaints about bad governance and mismanagement had led to the gradual withdrawal of support from the Council. A dispute between the chairperson and her rivals reached fever pitch in August 2005 when opposing leaders tried to evict her from the office. The government then intervened, saying that it needed to do so in order to redeem the image of the council and the NGO sector as a whole. The chairperson of the NGO Council insisted that she would not allow the government to gain control over the affairs of the council, and she locked herself in the council's office for nine days. The government dissolved the NGO Council's Executive and Regulatory committees and appointed a Caretaker Committee to carry out the core business of the organization. An audit was to be carried out, with fresh elections and a 'streamlined' membership. A fresh dialogue with the donors was to be held for resumption of financial support. The NGO Council officials were ordered to keep out of the offices of the council or face disciplinary action from the government.

These events have caused much concern within the NGO sector and among wider citizens. The dispute at the NGO Council is clearly not in the best interest of nurturing a vibrant NGO sector, nor is the government's intervention. Some NGOs, while they did not like the chairperson's leadership style, have condemned the government for ousting the chairperson from office. But NGOs also accept that it is civil society's job to 'trouble the government's conscience' and for NGOs to set a good example for the conduct of public life, and provide a framework for alternative leadership. Instead, at this time the sector was embroiled in squabbles that cast doubts on its ability to embrace democratic leadership. The governance crisis in the NGO Council in Kenya erupted at a time when the council had been expected to mediate in the review process of the new draft constitution. The majority of Kenyans felt that if the council risked losing its credibility at this time, it would also lack the authority to play any meaningful role in Kenya's public life in future. There is great danger, it was said, that civil society will be seen as 'the preacher of water who indulges in wine'. If NGOs cannot nurture internal democracy, it was asked, how can they challenge politicians and state leaders to be democratic?

Source: personal communication, Agnes Kithikii; also drawing on material from *The Standard*, 19 August 2005; *East Africa Standard*, 19 August 2005; *Daily Nation*, 22 August 2005.

or Gramscian perspective it is also possible in the Philippines to use civil society theory to understand how NGOs have ultimately helped to institutionalize contested political interests. Radical militant social movements which developed under the Marcos dictatorship have become diffused in the post-Marcos era, and NGOs have contributed to the reduction of this anti-state pressure by absorbing activists into more legitimate 'development' and human rights concerns, and by strengthening the state. But the contradictions in the liberal view of seeking to strengthen NGOs as a proxy for strengthening civil society, and the dangers of taking an apolitical view, point to the need for NGOs and donors to pay more attention to radical ideas about civil society in seeking to explain and inform development action.

Finally, there is another emerging discourse in relation to NGOs and civil society: that of the growth of 'global civil society'. Until comparatively recently, civil society had been discussed only in relation to the nation-state. However, it is now common to hear it argued that the nation-state is in decline and that civil society increasingly represents itself across nation-state boundaries through the formation of global institutions – such as formal links between parties, churches, unions; and informal networks among women's movements, peace movements and global organizations such as Amnesty International and Greenpeace (Shaw 1994: 649). For example, MacDonald's (1994) article examines the links between 'international NGOs, national NGOs and popular organizations' in international solidarity work and development support to Central America in the 1980s.

In Nicaragua, for example, the US government tried during this period to destroy an alternative economic form which emerged in the shape of the Sandinista regime in the 'backyard' which it had long been accustomed to controlling. Local grassroots organizations quickly developed in Nicaragua and made contact with international NGOs, which began to provide support in the form of finance, volunteers and political advocacy, and in MacDonald's view this action supported a decisive moment in Central American democratization. NGOs also lobbied other US allies to dissent from the US foreign policy line, and achieved some success in this. But two types of NGO eventually emerged: the first was relatively conservative, aiming to reduce the social tensions of the structural adjustment process, while a second group of more radical NGOs was interested in modifying the structure of power. MacDonald suggests that international NGOs like Amnesty International, Greenpeace and Oxfam might contribute to 'transnational counter hegemonic networks', through forming wider coalitions with other sections of civil society:

> The potential long term impact of actors in global civil society lies not merely in their material resources but also in their ability to create new identities, to contest established ways of thinking, and to create new linkages between peoples in different parts of the globe
>
> (MacDonald 1994: 277)

Global civil society theory is likely to be an important area for conceptual discussion and NGO action during the coming decades. It signals an optimism in some quarters about the role that NGOs, in conjunction with a wide range of other kinds of organization and networks, might play at a transnational level. For example, Kaldor (2003) argues that global civil society, which is 'both an outcome and an agent of global interconnectedness', brings a new form of politics which can 'supplement' democracy at the national level. It constitutes a realm of public debate and Kaldor suggests that in its 'activist' form (as opposed to other types or strands of global civil society which she analyses)[8] creates possibilities for democratizing and 'civilizing' the globalization process through demanding global rules and justice – including (a) a strengthened framework of international humanitarian law, (b) a shift from military force to 'international law enforcement', and (c) a stronger form of international policing in place of 'traditional peacekeeping'.

Clark and Themudo (2006: 50) argue that global civil society is being constructed and transformed by Internet-based 'dotcauses', described as 'cause-promoting networks whose organizational realm falls within internet space'. These organizations, concerned with issues as diverse as currency speculation and indigenous people's rights, but broadly linked with what has become known as the anti-globalization movement, have fed into debates about a range of issues, including the idea of 'global civil society' itself. Like most new concepts, the idea of global civil society also has its share of critics, such as Anderson and Rieff (2005), who argue that the lack of democracy within international relationships is perpetuated rather than challenged by the NGOs that make up much of the 'global civil society movement' and that there has been a 'severe inflation of ideological rhetoric' (2005: 26) around the concept itself.

FROM CIVIL SOCIETY TO THE 'THIRD SECTOR'

The rediscovery of the concept of civil society has run parallel to another conceptual discussion within organizational studies and public policy – the concept of the 'third sector'. This section takes the third sector concept as the entry point for considering NGOs as organizations before we move on in Chapter 3 to discuss the various roles which are being played by NGOs in development. There appears to be no precise moment of origin for the term 'third sector', which seems to date back to public policy discussions in the 1970s in the United States.[9] The US sociologist Amitai Etzioni (1972, 1973) is believed to have coined the term. Another important influence on third sector thinking was Theodore Levitt (1975), a writer on marketing management at Harvard Business School in the 1960s, who later went on in the 1970s to develop wider interests in the analysis of public policy. The idea of the third sector is useful to a discussion of NGO management because, while civil society provides an analytical framework for understanding the institutional arena in which NGOs operate, the concept of the third sector has its roots in the analysis of organizational difference and therefore draws useful attention to the ways in which NGOs and other third sector organizations are structured and motivated.

In his influential work on complex organizations, Etzioni (1961) set about analysing why people become involved in organizations, and the different kinds of power relationships which determine organizational forms. What emerged was a conceptual framework which sets out three different basic types of organizational form. This is based around the concept of 'compliance' as a central element of all organizational structure which explains the relationship between those who have power and those over whom they exercise it:

> Compliance refers both to a relation in which an actor behaves in accordance with a directive supported by another actor's power, and to the orientation of the subordinated actor to the power supplied.
>
> (Etzioni 1961: 3)

This determines commitment or alienation from the organization among those involved. Within most organizations there tend to be people with high levels of power who dominate, and those in subordinate positions with less power. Power relations differ in terms of the means used to achieve compliance, and usually take three forms: *coercive*, which is the application or threat of physical sanctions (such as pain or restrictions on the freedom of movement); *remunerative*, based on control over material resources and rewards such as wages or benefits; and *normative*, based on the manipulation of symbolic rewards and deprivations, the use of the power of persuasion, and on appeals to shared values and idealism.

While these types of power are not restricted to particular types of organization, one will tend to be the dominant force in any one organizational case, such that 'most organizations employ all three kinds of power, but the degree to which they rely on each differs from organization to organization' (Etzioni 1961: 6–7). Each type of power relation can then be equated with government, business and voluntary or third sector organization respectively. Following from this argument, Etzioni goes on to outline three kinds of involvement by people in organizations which he described as *alienative*, where involvement is kept to a minimum, such as among capitalists in foreign countries, prison inmates, enlisted recruits; *calculative*, where there is positive involvement of low intensity, such as business contacts and prisoners who have created relations with prison authorities; and *moral*, which indicates high-intensity involvement, such as devoted party members or parishioners in church, and followers and leaders in social organizations.

Although voluntary associations are highly diverse, Etzioni suggests that they chiefly use degrees of normative power to achieve compliance. They build commitment of workers, volunteers and members and compensate them primarily through symbolic reward. This line of thinking has led to the idea of a third sector as a loose category of organizations that are not government or for-profit businesses, but which are held together by the 'glue' of value-driven action and commitment. Najam (1996b) shows how Etzioni's schema of three different ways in which organizations mobilize resources – coercion and legitimate authority (the state), negotiated exchange in markets (business) and shared values in consensus-based systems (voluntary organizations) – can be used to argue that broad differences exist between the three sectors of institutional forms. Within policy circles, the discovery of the third sector has been seen as having several possible purposes: as another potential delivery system for services, as an area of 'private' activity into which government can shift responsibilities, and, as we saw earlier, the notion of an arena of 'civil society' in which individuals can organize social action.

There is another line of thinking which has led to the third sector concept which is based on the history of activist organizations. Levitt's (1975) book deals with the changes in the nature of protest and social movements in the United States, and represents one of the first documented uses of the term 'third sector'. It seems possible that Etzioni and Levitt both independently came up with the expression. Levitt traces the emergence in the 1970s of increasing social activism which was not just seeking 'specific reforms' as in the past, but was pressing for 'a more responsive society', with more 'benign behaviour' from government, business and educational bureaucracies than in the past, asking:

> Why suddenly have so many new organizations arisen to institutionalize this activism in order to tackle problems which for so many years were ignored by the other two sectors and generally tolerated by the rest of society? These new organizations – which I shall collectively call the Third Sector – demand our attention.
>
> (Levitt 1975: 7)

These demands centred on a greater emphasis on quality of life over material goods, a more equitable distribution of resources, higher levels of public participation in determining what is equitable, and on active interest groups and personal involvement rather than just on conventional politics. Levitt was writing in the context of the emergence of highly visible activism embodied in student groups, the Black Panthers, women's groups, environmentalists and the US New Left corporate responsibility movement. He claimed that:

> To treat the Third Sector, its outcries and demands, its assertions and its tactics, simply as a brief though influential phase in the so-called American revolution is to miss the possibility that fundamental new institutions are being created and new methods for achieving social change are being irrevocably manufactured.
>
> (Levitt 1975: 8)

The new ground which Levitt identified took many forms, including challenging the 'safe anonymity' and controlling functions of large-scale bureaucracies in public and private sectors, a critique of normal bureaucratic 'professionalism', and the idea that government is unwieldy and unresponsive to people's needs.[10] He points out that for too long policy makers and researchers have focused on only two broad sectors in a conventional taxonomy which divides society into public and private such that private is understood to be 'business', while 'public is presumed to be all else' (1975: 48).

> But that leaves an enormous residuum, which itself is divisible in many ways. . . . I have called this residuum the Third Sector . . . a bewildering array of organizations and institutions with differing degrees of visibility, power, and activeness. Although they vary in scope and specific purposes, their general purposes are broadly similar – to do things business and government are either not doing, not doing well, or not doing often enough.
>
> (Levitt 1975: 49)

There has always been a third sector, but it was ignored by social commentators – church groups, labour unions, sports clubs and music associations. They have purposes, like all other organizations, but they differ chiefly in the tools they employ to get things done. Without any explicit reference to Etzioni's work, Levitt goes on to outline the different 'rules of the game' found in the different sectors. In business the main tool employed to get things done is that of exchange, rational calculation of competitive economics and market. In government the main tool is that of law, the power of compulsion, even if it is not explicit – the formal codification of legitimacy, whether real or contrived. Finally, for the third sector, things run on voluntarism, donations of time and money and quiet persuasion. Participation, Levitt suggests, is not usually motivated by income (although the desire to protect income may emerge), while resources are mobilized by an organization's ability to seek and attract them voluntarily.

The concept of the third sector should best be seen as a guiding metaphor (Wuthnow 1991) or a Weberian 'ideal type', which provides an analytical framework for discussing organizational and institutional relationships, but which does not always correspond precisely with realities on the ground.[11] Najam (1996b) suggests that Nerfin's (1986) framework of three systems of power – the 'prince, the merchant and the citizen' – provides a useful 'way of seeing' by contrasting government and economic power with the power of 'citizens and their associations'.[12] The resultant notion of a three-dimensional web of the institutional landscape of society shows both the blurred boundaries which exist (for example between private sector business and some NGOs) as well as a set of quite distinctive concerns, such as the building of organizations in the third sector based primarily on social vision. As a guiding metaphor, it is also important to realize that while the concept is relatively new, the organizations of the third sector are not, and the concept allows us to reinterpret existing studies and data in a new light. As Levitt (1975) points out, despite being ignored as a separate 'sector', a vast literature arguing about its forms and taxonomies exists. For example, research by Smith and Friedmann (1972) – along with work by numerous anthropologists who have long focused on the organizational activity of communities in different parts of the world (Lewis 1999b) – offers a relatively long and detailed history of thinking about the third sector, to which it is always useful to return even if such work is not presented within the conceptual categories fashionable today.

With both mainstream and radical origins, the term 'third sector' is useful because it provides an analytical framework into which we can categorize NGOs as organizations based on a set of relatively clear conceptual distinctions in relation to government agencies and for-profit business. These boundaries are in practice unclear and overlapping, and use of a simple three sector framework may only serve to obscure fundamental historical differences between states and regions (Tvedt 1998). Another perspective on the third sector developed by Evers (1995) sees it not as a clear-cut sector, but as an intermediate area between state, market and household. It is an area within mixed systems of welfare in which a range of different kinds of organizations, including hybrid forms or new types of partnership, deliver services in new ways and challenge existing institutional arrangements. Whichever third sector tradition is adopted, arguably despite some limitations a three sector model is a start.

CONCLUSION

This chapter has reviewed the rise of NGOs and the changing contexts in which they operate. We have considered the background to the growth of NGOs, and the main reasons as to why these organizations have recently begun to interest researchers and policy makers. A brief sketch of the history of NGOs at international level was presented, and this history is shown to have far deeper roots than is often supposed. The different regional and national contexts and influences on NGOs in different parts of the world was also reviewed in order to show the high level of diversity among various NGO traditions.

We have also explored the challenge of defining NGOs, the often bewildering range of terminologies that have been used in the literature, and the conceptual confusion that this both reflects and creates. Making use of Najam's and Vakil's definitions of development NGOs, a distinction was made between a *broad* definition (NGOs as an umbrella term for third sector organizations concerned with improved services and wider social change, whether part of the aid industry or not, including both public benefit and self-help) and a *narrow* definition (NGOs as donor-funded intermediary organizations which support community-level membership organizations). Even the narrow definition covers a highly diverse group of organizations working in different societies, sectors and policy environments. The broad definition is adopted as being useful to our general discussion, because it allows comparison between different types of organization which nevertheless all still share certain common characteristics.

The chapter then traced the background to the recent rediscovery of the concept of 'civil society' which forms the backdrop for much of the current interest in NGOs, highlighting the liberal and radical traditions of civil society, and introduces the different ways in which NGOs are both part of, and contributors to, civil society. The chapter concluded by considering the concept of the 'third sector', which helps place NGOs as organizations more firmly on the map in conceptual terms.

Different parts of the world face very different relative profiles of state, market and civil society. It is important for NGOs to be seen not in isolation, but as development actors alongside many others. As Biggs and Neame (1995) point out, it is not always helpful to separate civil society from the state, and instead they argue for a focus on the relationships between the two in a given context. Nor should NGOs always be viewed as suitable vehicles for democratization since, as we have seen, both civil society and social capital have their dark sides. Neither the theory nor the practice of civil society makes sense without the state. Democracy and civil society are processes and arenas which continually evolve, and are not goods which can be 'delivered', as some development donors and NGOs sometimes seem to think. In the end, NGOs exist as one diverse set of actors within a set of complex, changing, context-specific social and political processes.

In terms of our conceptual framework (Figure 1.1), we have therefore begun exploring the outer circle – the context in which NGO management must be understood. In the next chapter, we continue this exploration by examining the world of international aid and its institutions.

REVIEW QUESTIONS

- Choose a specific national context that is well known to you and outline the origins and characteristics of its third sector, making clear whether and how its history is different from general understandings of NGOs and the third sector.
- What are the broad differences of origin and meaning between the concepts of the 'third sector' and 'civil society'?
- Which of the many terms used for different types of NGOs do you find most useful and why?

Chapter 3

NGOs and development

LEARNING OBJECTIVES

After considering this chapter, the reader will be able to describe and analyse:

- Relationships which exist between development NGOs and the wider 'aid industry' to which many of them are linked
- Main development NGO roles of implementer, catalyst and partner
- Challenges of judging the effectiveness of development NGOs' work

KEY TERMS

- Development
- Humanitarian relief
- Rights-based development approaches
- The aid industry
- Advocacy
- Empowerment
- Service provision
- Partnership
- Implementation

INTRODUCTION

This chapter examines the backdrop of the institutions and policies of international development assistance, against which many NGOs seeks to manage their work. For many people, the concept of 'NGO' has become inseparably linked with the business of international development – to the multilateral institutions such as the World Bank and the United Nations, to the bilateral donors such as the UK Department for International Development (DFID) or the United States Agency for International Development (USAID) and to a raft of specialized, development-focused international third sector organizations which channel funds from Northern governments and publics.

International aid, which became a prominent part of international relations in the period after the Second World War, tended to be based primarily around a set of bilateral and multilateral relationships between governments. Aid was channelled predominantly into large-scale, government-organized projects in the developing world. This began to change in the 1980s when donors began to pay more attention to NGOs, as we saw in Chapter 2. NGOs, according to Little (2003), were perceived to offer three 'qualities' that official aid was unable to provide. The first was that NGOs were not tied to the geopolitical interests of states, but were seen as more independent in the agendas they were able to pursue. The second was that NGOs offered ordinary citizens in the North an opportunity to engage with issues of poverty and social justice as supporters, volunteers or contributors to organizations and campaigns. The third was that NGOs could engage more effectively than governments with citizens in the developing world, particularly those such as women or minorities who found themselves excluded from economic and political participation within existing institutional structures.[1]

Yet the 'donor' view of NGOs, while definitely an important part of the story, can give a somewhat incomplete and oversimplified picture of the world of NGOs. While there *are* clearly a great many NGOs which depend on international development assistance, there are others which seek to 'go it alone', relying instead on the voluntary labour of their staff or members, on contributions from the local or the international community, or on using the market for other sources of income.[2] Indeed, Satterthwaite (2005: 2) argues that development aid has largely ignored or 'provided too little support to' the numerous local organizations that benefit and represent poorer groups, which remain largely 'invisible to development assistance'. There are also vast and generally unquantified private international resource flows in the form of remittances between individuals, families and communities which constitute an important though often unrecognized source of survival and development (Sogge *et al.* 1996).

NGOs AND THE 'AID INDUSTRY'

However, the NGO phenomenon cannot be discussed adequately without reference to the flow of development assistance and the organizations and institutions which sustain the aid system. NNGOs – many of which play the role of donors, project implementers or 'partners' working with SNGOs and community-based organizations – form an increasingly important element of the 'aid industry'. In the 1950s and the 1960s NGOs and official donors tended to pursue different development agendas and remained largely uninterested in each other's activities and occasionally suspicious of each other's agendas (ODI 1995). NGOs were seen as organizations which were useful in emergency work rather than as serious actors in development work. A few bilateral donors began to support NGO programmes directly in the 1970s, beginning with Canada and Norway, and this trend accelerated in the 1980s. This reflected a recognition by donors that NGOs could contribute to official aid objectives in the areas of poverty reduction efforts, environmental conservation initiatives and health and education work. It also reflected the growth of the 'new policy agenda' of governance reform and liberalized markets that was discussed earlier (Edwards and Hulme 1995). What most donors seem to want from development NGOs is summarized well by Carroll (1992: 177), who lists effective service delivery (of shelter, credit, healthcare and so on), the rapid disbursement and utilization of project funds, an assurance that funds will be handled and spent honestly, a sense of 'ownership' of intervention fostered among beneficiaries which will lead to sustainability, and finally an increased role for NGOs in service delivery as part of the desired privatization of the state.

In practice, it is very difficult to get accurate or up-to-date figures of aid flows to NGOs through official channels (Riddell and Robinson 1995; Wallace *et al.* 2006) (Box 3.1). Data from the Organization for Economic Cooperation and Development (OECD) do not include increasing amounts of multilateral funding through NGOs, nor do official figures include the money going to NGOs within official aid projects, nor the funds channelled directly to NGOs from official country programmes (ODI 1995). OECD figures showed that by the second half of the 1990s about 5 per cent of all official aid was being channelled through NGOs. The proportion of total NGO funds in a country that are drawn from official sources varies very greatly, from 85 per cent in Sweden to about 10 per cent in Britain. The pace of increase of official aid flowing to NGOs has been dramatic, such that between 1983/4 and 1993/4 Britain increased its official funding of NGOs by almost 400 per cent, to £68.7 million, with an increase of the share of total British aid to NGOs rising from 1.4 per cent to 3.6 per cent. By 1998/9 the DFID's funding to British NGOs had reached an estimated £182 million, even though British NGOs still take less from government than do many other European NGOs (Wallace *et al.* 2006).

Perhaps surprisingly given the regular outbreaks of public concern about the volume of resources NGOs control (see Box 1.1), the vast majority of official development assistance still does not go to or through the NGO sector, despite the large quantities of funds that go from some donors to some NGOs. According to Little (2003: 178), NGOs in fact control only 'a meaningful but small share' of the world's assistance to developing countries. But he argues that their significance lies in the fact that NGOs bring two qualities to international development assistance that cannot be achieved through mainstream official channels. The first is a measure of independence from the strategic and geopolitical interests that drive foreign policy, which can create more space for an NGO to pursue its own goals in terms of poverty reduction or rights. The second is they enable ordinary citizens from both North and South to engage with development and other issues, a capacity which is higher than that provided within the normal channels of development assistance. For these reasons, argues Little, NGOs play roles which go beyond that reflected by the monetary value of the resources they control.

Official development assistance flows to NGOs

It is almost impossible to get precise figures on the amounts of development assistance flowing to NGOs. According to figures from the Development Assistance Committee (DAC) of the OECD, the amount of official funds going to NGOs (for example through mechanisms such as the UK's Joint Funding Scheme or Sida (Swedish International Development Agency) NGO programme) currently stands at around 9 per cent of the total global flows. What makes it more complicated is that development funds also flow 'through' NGOs as NGOs are contracted to undertake official programmes or take part in official relief operations. If these resources are included, then the figure rises to approximately 15 per cent of global aid flows. From the early 1990s onwards, observers noted a tendency or humanitarian aid to impinge upon funding to NGOs for development purposes in times of humanitarian crisis. The 'diversion potential' away from development purposes in order to meet an international emergency situation remains high.

Although talk of 'compassion fatigue' among public giving to NGOs has been a regular cause of concern in Northern countries since the 1980s, recent crises have indicated high levels of public support for humanitarian efforts by NGOs, often dwarfing official responses. The devastating Asian tsunami, caused by an earthquake which struck on 26 December 2004, caused hundreds of thousands of deaths across South and South East Asia. The public response to the appeal by the Development Emergency Committee (DEC) of UK NGOs far outstripped initial government responses. By summer 2005, the British public had raised more than £350 million and the US public US$350 million, while the UK government offered £72 million in immediate relief funding and a further £65 million in longer-term support. However, by late 2005 after subsequent appeals for funds from the DEC for the famine in Burkina Faso and the earthquake in Kashmir had proved rather less successful, there were some who argued that the fact that Western holidaymakers had been directly affected by the tsunami and the dramatic media coverage that it received had been decisive factors in triggering the massive response earlier in the year.

Sources: Roger Riddell, formerly of Christian Aid, personal communication; D. Aycliffe and K. Roscoe, 'The truth about the Tsunami', *International Development Magazine*, London, Summer 2005, p. 37.

Official funding for NGO projects and programmes can follow several different routes. One model is that NGOs themselves put forward projects and programmes and get funding from donors. There are also forms of donor/NGO partnership agreement which are negotiated for block funding to particular organizations. Some funds are also channelled through international NGOs (such as the Red Cross) and to NGOs specializing in sending volunteers abroad. The second basic model is that of contracting, in which NGOs are engaged by bilateral donors to undertake specific roles and tasks in particular contexts, within donors' or governments' own projects and programmes. In these kinds of arrangement, which again may take many forms, it is common for donors to subcontract projects to NGOs and provide them with the funds required to carry them out. ODI (1995) figures suggest that in recipient countries with a strong NGO presence, about 5 per cent of total bilateral aid funds go to NGOs for subcontracting initiatives.

Multilateral donors such as the World Bank and the European Union continue to find ways to bring NGOs into their development work as 'partners'. The European Union for example has long viewed NGOs as a means to provide development services to poor and marginalized groups that may be bypassed by official aid programmes. EU co-financing with European NGOs has increased steadily to about 200 million euros annually in 2000 (Wallace *et al.* 2006).

The reasons for the growth of official funding to development NGOs are that:

- it follows from donors' earlier work with NGOs on humanitarian relief, and is in some sense a logical progression of such work;
- donors turned to NGOs as a result of the poor performance of their own projects and programmes in the 1960s and 1970s, the popularity of NGOs in particular in the health and education sectors, and stronger claims by NGOs themselves that they were able to reach the poor and improve their lives;
- donors have seen NGOs as a way of getting around the problem of lack of impact due to inefficient or corrupt governments, or of reaching people in countries where official aid programmes have been suspended.

There has been considerable discussion about the dangers for both Northern and Southern NGOs of having closer links with international development donors. Carroll (1992: 18) suggests that organizational learning and effectiveness might be reduced as the growth of 'contracting' places new administrative demands on NGOs, generated by contrasting administrative styles (the donor brings a more bureaucratic approach with complex accounting and reporting) and an emphasis on outputs rather than on longer-term learning and development. There may be a negative impact on grassroots organizational work, as donors are often reluctant to support long time horizons because they want to show rapid results to constituencies at home (Edwards and Hulme 1995). There may be a lack of clarity as to whether funds are contract payments (the donor decides what is to be done) or grants (the NGO decides what is to be done), as the Commonwealth Foundation's *NGO Guidelines* (1995) points out. Finally, most donors are reluctant to cover any of the core costs related to the projects, which may be unpopular at home (Carroll 1992). This can lead to NGOs which are under-administered and under-managed just because of a belief that NGOs do not need to spend much on these core costs. It makes NGOs feel that they are valued simply because they are seen as a cheap way of getting things done, not because of any creative skills.[3]

There have also been difficult questions in recent years, asked by both sides, of the changing relationship between Northern and Southern NGOs. By the late 1990s Northern NGOs found themselves operating in an increasingly complex policy environment. There are three main sets of changes which these organizations have in many cases experienced (Lewis 1998c). The first has been the steady shift from direct implementation of projects and programmes towards the idea of partnerships with local organizations. In these partnerships SNGOs would implement work on the ground with NNGO support. The second was the increase in direct funding by donors to Southern NGOs, which in some cases and contexts began to bypass the Northern NGOs which had been used to acting as intermediary organizations. The third has been the emphasis by donors on relief and emergency work in the 1990s, often at the expense of longer-term development activities. Combined with these pressures is the growing 'identity crisis' faced by some of these organizations which find themselves caught between 'one country's concern and the problems of people in another' (Smillie 1994: 184). This gives Northern NGOs an uncertain, hybrid character, since they are part of the third sector of the North, but work predominantly in the South.[4]

A further set of problems for NGOs in both the North and South involved with the aid industry is connected with what Smillie (1994) called 'the tyranny of the project'. A preoccupation with development projects, rather than wider, more open-ended and long-term approaches, emphasizes donor control, and, according to Campbell (1994: 3), this ultimately 'prevents the community from effectively managing its own programmes' because it is difficult to build local ownership of externally driven activities. Another common complaint – heard mainly from SNGOs – is a vulnerability to changing donor fashions (such as environment, sustainability, civil society or gender) which come and go for reasons which lie well beyond the control of the NGO. Finally, there are also cases where SNGOs which depend on foreign funding find themselves taken less seriously by their governments if they try to negotiate with them over policy changes or engage in lobbying (Bratton 1989). Furthermore, government dependency for the provision of basic services on NGOs, which are themselves dependent on foreign donors, may serve to undermine the basic rights of accountability of citizens to demand services from governments, since the resources which ultimately provide such services are controlled from outside the country (Wood 1997).

THE CHANGING FACE OF DEVELOPMENT AID

The aid industry has always been characterized by a rapidly changing set of ideas, approaches and terms, but there has been another substantial shift in the way international development agencies operate since the turn of the millennium, with some perhaps paradoxical implications for NGO managers. In the words of Hinton and Groves (2004: 4) a 'radical rethink' has been prompted by the recognition that development policy and practice has done little so far to increase living standards in poor countries:

> There has been a dramatic shift from a belief in the importance of projects and service delivery to a language of rights and governance. Among policy-makers there has been an evolving sense of the need to involve members of civil society in upholding their rights and working to promote transparent, accountable government. . . . Donors are emphasising the need to work in partnership with national government rather than create parallel structures for service provision. The 1990s witnessed a gradual increase in the flow of aid delivered through governments, as support for democratic national processes grew.
>
> (Hinton and Groves 2004: 4–5)

The result has been that, on the one hand, there has been a continuation of donor interest in NGOs and civil society as key actors in promoting rights and accountability, but on the other, the channelling of more aid directly to governments rather than to NGOs or projects. In other words, a partial return can be observed to the emphasis on government to government aid that earlier characterized international development assistance between the 1950s and the 1980s. What is different in this new scenario is the set of new policy tools that have been designed by the World Bank and others to promote coordinated donor support of coherent government policies (such as poverty reduction strategies and budget support) and improved accountability between civil society and government (such as participatory poverty assessments).

Let us explore these changes, and their implications for NGOs, in more detail. From the late 1990s onwards a 'rights-based approach' has steadily gained ground among many NGOs and donors (ODI 1999; IDS 2003). This has been a response both to progress at the international level in terms of new legal rights frameworks, and to the work of local-level activists and movements around the world that are using and adapting rights frameworks as means for claiming social justice. The shift to a rights-based approach has brought issues of economic, social and cultural rights centre stage, alongside existing concerns with civil and political rights. In fact, this new interest is better seen as a 'revitalization' of an older development and rights discourse which had emerged with the first UN World Conference on Human Rights in 1968 (Molyneux and Lazar 2003). The rights perspective has proved useful in linking poverty reduction efforts with citizenship, laws and accountability, and, in the case of humanitarian intervention, has highlighted the need to build local dialogue around protection of the rights. For NGOs choosing to take a rights-based approach (and for some funders this may increasingly be an area of conditionality), a focus on rights has far-reaching implications for most aspects of development work, including the content and process of community-level partnerships, and the need to focus on wider institutions of state, public accountability and law in campaigning work (Box 3.2).

In addition to changes in development ideas, the main ways of working have also shifted. Rather than the previous emphasis on projects, donors have moved towards current preoccupations with 'upstream aid' and the need 'to do more with less'. As Beall (2005: 4) writes,

> While projects remained tenacious, from the 1980s onwards they increasingly gave way to programme aid, usually directed at particular sectors such as health and education or public sector reform. . . . Currently there is a growing trend towards the delivery of aid through Direct Budget Support (DBS), where financial support is channelled directly to a recipient government, usually through a ministry of finance, in a context where conditionality is arguably less oppressive and negotiated in advance in the context of policy dialogue and development partnerships.

Following the lead of the World Bank, donors such as DFID have in recent years left projects behind and looked for ways to influence directly recipient governments in more coherent and comprehensive ways. It has long been a criticism of the way that donors work that they do not coordinate effectively. So, for example, sector-wide approaches (SWAPs) are designed to bring donors together in support of national health or education policies to provide resources and consistency throughout the policy-making process. In a similar vein, the poverty reduction strategy papers (PRSPs) are intended to build donor support at the

Some implications of the rights-based approach for NGO practice

Increased transparency: the need for an NGO to be explicit in relation to its principles and values when it deals with other development actors and local people. A key area is making partnerships with other agencies more accountable and responsive.

Shifting from beneficiaries to partners: seeing people with whom an NGO works as active citizens rather than as voiceless recipients of assistance.

The analysis of power relations: NGOs require a sophisticated understanding of how local institutions operate within a given context and the complexities of local politics.

Building new skills in political analysis and diplomacy: since the rights-based approach is one that implies a deeper engagement with local laws, social norms and political systems it brings with it a high level of sensitivity and added risks of allegations of interference.

An emphasis on working with the poorest: the rights-based approach draws renewed attention to people who remain hidden or 'to whom no one listens' in their local struggles for justice on the broader landscape of development activities.

Engaging more fully with legal systems: this can provide NGOs with the means to help build people's awareness of their rights, through for example legal aid provision and rights awareness training.

Encouraging better accountability between governments and citizens: examples here would include supporting the right to information, and exploiting the potential of the PRSP process.

Source: adapted from IDS 2003.

national level across ministries, private sector and civil society to develop a single national plan to tackle poverty which can be more strongly 'owned' by the recipient government and its citizens. The move by many development donors in recent years away from free-standing projects or programmes towards broader support for budgets and policy reform within recipient governments – sometimes seen as part of what has been termed 'the new architecture of aid' – seems set to continue, despite recent setbacks in countries such as Ethiopia and Uganda.

Alongside this process there has been an effort to try to reduce the transaction costs of development assistance, by disbursing large lump sums to local organizations through forms of subcontracting. Funding to NGOs in particular, especially when large numbers of smaller organizations are concerned, can require enormous amounts of donor staff time to disburse and monitor. One current model is that of the local fund in which an NGO or a mixed consortium of organizations 'manages' a fund on behalf of donors and within which NGOs compete with each other for funding on themes or areas that are specified by donors (Box 3.3). Another new funding model is the growth of what DFID calls programme partnership agreements (PPAs). These arrangements were introduced in 1999 and were designed to replace the older block grant system and widen NGO participation beyond the well-known large UK NGO group of Oxfam, Christian Aid, CAFOD, SCF and VSO to more than fifteen organizations. Although described as partnerships, these can also be seen as a form of contracting in which an NGO is given responsibility for a set of tasks that contribute to DFID's overall objectives in a particular country or sector for a specific time period (Wallace *et al.* 2006). PPAs are also designed to help donors to try to reduce transaction costs and improve local 'ownership' through the dispersal of a smaller number of larger grants. In the PPA system, an NGO develops an individually tailored partnership agreement with DFID. For example, for Christian Aid the PPA which lasted until the end of 2005 provided approximately £3 million a year, while the NGO also continued to access other budget lines for specific pieces of work, for one-off development and humanitarian work.

In Britain, since 2000 there has also been a Civil Society Challenge Fund (CSCF) which forms a competitive means of project funding for organizations which do not have PPAs.[5] Although providing smaller grants than the PPA, the CSCF is currently worth about £10 million annually. Ostensibly, the idea was to broaden participation beyond NGOs to include a more diverse set of civil society actors – which have to be registered as charities in the UK – such as trade unions, universities or church groups, but in practice the main recipients have remained the more standard types of NGOs (Wallace *et al.* 2006).

Finally, a key element of the recent changes in the aid system is the new emphasis on internationally agreed targets for poverty reduction. The emphasis on targeting is embodied in the UN's Millennium Development Goals (MDGs). This phenomenon is of course part of a much broader trend within public life towards an 'audit culture' and the use of performance indicators. Donors have affirmed commitment to the MDGs – including halving poverty and hunger, universal primary education, and halting and reversing HIV/AIDS. While this is a good basis for organizing around common basic themes and has undoubtedly helped to bring a much-needed focus to international efforts at global poverty reduction, there are also concerns about whether or not these targets may obscure important qualitative criteria (such as gender and social attitudes, or the quality of schooling in a particular education system) and about who is involved in setting and measuring such targets. There are also concerns that in seeking to achieve maximum impact in meeting the goals overall, donors are reprioritizing their efforts towards areas of the world where the largest concentrations of poverty are found – mainly Africa and South Asia – at the expense of substantial minorities of people in middle-income countries who remain poor and marginalized.

What does this mean for NGOs? Although there may be opportunities for seeking influence within the implementation of measures in support of meeting these targets, NGOs are also asking whether or not these kinds of generalized measures have an impact in relation to poor people 'on the ground'. One positive suggestion for this kind of approach is to work to ensure adherence to the 'spirit' of the MDGs rather than the formal specifics (Naschold 2002). For NGOs seeking to initiate or continue donor support, it has also become necessary to find ways to monitor more closely the ways in which the targets may bring changes to donor priorities at national and sectoral levels.

New donor approaches with NGO funding: Manusher Jonno, Bangladesh

Manusher Jonno (MJ) – which means 'for the people' – began life as a small consortium of local and international agencies coordinated by CARE and funded by DFID to the tune of £13.5 million. DFID wished to fund a wide range of innovative human rights and governance work in Bangladesh but wished to avoid incurring the transaction costs of funding large numbers of often small civil society organizations that would deliver this kind of cutting-edge work. Instead, DFID tendered for the management of the project in order to find the most cost-effective and decentralized way of working. In 2002 MJ began work; establishing a small secretariat in Dhaka, it developed administrative systems and a set of criteria for funding and advertised for project proposals. MJ was immediately deluged with applications from all kinds of organizations for a wide range of types of project and at first found it difficult to cope with the demand. In particular, there were many applicants whose proposals did not fit within MJ's brief – since human rights and governance work was a relatively new framework for many local NGOs – and large amounts of time were needed to better inform applicants about MJ's objectives and to provide capacity building to NGOs around human rights and governance themes. By late 2005 MJ had developed robust operating systems for dealing with applications and monitoring the progress of more than 120 partners. A key lesson nonetheless was the severe underestimation of the massive administrative workload which was passed down from DFID to the decentralized MJ secretariat. In 2006 MJ achieved the status of an independent, local trust separated from both DFID and CARE. Other donors have begun to contribute to its funds in addition to DFID. MJ will act as a local funding point for organizations in Bangladesh seeking support for human rights and governance work.

Sources: author's own field notes; Beall 2005.

There is also growing recognition of a changing and more diverse landscape of donorship in other areas (Harmer and Cotterrell 2005). Particularly in relation to humanitarian intervention in natural disasters and complex crises, it is no longer the case that it is only the rich industrialized nations of the DAC that are seen to provide resources. Aid is now also provided, and has become more visible, through a range of 'non-DAC' nations that includes Gulf states, areas of central Asia and central Europe, South Africa and some Latin American countries. There is a realization among Western donors that regional groups of donors such as the League of Arab States, the Association of South East Asian Nations (ASEAN) and the African Union are playing important roles and that previous policy dialogue between the DAC, the UN and the EU needs to be substantially widened.

It is not simply the case that NGOs will need only to find ways to respond to these changing donor agendas. There is also ample evidence that NGOs themselves have contributed to changes within donors' agendas as well. Issues which were previously seen as mainly NGO concerns are now far more deeply entrenched within mainstream official donor activities – issues such as the concept of participatory planning, the gender dimensions of development and environmental concerns. Rights-based development, discussed earlier in this section, is also an example of successful influencing of the wider development agenda in part by NGOs.

While many donors have long included NGOs in the implementation of their projects, it is becoming more common for them to consult NGOs on policy. For example, Norway consulted many NGOs when drawing up its bilateral programmes in Nicaragua and Ethiopia in 1993, and in 2000 the DFID completed what it called a civil society consultation exercise with a range of third sector organizations in the North and South. Donor concern with the issues of human rights and 'strengthening civil society' is in part another reflection of this 'reverse agenda' (Riddell and Robinson 1995). Many NGOs nevertheless remain sceptical of these developments and claims, seeing them more as a convergence of 'language' (and subversion of radical discourse by more powerful development actors). For example, NGOs such as Oxfam remain on the whole highly critical of World Bank structural adjustment policies, despite the Bank's recent moves towards consultation with civil society organizations in many of the countries where it works.

For some analysts such as Biggs and Neame (1995), NGOs run the risk of being co-opted by the new orthodoxy, and it has often been pointed out that 'he who pays the piper calls the tune'. Concerns have been raised about the ways in which NGOs' position within funding chains can contribute to the gradual 'depoliticization' of their ideas about and approaches to poverty, and their abilities to reach and work with the poorest groups on the ground (Bebbington 2005). Also important is the possible 'closing off' of more independent NGO options and strategies by the preoccupation of many of the donors with linear, planned, mainstream projects rather than the complex and multidimensional processes required for sustainable development. According to Biggs and Neame (1995) this may threaten the long-term effectiveness of NGOs by pulling them away from the wider context in which they operate and from the links which develop over time with other actors and organizations. NGOs will need to retain their room for manoeuvre to adapt, innovate and maintain a range of accountabilities with different constituencies. NGOs will need to manoeuvre carefully around vested interests if necessary, by building links with the public sector, by using trustees to negotiate around key power holders and by carefully building wider alliances and networks (Biggs and Neame 1995). The danger is that NGOs will lose, or will fail to develop, these abilities and strategies.

The new donor approaches may have potentially important implications for the ways in which Northern NGOs approach partnership and advocacy, as more points of policy influence are opened up. For example, there may be opportunities to influence donor priorities 'from above' in the ways in which they approach budget support issues, but at the same time there may be opportunities for their SNGO partners 'from below' to influence spending priorities at national and local levels – for example through participatory budgeting initiatives and decentralization processes. While it remains the case that many NGOs are becoming more tightly institutionalized into government and donor systems, more research is needed to understand better the ways in which both NGOs and these wider systems may be changing (Nelson 2006).

NGOs AND THE CONTEXTS OF 'DEVELOPMENT' AND 'RELIEF'

The concept of 'development' is one of the most problematic and contested terms of the current age, and this is not the place to undertake a systematic review of the different perspectives which exist.[6] In this book, development is defined, as here, as deliberate efforts to secure positive changes in people's quality of life in economic, political and social terms. This includes the more conventional concepts of development in economic terms as well as the more recent empowerment and rights-based approaches (e.g. Friedmann 1992) or the new interest in the concept of 'social exclusion' (Bhalla and Lapeyre 1997).[7] Edwards (1999b: 4) defines development as: 'the reduction of material want and the enhancement of people's ability to live a life they consider good across the broadest range possible in a population.'

Alongside the concept of development, we also find NGOs frequently associated with the related field of relief and emergency work (Box 3.4). In contrast to the longer-term challenge of development, relief work was commonly seen simply as an immediate response to natural or man-made disasters in terms of the relatively unproblematic challenge of distributing resources to those in need in the form of goods, services and technical assistance. Disasters were understood as interruptions in the linear process of development, after which 'normal' longer-term development work could be resumed (Macrae and Zwi 1994). In this model, the concept of 'rehabilitation' formed the bridge between relief and development. But development is increasingly understood in terms other than as a linear process, and the causes of disasters and famines are now seen as being far more complex. The emergence of the term 'complex political emergencies' signals a recognition that there are areas of the world where insecurity, instability and disorder are more or less permanent conditions (such as in Somalia or Afghanistan) and where conventional thinking about 'development' or 'relief' interventions may be of very limited value.

New thinking about relief therefore problematizes it in three ways. The first is that relief is increasingly understood as not – as was once believed – politically neutral, because political factors limit access to resources, and aid itself becomes a political resource. The second is the recognition that even after a problem or hazard has passed, the capacity of communities to access resources may be impaired and people may remain vulnerable. The third is the idea that relief and development tend to have different objectives, with the former concerned with physical survival and the latter aiming at sustainability and the building of appropriate social and economic systems. How can a process of 'rehabilitation' link these differing objectives?

Although it is in the countries of Africa, Asia and Latin America where the scale of poverty is most severe and where needs are greatest, it may also be important to recognize that 'development' is not only something which is being pursued in the 'developing world', as Gaventa (1999) has shown in his work on the growing links between economically marginalized communities in the USA and countries such as Mexico and India. What has been termed 'globalization', in which international flows of trade, finance and information are taking place at an unprecedented rate, may be important in contributing to this trend. This is also true of relief – the Kobe earthquake in Japan in 1995 was a disaster which required massive emergency efforts and generated an unprecedented response from and profile for

From emergency to development – building partner capacity in post-tsunami Sri Lanka

Over 38,000 lives were lost and 5,637 people were declared missing when the tsunami wave struck Sri Lanka on 26 December 2004, causing destruction estimated at US$ 1 billion. Thousands were left homeless and jobless. A massive international fund-raising appeal generated a huge influx of resources, while Sri Lanka, an accessible tropical tourist destination, also attracted numerous volunteers, students, tourists and aid workers who arrived to work alongside local communities and the military in the relief and rehabilitation effort. It was against this backdrop that the development arm of the Sri Lankan Conference of Catholic Bishops, the Caritas Social and Economic Development Center (SEDEC), with five of its thirteen diocesan centres located in affected areas, joined the efforts of local communities to respond to emergency needs. Caritas Sri Lanka (CSL) had long experience with disasters and emergency work, having worked in the ongoing conflict in the north and east of the island and aided victims of previous floods. Diocesan social centres had also been active in several of the devastated communities for many years, implementing development programmes focused on rainwater harvesting, sustainable agriculture, women's savings groups and micro-credit. However, they lacked adequate staff, systems and logistics capacity to respond to the enormous scale of food, shelter and livelihoods needs.

By January 2005, the Sri Lanka Bishop's Task Force agreed a structure for partners in the Caritas Internationalis (CI) network worldwide to join with CSL to provide financial resources and use international staff for capacity-building support. Capacity building in an emergency setting proved to be difficult work. In addition to meeting the needs of tsunami victims, the CI and Caritas partners needed to recruit and train the required staff, establish sub-offices, procure emergency materials, purchase necessary office equipment to support communication and transportation, host journalists and visitors, and maintain records and reports of how donor funds were spent. Staffing levels increased ten-fold. CI partners brought technical and organizational strength to complement the local knowledge, experience and grassroots network of Sri Lankan partners. While financial resources were plentiful, the main constraints proved to be lack of time and having to work within an environment often characterized by weak coordination, lack of communication and inappropriate government policies.

One year after the tsunami, partner capacity building continues and is projected for several more years as CSL embarks upon an ambitious three-year strategy to construct and repair over 9,000 permanent houses for tsunami victims, rebuild communities, and enhance and strengthen livelihood capacity. However, parallel to the shift from emergency to rehabilitation/development, the capacity-building focus has transitioned from rapid staff recruitment and rehabilitation of office space to supporting quality programme design, planning and implementation, monitoring and evaluation, and designing systems and policies to promote healthy organizational development. Staff training, information sharing between offices, and use of tools such as log-frames, indicators and budget tracking characterize the present programming priorities. ➤

The key challenge now is to find ways to avoid disempowering partners and creating dependency. Staff and agencies acting in an advisory role are assessing the risk or benefit of scaling back capacity-building support in favour of empowering and promoting the growth and development of the partner. An additional challenge for the agency is balancing continuing development of pre-tsunami programmes with the finance and human resource intensive tsunami work. Many pre-tsunami staff were reassigned to tsunami programmes, so care will be needed to ensure that this pre-tsunami work remains adequately staffed. The 'do no harm' principle must therefore be applied not just at the community level, but also among the agency itself and its partners.

Source: Alisha Myers, personal communication.

the Japanese 'third sector' (Kawashima 1999). The Turkish earthquake in 1999 had a similar galvanizing effect on citizens and civil society and shifted people's expectations about third sector roles, and, just as importantly, the responsibilities of the state itself (Box 3.5).

Since the 9/11 terrorist attacks on the USA in 2001, and the subsequent policy shift towards the so-called 'war on terror', there have been further changes within the aid industry which threaten further the capacity of NGOs to maintain this room for manoeuvre. For example, the political context of humanitarian assistance is changing. While strong and growing links between conflict and poverty were observed and documented throughout the 1990s, this relationship has become more widely acknowledged since 2001 and has been translated into new aid policies. One result has been what Harmer and Macrae (2003) call the increased 'securitization of aid', which includes the following trends: (a) renewed engagement by the USA with 'failed states' to reduce security threats (as opposed to previously investing in states that were willing to embrace reform); (b) an increased linking of military, political and humanitarian responses to instability; and (c) closer to the 'third sector' perhaps, a closer intertwining of military and welfare roles within radical Islamic groups. In Iraq, food aid in particular is viewed as an integral part of the reconstruction and stabilization process requiring arrangements for engagement with occupation forces. Although NGOs are not yet involved to a significant degree, they could become more so in the future.

A key tension exists between the 'war on terror' and the challenge of state building. The wars in Afghanistan and Iraq are raising very difficult questions for NGOs seeking to provide humanitarian assistance at the same time as engaging with transitional administrations with weak capacity and legitimacy. Some now suggest that the war in Iraq, and the current 'post-conflict' situation, may be ushering in a new era in which humanitarian organizations will in the future compete with a new private 'humanitarian industry' working in infrastructure and services, such as health education and water, based on for-profit provision (Harmer and Macrae 2003). These authors conclude that humanitarian actors will face a more complicated operating environment, and may need to make increasingly difficult judgements about the legitimacy and legality of struggles and conflicts if 'universality, impartiality and neutrality' principles are to be maintained.

The present book tries to avoid taking a prescriptive position with regard to any particular stance on development or relief issues, but instead seeks to analyse the efforts of different kinds of NGO to organize and manage work within a broad development focus.

The Turkish earthquake and the NGO sector

On 17 August 1999, an earthquake shook the eastern edge of the Marmara Sea, some 80 kilometres from Istanbul. Official figures state that there were over 17,000 deaths and half a million people made homeless. There was an unprecedented mobilization of NGOs and other civil society actors and this was an arguably positive outcome of the disaster, because NGOs and the media forced changes at the state level and acted as advocates for survivors. The challenge of civil society actors resulted in the state eventually providing for many of the immediate needs of the survivors. The initial response by the state had been very ineffective. It was two weeks before the state was able to coordinate its relief efforts, since it centralized its service delivery, marginalizing all but a very few 'state-friendly' NGOs from operations. But by the end of the year, state-led efforts gradually improved and tent-cities were run efficiently and basic needs of residents adequately met.

This change was the result of civil society pressure and the fact that NGOs were able to demonstrate their effectiveness through the media. Among the NGOs, Arama Kurtarma Dernegi (AKUT), which means 'Search and Rescue Association' and was previously concerned with mountain rescue, became a favourite with the public and rescued over 200 people. NGOs also demonstrated impressive coordination skills, with over thirty NGOs establishing a civil coordination centre and making use of an independent radio station in order to facilitate the distribution of resources. NGOs reacted to attempts by the state to limit their activities by taking a proactive stance. A manifesto was published in all the major newspapers, appealing to the state not to over-centralize relief efforts and to recognize the value of the NGO contribution to the relief effort. This manifesto, signed by over one hundred NGOs, represented a highly significant and unusual initiative that challenged prevailing norms in Turkey, and it reflected a changing public mood which allowed for citizens to criticize the state where criticism was due.

By providing an effective practical response and demonstrating their commitment and effectiveness, and then gaining legitimacy to make criticisms of the state when it made mistakes, NGOs successfully challenged the state to regain its legitimacy by improving its response to the earthquake and providing better services, which it gradually did. The magnitude of the efforts undertaken by the government should not be underestimated; at the time the World Bank described the earthquake as 'the most difficult emergency management crisis faced by any nation in recent history' (1999: 8). The unprecedented mobilization of Turkish civil society was a major component in meeting the challenge, and one remarkable result of the disaster was the 'coming of age' of the NGO sector.

Sources: personal communication from Markus Ketola; Jalali, 2002; World Bank 1999; Kubicek 2002.

ANALYSING NGO ROLES: IMPLEMENTERS, CATALYSTS AND PARTNERS

We move now from a discussion of the general context in which NGOs operate to begin to examine NGOs as organizations and the roles they play in development work. The following section focuses on what development NGOs actually *do*, and argues that what they do can be summarized broadly in terms of three main overlapping sets of roles: those of *implementers*, *catalysts* and *partners*. Of course, each role is not confined to a single organization, since an NGO may engage in all three groups of activities at once, or it may shift its emphasis from one to the other over time or as contexts and opportunities change.

The *implementer* role is defined as the mobilization of resources to provide goods and services, either as part of the NGO's own project or programme or that of a government or donor agency. It covers many of the best known tasks carried out by NGOs and includes the programmes and projects which NGOs establish to provide services to people (such as healthcare, credit, agricultural extension, legal advice or emergency relief) as well as the growth of 'contracting', in which NGOs are engaged by government or donors to carry out specific tasks in return for payment. The role of *catalyst* is defined as an NGO's ability to inspire, facilitate or contribute towards developmental change among other actors at the organizational or the individual level. This includes grassroots organizing and group formation (and building 'social capital'), empowerment approaches to development, lobbying and advocacy work, innovation in which NGOs seek to influence wider policy processes, and general campaigning work. The role of *partner* encompasses the growing trend for NGOs to work with government, donors and the private sector on joint activities, as well as the complex relationships which have emerged among NGOs, such as 'capacity building'. The new rhetoric of partnership now poses a challenge for NGOs to build meaningful partnership relationships and avoid dependency, co-optation and goal displacement.

NGOs as implementers

Implementation for NGOs usually involves the delivery of goods and services. As Carroll (1992) points out, service delivery is perhaps the most directly observable, visible role as NGOs attempt to provide goods and services that are wanted, needed or otherwise unavailable. An NGO can be engaged in providing services to its clients through its own programmes, it may be 'contracted' by government to provide services formerly provided by the state, or it can be contracted by a donor to provide services within a project structure. Increasingly, NGOs do not always provide the services to their target groups or clients, but may also provide services such as training or research to other NGOs, government or the private sector. Since the late 1980s, NGOs have been brought into World Bank structural adjustment programmes to provide a social 'safety net' to vulnerable sections of the population.

There has been a tendency for many to devalue the NGO implementation role. Korten (1990), for example, implies that his 'public service contractor' category of NGO is far from the creative, value-driven NGO ideal. Instead, NGOs are criticized for becoming closer to being private sector businesses, and therefore run the risk of being deflected from their original broader, value-driven goals by concentrating on services (Carroll 1992).[8] However, for many NGOs, implementation and service delivery have been areas of relative success. For example, in agriculture NGOs may be engaged in the delivery of services to people in 'unreachable' areas such as the fragile, complex or risk-prone lands for which government outreach is poor (Chambers 1987; Bebbington 1991; Kaimowitz 1993) and NGOs may achieve this using local field staff rather than relying on outside 'experts'. NGOs may also go on to strengthen wider systems of delivery through training, research and innovation, particularly with government staff whose skills and outlook can be improved through the formation of NGO 'bridges' with groups of local farmers.

An example is the work of the Baptist Rural Life Centre (BRLC), in Mindanao in the Philippines, which centres on the identification of soil fertility problems with poor upland farmers in communities that have been largely ignored by government extension service workers who are more interested in richer farmers who grow cash crops. The NGO developed a simple but effective technology, which would allow farmers to make the soil on sloping lands more secure and productive as well as providing a varied yield of essential foodstuffs throughout the year. Once this sloping agricultural land technology (SALT) had been tried and tested, the NGO then set about working to ensure it was utilized by other organizations and by government through demonstration events and training work (Watson and Laquihon 1993).

One reason for the criticisms has been misgivings about the accountability and the sustainability of NGO service delivery work. Criticisms revolve around the relationship to government and whether NGO services are supplementing, undermining or replacing public services. Since some NGOs may be dependent upon foreign development assistance, it is not desirable for basic services to pass into the hands of NGOs whose lines of accountability are not clear. Carroll (1992) is certain that NGOs 'should emphasise capacity building or viability upgrading services, not routine services' and this is a view backed up by Brown and Korten (1989: 11), who state: 'unless they [NGOs – MSOs (membership support organisation) and GSOs] are developing the capacity of indigenous organizations to replace them in their functions on a self-sustaining basis . . . they cannot claim to be doing development work.' This is close to the ideas developed by Evans (1996), who argues that rather than NGOs and government merely complementing each other's work, a more useful 'synergy' can be created if the relationship is a mutually reinforcing one based on a clear division of labour and mutual recognition and acceptance of these roles. Robinson and White (1997) provide a useful framework in which to analyse these relationships, based on three basic processes within the public–private relationships around service provision: the *determination* of which social services are to be supplied, the *financing* arrangements for these services and their actual *production*.

Some of those who advocate an increased level of NGO contracting for essential service delivery have taken on board such criticisms and instead advocate a 'pragmatic' involvement by NGOs. This stresses a limited timescale, and the ultimate goal of having the state (or the private sector) take over provision once new skills and approaches are acquired and resources mobilized (e.g. Poole 1994). While there may be good short-term reasons for 'gap filling' in public provision, NGO service delivery should ultimately be judged on its developmental impact: 'while service delivery has a strong intrinsic value, it should really be evaluated on the basis of its instrumental value as a catalyst for other developmental changes' (Carroll 1992: 66).

For optimists, the increasing profile of NGOs as service providers is seen as part of the growth of 'civil society', which will strengthen wider democracy and ultimately improve the efficiency and accountability of the state. In Africa, for example, Semboja and Therkildsen (1995) outline a scenario in which, following economic growth and 'successful' structural adjustment, the state will create an appropriate 'enabling environment' to allow the NGO sector to prosper, with the result that the quality and sustainability of services increases. However, the same authors also outline a pessimistic (and perhaps more realistic) scenario, in which it is not always clear who or whose values NGOs represent, and where NGO links with donors, elite and state patrons create ambiguity as far as their role in democratization is concerned.

There are two main sets of issues for NGOs in terms of longer-term thinking about implementation questions. For those emphasizing pluralism, the growth of NGOs as service providers increases choice. For example, Brett (1993) points out that NGOs, alongside the state and private sector, exist within a pluralistic organizational universe, which will expand the range of social choice and potential as relatively autonomous agencies existing within an open society. The challenge is for NGOs to achieve accountability and performance levels comparable with the other two sectors. However, for those stressing the role of NGOs in promoting development and change, there is concern that NGO potential strengths might be underused. After all, even when the quality of services is high, most NGOs offer limited, piecemeal or patchy provision which can never compete with the state in terms of coverage.

One future possibility is the increasing specialization and differentiation between two types of organization – between contracting NGOs and organizations with a more developmental focus (Edwards and Hulme 1995). For Carroll (1992), the key question is whether service delivery is a 'means' or an 'end' for development NGOs – a question which leads us neatly on to a discussion of the NGO role of 'catalyst'.

NGOs as catalysts

For many development NGOs, a key strategic choice (or perhaps balance) is between what Korten (1988: 6) calls 'the output vendor versus the development catalyst'. This section discusses what the development catalyst role might mean for NGOs.

Starting at the community level, many development NGOs speak of 'empowering' their clients or beneficiaries. The word 'empowerment' has many meanings, from the radical transformative sense in which Freire's education ideas have been adapted by many NGOs to the personal 'self-improvement' sense in which it is used in countries such as the United States.[9] While the latter is of limited relevance to NGOs, there is still widespread variation in the ways in which 'empowerment' is used. Showing how the term has multiple origins from Western counselling work to Gandhian philosophy (as well as Freire's work), Rowlands (1995) points out that it is seen always in terms of a process which includes becoming aware of the power dynamics in one's life, developing skills and capacity for greater control, exercising control without infringing rights of others, and supporting empowerment of others in the community. In this view, the process involves moving from insight to action, and from individual to collective action.

Empowerment has become central to ideas of 'alternative' development theory and practice. For example, Friedmann (1992: 31) shows how households are concerned with three different kinds of power: social (access to information, knowledge and skills, participation in social organizations, financial resources); political (access by individual household members to decision-making processes singly or in groups, e.g. voting, collective action, etc.); and psychological (an individual sense of power and self-confident behaviour, often gained from successful action in the other levels). As its central process, an alternative development seeks the empowerment of households and their individual members in all three senses.

Empowerment-centred approaches have also been used by development policy researchers to bring out the importance of gender and power in development. For example, Moser's (1989) view of empowerment rests on a generative view of power and links empowerment to problems of exclusion and participation, with an emphasis on bringing in people who are usually outside the decision-making process, as well as going beyond the formal institutions of political and economic power into the dynamics of oppression in the personal sphere. Moser's ideas also show that alternative development approaches, if they focus on the household, need to recognize that unequal access to decision making and resources exists within households as well as between them.

Freire's ideas of 'conscientization' placed emphasis on the role of an outside, professional facilitator who played an educational and ultimately catalytic role in creating the conditions for action towards change to take place. For some NGOs, this role is played by the NGO itself as it organizes and educates people and later withdraws. Case studies of the early work of the Bangladesh NGO Proshika illustrate the different ways in which this approach helped generate local efforts to act collectively to bargain for higher wages from landowners, to occupy land intended for redistribution to the landless but occupied by local elites and for action to be taken by local police to support women's rights (Kramsjo and Wood 1992).

Thomas (1992) provides the example of ASSEFA (Association of Sarva Seva Farms) which takes such an approach, combining it with Gandhian ideas. This Indian NGO is a good example of local grassroots action based on Gandhian action. Formed in 1969, ASSEFA develops land given to the landless through the Gandhian Bhoodan 'land gift' movement. It initially worked on settling communities on this land, but now works for rural industries, education and health and works in five states. Its field staff work for many years with communities on 'empowerment' before moving on and leaving villagers to address their own problems in their own ways, having altered the balance of power. One previously landless villager remarked: 'We have gained recognition in the village. Other castes, who were our masters earlier, now not only listen but pay attention to what we say' (Thomas 1992: 121).

Although such an approach characterized earlier work in the 1980s and 1990s by many NGOs (see for example Hashemi and Hassan 1999, on Bangladesh) and provided a strong influence on the shaping of NGO philosophy (and rhetoric), most of these kinds of organization have now gradually moved towards a less radical, more market-based version of empowerment, which emphasizes empowerment through economic activity as well as through political activism. For example, the well-documented Grameen Bank links women's empowerment to access to credit and participation in small-scale productive activities, although questions have been raised as to how far women's decision-making power within the household is affected (Holcombe 1995; Goetz and Sen Gupta 1996).

For Friedmann, NGOs are seen as vehicles which can link local action back into national and structural change. This takes us to another key NGO role as catalyst – that of advocacy. By the mid-1990s, advocacy had become widely acknowledged as an important NGO activity in building sustainable development (Covey 1995), and NGOs had come to see advocacy as a means for improving their effectiveness and impact, and as a potential strategy for 'scaling up'. Korten (1990) sees advocacy as a mature and developmentally sound NGO activity, particularly for NNGOs, because it addresses the structural roots of poverty rather than the symptoms, and because it moves NNGOs away from direct implementation in the South and towards engaging with power structures based closer to home. Jenkins (1987: 267), writing from the US non-profit perspective, defines policy advocacy as: 'any attempt to influence the decisions of any institutional elite on behalf of a collective interest'.

For some development NGOs more used to service delivery, this may be a relatively new challenge requiring a reorientation of the organization (see Box 3.3 on Manusher Jonno). It also raises new challenges of assessing impacts. In her discussion of four SNGO case studies in the Philippines and Mexico, Covey (1995) assesses the effectiveness of advocacy not just in terms of achieving the desired policy impacts, but also in terms of the process itself, which is seen as making a contribution to a healthy civil society. This is connected to ideas about building 'social capital' advanced by Putnam (1993) and with ideas under the new policy agenda to build democratization processes within the South. As we saw in Chapter 2, the results are not necessarily developmentally sound, and a form of interest-group 'gridlock' can be the result of an active civil society meeting a weak state (Blair 1997). However, what comes through clearly from Covey's work is that NGOs can balance power in multi-organizational alliances by playing a 'bridging function' (Brown 1991) which links grassroots level and national or international action, and different kinds of organization.

For Northern NGOs there is a long tradition of advocacy work, though results have been mixed. Edwards identifies advocacy as a distinctive type of activity for NNGOs:

> it is an attempt to alter the ways in which power, resources and ideas are created, consumed and distributed at global level, so that people and their organizations in the South have a more realistic chance of controlling their own development.
>
> (Edwards 1993: 3)

There have been some successes, such as the instituting of a baby milk marketing code, the drafting of an essential drugs list and the removal of restrictions on international trade for some items, for example on the textile quotas from Bangladesh, which helped create new women's employment during the 1990s (Clark 1992). More recently, in 2005, the Make

Poverty History campaign supported by NGOs such as Oxfam GB achieved a high profile in relation to the building of a social movement seeking to influence the G8 countries, the European Union, the IMF and the World Bank in relation to fairer trade, debt cancellation and increased levels of international aid.[10]

Advocacy has also become an important activity for Southern NGOs, where campaigns such as that against the Narmada Dam in India have been established by local organizations with international links. But according to Edwards (1993), in general results of Northern NGO advocacy have been rather disappointing, and in a harsh critique Edwards suggests that NNGO potential has not yet been fulfilled due to the absence of clear strategy, the failure to build strong alliances, an inability to develop alternatives to current orthodoxies and the dilemma of relations with donors. Work on the efforts of both SNGOs and NNGOs at the UN global summits has presented a more positive picture, showing how NGOs have achieved influence through lobbying, particularly in the base of 'low salience' policy issues such as the environment, gender and poverty, as opposed to 'high salience' policy issues such as military spending, human rights and economic reform (Van Rooy 1997). Covey (1995) concludes that SNGOs need good links with the grassroots for an advocacy strategy to work, along with a stable and responsive government with which they can develop a dialogue.

NGOs as partners

In the context of international development policy and practice, the concept of 'partnership' is increasingly in vogue amongst policy makers and practitioners. A British government White Paper on development is full of references to partnerships – between countries, donors, governments, NGOs and business – but offers no definitions and is vague as to the forms such partnerships might take (DFID 1997). The World Bank in Bangladesh began advocating partnership between the government and the NGOs under the title 'Pursuing Common Goals' (World Bank 1996).

Much of the interest in partnership in development circles since the 1990s has been aimed at seeking to build links between the work of government agencies and NGOs in development projects (Farrington and Bebbington 1993). Brown and Ashman (1996) suggest that cooperation between government and NGOs needs to span gaps of culture, power, resources and perspective if they are to be successful. In broad terms, the creation of partnerships is seen as a way of making more efficient use of scarce resources, increasing institutional sustainability and improving beneficiary participation. At a more general level, creating links between government agencies and NGOs may have implications for strengthening transparency in administration and challenging prevailing top-down institutional culture, both of which may contribute to the strengthening of the wider 'civil society' and for example Bangladesh's fragile process of democratization (Lewis 1997). On the other hand, the increased interest in NGOs as vehicles for service delivery is strongly linked to demands for privatization within what has been termed the 'new policy agenda' (Robinson 1993) discussed in Chapter 2. At the same time, some models of partnership have been transferred from rich country contexts to developing country or transition contexts with mixed results (Box 3.6).

Afghanistan: recent concerns about performance-based health partnerships

A World Bank proposal for an experimental performance-based partnership model for rebuilding health services in Afghanistan has come under criticism for its unproven assumptions and a set of ethical concerns. The proposal is one to subcontract the delivery of health services to NGOs, according to the NPM principle that governments should increasingly move from actually doing things to instead 'making sure that things get done'. The problem is that in Afghanistan the state is virtually non-existent, and therefore an assumption of the relative strengths and weaknesses of public and non-governmental agencies of the kind made in some Western countries is highly problematic. Since the state will be unable to manage performance-based partnerships effectively, it is argued that the result will be the complete privatization of health services and the further marginalization of a state that already lacks the confidence of many of its citizens. Evidence from earlier schemes in Ghana and Thailand showed important limitations in the way contractors monitored progress and results, while in South Africa evidence indicated that contracting out produced lower cost provision of some services but was found to conceal high transaction costs for the state. The introduction of user fees (suggested for Afghanistan) has been shown in several contexts to be an inequitable way to finance health services since it excludes the poorest. On an ethical level, there are also concerns voiced that the proposed policy experiment will be funded as a pilot using donor loan money that will eventually have to be repaid, in part by those citizens who may be disadvantaged if things go wrong.

Source: Ridde 2006.

It is not therefore surprising that 'partnership' tends to mean different things to different development actors, and there is in practice a wide gap between rhetoric and reality. We can use the term 'partnership' to refer to an agreed relationship based on a set of links between two or more agencies within a development project, usually involving a division of roles and responsibilities, a sharing of risks and the pursuit of joint objectives, in this case between government agencies, NGOs, donors and farmers. The term 'linkage' is used to refer to specific points of the partnership at which activities are shared between different agencies and stakeholders at different levels of the project. A project which involves partnership is likely to have a range of inter-agency linkages at various levels. The use of the word 'partnership' covers a wide range of different relationships between agencies which may have either an *active* or a passive, *dependent* character, and this is discussed further in Chapter 6.

Active partnerships are those built through ongoing processes of negotiation, debate, occasional conflict, and learning through trial and error. Risks are taken, and although roles and purposes are clear, they may change according to need and circumstance. Dependent partnerships, on the other hand, have a blueprint character and are constructed at the project planning stage according to rigid assumptions about comparative advantage and individual agency interests, often linked to the availability of outside funding. There may be consensus among the partners, but this often reflects unclear roles and responsibilities rather than the creative conflicts which emerge within active partnerships.

The origins of the partnership (such as compulsion, agreement or financial incentive) may hold the key to its success or failure, and may limit the scope for subsequent process monitoring. For example, agencies may enter into relationships in order to gain access to external resources which are conditional on partnership. Agencies can drift into partnerships without adequately considering the wider implications. For example, new roles for staff may have to be created in order to service the partnership properly, or management systems may be required to monitor the progress of new activities. NGOs in particular are vulnerable to being viewed instrumentally, as agents enlisted to work to the agendas of others as 'reluctant partners' (Farrington and Bebbington 1993). Partnership may bring extra costs which are easily underestimated, such as new lines of communications requiring demands on staff time, vehicles and telephones; new responsibilities for certain staff; and the need to share information with other agencies. Building partnerships is likely therefore to be difficult.

While partnerships between different actors are usually seen by development agencies as essentially positive, there is a view, particularly among some NGOs, that 'partnership' may be becoming a degraded term. Clearly, any new thinking on forms of partnership is to be welcomed. In particular, mechanisms are needed for monitoring how the partnership is measuring up once the linkages are in place, and developing the means to achieve appropriate 'course corrections' when necessary. Many partnerships begin with a dependent character but can be made more 'active'. Essential to any notion of the value of deploying partnership as a tool for achieving project objectives is the idea that agencies acting together are able to achieve certain objectives which they would be unable to manage singly. This idea is the key to 'measuring' the success of any partnership.

Linking management challenges and roles

If we return to our conceptual framework (Figure 1.1) it is possible to link all of these roles with each of the three interlocking circles of the NGO management challenges in terms of *organization*, *activities* and *relationships*. For example, acting as a catalyst in relation to community empowerment will require an NGO to manage an appropriate set of internal organizational arrangements, to design a set of appropriate activities to meet the goals of the intervention, and to negotiate suitable relationships with relevant people and organizations.

EFFECTIVENESS: ARE NGOs ANY GOOD AT WHAT THEY DO?

There are many arguments which have been made in support of the assumed advantages of NGOs over other types of organization (Anheier 1987). There is a social argument which is based around equity issues: the idea is that NGOs can encourage and facilitate participation of the poor and can reach strata of the population which have hitherto been left untouched or bypassed by public service delivery systems. This is because government sector agencies suffer from shortages of resources and face social and cultural access problems, and government decision making is over-influenced by the interests of elites. There is an economic argument, based on the concept of efficiency, which argues that NGOs provide services more cost-effectively than government agencies can, and that NGOs are able to generate self-sufficient, self-reliant and sustainable interventions. For example, Smith (1987) found that NGOs were generally more efficient than government projects, based on a greater cost advantage due to lower labour costs and incomplete pricing (relying on voluntary local inputs, taking no provision for depreciation, leaving out transaction costs such as site selection, grant seeking, information gathering, and the exclusion of long-range recurrent costs).

The political argument is that NGOs are less vulnerable to sudden and unexpected political upheaval and change than government agencies, and that government agencies tend to have a 'hidden' political agenda which seeks to win votes or build patron–client relationships. NGOs are therefore seen as being more honest in that they are less likely to be guided by these types of political considerations in their work. Finally, the cultural argument points out that NGOs (and Southern NGOs in particular) are more embedded in the local culture and that they therefore can be more sensitive to assessing and meeting local needs. NGOs can also support local organizations in their own original contexts rather than building new ones or imposing their own large-scale organizations from outside on local communities. Each of these arguments can be shown to have some merit, but none can be taken for granted or assumed, and it is necessary to pay careful attention to specific cases and contexts. To make matters worse, there is surprisingly little data about the effectiveness of NGOs in either development or relief work (see Boxes 3.7 and 3.8). What we find in the literature is a set of writings which tends to take either a 'pro-' or 'anti-' NGO case based on limited generalized evidence or a specific narrow example.

One of the earliest examples of the pro-NGO case is Michael Cernea's (1988) report which was written for the World Bank. Cernea sees NGOs' main contribution as one of strengthening local organizational capacity, and he notes that 'the NGO priority on first organizing the people embodies a philosophy that recognizes the centrality of people in development policies and action programs and the importance of self-organization' (Cernea 1988: 8). NGOs therefore seek to organize people to make better use of local productive resources, create new resources and services, promote equity and alleviate poverty, influence government actions towards these same objectives, and establish new institutional frameworks to sustain people-centred and action-centred development. NGOs therefore possess a 'comparative advantage' over government agencies, according to Cernea, in four main areas:

1   NGOs reach the poor in remote areas where government reach does not exist or is ineffective;
2   NGOs operate at lower cost due to the voluntary nature of their activities and lower technological overheads;
3   NGOs promote local participation by working with community groups as partners, emphasizing self-help initiatives and local control of programmes;
4   NGOs innovate and adapt to local conditions and needs.

Lack of agreement and evidence about the effectiveness of NGOs

There are many perceived strengths of NGOs, but little hard data to support the claims which are often made. It is claimed that in comparison with government the main advantages of NGOs are social (a greater gender and poverty focus); economic (greater performance and efficiency, the ability to innovate and adapt); political (an emphasis on participation and human rights and an independence from government agendas); and cultural (a sensitivity to need and a focus on appropriateness of interventions) (Cernea 1988; Anheier 1990). However, many of these claims remain unsubstantiated. Vivian and Maseko (1994) also show that evidence for NGO performance is somewhat scanty. Judith Tendler's (1982) oft-quoted study provides an important critique of NGOs drawn from a wide USAID survey: NGOs were often top-down in their decision making, villagers were in practice only rarely involved in project designs, local elites might well influence or control NGO programmes, and most NGOs tended to use well-known techniques and only rarely innovated. Other critiques stress the role of NGOs as resource brokers rather than change agents (McGregor 1989; Hashemi 1989); as palliatives to real structural change (Arellano-Lopez and Petras 1994); the vested interests which exist between donors, NGOs and states (Hanlon 1991; Sanyal 1991); NGO limitations in relief work (de Waal and Omaar 1993); and NGO problems with sustainability and impact.

Source: UNDP 1993.

The 1997 DAC donor evaluation of NGO impact

A study of donor and NGO evaluations of projects and programmes concluded it was still difficult to assess the impact of NGOs because few organizations kept benchmark data or maintained effective monitoring systems. Most evaluations were weakened by a preoccupation with 'impact' rather than learning, and the report argued that this led to a reduction of risk taking and innovation because funding had come to depend only on impact. The results of the evaluation showed that while NGOs may be more effective than government in reaching the poor, they tend not to reach the very poorest section of the population; that more than 85 per cent of projects met their objectives (which is much higher than government); that the rate of innovation was less than is often assumed or claimed; that assessments of cost-effectiveness were inadequate because fixed costs were usually ignored in the calculations; that sustainability was difficult to assess because few NGOs collected data after a project had ended, but that the poorer the people involved, the less likely was sustainable impact to be achieved; that NGOs were more gender focused; and finally that replicability was rarely considered in evaluations.

Source: drawn from Riddell 1999.

In many ways Cernea's analysis serves as a useful benchmark against which the claims on behalf of NGOs can be measured.

There is also a growing literature which offers a comprehensive critique of the NGO phenomenon. The first of these to receive widespread attention was Judith Tendler's (1982) analysis of donor evaluations of seventy-two NGO projects from around the world, which found that many NGOs were often top-down rather than participatory in their decision making, that villagers were marginally (if at all) involved in NGO project design; that local elites often influenced or controlled NGO programmes; and finally that NGOs tended to introduce known techniques into new areas rather than actually 'innovate' themselves. This study has been influential in acting as a counterweight to the strongly idealistic pro-NGO literature which developed during the 1990s. Since then, many other writers have been critical of the attention which NGOs have received, and have pointed out that very little documentation from the field exists with which the pro-NGO lobby can support their claims.

The growing critique argues that within the aid industry there is too much overlapping of vested interests (donors, NNGOs and development idealists) to allow for real analysis of the issues or honesty (Sanyal 1991). There is also a suggestion that NGOs and their groups do not constitute real movements of the poor, but are simply groups of people brought together around provision of resources from outside, i.e. NGOs as the new patrons (in the Bangladesh context Hashemi 1989 and McGregor 1989). Such NGOs are not sustainable and fade as soon as their resources no longer flow; they also have little independent potential for decision making or action. Others have argued that NGOs actually harm the interests of the poor since they are a palliative – by defusing possibilities for genuine radical action by people who are poor they actually worsen the position of people by keeping them just above the poverty line (Arellano-Lopez and Petras 1994). The neocolonialist critique goes further and sees NGOs simply as the servants of foreign capital serving its interests in the Third World.

Another set of criticisms focuses on the small scale of NGOs. NGOs cannot ever meet the needs of the whole poor – that is the role of government. They are too piecemeal and too small. In Bangladesh, where the NGO sector contains some of the most large-scale, influential NGOs anywhere in the world, the total combined NGO effort may only reach about 20 per cent of the functionally landless population of the country (which numbers about a half of Bangladesh's 130 million people) – leaving about 40 million people out altogether (Lewis 1992). And that is with diverse, unsystematic services. In fact, what NGOs end up doing is weakening government in the long run and perpetuating its inefficiency (UNDP 1993).

One of the most hard-hitting critiques of NGOs centres on the problem of accountability. NGOs are seen as relatively unaccountable to local citizens, and their receipt of increasing amounts of foreign funds conflicts with the sovereignty of the state (Sogge *et al.* 1996; Wood 1997; Tvedt 1998). In fact NGO accountability may shift towards foreign governments and NNGOs, and away from local people and local structures. Some of the most compelling arguments emerged from Northern NGO experiences in Africa during the humanitarian crises in Somalia and Sudan in the late 1980s. Some made the argument that NGOs' relief efforts may serve a purpose in the short term, but do not have much longer-term development impact because NGOs interact poorly with government and weaken local institutions (Abdel Ati 1993; de Waal and Omaar 1993).

Other criticisms of NGOs have been concerned with efficiency issues, and there is evidence that NGOs may not be particularly cost-effective. Ellis (1984) suggests that NGO projects often have poor cost–benefit ratios, are not sustainable in the long run and are not very replicable within the wider society. NGOs actually spend far more in their service delivery than governments do, so when NGOs claim better results it is not really surprising. They have far more resources, and if government had these levels of funding, according to this line of reasoning, they would manage the same level of success.

It quickly becomes clear from this brief summary of the various discussions about NGO strengths and weaknesses that NGO positive and negative qualities are often both sides of the same coin (Annis 1987). For example, what is seen as flexibility and spontaneity by some people can easily be viewed as amateurism by others. Those who argue that it is useful to compare NGOs and governments perhaps miss the point. The broad value of NGOs is summed up most effectively by Brett, who argues that NGOs need to be seen alongside government and private sector organizations in a 'pluralistic organizational universe', and therefore selected for specific tasks on the basis of some common criteria for performance judgement:

> Significant similarities exist between the three kinds of organization, which enable us to apply theories developed across the whole range; but real differences in philosophy and practice still remain between them, and this makes it possible for each to solve particular kinds of problems more effectively than the others. Thus, providing support selectively to all of them is likely to produce a pluralistic organizational universe which will expand the range of social and individual choice and potential.
>
> (Brett 1993: 298)

An evaluation study by Edwards (1999a) of four organizations in South Asia is a revealing and balanced study which seeks to identify the criteria which contribute to successful NGO initiatives in terms of impact, sustainability and cost-effectiveness. The results uncovered a large variation in all three criteria, which can be understood as the result of the interaction between the context in which the NGOs operate and the *external influences* on their work, and a set of *internal influences* based on the organizational choices which the NGOs make. Although the contexts of, for example, the Indian state of Orissa and that of rural Bangladesh offer different levels of opportunity and constraint, the high variation in NGO performance was attributed more strongly to the different strategies selected by the NGOs, such as the ability of an organization to combine clarity of purpose with a sustained, long-term commitment to its work, a balance between material provision and community organizing, good organizational learning and communication, and the use of strong external linkages for leverage and ensuring resource flows.

The point is not only that NGOs deserve to be seen alongside a range of other actors in development, but also that it makes little sense to generalize about organizations which vary enormously within and between contexts. Fisher writes:

99

> Despite the remarkable similarities among NGOs in different parts of the Third World, the time for 'feel good' generalised discussions of 'North–South partnership' is past. Country-specific field research on 'who is doing what where' is an urgent necessity, given the global need for sustainable development.
>
> (Fisher 1994: 139)

This is perhaps true of not only partnership issues between North and South, but also the entire discussion on NGOs. However, it is also wise to keep in mind the critics of NGOs, such as Tvedt (1998) who argues that the diversity of the NGO community is often exaggerated (if it existed at all). There may be an isomorphic trend towards routine NGO service delivery – and credit delivery in particular – that may narrow the wide-ranging array of activities usually claimed for NGOs by their supporters.

CONCLUSION

This chapter has moved on from the broader contextual discussion of Chapters 1 and 2 to focus more clearly on the organizational dimensions of NGOs and their roles in development. The chapter has outlined the main NGO roles in development, seen here as implementation, catalysis and partnership, and it has considered different views of the effectiveness of NGOs in these roles. These roles have also been linked back to the conceptual framework of NGO management (Figure 1.1) that was set out in Chapter 1, since each element of the management task – organization, activities and relationships – is likely to involve combinations of these roles.

A recurring theme throughout the book is the need in our analyses to appreciate the diversity of NGOs as organizations, and to recognize that this diversity is central to the creative ideas, insights and approaches that NGOs can bring to development. Finally, there is a firm need to locate our discussion of the problems and issues of NGO management within specific historical, cultural and political sectoral and country contexts.

This means that there is no general 'blueprint' for either understanding or managing an individual NGO and its activities. But as we saw earlier in Chapter 2, and will discuss in more detail in Chapter 4, Korten's (1990) generation model sets out the idea that NGOs are dynamic, changing organizations that tend to move through a sequential learning process as they develop and grow. For example, while many NGOs may owe their origins to relief and welfare work, they often gradually tend to move over time into more developmental roles. Korten's theory of NGO generations and strategies seeks to explain how NGOs emerge, change and manage a variety of tasks. While this framework should not be taken to imply unidirectional change or standardized NGO patterns or organizational change, it does perhaps provide one useful window of understanding on the different ways in which development NGOs have approached their work.

REVIEW QUESTIONS

- Discuss the advantages and disadvantages for a development NGO of building a funding relationship with the aid industry.
- Review the work of an NGO known to you in relation to the three central roles of implementer, catalyst and partner.
- What are the factors that make the judgement of NGO effectiveness such a complex task?

Chapter 4

Culture, ambiguity and NGO management

LEARNING OBJECTIVES

After considering this chapter, the reader will be able to describe and analyse:

- Key areas of organization theory as they relate to development NGOs
- Leadership issues within development NGOs
- Challenges of cross-cultural management in the NGO context

KEY TERMS

- Resource dependence theory
- NGO generations
- Organizational learning
- Organizational culture
- Life cycles

INTRODUCTION

Social structure is concerned with the social relationships which exist within an organiza-tion, while culture refers to the shared ideas and values which people bring to these relationships (Jones 1996). This chapter explores the ways that the study of organization theory, with its perspectives on structure and culture, open up important areas for analysing NGO management. In particular, theoretical perspectives on culture and values in organ-izations can assist us in understanding distinctive aspects of NGO work. They can further enrich understandings of NGO management if they are combined with insights from the anthropology of organizations, which brings ideas not just about how organizations work as communities, but also the ways in which NGO management involves the recognition of a range of distinctive tensions and ambiguities. This ambiguity is explored in the second half of the chapter.

As we saw in Chapter 1, it has been common to distinguish between two main groups of approaches to management. The first is top-down management, which stresses control, hierarchy and instrumentality; while the second is enabling management, which emphasizes process, flexibility and participation. For many development activists, the concept of management was strongly associated with the first tendency. Management has therefore often been problematic for people working in third sector organizations, many of whom wish to distance themselves from the 'mainstream values' with which it is often associated. This type of management tradition alienates many of the senior staff in third sector organ-izations, who may instead choose to see themselves as 'facilitators', 'organizers' or 'coordinators'. For example, in a survey of the directors of US development NGOs under-taken by Stark Biddle (1984), there was a clear reluctance among most of these managers to accept that their NGOs could be run like other organizations, because they somehow felt that their organizations were different. This sense of 'difference' was based on a belief in the ideals and values of participation, closeness to the poor and flexibility, and on an assump-tion that top-down management ran contrary to such a belief. These managers felt that they would become contaminated by the mainstream values of hierarchy and authority, but, as Stark Biddle points out, this stance ironically left many of these NGOs with a set of basic management weaknesses.

NGO CULTURAL ATTITUDES TO MANAGEMENT

The culture and values of some development NGOs have not always fitted easily with a mainstream management perspective. Korten argues that the origins of many NGOs lie in the efforts of key individuals to mobilize efforts based on altruism:

> They have relied upon high moral purpose, good will, hard work, and common sense to make them successful. Until recently the application of effective profes-sional management techniques, and in some instances even the acquisition of technical competence, has not been seen as relevant to their purposes. These particular NGOs are best described as being at a pre-bureaucratic stage, lacking adequate development of basic management systems and procedures.
>
> (Korten 1987: 155)

103

The reluctance of some NGOs to take management seriously has sometimes been based on the fear, as we saw in Chapter 1, of the oppressive characteristics of management itself. Management was identified closely with what Chambers (1994) calls 'normal professionalism', and was viewed as running counter to many of the cherished principles of NGO work – such as valuing things over people, quantity over quality, blueprint over adaptation, or the powerful over the weak.

From the work of Chambers and others, Korten identified a set of emerging 'alternative management approaches associated with the new development professionalism':

> Rather than supporting central control they support self-assessment and self-correction, driven by a strong orientation to client service and a well-defined sense of mission. Highly developed management systems provide rich flows of information to facilitate these self-management processes.
>
> (Korten 1987: 156)

An example of this is the difference between the concept of 'strategic planning' (in which a specialized planning unit makes a plan which may often be resisted by other parts of the organization) and that of 'strategic management', which requires a more inclusive process to bring staff at all levels of the organization into the identification and implementation of organizational choices. Korten makes a connection between the level of interest in management in an NGO with its stage of growth, and these ideas are discussed in relation to the NGO generation concept later in this chapter.

Whatever some idealists may have said, there are still those who claim that basic top-down management can be useful to NGOs in certain circumstances. Dichter (1989a) provides an example of a dysfunctional large savings and credit society which had failed to produce a dividend for seven years and whose leadership was widely seen as corrupt. Employing what was essentially a set of top-down, 'blueprint' management approaches, an international NGO was asked by a presidential commission to reorganize the society. Over an eighteen-month period, a country national was appointed as transitional interim manager, and removed seven senior staff from their jobs and organized for key headquarters staff to be trained in new administrative systems, basic financial controls and computer systems. The result was that the society's assets increased by 100 per cent and membership increased by 560 per cent, and five years later the cooperative remained successful.

There are also sections of the NGO community that have apparently gone to the other extreme. Revising their negative opinion of 'management', some have rushed headlong into trying to import the latest management techniques (usually from the private sector) in an attempt to address organizational problems through the application of a managerialist 'quick fix'. For example, it was common for many Northern NGOs during the 1990s to emphasize the need to develop systems for strategic planning, precisely at the time when private sector management theorists such as Henry Mintzberg (who was one of the originators of the concept of strategic planning in the 1970s) were giving up on it as a useful tool (Mintzberg 1994). In an article on the US non-profit sector, Mulhare (1999) shows that the adoption of strategic planning techniques took place in the 1990s despite the growing critique of the concept in the business world. He suggests that this was due not so much to evidence that the technique was a successful one, but to the growing 'professionalized' culture of the non-profit sector which made it important to signal to donors and government the adoption of business methods and ideas.

While there may be tensions between different approaches to management, there are also issues arising from the different cultural contexts and values which inform management practices. As we saw in Chapter 1, Dichter (1989a) notes that both the top-down and the enabling approaches to management are derived essentially from the Western private sector – although development NGOs may often be unaware of this – and suggests that while NGOs need to pay attention to basic management principles, it is important to consider the different contexts in which NGOs operate. Meanwhile Campbell's (1987) framework for understanding NGO management emphasizes cultural difference as a key element.

The next section goes on to discuss selected aspects of organization theory in relation to NGO management, focusing on resource dependence, leadership and life cycles, organizational culture and learning as critical issues for development NGOs.

ORGANIZATION THEORY

This section moves us on to a discussion of selected issues in the field of organization theory which may be relevant to the study of NGO management. This is a largely new approach, because organization theory has not traditionally identified third sector organizations as being distinctive, and NGO researchers have been slow to consider whether organizational theory might offer insights into how NGOs are managed. This chapter does not therefore pretend to offer a comprehensive review of organization theory, which is a vast field, but instead reviews actual and potential points of interaction between the two.

While most organization theory has its roots in the business sector, many of its ideas are relevant to NGOs. At a very basic level, organization theory allows us to break down an organization into its constituent parts. Hatch (1997) presents a conceptual model of 'the organization', represented as the interplay of four interrelated elements: culture, social structure, physical structure and technology, and suggests that all of these are 'embedded in and contributing to an environment'. Such frameworks are now becoming part of the discourse around NGOs, particularly in connection with the growth of interest in NGO 'capacity building', discussed below in Chapter 7. Hatch's framework serves as a useful one within which to analyse NGOs as organizations.

Like all research fields, organization theory is a far from unified body of work, and different approaches and traditions compete with each other for explanatory power. Hatch describes the multiple and often contradictory perspectives offered by organization theory by summarizing three main research traditions – which she terms *modernist*, *symbolic-interpretative* and *postmodern* (Box 4.1). Hatch argues that these three traditions are not mutually exclusive and suggests that a 'multiple perspectives approach' can allow each one the potential to illuminate different aspects of organizational life. This approach resonates strongly with what we know about NGOs, which reveal themselves as highly complex organizations working in increasingly diverse and rapidly changing environments. For example, this chapter will discuss the strong interest among NGOs in 'organizational learning', which has emerged strongly in the symbolic-interpretative tradition. In Chapter 7, the importance

105

Research traditions in organization theory

Modernist organization theory has its roots in several thinkers from the first part of the twentieth century. The sociologist Max Weber's theory of rational-legal authority exercised through an objective and impersonal bureaucracy is a cornerstone of modernist organization theory. The ideas of F. W. Taylor and his notions of 'scientific management', and Henri Fayol's theory of the rational administration of organizational activities, both of which emphasized structure, hierarchy and control, have also been influential. Later, open systems theory brought with it the idea of organic growth and development of organizations, their different levels of activity and the interconnectedness of organization and environment.[1]

The *symbolic-interpretative* perspective emphasizes the subjective realities of organizational life and shows how organizations are built from negotiations and understandings of the world. In this view, organizations are seen as socially constructed and can therefore be changed, assuming we can become more aware of our participation in organizational processes. The importance of ambiguity is recognized as being a source of both power and creativity, as well as perhaps an area of danger and confusion.[2] The anthropologist Clifford Geertz's (1973) concept of culture as socially constructed and open to continuous change has been used to explore how people within organizations create and maintain 'organizational culture' through the use and interpretation of symbols.

More recently, the *postmodern* perspective on organizations evolved as a critique of the modernist quest for universal explanations for organizational life, and concentrates instead on complexity, fragmentation and contradiction. For theorists within the complexity and management field, for example, the focus is on the disjuncture between what managers feel they ought to be doing and what they actually find themselves doing, and they point out that:

> life in organizations is essentially paradoxical. Managers are supposed to be in charge and yet they find it difficult to stay in control. The future is recognizable when it arrives but in many important respects not predictable before it does. We sense the importance of difference but experience the pressure to conform
>
> (Stacey *et al.* 2000: 5)

In the postmodern view, organizational change is becoming less predictable as information is exchanged more rapidly and more frequently, and organizations themselves are becoming more informal, flexible and participatory in response to uncertainty. At the same time, the radical critique of power in organizations within the postmodern approach has led to the need for self-reflexive organizations and for means through which 'voice' can be achieved for those who are marginalized or excluded within organizations.[3]

Source: most material drawn from Hatch 1997.

of postmodernist ideas to organizational change within NGOs is considered, and we will also analyse the work of third sector researchers such as Billis (1993a) who has built upon Weber's ideas on bureaucracy in developing a theory of the voluntary sector in the UK context.

Resource dependency perspective

An area of organization theory which has been employed to improve understanding of the ways in which NGOs are managed is the 'resource dependency perspective' (Pfeffer and Salancik 1978). The theory is based on the idea that instead of seeing organizations as relatively autonomous, the environment is a strong constraining influence which limits room for manoeuvre. All organizations depend on the environment for the resources they need, and to do this they must continuously negotiate and exchange, and in this sense are to a large degree 'externally controlled'. Organizations try to reduce this dependency by controlling the flow of information about themselves to outsiders and by diversifying their sources of resources. Environmental contingencies also therefore help determine internal management factors, such as succession to leadership positions. The function of management becomes the need to direct an organization towards a more favourable relationship with its environment through three kinds of management action – symbolic, responsive and discretionary. *Symbolic* management refers to actions which make little or no difference because outcomes are in reality determined mainly by the context, such as replacing a leader. This only alters appearances, but if people believe a new leader has some power (even if they don't) it may relieve the pressure. *Responsive* management refers to actions taken by managers which do make a difference, even though they are undertaken within the constraints created by the environment. The *discretionary* role is the successful balancing of these constraints in the interests of the organization, based on good 'scanning' of the environment for information. Hudock (1995) shows how this theory is useful when applied to NGOs which are highly financially dependent on donors. Hudock shows how SNGOs in West Africa are extremely vulnerable to goal deflection and unplanned structural change in the struggle to meet external demands. However, Billis (1993a: 213), writing in the UK third sector literature, is somewhat critical of the resource dependency perspective for depicting organizations 'at the mercy of powerful and almost uncontrollable forces', and argues that organizations should be seen as having real choices. This is supported by research by Dechalert (2002) among NGOs in Thailand, and by Themudo (2003) in Portugal and Mexico, which highlights the importance of decision-making processes within organizations that can produce different outcomes despite similar resource environments.

Leadership and life cycles

Another area of organization theory which has proved influential in the NGO context is the evolutionary view of organizational life cycles, often used to help understand patterns of organizational change and leadership. Life-cycle theories of organizations have a long history in organizational studies, and allow reflection on organizational change not just in terms of values and approaches, but also in terms of changing structure. According to Hatch (1997), it was Greiner in the early 1970s who first used the metaphor of the human life cycle to help understand the structural changes experienced by organizations over time. Greiner set out a series of five phases through which most organizations will pass, and termed these the entrepreneurial, collectivity, delegation, formalization and collaboration phases. Each phase is dominated by a distinctive focus, and Greiner suggested that transition to the next stage was usually triggered by a serious crisis which threatened the very survival of the organization. The reasons for each crisis also followed a sequential pattern which started with a leadership crisis, followed by one of autonomy, control, red tape and finally by a crisis of renewal. In this way, according to Hatch (1997: 177), 'every stage of an organization's development contains the seeds of the next crisis'.

Life-cycle theories have influenced David Korten's outline of NGO generations discussed briefly in Chapter 3. Korten (1987) suggested a model of organizational evolution through a series of stages of development based on incremental learning. This leads to a chain of increasingly sophisticated approaches to working with poor people in terms of sustainability, self-reliance and participation. Korten's original paper outlined three distinct generations of 'private voluntary development action' based on three kinds of programming strategy.

The NGOs which Korten analysed tended to move along through a threefold sequence of stages of organizational development and programming strategies based on growing awareness of broader ranges of possibilities. The first generation is that of relief and welfare. The aim is that of meeting immediate deficiencies among beneficiaries for food, healthcare or shelter. At this stage the NGO is the 'doer' and there is a largely passive role for 'beneficiaries', and the main management needs are skills in operations and logistics management in the delivery of welfare services. The result of the work of most first-generation NGOs is the temporary alleviation of the symptoms of poverty, but it does not really address the root causes. The second-generation NGO approach is that of small-scale, self-reliant local development, in which NGOs seek to transform themselves into development agencies and focus on 'community development' work aimed at creating self-reliance and sustainability of projects.

In the cases reviewed by Korten in the 1970s, the growth of donor support to NGOs brought about a need for these NGOs to focus more strongly on the need to develop better project management skills. These NGOs moved from being primarily 'doers' towards a mobilization role. The problem which then emerged was that many NGO efforts turned out to be largely unsustainable after the withdrawal of the NGO, and amounted to little more than 'handouts in a more sophisticated guise'. This led to new thinking and a subsequent focus on sustainable systems development as the third-generation stage. At this point, the NGO looks beyond the immediate community in which it works to also seek changes in the institutional and policy context to create an 'enabling' environment for greater local control and initiative. The NGO realizes that gains made still depend on the continued presence of the NGO and donor funds, and that by acting on its own, only local, piecemeal impact can be achieved. The NGO may seek to establish links with larger institutions to provide services on a more sustainable basis, such as a collaboration with a bank or a link with a government agency. In this model, which has been highly influential, a development NGO gradually moves from being primarily a service provider to being a catalyst which seeks to gain leverage over policy discussions in favour of poverty reduction and which 'bridges' the efforts of community-based initiatives and other development actors.

Korten (1990) later began also to speak of 'fourth-generation' strategies for NGOs in which they experimented with wider alliances with social movements and subordinated their organizational identities within these wider social forces.[4] This is based on a refusal by NGOs to be simply 'patching up' wider development problems, and instead to reach for an alternative development paradigm. In doing this, some NGOs are therefore now turning their attention towards social or 'people's movements' – helping to create changes in public consciousness which will mobilize voluntary action on a national or global scale – women's movements, peace movements and environmental movements. But, as Korten points out, movements have a history of becoming institutionalized once they burn out their initial energy, such as in the case of the Chinese Mass Education movement. This was started by James Yen in the 1920s, and gradually took on a momentum of its own, with several hundred volunteers teaching literacy to five million villagers around the country. Gradually it was identified by outsiders as a successful venture, and public funding and US support led to its institutionalization. By the time the communists came to power in China the original spirit of voluntarism had gone. NGOs have only recently begun to accept the challenge of the fourth generation, which is for the NGO 'to coalesce and energise self-managing networks over which it has no control'.

In a footnote, Korten explains that the generation concept is drawn from a notion of the human family, in which new generations take their place alongside the older ones. What drives the changing orientation of these organizations is, according to Korten, not necessarily a series of organizational crises, but a combination of the growing awareness of local community needs and a clearer definition of the NGO's own 'purpose and distinctive competence'. Korten sees this purpose as ultimately leading towards the 'catalyst' role. Although these different approaches may all be present within the wider NGO community (or even within one single organization at any one time in different programmes), Korten (1990: 147) presents the framework in terms of an evolutionary scheme: 'there is an underlying direction of movement that makes it appropriate to label these orientations as first, second, and third generation'. Although Korten is not very specific about how these changes take place, it seems to imply 'evolution and adaptation to the socio-economic context' (Senillosa 1998: 46) as a result of some combination of internal and external forces. Indeed, Korten ends the article with a set of comments about the need for NGOs to improve their management systems and structures in order to improve their effectiveness (see below). The generation framework has been influential and has been widely cited by writers on NGOs (e.g. Vakil 1997; Clarke 1998).

Senillosa (1998) makes important criticisms of the 'generation' idea, pointing out that several different generations can coexist within one organization, rendering the concept rather imprecise, and suggests some of the different ways in which NGOs may evolve in different contexts. For example, at a workshop in Nigeria which I attended in 1999, several education NGOs were discussing the need to move away from solely concentrating on advocacy work (their original purpose) towards service delivery through which real and immediate needs could be met, and which many felt would give organizations more credibility both with local communities and with policy makers.

The idea of evolutionary models of organizations has also been criticized by those who point out that linear models tend to oversimplify a complex reality. Critics of life-cycle theory have pointed out that organizations do in fact have 'room for manoeuvre', and that different outcomes merge from different choices that are made by managers. They suggest that organizations do not change along predefined paths and have drawn attention to the importance of the environment, structures and the human resources of organizations in determining patterns of change. There is also a problem of subjectivity in the generations idea, in terms of the implicit assumption that as it evolves, the NGO becomes 'better'. This becomes apparent in that while Senillosa states that there need be no hierarchy in the different generations of NGOs – 'the first generation is no worse than the fourth' (1998: 46) – he is at the same time making the claim for fourth-generation NGOs that they hold the key to the future. Like much of the writing on NGOs, the theory contains an at-times-difficult combination of subjective tone (which seeks to identify an 'ideal' path along which NGOs might move) alongside the presentation of an 'explanation' of how NGOs as organizations change over time.

Despite the argument that the increasing sophistication of NGO approaches moves organizations towards the 'fourth-generation' strategy, some research suggests that funder pressures in the 1990s pushed many international NGOs towards a welfare approach (Atack 1999). Avina's (1993) article which related the life-cycle idea to NGOs specifically presents a somewhat different framework (though still within the overall terms of the life-cycle metaphor). This framework is drawn from his own observations rather than from the literature, and seeks to set out a four-stage life cycle of NGO evolution, suggesting that both external factors and internal factors can help determine movement from one stage to another: start up, expansion, consolidation and finally close-out. These stages are presented by Avina in order to provide NGO managers with a 'map' with which an organization can plan and adapt its structure and strategies, and perhaps resist external pressures for change. In this way the generation concept can be seen to have implications at the level of NGO strategy, while the life-cycle concept has meaning at the level of particular organizational trajectories. However, both concepts need further elaboration if they are to help us understand where NGOs are going.

Other criticisms can be made from the perspective of organizational choice. For example, writing in the UK non-profit literature, Billis (1993a) argues that the life-cycle model is too mechanistic and needs to be set against internal organizational choices which are downplayed by life-cycle theories. This, he argues, has a crucial bearing on the trajectory taken by an organization because there is always an element of choice – albeit often constrained – in the decisions taken about how an organization changes its structure or diversifies its activities.

At the level of the individual, the concept of generations also leads us to reflect on the changing roles of charismatic leaders and followers (often a defining feature of many development NGOs) as well as the changing character of different generations of NGO staff. Writings on NGOs have revealed a tendency for these organizations to be centred around strong, often 'charismatic' founder leaders, who use their contacts to mobilize resources and to manage the political environment in which their organizations operate. There may be a few founder individuals who 'retain charismatic control over the organization as it grows' and who tend to monopolize contacts with other agencies and with the government

110

(Wood 1997). A remark made by an NGO staff member on a trip to Bangladesh (where many of the main NGOs are still led by their original charismatic founder-leaders) a few years back made this clear to me: 'People say that we are unfortunate in Bangladesh that we have yet to experience the death or retirement of a major NGO leader.' What was meant was that the main NGOs had not yet been 'tested' by a leadership crisis (in Greiner's sense) and the suggestion was that NGOs were not yet in this sense mature.

Bryman shows that work on leadership in organizations has revived interest in the 'charismatic leader', creating an emphasis on heroic individuals or the roles of top executives in organizations rather than on the contextual factors which influence leadership, such as organizational structure and systems (Bryman 1992: 157). There has been very little research as yet on the role of NGO leaders, though it would seem from casual observation that the 'charismatic' leader is a vital component of many an NGO, particularly in its early years. Edwards's (1999a) study of South Asian NGOs found that the more successful NGOs tended to have 'inspirational but not overbearing' leadership, which was able to guide the organization through crises and provide a clear sense of direction while allowing room for initiative and ideas from throughout the organization and its clients.

At the same time, contingency theories of leadership – which stress context rather than any innate human qualities of leadership – can also be seen to be important for NGOs. In the Bangladesh context, some of the major NGO leaders are clearly charismatic individuals supported by their class background, social status and levels of education. Others draw some of their power from contextual factors such as having been student activists in the pre-independence period, while others were returnees who came back to their country from overseas in order to put into practice humanitarian or development-oriented programmes. Hailey's (1999) work on South Asian NGO leaders highlights the 'chameleon-like' qualities displayed by successful individuals who operate with different kinds of 'intelligence', which they need to continuously combine if they are to maintain their position and their success. Hailey terms these types of intelligence aspirational, rational, environmental and interpersonal. Wood (1997) points out that charismatic NGO leaders may use personal networks and extended kin ties as management tools, often producing strong centralizing tendencies in which even comparatively trivial decisions need to wait for decisions from the top. While such practices may raise problems of nepotism and inefficiency, they can also nevertheless be seen more sympathetically as organizational adaptations to a frequently hostile institutional environment.

The challenge for understanding NGO leadership issues is to move beyond the 'one best way' tendency of some of the new leadership studies brought about by the Peters and Waterman line of thinking (the 'guru' approach to organization studies) and accept that there is no one way of providing effective leadership, as contingency theory convincingly showed (Bryman 1992: 157). Does the leadership succession question raise important questions about the future of NGOs? Or will such conflicts be negotiated in ways so far unidentified? Leadership problems, after all, have been successfully negotiated by older NGOs such as Amnesty International or Oxfam, where the profile of the actual organization has long since superseded that of its leader at any particular time.[5]

Organization theory may be a useful analytical lens through which to assess the changing roles and structures of NGOs by focusing on what goes on inside the organization rather than, as much of the research on NGOs tends to do, focusing exclusively on the work which NGOs carry out. The 'generation' concept raised by Korten brings forward three issues which are now crucially important for research on NGOs. First, what drives the changing orientation of NGOs, a fact not specified by Korten's work (which is a major weakness of this and many other life-cycle theories)? Second, a useful link is made within the generation discussion with the need for closer attention to be paid to NGO management issues. Third, the role of individual leaders in relation to the life cycle is highlighted by these debates. But the concept of the organizational life cycle and the NGO generation idea are likely to have crucial limitations if they are used to predict the organizational trajectories of development NGOs, where evidence points to non-linear, multi-directional changes based on a combination of outside pressures and internal choice and decision making. The life-cycle model also arguably focuses too strongly on the role of leadership, and has been criticized in this regard by Hatch, who shows, drawing on ideas about 'open systems' ideas, the importance of organizational structure for organizational effectiveness.

Organizational culture

One of the organizational characteristics which strongly influences levels of organizational learning is that of 'organizational culture'. Handy (1988) points out that the concept of 'organizational culture' only emerged relatively recently in management studies, due to the earlier predominance of the 'engineering model' of management, which tended to conceptualize organizations as essentially rational and similar, and offers a simple common-sense definition of 'organizational culture':

> If organizations are communities, mini-societies, rather than machines, then it is natural to expect that each community will have its own taste and flavour, its own way of doing things, its own habits and jargon, its own *culture*.
>
> (Handy 1988: 85)

Handy's particular contribution has been to distinguish four organizational cultural styles – power, role, task and person – which help categorize the ways in which people within organizations believe they should work. Within 'power culture' there tends to be a dominant central leader and an emphasis on individuals over roles and procedures, as might be found in a small company or a trade union. 'Role culture' is present where an organization is essentially bureaucratic and specialized according to specific roles rather than individual people, and such organizations are secure and predictable, such as a tax office. The third type is 'task culture', in which judgements are made by results based on the power of experts and the organization often displays a flexible team culture – such as a consultancy team – though it may often be quite hard to manage in practice. Finally there is 'person culture', in which an organization exists mainly for the good of people within it, has no particular goal beyond this one and seeks management by mutual consent. Handy suggests that there are many third sector organizations which display this type of organizational culture.

An understanding of these four styles of organization culture has been influential in both business and development management fields, and can be used to help analyse what goes on within NGOs (Lewis 2002b). For example, in the case of some small-scale informal organizations, or those at an early stage of development, person culture may dominate and lead to a situation where the staff feel that although they are getting something out of the NGO there are questions to be asked about its overall effectiveness. In the case of a more bureaucratic, formalized NGO, the dominance of role culture may inhibit learning and creativity within the organization. For NGOs that retain a strong charismatic leader or a founder-leader, the price of a dominant power culture may be an inhibition of the abilities of other staff to play an effective role in the organization. The challenge may often be the building of a 'task culture' which allows NGO staff to work flexibly in the context of their specific competencies, within work teams in a more satisfying and stimulating environment which in the end will produce better results (Maxwell 1997).

Such analyses draw heavily upon the symbolic-interpretative perspective outlined in the previous section by Hatch (1997). But the postmodern perspective has also been influential in the analysis of organizational culture. For example, Alvesson (1993) outlines the debate as to whether or not organizational culture – a shared, unifying system of values, meanings, understandings – is the binding force in organizations, or whether, as a postmodern view asserts, it is instead the concept of 'ambiguity' which plays the central organizing role through the need to manage contradiction and confusion within organizations. An interesting example of the use to which the postmodern perspective can be put in the third sector context can be found in the work of DiBella (1992), who shows how planned organizational change did not take place within an international NGO due to the existence of a range of 'subcultures' within the organization based on fragmentation and difference, which produced a kind of 'organized anarchy'.

Multiple cultures may therefore exist within an organization (and this may be particularly apparent in the case of third sector organizations), say, between those who are concerned with mission and values and those with bureaucratic tasks such as basic administration. Alvesson (1993: 118) argues that neither a sole emphasis on a unitary culture nor one simply on the organizing power of ambiguity is adequate. Instead he suggests a 'multiple cultural configuration view', which sees organizational cultures as mixtures of cultural manifestations at different levels and of different kinds. In this view, different cultures and subcultures overlap in an organizational setting with profession, gender, class or ethnic group. Box 4.2 examines this issue in relation to the concept of gender.

One of the few studies in the third sector literature focusing on this issue is Brown and Covey's (1983) analysis of an NGO as a 'microcosm' of its environment, containing diverse cultural perspectives, such that it may reproduce internally ideological conflicts characteristic of the wider society. The authors highlight the 'ideological negotiation' that took place within a US-based third sector organization working in development education, project management and government lobbying. For example, tensions between staff from different ethnic groups (with white males dominating senior management) and between clerical workers and managers (the former with low salaries and little input into decision making) were found to be basically ideological and rooted in the racism located in wider society. Brown and Covey (1983: 246) concluded that 'organizations cannot be efficiently co-ordinated without recognizing and managing ideological diversity rooted in the cultural origins of organization members'.

Gender and organizational culture

The social science definition of 'gender' distinguishes the *social* from the *biological* construction of differences between men and women, focusing on the rules, traditions and norms which help determine the values and attributes which are considered 'feminine' and 'masculine', and the ways in which power is allocated and used differently by women and men. Fowler (1997) reviews the ways in which roles and power are divided along gendered lines within NGOs, and the degree to which 'female' and 'male' principles are reflected and valued in an NGO's organizational culture. Many NGOs have paid little attention to gender inequalities within their own organizations, and have preferred to see the importance of gender in their sectoral work. NGOs have an 'immediate sainthood', but often the culture of masculine exclusiveness and sexual harassment are as common in NGOs as elsewhere (Ashworth 1996). Some NGOs have 'gender units' but these are often marginalized or used as 'alibis'. Recognizing this, some NGOs such as ACORD (Agency for Cooperation and Research in Development) are working hard to develop a gender policy, but with mixed results so far (Hadjipateras 1997). In the North, there is often discussion of 'equal opportunities' (Osborne and Homer 1996). Liberal and radical perspectives can be contrasted here. The Western management literature is increasingly focusing on women and business leadership and the challenge of increasing women's 'presence' (e.g. T. Morgan 1994). Wallace (1998) documents efforts to 'institutionalize' gender within some Northern NGOs' structures as well as within their programmes, finding that male trustees and directors still dominate the organizational culture, even if there has been some success with programmes and staffing. Preconditions of success of building a gender policy include: leadership should not be actively opposed; resources must be allocated, activities must not be seen as an add-on; responsibility for change management must be allocated and indicators of progress agreed (Fowler 1997). In the South, research on gender issues within BRAC is beginning to appear. Rao and Kelleher (1995) analyse BRAC's Gender Quality Action-Learning (GQAL) programme, which seeks to sensitize its field staff to gender issues. The research highlights tensions between the twin tasks of 'lending money' and 'empowering women' that BRAC undertakes. Goetz (1997) examines the issues of 'gendered time and space' within BRAC and its implications for men and women staff. Some writers have suggested that NGOs may have 'a feminine development approach and masculine organizational culture' (e.g. Fowler 1997: 79) in which cultures of action and control take precedence over cultures which value communication and participation.

The authors argue therefore that the challenge is to build ideologies that appeal across cultural boundaries and encourage constructive ideological negotiations. However, the challenge of building and sustaining common ideas and meanings is not just a difficult challenge within organizations, it is also made more complex by the rise of partnerships and multi-agency development projects. As Lewis *et al.* (2003) have shown in relation to inter-agency World Bank projects, combinations of non-governmental, public and private actors can create projects which become fragmented through tensions over issues of culture and power among different perspectives within and between different types of project actors. From organizational culture we turn now to the related topic of organizational learning.

Organizational learning

The open systems approach to understanding organizations brings us to an area of organization theory which has been enthusiastically embraced by many NGO writers. The concept of 'organizational learning', which during the 1990s bloomed into a wide-ranging area of theory and practice, has engaged the attention of both management thinkers and NGO activists, though it has its origins in the private sector. There are many different writers and approaches to organizational learning, but Peter Senge is the 'management guru' who became strongly associated with the idea when his (1990) book *The Fifth Discipline* became a management bestseller. Senge's argument was that organizations need certain skills if they are to survive in a rapidly changing world, but that many are held back by a set of 'learning disabilities'. This idea draws upon the work of Argyris and Schon (1978), who showed how people in organizations face contradictory pressures on their behaviour which produce unhelpful 'defensive routines' which inhibit learning and lead them to resist change. For example, control systems in organizations can generate a paradox in which staff are told at the same time to take initiatives and risks, but not to violate rules and regulations, and this leads to a profound tension between the need for stability and the need for change.

These disabilities include the tendency to learn only from experience (when it is also necessary to learn indirectly from the experiences of others) and the tendency of individual staff not to see the whole picture above their individual concerns. Senge set out five key skills, which he called 'disciplines', for managers to acquire: personal mastery (the need for staff to learn self-discipline and self-awareness); flexible 'mental models' which avoid the pitfalls of stereotyped thinking and reveal an openness to new ideas; the building of a shared vision about what the organization wishes to achieve; a commitment to team learning in which people overcome the tendency to simply defend their own 'patch' and learn to share and cooperate; and finally a form of systems thinking which takes into account both long- and short-term outcomes of decisions, an awareness of the complex interrelationships between different levels of organizational activity and the need to address root causes of problems rather than symptoms. Together these skills, according to Senge, help to build a learning organization.

Korten (1980) was an early exponent of the 'organizational learning' approach to NGOs, where he identified the NGO problem of successfully translating ambitious plans into practical activities. Under the earlier 'blueprint' approach to development management, Korten argues, attempts to intervene in favour of the poor tend to fail and end up strengthening local elites who 'capture' new resources and opportunities. But the example of a number of South Asian NGOs, such as BRAC, showed that this outcome is not inevitable. An NGO can learn from its mistakes if it has suitable systems in place which produce improvements in the 'fit' which can be achieved between needs, programme outputs and the competence of the assisting organization: 'The key was not pre-planning, but an organization with a capacity for embracing error, learning with the people, and building new knowledge and institutional capacity through action.' Korten went on to outline a 'learning approach' for NGOs, in which he saw three stages through which an effective NGO should aim to proceed. The first of these was 'learning to be effective', in which an NGO considers how a task should best be performed. The second was 'learning to be efficient', which referred to asking questions about how a task can be performed so that it produces desired outcomes at an acceptable cost. The third was 'learning to expand', during which the NGO reflected and found ways to increase the impact of its work through replication or by increasing the scale of its activities.

The concept of organizational learning made a considerable impact on many studies of NGOs and management.[6] The concept of learning is central to Brown and Covey's influential (1987) study of US NGOs, which identified four kinds of core organizational activities: attracting resources, empowering beneficiaries, undertaking public education and doing advocacy work. The authors analysed four areas of NGO management task through which the NGOs undertake this work. The first was the NGO's mission and its implications for management, particularly as the mission changes from relief to development. The second was the linkages established by the NGOs with diverse constituencies and the complex environments in which they operate, i.e. funders, beneficiaries and other stakeholders. The third was the nature of the organizing mechanisms used to regulate behaviour – such as leadership, formal structures, informal cultural mechanisms and values. The fourth area was the key organizational dynamics such as strategic planning and decision making. The authors argued that to be effective, NGOs must play *bridging roles* across the gaps between different constituencies, and that NGOs are good at this in terms of national and international social integration in times of rapid change or upheaval. The bridging metaphor is an alternative to hierarchical and bureaucratic models, with multiple bridges between headquarters, country office, SNGO and beneficiaries, for example. They also seek to *change* the social and economic environment in which they operate, rather than simply supporting the status quo. The NGOs which have been successful have acted as catalysts of social energy and entrepreneurship, thus increasing 'social capital for development' (1987: 56). However, the problems which exist are:

- conflicts between units and sub-units;
- decision making of various kinds (participation, top-down leadership, incremental trial and error); and
- the struggle of the leadership to embody the NGO's culture and core values to maintain legitimacy.

According to the authors, organizational learning is the key to survival for these NGOs, due to their complex tasks and the turbulent, changing contexts in which they operate.

Ironically, there are those NGO writers who point out the reality that NGOs – in practice – often find it rather difficult to become 'learning organizations', and this inability to learn has been identified as a key management problem. This is one of the most important lessons which development NGOs still need to learn if they are to improve their effectiveness and indeed survive:

> An almost universal weakness of NGDOs is found within their often limited capacity to learn, adapt and continuously improve the quality of what they do. This is a serious concern . . . if NGOs do not learn from their experience, they are destined for insignificance and will atrophy as agents of social change. NGDOs urgently need to put in place systems which ensure that they know and learn from what they are achieving – as opposed to what they are doing – and then apply what they learn.
>
> (Fowler 1997: 64)

Smillie (1995) also writes of the common problem that NGOs have of the 'failure to learn from failure', and suggests that 'there are few reasons to disseminate the positive lessons of development, and many more powerful reasons to conceal and forget the negative ones'. Failure may be common to many third sector organizations, but there is an understandable reluctance among staff to engage with it. Anheier (2005: 254) argues that there is evidence that many non-profit organizations may remain locked into a kind of 'stalemate' 'state of hidden failure' since there is a lack of influence from the market or from an electorate to check on organizational performance. In his influential study of public management, Hood (1998: 23) places considerable emphasis on the idea that 'sharp thinking' is far more likely to result from a confrontation with perceptions of failure than 'reasoning about "how to create value" on a blank page'.

Britton (1998) sets out a series of internal and external barriers which make learning difficult for NGOs, such as funding competition, the pressure to show low rates of administrative overheads, poor incentive systems and an activist culture which tends to value the present over planning for the future. Britton is concerned to apply the concept of organizational learning to strengthening the capacity of NGOs. One of the key problems NGOs face is the development of information systems which allow all staff to access the valuable knowledge which often remains locked up within particular individuals' heads. For example, during a recent evaluation by the author of an NNGO working in Uganda, it became clear that as senior expatriate staff came and went from the organization every two years or so, similar mistakes were repeated because local middle-level managers did not have an opportunity to share what they knew with the incoming senior managers. Box 4.3 explores work on learning and information issues within NGOs.

This organizational learning approach advocates an 'enabling' model of leadership, in which managers seek to create an environment for sharing and thinking systemically, rather than the charismatic 'hero' style. In the following section, we move to consider management challenges across different cultures, an important topic for many development NGOs.

Culture and organization

The study of management in recent years has been characterized by the recognition that economic, social and technological change at the global level has dramatic implications for the management of all types of organization. As Barbara Parker remarks in the introduction to her influential textbook:

Learning and information management

Two main kinds of information exist within NGOs. The first is *product data* that is easily measurable (e.g. financial progress reports, narrative reports, annual budgets, workplans and baseline data). The second is *process data*, which is qualitative, context specific and more effective at capturing gradual change (e.g. information generated by participatory rural appraisal, process documentation, field diaries, community meeting notes). Ebrahim found NGOs ready to share product data with funders, but they shared process data only so far as it related to 'success story' case studies. Less straightforwardly positive experiences were withheld, either for practical reasons (product data can be more quickly read and analysed) or political expediency. NGOs therefore come to pay disproportionate attention to the collection of product data. Because it is available and manageable, it becomes central to decision making. Process data, if it exists, comes to play a secondary role. It was found that the dominance of product data has a depoliticizing effect overall, since it decontextualises NGO work away from social and political dynamics.

This pattern is compounded by donor information requirements. Focusing on a European Community grant aimed at supporting more systematic data collection within NGOs, Ebrahim shows how a heavy emphasis was placed on financial progress documentation and baseline impact data through standardized reporting formats. This was by no means a bad thing, since one NGO involved had no prior experience with target setting, and gained new, more efficient ways of planning and budgeting. But it produced a systemic rigidity which tended to limit information management within certain prescribed formats, such as the logical framework tool. In the logframe, objectives, purpose and results are hedged by 'assumptions', so that uncertainties are sometimes assumed away. This then tends to reinforce the exclusion of process data. In one case, an NGO agreed to measure 89 different indicators. Many indicators were useful in terms of justifying their work to the funders, but of little value to the NGO itself. And the large scale of the data collection that was required ended up restricting the NGO's capacity to focus on other work.

Ebrahim concludes that funder demand for information may strengthen NGO information systems, but at the cost of process data. It emphasizes forms of information that enable easily quantifiable valuations of success and failure, and these forms then come to feature disproportionately in decision making. At the same time, NGOs may consciously attempt to avoid excessive funder influence by the 'symbolic' generation of information to satisfy funder needs, selective sharing of information and the use of outside professionals to enhance the legitimacy of the information provided. The above combination of funder demands for information, NGO resistance to external interference and bias towards more manageable forms of information, all serve to further entrench existing information systems.

Source: Ebrahim 2003.

> The world increasingly resembles a global market place where integration across 'traditional' borders is evident in almost every dimension of life. . . . Increasingly a world with fewer boundaries calls for organizations able to transcend vertical and horizontal boundaries and create hybrids that are both cost effective and responsible to local, regional, domestic, international and global communities of interest.
>
> (Parker 1998: x)

One important area of reduced boundaries is in the tendency for crossing traditional borders of space, time and cultural assumptions. This means that new relationships are being constantly generated both within and between organizations. Third sector organizations are now facing more and more internal diversity in human resource terms, and are developing new and more intense cross-cultural relationships and linkages across shifting global landscapes. These differences should not simply be conceived in terms of a polarity between Western and non-Western contexts, however: a study by Olie (1996) shows a surprisingly high level of cultural variation in relation to management practices *within* Europe, for example. Furthermore, there is a high level of diversity within cosmopolitan cities such as London or New York, which we would expect to be increasingly reflected within organizations working in such cities.

Of course, these issues are not new for international NGOs, because there is a long tradition of Northern agencies going to work in the countries of the South, where they face dramatic differences in culture and context. The development industry has long been characterized by cross-cultural encounters between Western developers and (usually) non-Western 'developees'. There has periodically been concern voiced around this topic, as the work of Jaeger and Kanungo (1990) illustrates, because such encounters have often been characterized by imposition of ideas and practices, lack of sensitivity to difference and by misunderstanding. They make the case for thinking more deeply about the need for 'indigenous' management in developing countries, a line of thinking that is particularly appropriate for NGOs: 'Uncritical transfer of management theories and techniques based on Western ideologies and value systems has in many ways contributed to organizational inefficiency and ineffectiveness in the developing country context' (Jaeger and Kanungo 1990: 1).

The basic premise is that the external environment in many developing countries is different to that of the developed countries, where certain development ideas and techniques are developed, and that the process of 'transfer' of ideas, techniques and practices is therefore misguided. Yet these are not issues that only affect NNGOs, since cultural differences can also be important within countries. The encounter between a middle-class urbanized Southern NGO staff member and a rural villager may also be characterized by difference, misunderstanding and complexity. At the same time, there are Southern NGOs working transnationally in some areas of the world. The Bangladeshi NGO BRAC has worked in Afghanistan since 2002, and is currently establishing development programmes in several sub-Saharan African countries.

The study of relationships between culture and organizations in the management literature is dominated by the work of Geert Hofstede, a Dutch social psychologist, who in the 1970s undertook a massive study of the US-based multinational IBM, which was then

119

operating in more than forty countries. The study explored the work-related values held by employees working for the corporation, and found wide-ranging national cultural differences in its offices around the world within the overall organizational culture of IBM (Hofstede 1991). These variations led Hofstede to build a theoretical framework in order to analyse the contours and dynamics of these different 'national cultures', suggesting key differences along four sets of general variations: power-distance (the distance staff feel from their superiors), uncertainty-avoidance (the ways in which staff deal with novelty and risk), individualism (the level of integration of individuals into collectivist groups), and masculinity (the valuing of performance and ambition compared and contrasted with the valuing of quality of life and role flexibility).

Different cultures were then mapped across these four dimensions, and Hofstede argued that we should not assume that management prescriptions operate in the same way in different national contexts. One useful example discussed by Hofstede is the history of 'management by objectives' (MBO) which was developed in the United States in the 1960s as a planning tool.[7] This example shows the potential pitfalls for NGOs of applying a management tool developed in one cultural context to an organization within a different cultural setting. Hofstede shows that this particular Western-designed piece of management technology requires low 'power-distance' and 'uncertainty-avoidance', since it requires that subordinates negotiate forcefully with their superiors, and that risks must be accepted by all levels of staff if it is to operate effectively.[8] The evidence he presented suggests that MBO was introduced far more successfully in Britain than in France, where power-distance and uncertainty-avoidance were found to be higher. Jaeger and Kanungo (1990) make the point that if MBO is used in the 'wrong' context, then it may actually be *dysfunctional* because it can create distrust between senior and junior staff. It is not difficult to see why Hofstede's work has received wide circulation within organizational studies: 'The importance of Hofstede's work is not only that it identified specific cultural differences between nations, but Hofstede also showed that organizational culture is an entry point for societal influence on organizations' (Hatch 1997: 210).

Hofstede also of course has his critics. Some researchers within the organizational studies field have been critical of both his methodological approach and some of his assumptions. For example, McSweeney (2002) argues that despite the large volume of questionnaires deployed overall in this massive study, Hofstede's samples in many countries were in practice extremely small. The research was also restricted only to employees of the IBM corporation, so that any generalization derived from the characteristics of this self-selecting subgroup to those of the larger national population of an entire country may be open to criticism.

This is difficult ground, and there have also been unhelpful overgeneralized characterizations of the cultural encounter between 'developers' and 'developees'. For example, Jaeger and Kanungo (1990) are highly critical of the notions of 'traditionalism' propounded by authors such as McClelland (1961), which insisted that cultures which emphasized familism and fatalism were antithetical to development because they could not espouse 'modern' values, a line of thinking which informed much of the 'modernization' theory of the 1960s and 1970s. Some of this thinking, however, has been challenged by the economic success of countries such as Singapore and Japan, which led to a range of debates about the ways in which linking formal management styles with local values had the potential to bring success on non-EuroAmerican terms.[9]

A key challenge for mainstream management has been to find ways of relating ideas about wider cultures with the concept of organizational culture. Hofstede argues that 'organizational cultures', the set of values and norms which are constructed within organizations, may be more malleable than national cultures and can be drawn upon within organizations to build bridges between different national cultures through the acquisition and deployment of intercultural communication skills.[10] Tayeb (1988) undertook a study which compared India and Britain in order to explore the relationship between national cultural contexts and organizational culture. In an analysis of the main approaches to the cross-national study of organizations, he shows that a set of different factors helps to determine the structures and activities of organizations, within which culture is just one. First, a 'contingency perspective' is important, since it focuses on securing a fit between structure and context which is fundamentally necessary for any organization's survival. Second, a 'political economy' focus is needed in order to examine the social and economic structures which also help determine aspects of the organization. Finally, the 'cultural perspective' highlights the ideational process in which attitudes and values of individual members help determine the organization's structure. For NGOs, all three levels are important for cross-cultural management.

The management literature therefore highlights the importance of linking ideas about culture with the ways in which organizations are managed. It also presents an increasingly detailed analysis of management and globalization, which shows how even within the business world the management assumptions embodied in Western business school training are increasingly under challenge. Parker (1998: 25) cites research which suggests that large numbers of successful though little-known companies operate using new models of management, for example combining Western-style accounting systems with non-Western team structures, and with authoritative leaders who nevertheless give local managers a high degree of autonomy and flexibility.

ANTHROPOLOGICAL PERSPECTIVES

So far this chapter has provided a brief review of selected aspects of organization theory in relation to the management of NGOs, and this has proved a fruitful approach to analysing important aspects of the subject – from organizational learning and change through to organizational life cycles and leadership. As NGO management has taken on an increasingly transnational character, we need to draw ideas both from organizational theory and from what has been termed the 'anthropology of organizations' (Wright 1994). An anthropological approach can potentially make a distinctive contribution to the understanding of NGO management. This is particularly the case when we bear in mind that most NGO work is undertaken in non-Western contexts, and that development interventions frequently take the form of a cultural encounter at the level of both organization and individual. The need to investigate more deeply questions of context takes us back to our conceptual framework set out in Chapter 1.

Social anthropology (or cultural anthropology, the term used in the USA) can enrich third sector studies in two main ways: by generating and sharing ethnographic data about organizations and the contexts in which they work, and in bringing distinctive theoretical and methodological approaches (Lewis 1999b). Social anthropology has traditionally been associated with the study of 'traditional' or non-Western communities, particularly those which were subordinate, marginalized or geographically remote. There are rich ethnographic descriptions of non-Western third sector organizations contained in anthropological monographs which go back many years. However, the narrow view of anthropologists as purveyors of the exotic is now agreed to be long out of date. Anthropologists as long ago as the 1950s began to focus on organizational studies in industrialized societies and the idea of studying organizations as communities. More recent anthropological research has been concerned not just with communities 'at home' but with community relationships with wider policy issues of education, health and bureaucracy or with international development institutions (Wright 1994; Lewis and Mosse 2006). Anthropologists have moved away from preoccupations with marginal or remote people to 'study up' instead, by focusing also on the powerful and the mainstream (Gardner and Lewis 1996).

Anthropologists bring a distinctive research methodology to third sector research – an approach which seeks to understand small-scale communities primarily through long-term 'fieldwork' to facilitate face-to-face data collection, often using a qualitative 'participant observation' research methodology. This small-scale, interpretative approach to research has tended to distinguish anthropological work from that of sociologists. Of particular interest to research into NGO management is the practice of 'organizational ethnography', in which organizations and their relationships are treated as units for research using participant observation. Organizational anthropology of this kind, while popular in the 1950s and 1960s, has become less common in recent years, and the dialogue between anthropologists and organizational theorists about the workings of organizations has waned (Bate 1997). As Bate argues, ethnographic research is at the core of anthropology and provides a methodology, a way of thinking and way of writing which can enrich much of the current writing about organizations, which is frequently weakened by a tendency to essentialize the concept of culture in organizations in the search for quick-fix management solutions.

For researchers on NGO management, anthropology offers more than the participant observation research methodology, which is now widely used by other types of social scientist. Gledhill (1994) shows that the distinctive contribution of anthropology to social science is primarily a theoretical one which:

> attempts to examine social realities in a cross-cultural frame of reference. In striving to transcend a view of the world based solely on the premises of European culture and history, anthropologists are also encouraged to look beneath the world of appearances and taken-for-granted assumptions in social life in general. This should help us to pursue critical analyses of ideologies and power relations in all societies, including those of the West.
>
> (Gledhill 1994: 7–8)

The study of Western third sector organizations, whether US non-profit organizations, UK voluntary agencies or international development NGOs, brings with it a set of assumptions and biases rooted in the history, values and cultures of the West (see Box 4.4). These are

NGOs and organizational development (OD) in Malawi

James (2003) has documented his own international capacity-building work with NGOs in Africa and provides a set of valuable insights into the realities of organizational change. One is the importance of understanding context. The recent history and politics of Malawi has created an environment in which the authoritarian style of Banda's thirty-year dictatorship (itself following on from a long era of colonial domination) brings certain distinctive organizational implications. It has contributed to a cultural climate in which hierarchies are strong, interpersonal trust has been eroded and sensitive disputes between staff in organizations are often resolved behind the scenes rather than in public. It also helps structure relationships between staff and 'experts' from outside, creating circumstances in which current Western-style participatory management styles and OD techniques cannot easily be transferred in any straightforward 'one size fits all' manner. But, as James is able to show, this does not mean either that the concept of organizational development is irrelevant or inappropriate. Taking an ethnographic approach which seeks to understand better the structures, relationships and ideas within African NGOs *on their own terms*, he examines the ways local organizations operate. He finds that forms of democratic decision-making within organizational change processes are differently structured, such as through private one-to-one conversations rather than open plenary discussions.

James also engages with the particular language of change within these organizations through which OD is being imagined and managed, and shows how the language of Western OD used by outsiders needs to be adapted or changed if it is to be understood in local contexts. To give a simple example, James points out that to speak of an organization as an 'iceberg', with the bulk of its structure hidden out of sight, as many trainers do, is a metaphor less relevant to the everyday life of people used to a tropical climate, than to speak of an organization as a 'hippo', similarly partly submerged. Going deeper, James explores some of the counterpart ways in which local thinking about organizational change have long existed in these communities, which have their own language, terms and ways of thinking about change. These range from a tradition which accepts the need for outside facilitation to solve organizational problems ('the stranger brings the sharper blade') to the recognition of the need for cooperative problem solving ('one finger does not squash a tick'). These ways of thinking about organizations are in many cases much older than Western discourses of organizational change, and there are important ways in which outside 'experts' may also learn from them. For example, the role of story-telling as a method for addressing organizational problems comes through strongly from James's data. In the West, the importance of story-telling as a method for business management and participatory learning and action in development has only recently begun to be recognized (e.g. Denning 2000).

James shows the ways in which concepts of OD can be translated and interpreted between 'Western' and 'African' contexts, if this is attempted with openness and sensitivity. But James also implicitly questions the principles of simple 'technology transfer' embodied in much of NGO 'capacity building' literature and its associated practices by drawing attention to the existence of important 'counterpart traditions' of participation and organizational change in other contexts. The possibilities for a more genuine 'two-way learning' within international development relationships, he argues, is thereby opened up.

Source: James 2003.

only now beginning to be questioned as non-profit studies begins to widen and internationalize its focus. The discussion about the types of third sector organizations which 'belong' and those which do not has become a lively debate in the efforts of the Johns Hopkins comparative non-profit research project, as the project has moved beyond the context of North America and Europe (Salamon and Anheier 1997).

Cross-cultural management

Cross-cultural studies of organizations are on the rise amongst organizational anthropologists (Hamada 1992). One obvious area in which anthropological research can contribute to NGO management is in the study of cross-cultural encounters created through the work of international NGOs, as Wright (1994) suggests. For example, what are the management challenges and organizational implications of deploying expatriate NGO staff from the North to work in Southern country contexts?[11] What is the consequence of conflicts between different cultures and values? Where NGOs from the North are seeking to work with Southern NGO partners, should the Northern organizations be driven primarily by their own values or by the non-Western values of the partner organization?

Another key area in which 'anthropological' ideas can be applied to internal management questions is through the importance of the concept of 'ambiguity' in management, which may have particular relevance to NGOs. Within organizational theory, the management of ambiguity has also been seen as a key to understanding the challenges faced by organizations in the postmodern world, in contrast to earlier 'rational scientific' theories of management (Peters and Waterman 1982; Morgan 1997). Martin and Meyerson (1988) show how ambiguity can bring both paralysis and innovation within organizational culture. More recently, the emphasis on the management of shared meanings in current organization theory highlights the need for managers to clarify and project the desired future organizational identity and image, in order to guide organizational change (Gioia and Thomas 1996). Indeed, the concept of ambiguity has long been identified by anthropologists as a source of both creativity and danger. It has been viewed as central to explanations of how cultures, ideas and activities are constructed, negotiated and reworked through processes in which both tension and creativity may be present (Wright 1994; Curtis 1994).

Managing ambiguity

Some third sector researchers, influenced by both the anthropological and the organization theory traditions, have been drawn to the concept of ambiguity. For example, drawing upon the work of the anthropologist Edmund Leach, Billis (1993a) has argued that organizations may exhibit a set of organizational problems created by the existence of an ambiguous zone between the bureaucratic and associational 'worlds', which tend to operate through very different sets of rules (discussed in more detail in Chapter 7). For example, the 'bureaucratic world' operates according to the rules of Weberian hierarchy and role specialization, while by contrast the 'associational world' is characterized more by face-to-face egalitarian relationships and multifaceted, informal roles. Many third sector organizations as they grow

124

become caught in the ambiguous zone between the two, bringing confused roles and identities. Following from this approach, the idea of ambiguity has also been applied to the analysis of the sectoral boundaries between state, business and third sectors (Billis 1993b). Carroll (1992: 138) shows that 'socially-oriented businesses' are under constant tension between their profit-making and their equity-promoting selves. A recent study of 'community trade' work undertaken by the Body Shop (Lewis 1998a; see Box 6.5), a UK-based 'social' business in collaboration with South Asian NGOs, alternative trading organizations and producer groups, illustrates the relevance of the concept of ambiguity in understanding the complex management challenges involved for both NGOs and business when attempts are made to link poverty reduction objectives to the action of commercial market forces – on the boundary between the for-profit and non-profit sectors, as we will see in Chapter 6.

Anthropological perspectives also offer a critique of the 'one best way' tendency in some management thinking – whether in the form of top-down or enabling forms – which may be another way of extending Western cultural hegemony through the co-optation of local value systems (Marsden 1994). What anthropology may be able to do is open us up to the possibilities of the roles which might be played by indigenous management styles and local understandings of 'organization' and 'development' as appropriate foundations for development efforts (Marsden 1994: 35). For example, in one well-documented case the Philippines Irrigation Authority (PIA) managed to restructure an inefficient top-down bureaucracy by decentralizing water provision to locally developed irrigation management structures, which drew upon the capacity of organized groups of local farmers to manage their own community irrigation systems (Korten and Siy 1989).

CONCLUSION

This chapter has explored some of the ways in which organization theory – most of which originates from the business sector – can be applied to the analysis of NGO management. The chapter has focused on selected issues in organization theory which have engaged the attention of writers on NGOs, such as ideas about the organizational life cycle, theories of organizational learning and change, and perspectives on resource dependency. Each of these ideas can contribute to a better understanding of the challenges faced by NGO managers as they consider the development, performance and access to resources of the development NGOs in which they work.

Yet there is also growing awareness that formal strategies for organizational change need to be supported by a strong focus on culture and values at the individual and the organizational levels. As Owusu (2004: 108) observes from the perspective of many years of experience of practice and reflection within the NGO sector:

> Change must begin from within development organizations themselves and must go beyond just restructuring when things appear not to be working. Often development organizations are quick to embark on restructuring in the belief that adjusting organizational structures is enough to solve underlying problems. But new structures do not, in themselves, herald new dawns. Rather, it is the attitudes,

125

behaviours, values and commitment that underlie these structures that hold in them the seeds of success or failure.

Of particular relevance to NGO management then is the need to reflect on organizational culture and cross-cultural management issues, particularly under conditions of increased globalization. Many development NGOs seek to build an internal organizational culture and a way of working that can reflect, and is appropriate to, the values of strengthening social justice and achieving poverty reduction. At the same time, NGOs, perhaps more than any other type of organization, are seeking to manage complex cross-cultural encounters both *within* their organizations as staffing becomes more diverse, and *between* themselves and their clients, since organizational success depends on working closely with communities, individuals and institutions with which they may be unfamiliar.

This chapter has explored the idea that both organizational theory and organizational anthropology can provide useful and potentially complementary insights for NGO management.[12] There is still comparatively little research available on many of these themes in relation to the NGO world. More empirical research is needed if we are to gain a better understanding of the ways in which development NGOs can build and maintain their influence in a rapidly changing world.

REVIEW QUESTIONS

- Why has the relationship between development NGOs and mainstream management often been complex and difficult?
- Does the resource dependency perspective suggest that NGOs are more vulnerable to external resource flows than other types of organization?
- Explore how you would go about designing a research project that would explore important key areas of NGO management culture that have not been discussed here.

Part II

The practice of NGO management

Chapter 5

Advocacy and service delivery

LEARNING OBJECTIVES

After considering this chapter, the reader will be able to describe and analyse:

- Key issues in the management of the two central NGO activities of service delivery and advocacy
- Importance of innovation in relation to the work that NGOs undertake
- Challenges of evaluation and the questions of whether and how to attempt the 'scaling up' of successful interventions

KEY TERMS

- Power
- Empowerment
- Participation
- Contracting
- The policy process
- Evaluation
- Innovation
- Scaling up

INTRODUCTION

This chapter is concerned with the main activities undertaken by development NGOs. As the preceding chapters illustrate, there is an immense diversity of such activity, and this needs to be understood in relation to the wider policy context in which NGOs operate. Najam (1999) makes the case for seeing NGOs – or 'citizen organizations' as he prefers to call them – as 'policy entrepreneurs' seeking to influence and change policy in innovative ways in support of poverty reduction.

Najam sets out three stages of the 'policy process', which is the process of conceiving, designing and implementing public action. In his analysis, the policy process is a three-stage process: *agenda setting* (the agreement of priorities and issues), *policy development* (making choices among possible alternatives and options) and *policy implementation* (undertaking actions to translate policies into practice).[1] Within the policy process, Najam suggests that there are four distinct types of NGO role which may be undertaken: service delivery, advocacy, innovation and monitoring. He therefore characterizes NGOs as 'policy entrepreneurs' balancing and combining elements of some or all of these roles in the pursuit of social change. There are in this model four potential NGO roles within the 'policy stream': *service providers* (acting directly to do what needs to be done); *advocates* (prodding government to do the right thing); *innovators* (suggesting and showing how things could be done differently); and finally *monitors* (trying to ensure that government and business do what they are supposed to be doing). This chapter focuses primarily on the first two roles, which are the most prominent NGO roles to feature in the literature, but it concludes with a discussion and some examples of the other two.

RELATIONSHIPS BETWEEN SERVICE DELIVERY AND ADVOCACY

The first part of the chapter addresses the implementation of service delivery, in which development NGOs provide goods or services to people who need them. For example, in many developing countries NGOs are operating primary healthcare services, delivering non-formal education programmes or extending forms of micro-credit at the local level. Some focus on a single specialized service, while others may bundle together several types of services within multifaceted interventions. Whatever the services that are delivered by NGOs, several crucial management issues are raised: to whom should such services be provided, and at what cost? How should the NGO manage relations with other service providers, such as the state? And how participatory should the relationships be with the users of these services, and how accountable?

The second part of the chapter is concerned with the catalytic role of advocacy and campaigning, in which NGOs seek to exert pressure on individuals and institutions in pursuit of wider change. For example, efforts by NGOs to change the government's education policy, or international action to urge debt relief for impoverished nations, are common strategies of this kind. These activities require another set of management skills and approaches as NGOs need to select issues, maintain accountability to stakeholders, manage information and complex relationships with other agencies, and seek 'leverage' with which they can achieve influence. NGOs may conduct advocacy locally, or they may be part of large, transnational networks in which gaps of space and culture must be carefully negotiated.

Although there are some NGOs that only do service delivery and others that specialize in advocacy, these two roles are not mutually exclusive in practice, and may often be combined within one NGO. For example, Proshika in Bangladesh has built up long-standing relationships with its group members across the country, based in part on providing them with services such as credit. Proshika has from time to time taken on advocacy work in response to local problems and needs expressed by these group members, such as when they requested the government to implement a ban on the importation of certain dangerous pesticides that were causing local health concerns. In a study of advocacy work in Kenya and Mozambique, it was found that local-level community work is often an essential ingredient of advocacy work for African NGOs: 'Service delivery is often important, not only in itself, but as a way of gaining legitimacy and as an entry point for advocacy' (Kanji *et al.* 2002: 32).

This makes the question of 'balancing' different tasks a crucial one for NGO managers – and Fowler (1997) calls his overview of NGO management issues 'striking a balance'. The strategy of providing services to a section of the community which is otherwise excluded from government service provision, for example, while simultaneously exerting pressure at the policy level for improvements in provision in the longer term, is one such balanced strategy. Another type of strategy is the entering into of a formal contract between an NGO and the government to provide a specific service for an agreed length of time which may help to build trust between the NGO and the government, and create opportunities for influence. On the other hand, there are some NGOs which find that the balance is not sustainable, and that entering into a contract with government simply robs them of their spirit and their independence.

Common to both activities is a set of three related questions. The first of these is the problem of judging the 'success' or 'failure' of an NGO's work, which raises the complex question of evaluation. The second is the issue of achieving impact, where NGOs may need to make complex trade-offs in the balance between local small-scale effectiveness and the challenges of wider and larger-scale influence, and which has led to discussions about the possibilities of 'scaling up' NGO work. The third is the issue of innovation, which is frequently an assumed characteristic of NGO work but is one that requires careful appraisal. For NGOs that consciously seek to innovate, a further question is raised: exactly how innovative should NGOs be, and how can they balance innovative responses to important problems with the dangers of 'innovation for innovation's sake', especially when pressure from funders may lead NGOs to demonstrate that they are always doing something new?

SERVICE DELIVERY: MEANS OR END?

Carroll (1992) points out that service delivery is perhaps the most directly observable and clearly visible role which NGOs play in development work. In this role, goods and services that are wanted, needed or otherwise unavailable are provided by NGOs to a particular section of the community. Sometimes the NGO itself takes a decision to provide services to its clients in order to meet hitherto unmet needs, while in other cases an NGO may be 'contracted' by the government to take over the provision of services which were formerly provided by the state (see Box 5.1). There are also cases where NGOs do not provide services to clients at the grassroots but instead provide training services to other organizations or to government, or offer research or conflict resolution services to other agencies.

NGOs are involved in service delivery activities primarily in the agriculture, health and education sectors, but are becoming increasingly active in less-documented areas such as housing, legal services, research and conflict resolution. There are three main roles which NGOs can play. These can be illustrated with reference to agricultural development as follows. The first role is as an implementing agency which actually delivers the services to people. An example of this is NGOs working with farmers in remote, difficult-to-reach areas who may be farming fragile, complex or risk-prone lands for which government outreach is poor (Bebbington 1991). In undertaking this kind of work, NGOs often draw on the use of local field staff whose knowledge can bring a better 'fit' with local people than can be the case with professionals or outside 'experts'. The second role is that of strengthening the already existing public delivery systems through providing research into unmet needs and innovative responses to delivery problems, and through training services, particularly to government staff, whose skills and outlook can be upgraded through ideas and information learned by an NGO which has successfully built bridges with local grassroots communities. The work of the Mindanao Baptist Rural Life Centre (MBRLC) in the Philippines, which worked jointly with farmers to develop a technology (SALT) for farming degraded sloping agricultural land which improved poor local farmers' yields, illustrates this

---

NGOs IN ACTION 5.1

Growth of non-state actors in health service delivery in Africa

NGO service provision can take two main forms – *direct service provisioning* and *self-help from below*. During the 1980s and 1990s the adoption of structural adjustment policies by many African governments led to drastic cuts in the provision of social services, with the result that third sector organizations have attempted to fill the resource gap. Church-based NGOs have been particularly prominent in providing health services. In Zimbabwe, church missions provide 68 per cent of all hospital beds in rural areas, while in Zambia the third sector – which is mostly church-based – provides 40 per cent of health services in rural areas. Self-help initiatives have emerged as citizens have addressed the resource shortfall themselves. For example, in Kenya the *harambee* self-help movement (which was originally established by President Kenyatta) has helped to create a network of health infrastructure in rural areas, though grassroots involvement in construction and maintenance later declined. In Uganda, self-help initiatives in the health sector have emerged from below, while many rural schools are being managed and funded by parent – teacher associations, despite being still nominally under the control of the state.

Source: Robinson and White 1997.

role very well: after innovating the new approach, which was relatively simple and low cost, the NGO began training government agricultural extension workers and other NGOs in the new approach in an effort to get it promoted and adopted more widely (Watson and Laquihon 1993).

The third approach is that an NGO can work with its clients in the community to assist them in generating pressure or 'demand pull' so that people can claim better services from government and hold government agencies more accountable. Cases from Bangladesh collected by Kramsjo and Wood (1992) illustrate this approach in action, such as when the NGO Proshika helped to organize local women to take action against a local magistrate to demand justice in a case of violence against a group member. NGOs can also achieve this third objective by acting as 'bridges' (Brown 1991) between clients or beneficiaries and specialized service providers such as legal advisers. A good example of this role is that of PROTERRA in Peru (Bebbington 1991), which provided services to recently resettled marginal farmers who not only needed help with finance to begin farming the new lands, but also needed to ensure that their land titles were quickly formalized so that they would not be illegally removed from the land. This is also an approach used by the PDI (2004) in the Philippines in its efforts to keep pressure on government to maintain implementation of its agrarian reform policy, while at the same time assisting farmers with practical help in taking possession and commencing cultivation of the new land they receive (see Box 5.3).

Some policy makers assume that NGOs have specific organizational advantages – such as flexibility, commitment and cost-effectiveness – which can make them particularly well suited to the service delivery role. However, it is difficult to find systematic studies which can provide evidence to support this claim in any general sense. One exception is Carroll (1992), who found in a survey of thirty Latin American NGOs engaged in rural develop-ment activities that all appeared to show an outstanding capacity to implement projects compared with other kinds of agency. Activities were typically completed on time and with reasonable efficiency so that seeds, tools or fertilizer were distributed before planting, requests for credit were processed in a timely manner, and demonstrations for farmers of new techniques were effectively organized. None of these achievements, Carroll argues, are typically characteristic of public or private national-level service providers in most Latin American countries. The skills possessed by NGOs which allowed them to manage this were derived from effective internal management systems such as relatively 'flat' (as opposed to hierarchical) organizational structures with smaller gaps between the office and the field than is typical in other types of agency; participatory modes of decision making which reflect the ideas of both managers and field staff; a strategy of 'organizational learning' which incorp-orates feedback from the field and distils the lessons learned from success and failure in order to improve future performance; and finally, the importance of finding a distinct niche for the NGO's work which allows it to develop a specialized role where as an organization it can build a competitive advantage.

There is some evidence in the literature about the cost advantages of NGO service delivery as well as better 'targeting'. The example of Bharatiya Agro-Industries Foundation (BAIF) illustrates that NGOs can be more cost-effective than government in performing certain service delivery tasks. It is not often possible to make straight economic compar-isons between NGOs and government, but BAIF's efforts to produce cross-bred dairy cattle in six states of India were in this case compared with a similar government programme in Tamil Nadu, and the overall costs of developing inputs came out as 66 per cent those of government, due probably to lower labour productivity in the government sector (Satish and Prem Kumar 1993).

Another key strength that Carroll (1992) identifies is the ability to influence and gain leverage over other actors in the development environment such as banks, government agencies and private suppliers. These arguments lend weight to the 'comparative advantage' view of NGOs in which they are seen as having strengths in relation to other development actors, but as Biggs and Neame (1995) warn, it is probably unwise to interpret such claims too literally. This is because of the wide diversity of NGOs of varying quality that exist and the fact that it is often the *relationships* between NGOs and other types of organizations that generate creativity rather than simply the activities of NGOs themselves. The importance of synergistic combinations of different actors such as central government, local municipal authorities and NGOs in improving healthcare services in north-east Brazil has been documented by Tendler (1997). For every case of the effective NGO it is usually possible to point to another NGO which has high administrative overheads, poor management and low levels of effectiveness. Nor are such characteristics fixed: Seckinelgin (2006) has argued that while some HIV/AIDS NGOs have been drawn into donor-funded interventions in Africa based on their closeness to local communities, it is precisely this closeness that becomes lost once these NGOs become institutionalized within international systems.

Despite the positive stories about service delivery, there is also a trend in the NGO literature which sees NGO service delivery as a source of concern, both in terms of the sustainability issues and the undermining of the state and the problems of citizen accountability this generates (Fowler 1997). There is also something deeper – the argument that as NGOs turn into service providers they may lose part of their essential, voluntaristic, value-driven identity (by moving towards the market) and they may become simply the instruments of governments or donors. The dilemma for NGOs is therefore the question of whether service delivery is a means (to provide people with services to meet immediate needs, but with an eye on influencing and improving wider delivery systems so that the NGO's role is essentially a temporary, transitional one) or an end in itself, in which NGOs as private providers become one set of actors among many who are contracted to deliver services.

In Britain, a gradual shift in the 1980s and 1990s towards using private social service delivery with a reduced government role was termed 'the mixed economy of welfare'. It has had somewhat uneven results in terms of the quality of provision, despite making more government resources available to the third sector (Kendall 2003). A similar dilemma is at the root of the uncertainties in parts of the NGO literature. The question for many NGOs and policy makers has been the tension between what Korten (1987: 146) calls 'the output vendor versus the development catalyst'. This concern remains highly topical. As we saw in Chapter 3, trends in the aid industry towards budget support means that a greater proportion of donor funds increasingly go directly to governments which then fund NGOs in service delivery roles through contracting arrangements. Korten (1990: 102) identified the 'public service contractor' NGOs as problematic because they are 'driven by market considerations more than values, and are therefore more like businesses than voluntary organizations'.

There are many examples of NGO service provision being characterized by problems of quality control, limited sustainability, poor coordination and general amateurism (Robinson and White 1997). Carroll (1992: 42) argues that while many development NGOs can simply remain as efficient service providers, opportunities may arise for them to do much more than that, such as promoting participatory values or supporting democratic principles, but he also acknowledges that this may in practice be very challenging:

> The problem is that GSOs and MSOs often face so many difficulties and complications in providing services that they tend to neglect their broader goals. Thus services that were intended as a means frequently become an end.

NGO service delivery is often carried out as part of a particular project, which by definition will have a finite end, after which services will need to be made sustainable otherwise they will no longer be available. The ways in which they might be made sustainable will vary, but range from the imposition of user fees, the development of community ownership and operation on a voluntary basis, to the substitution of the NGO role by the government. As a result, Carroll (1992: 66) argues that the effectiveness of NGO service delivery should be judged on its developmental impact: 'while service delivery has a strong *intrinsic* value, it should really be evaluated on the basis of its *instrumental* value as a catalyst for other developmental changes.'

This point brings us back to the discussion in Chapter 1 about the instrumental and the expressive aspects of management, and the particular importance of this distinction for third sector organizations. While it may be very important and useful that an NGO delivers services to a particular section of the community, it is also crucially important to examine *how* these services are delivered. This brings us to consider some of the factors that influence the quality of the relationship an NGO is able to build with its service users.

Empowerment and participation

Two terms which are frequently used in connection with NGOs are those of 'empowerment' and 'participation', and both have relevance to a discussion of service provision and NGO implementation issues. According to Carroll (1992), if NGOs implement service delivery in a certain way it can be empowering and act as a catalyst for other developmental changes, and this will avoid the less desirable outcome of simple 'substitution' of services previously provided by other agencies. The concept of empowerment is linked to that of participation, which speaks of involvement rather than passivity, and a role for people in decision making instead of being 'acted upon' in the name of progress or development.

The term 'empowerment' is now widely used by NGOs and other agencies working in development, but its meaning is imprecise. In the social work/counselling context, empowerment arose as a tool for understanding what is needed to change the situation of poor and marginalized people – a process which involves personal development, moving from insight and understanding to action, individually and then collectively (Rowlands 1995) and has roots in work with oppressed communities in the USA (Solomon 1976), with Gandhian values in India (Thomas 1992) and with the radical Brazilian educator Paulo Freire, whose

theory of 'conscientization' has influenced many NGOs. What is common to these ideas –
which do not in practice really form a coherent ideology or set of practices – is an emphasis
on process, with a movement through a series of developmental stages: becoming aware of
the power dynamics in one's life, developing skills and capacity for greater control, exercising control without threatening other people's rights and then going on to support the
empowerment of others in the community.[2] In the management sense, the term is also used
widely in business where managers want to empower their workers and unleash their
creativity for greater profit; bureaucracies want to empower their front-line staff who deal
with clients and provide them with more responsibilities (Wright 1994). Many NGOs now
speak of an empowering or participatory management style in which operating staff are seen
as the starting point for action, as a source of skills and capacities, and are encouraged to
take initiative in solving problems (Holcombe 1995).

In order to understand empowerment, we need first to analyse the concept of *power*.
Rowlands (1995) argues that it is useful to distinguish 'power over' (control or influence
by some people over others, such as men over women, dominant caste over low caste) from
'power to' (a generative view of power in which people stimulate activity in others and
raise morale). She argues that genuine empowerment implies gaining 'power to' in order
to resist and challenge 'power over'. This process has three dimensions: personal, with the
growth of greater self-confidence; relational, in the ability to renegotiate close ties and gain
greater decision-making power; and collective, in building links to work together and cooperate with others locally or nationally.

In Friedmann's (1992) book, the concept of empowerment became central to alternative development theory and practice, and he identifies three different kinds of power: social
(access to information, knowledge and skills, participation in social organizations, financial
resources), political (access by individual household members to decision-making processes
singly or in groups, e.g. voting, collective action, etc.), and psychological (individual sense
of power and self-confident behaviour, often from successful action in the above domains),
each of which is necessary for building an alternative approach to development which focuses
on more than simply material well-being. A recent example of this is the progress made in
decentralized local governance in Porto Alegre, Brazil. Participatory healthcare interventions in the city have been assisted by a greater recognition of the 'psychosocial' dimensions
of poverty, such that locally marginalized people have gradually become empowered to
better state their needs and ideas within a more open local public sphere (Guareschi and
Jovchelovitch 2004).

The work of the Association of Sarva Seva Farms (ASSEFA), a Gandhian NGO in India
as presented in Thomas (1992), illustrates both the potential and the problems with the
empowerment approach. Formed in 1969, ASSEFA develops land given to landless low-
caste households through the Gandhian *bhoodan* 'land gift' movement and helps to build
self-reliant communities through provision of credit and supply of agricultural, industrial
and health services alongside organization building and awareness raising. The work is careful
and slow. First, ASSEFA's field workers spend up to three years in a village listening to
local concerns, and an initiative must come from the villagers themselves because they will
bear the risks. A pilot project is then set in motion for two years to test the extent of cooperation and build trust, and then a larger project proposal is drawn up. Training in

self-management and other skills is provided, if necessary, by the NGO, so the project is a result of collective endeavour, not external resources, and group members are required to donate their labour and organization. Then a phase of complementary activities is undertaken – agro-industries or spin-offs in local communities – for three to four years, and ASSEFA gradually withdraws its advice and support. When self-sufficiency is achieved (such as through sales of produce) the NGO's investment is gradually paid back and can be reused for new projects. In addition to the economic improvement, there are political changes too, with one family member pointing out: 'We have gained recognition in the village. Other castes, who were our masters earlier, now not only listen but pay attention to what we say' (quoted in Thomas 1992: 121).

However, there is a range of problems which have been identified with the empowerment approach. NGO achievements in this area tend to be small scale. Thomas (1992) quotes data to suggest that at the present rate of activity it will take several hundred years to develop the 1.3 million acres of *bhoodan* land already distributed. There is a tendency for NGOs to hold on to groups for too long – there is seldom sustainable, autonomous group action (Carroll 1992: 113) and the contribution of labour is taken to be participation rather than collective commitment. There are issues of responsibility for NGO 'animators' if violent conflict ensues. Hashemi's (1995) account from Bangladesh, where an NGO was fielding landless candidates for local elections, describes arrests and injuries and quotes a local government officer as saying: 'all of us want to help the poor and provide charity for them. But when the poor get uppity and want to sit on the head of the rich, when they want to dominate that cannot be allowed' (Hashemi 1995: 106). As Thomas points out, there are limits to the NGO empowerment approach, especially when we consider the more radical ambitions behind some such initiatives.[3] The success of ASSEFA's work depends on factors outside the sphere of local direct action: landowners forgo land rights collectively; some state and local government resources are made available; resources come from international NGOs and Gandhian activists are recruited.

Moser's (1989) discussion of empowerment and gender links empowerment with the concept of 'participation'. The concept of participation can be traced back to Selznick's influential public sector study of the barriers to public participation in the Tennessee Valley Authority, which he found in the form of informal groupings within the organization and in the form of powerful vested interests outside it (Selznick 1966). The act of bringing in people who are outside the decision-making process can lead to a focus not only on the formal institutions of political and economic power, but also on the dynamics of oppression in the personal sphere. The concept of participation is widely used in development and, like 'empowerment', has both a development sense (the involvement of beneficiaries in development programmes) and a management sense (in which staff and partners are involved in decision-making processes). Within NGO service delivery strategies, the level of participation can influence both the quality of the service that is being provided and the likely outcome in terms of empowerment and sustainability.

The origin of the concept of 'participation' was in part a reaction to top-down statism during the 1960s and 1970s, when dissatisfaction among development personnel grew in the face of government's inability to take responsibility for promoting social development (Midgley 1995). This failure was due in part to the creation of large bureaucracies, the selection of wasteful projects and the involvement of corrupt politicians. In the prevalent top-down approaches of the time, projects did not involve people in the processes of their design and execution. A view emerged that 'development' could be better fostered through community participation in which 'ordinary people are mobilised to establish projects that serve their local communities and . . . are actively involved in these projects' (Midgley 1995: 60). These ideas, at least in their more radical form, were also associated with the ideas of alternative people's self-development of activist writers such as Freire. However, as Cornwall and Brock (2005) have shown, participation quickly became a broad catch-all term (a 'development buzzword' par excellence) covering both mainstream ideas about involving people as well as more radical ideas about collective action, negotiation with the power structure and building self-reliance.

There have been many critics of the ways in which the concept of participation has been used. Rahnema (1992) argues that the realization in the 1960s that growth did not reach the poor led to a reassessment of top-down strategies, with an incorporation of ideas about participation as a means of merely involving people in activities that had already been initiated by the state or by development organizations. As a result, Rahnema argued that the idea of participation lost its threat and became a potentially contradictory concept that can sometimes be perversely used to actually rob people of their ability to act together in their own best interests. In this view, participation can be used to import into communities ideas which are then attributed to those communities, to secure the token involvement of people in order to display a level of participation to outside agencies, and as such it can be cynically used merely for the legitimization of outsiders' decisions.[4] A collection of papers by Cooke and Kothari (2001) echoed and extended this critical view by speaking of the 'tyranny' of participation in relation to the ways in which participatory development has become a technical approach that serves to downplay the role of power and politics.

In the face of complex arguments for and against participatory approaches, Sarah White's (1995) conceptual framework for thinking about participation provides very useful arguments for unpicking its complexity. She argues that participation initially arose as a form of protest, but became mainstreamed and lost its political meaning, which now needs to be recovered. There are two levels to the politics of participation. The first is 'who participates?', since communities are not homogeneous, and the second is 'at what level?', since implementation is not enough and some power over decision making is also needed. White suggests four forms of participation. The first is *nominal*, such as when government-formed groups are created, but their main purpose is a tokenistic display. The second is *instrumental*, and this can be a way of providing labour under resource shortfalls created by structural adjustment, which then counts as a cost to local people. The third is *representative*, where, for example, a certain group within the community gains some leverage within a programme or project by gaining access to the planning committee and is able to express its own interests. The fourth and strongest form is *transformative*, in which people find ways to make decisions and take action, without outsider involvement and on their own terms. Only this final form is truly 'empowering' in a political sense. But top-down interests in participation are different from bottom-up interests, and participation is therefore a 'site of conflict' which might have positive or negative outcomes for the poor. Like empowerment, participation is also a process, and people may stop participating if they do not feel their interests can be met.

Can the concept of participation survive as a mainstream concept for NGOs? Hickey and Mohan (2004: 239) suggest that it can, so long as a focus is maintained on the political rather than just the technical dimensions of participation:

> understanding the ways in which participation relates to existing power structures and political systems provides the basis for moving towards a more transformatory approach to development; one which is rooted in the exercise of a broadly-defined citizenship.

The link between participation and citizenship therefore allows for the concept to be both broadened and focused, and connects participation more explicitly with the new emphasis on rights-based development in which development can be seen as seeking to increase people's agency, status and capacity to increase their control over social and economic resources.

Managing the dilemmas of service delivery

The environment in which NGOs work, as well as internal factors arising from the organization's own dynamics, produces pressures which can all too easily produce what is termed 'goal deflection' in the organizational literature, as NGOs lose their original objectives and become involved in other, often less ambitious, goals. The classic example of this is the gradual homogenization of relatively diverse communities of development NGOs in some country contexts into predominantly credit service providing organizations. According to Korten (1990), these pressures may be the result of becoming tired of surviving at the financial margins and struggling for funding, the frustrations for activists of long-term struggles against established interests, the sense of obligation which emerges over time to improve job security for staff, and finally the belief that service contracting can eventually buy time and bring more funding and therefore the opportunities to do more varied or 'important' work later on.[5]

A common set of external pressures comes from donors, who may want NGOs to undertake certain kinds of service delivery work such as credit provision, which allows them to show quick, measurable results rather than the messier, less quantifiable activities like awareness raising about rights or about preventive healthcare. Because NGOs are highly dependent on official funding, they have been subject to the influence of Northern domestic politics, which is currently engaged in most countries in defining the nature of public and private responsibility in society, reallocating delivery of what were previously publicly funded services to market or non-market providers, and 'contracting out' services which are to be financed from public funds, such that non-profit organizations are the main recipients (more than 50 per cent of US non-profits now receive more than 50 per cent of their funds from public sources).[6] In general, only a small amount of official aid goes to NGOs doing democratization and advocacy work, because results are hard to measure and in any case they may finance mobilization against their own policies. Besides, many NGOs are reluctant to put it at the centre of their programmes for fear of political problems. For example, this has been a source of tension between NGOs and government in Russia (see Chapter 2) and in Bangladesh where government approval of MJ human rights and government partner projects (see Box 3.3) has been found to be more forthcoming if activities such as voter education and citizenship training are avoided.

There is therefore growing acknowledgement that the limits to NGO roles in service delivery are all too apparent and should be recognized. For example, North (2003: 17) writes in relation to NGOs and poverty reduction efforts in rural Ecuador:

> It is states and global forces that set the parameters for development. . . . To be sure, NGOs can still play important roles. For example, NGO assistance was critical in the construction of infrastructure and the provision of services in two of the cantons . . . but NGOs do not have the resources to finance such programs in all of Ecuador's poor rural municipalities. Only the Ecuadorian state can do that.

In the light of these different perspectives on NGO service provision, Poole (1994) tries to make a pragmatic case for NGOs to get involved in service delivery in contexts where services are in short supply, and where the needs of the poor are not being met. In countries which are undergoing economic adjustment, the promotion of agriculture, education and health sectors is constrained by limitations on resources such as finance, human capital and institutional capacity. If the state is unable to provide essential services (e.g. agricultural extension and research) there is the possibility that the resultant gap can be filled by specialized organizations within the NGO sector.

According to Poole (1994) 'contracting out' is in many cases to be welcomed by NGOs as an opportunity to specialize and take over activities which may previously have been either non-existent or else the responsibility of ineffective government or private sector agencies. For example, agricultural research and extension are investment items which cannot be left to the private sector because they are 'public goods' – commercial profits would be limited because there are only limited markets through which communal benefits can be translated into profits by entrepreneurial activity. So by 'privatizing' them in the narrow sense, only limited impact would be achieved, but for the government to charge a fee would act as a disincentive to improving agricultural practices. In many countries the public agricultural system has failed to appreciate either the complexity of farming marginal, risk-prone lands, or the socio-economic constraints such farmers face (Chambers 1987). According to Poole, NGOs can function as:

> alternative providers of such services, financed by the state, and/or by international donor agencies where the state is economically too weak. Besides making a unique contribution to agricultural development, the NGO sector can supply other benefits. Diversity in the provision of agricultural technology and services is likely to promote efficient competition, and to stimulate the process of institutional and democratic evolution that are themselves dimensions of national development.
>
> (Poole 1994: 105)

In this argument, the respective roles of public and private sectors should be determined by the comparative advantage of each. Such a view is implicit in Brett's (1993) study, which argues that we are finally starting to develop methods of accounting for the relative efficiency of different kinds of institutional actors, and therefore envisages a plurality of institutional actors, based on their relative strengths and weaknesses, as the ideal. The issue of consumer choice is also relevant *within* the NGO community itself. How far might it be advantageous for local people to be able to choose the best services from among a range of different NGOs, rather than having to be aligned with the particular NGO which turns up in their locality?[7] Carroll (1992: 105) discusses this question in the case of Costa Rica, where the strength of a local democratic tradition has led to a situation in which many of the households he selected for a set of case studies were found to be part of a range of civic groups and NGOs which give people more options and choices. However, in many other resource-scarce environments this is unlikely to be the case, since development NGOs and other service providers remain thinly spread.

There is considerable debate as to whether NGOs should be 'complementary' or 'alternative' service providers, and Poole (1994) suggests that in some cases it might be advantageous for some NGOs to become alternatives for services which are public goods. Some of the benefits of 'contracting out' at the policy level are that absolute cuts in provision under adjustment conditions might be prevented at least in the short term, efficiency can be improved by making use of skills and resources locked up in the NGO sector, and if done competitively, contracting might lead to improved efficiency among public sector agencies.

At the human resources level there may be other advantages in that the drain of high-calibre staff from government to overseas posts might be prevented, the organizational complexity of the government sector could be reduced, leaving a few key positions in the higher echelons, and there might be efficiency gains which may permit better remuneration of government staff and reduce corruption by making malpractice less attractive. For this to make a positive contribution to agricultural development, contracting out would have to incorporate social and equity objectives to ensure that gender, ethnic and regional policy issues were addressed, and have a fixed time frame for at least three to five years to prevent the negative effects on tendering organizations and local communities of erratic funding and repeated proposal submission. There would also need to be work by NGOs to build social capital, such as stimulating the development of local grassroots organizations of users through training to help meet demand. Since NGOs are using foreign money, it is therefore undesirable for them to *replace* government services. Carroll's view is that NGOs 'should emphasize capacity building or viability upgrading services, not routine services'. This is a view supported by Brown and Korten (1989: 11): 'unless [NGOs] are developing the capacity of indigenous organizations to replace them in their functions on a self-sustaining basis . . . they cannot claim to be doing development work'.

The case made by Poole (1994) is for appropriately specialized NGOs to become more involved in service provision during periods when resources are constrained in the government sector, not that the whole NGO sector should move this way and ultimately compromise its independence. Indeed, it is argued that little is to be gained by trying to increase state responsibilities if resources are constrained and key government personnel are leaving for other jobs – in fact it would be 'negligent'. Semboja and Therkildsen's (1995) study of service provision in East Africa illustrates the complex ways in which the provision of services for the majority of the population now depends on joint action by the state, NGOs and community-based organizations. Under the macro-economic conditions of structural adjustment, links between the state, international donor agencies and the third sector are becoming more important as the government role declines in health, education and the maintenance of law and order. Many governments were initially hostile to NGOs in many African countries because the government's legitimacy traditionally depended on its provision of services in the postcolonial social contract between state and people. The role of donors in this process has been central, but the NGOs, and therefore also a range of key services, still remain dependent on outside funding.

In Bangladesh, where NGOs funded by bilateral and multilateral donors are taking over key services from the state in health, education and agriculture, the phrase 'franchise state' was coined by Wood (1997) to illustrate the dangers which threaten political accountability when citizens are no longer able to exert pressure on government for services, but instead become dependent upon NGO intermediaries and the international donors which fund them. The increasing involvement of third sector organizations in service provision is not confined to developing countries, but is still for example a live issue in the UK. The neo-liberal ideology of privatization and 'rolling back the state' pursued by Margaret Thatcher in Britain during the 1980s ushered in a new period of resource availability and increased profile for the service-providing section of the UK voluntary sector, but also generated dilemmas of quality control and accountability that have continued under the New Labour era, such as goal deflection and inappropriate regulation (Kendall 2003).

Theories of the origins of the third sector have tended to focus on the issue of service provision and have frequently attempted to explain the general emergence of NGOs around the world in terms of either market failure or state failure (Kendall and Knapp 1999). Within public goods theory, such as that of Weisbrod, third sector organizations emerge because there are unmet needs among sections of the population, either because there are minority interests which 'standardized' government prescriptions tend to exclude (for example, the needs of people with highly specialized health problems) or which the private sector finds unprofitable to address (such as the agricultural input needs of poor farmers on marginal or risk-prone lands). By contrast, other theories such as Hansmann's trust-based theory, emphasize the issue of trust in countries which provide tax incentives for 'not-for-profit' organizations (Anheier 2005). This 'non-distribution constraint' on third sector organizations creates a situation in which the public is more inclined to trust 'non-profits' than for-profit businesses to do a good job in the provision of services, such as in the case of residential care for the elderly.

These are highly contentious issues where there is little agreement and, as Chapter 2 reminds us, it is important to recognize both the diversity of third sector activity and the historical and political specificity of different country contexts. For example, in the USA, Salamon (1994) has argued that there has for many years been an essentially symbiotic relationship between the state and the third sector. Government has used its resources and ability to monitor quality deliberately to foster the growth of a 'community' of third sector organizations which possess the flexibility and responsiveness to identify needs, and this in turn has helped create 'stakeholders' who will support government programmes. The US third sector has therefore played an essential role in public policy in terms of the implementation of services, a fact which has overshadowed even the cost-effectiveness and efficiency arguments often used elsewhere to justify third sector involvement. This line of argument of course challenges earlier theories of state failure and market failure as likely explanations of the evolution of third sector organizations, at least in the context of the USA. A similar line of thinking from the development literature is found in Sanyal's (1991) influential and still highly relevant work on the very different context of Bangladesh, where the concept of 'antagonistic cooperation' is used to show the ways in which – despite frequent tensions and problems – the government, NGOs and donors all need each other because the perceived differences between each one helps to justify the legitimacy of all three types of development actor.

If resource pressures on NGOs continue the way they have been during the past decade we might expect some NGOs to begin to lose their multiple identities and specialize in service delivery to the detriment of other activities. This is the hazard outlined by Carroll (1992), and there is some legitimacy lent to the prediction in the work of Edwards and Hulme (1995). In a controversial study of the history of the NGO sector in Bangladesh, Hashemi and Hassan (1999) traced the 'de-radicalization' of the NGO sector away from its Freirean roots of 'conscientization' towards the almost universal pursuit of micro-finance delivery by almost every major NGO in the country. The new emphasis on budget support by funders is now producing additional pressures for NGOs to enter into externally driven contracting relationships around services. A related issue was highlighted in an influential and still relevant independent report on the British voluntary sector by Knight (1993) as contracting became more common. Will two distinct types of NGO therefore emerge, one focusing on advocacy and another on service delivery? This point is considered later in the chapter.

NGOs AND ADVOCACY: STRATEGIES FOR STRUCTURAL CHANGE

The second major NGO role is that of advocacy, in which NGOs seek to advance the interests of underrepresented groups through negotiations with powerholders, such as governments or corporations (see Box 5.2). Advocacy involves an NGO making arguments for or against a particular cause or a course of action. In this way, a discussion about NGO advocacy draws us further into the 'influence' sector of de Graaf's (1987) conceptual framework of NGO management set out in Chapter 6.

For Najam (1999) advocacy is the attempt by NGOs as 'policy entrepreneurs' to 'prod government to do the right thing', though it can be a strategy which can be equally directed at the private sector. Advocacy NGOs differ from service delivery organizations in that they are primarily seeking to try and change the wider status quo rather than meeting people's immediate material needs, although as we have seen, there are many NGOs which seek to combine both roles (Young 1992). For example, while Oxfam seeks to respond rapidly to a natural disaster such as an earthquake, it is at the same time engaged in a range of campaigns such as the Make Poverty History initiative. We can draw upon Hirschmann's

NGOs and international advocacy roles

NGOs contributed to the campaign for the abolition of the slave trade in the nineteenth century, to the rise of international humanitarianism in the form of the Red Cross movement, and to the emergence of international human rights law, such as the UN Convention on the Rights of the Child. Advocacy work by Northern NGOs has been part of the post-Cold War development policy agenda that has aimed to help build democratization processes within both the developing and 'post-communist' worlds. Advocacy has also become an important activity for Southern NGOs, whose environmental campaigns such as that against the Narmada Dam in India have been built by local organizations with international links. The efforts of NGOs from both the North and South at the UN global summits such as the Rio Earth Summit on Environment and Development (UNCED) or the Beijing Women's Conference indicated growing NGO influence through lobbying work on policy issues such as environment, gender and poverty.

In the global environmental arena, NGOs also have a history of playing important roles, from the 'green' perspectives of the 1970s to the sustainable development paradigm of the 1992 UN Rio conference. The emergence of codes of conduct for national and international business is one such strategy pursued by NGOs in conjunction with social movements, religious groups and investors. For example, the Coalition for Environmentally Responsible Economies (CERES) in 1989 established a ten-point environmental code of conduct for corporations based on what were termed the Valdez principles after the *Exxon Valdez* oil disaster of that year. However, progress with cooperative and voluntary strategies for engagement with the corporate sector were dealt a severe blow by the failure of some countries, and in particular the United States, to endorse the Kyoto Protocol on climate change.

In the field of conflict and disarmament, NGOs played a key role in the International Campaign to Ban Landmines (Scott 2001). This was a coalition of NGOs that mobilized campaigning across the world which led to a 1997 convention signed by 122 states in Ottawa, Canada that banned anti-personnel landmines, later adopted as a treaty within the United Nations. It showed the growing power of NGOs within international politics, leading to tangible results within the space of just a few years of action. But it also showed the diversity of interests among the NGO community since the US National Rifle Association – also an NGO – put up considerable resistance to the attempt to control international arms flows.

Such NGO advocacy roles seem set to grow, as shifting frameworks of global governance increasingly allow space for non-governmental actors to build stronger voices for local and global citizens.

Source: Lewis 2006.

(1970) influential ideas of 'exit', 'loyalty' and 'voice' in decision making in the analysis of NGO advocacy and policy issues, since the aim of advocacy is to secure voice within the policy process. According to Bratton (1990), this needs to be more than just NGO claim making. Achieving real voice is about influencing those seeking to introduce a new programme or policy, or altering the goals or terms of an existing one.

Covey (1995) points out that the importance of the NGO advocacy role began to resurface in the development world in the early 1990s, and has since gained momentum such that it is now assumed by many people that advocacy is an important NGO activity in building sustainable development.[8] For those like Korten (1990), who argue that development is about addressing root causes rather than trying to simply cure some of the problems or symptoms, advocacy is seen as a crucial direction for NGOs to move in, particularly those in the North. Within Korten's NGO generation framework, the move into advocacy and away from simply attempting to meet people's immediate needs through service delivery is seen as a sign of an organization's growing maturity. Enthusiasm for the NGO advocacy role is also found increasingly among those who see the challenge of 'scaling up' NGO activities as the crucial priority for the future (Edwards and Hulme 1992). NGOs have increasingly embraced the advocacy role, to the extent that Clark (2003a: 147) has observed:

> When I was newly in charge of Oxfam campaigns, some of our trustees and managers feared that moving into campaigning might lose Oxfam support, including perhaps the strong funding from the aid industry. Now the opposite is the case; an NGO is penalized if it isn't energetic in lobbying and policy work.

What is policy advocacy? According to Jenkins (1987: 267), writing in the context of the non-profit sector in the United States, advocacy is 'any attempt to influence the decisions of any institutional elite on behalf of a collective interest'. For Lindenberg and Bryant (2001: 173):

> Advocacy work entails moving beyond implementing programs to help those in need, to actually taking up and defending the causes of others and speaking out to the public on another's behalf. In our analysis of NGO advocacy we further define the term to refer specifically to speaking out for policy change and action that will address the root causes of problems confronted in development and relief work, and not simply speaking out to alert people of a problem in order to raise funds to support operational work.

From the point of view of NGO management, advocacy links us back to our conceptual framework in which activities, organization and relationships are set within a broader context. We can also link the subject of advocacy to de Graaf's (1987) influential ideas about the challenge of trying to both control and influence factors in the environments in order to achieve objectives (which is discussed in more detail in Chapter 6): 'efforts to maximize control over the factors that affect the realization of shared goals, and seeking to influence – through lobbying or alliance building – those factors which cannot be directly controlled' (Bratton 1990: 91).

In this way advocacy can be distinguished from mere policy 'implementation', since it involves the articulation of a set of demands or positions in relation to policy, but not necessarily the enactment of such policies, though this will of course be the ultimate aim. Advocacy later needs to be converted into implementation. Jenkins (1987) argues that many non-profits see themselves as having legitimacy to represent the non-commercial interests of the general public as opposed to the special economic interest groups within the rest of society, such as commercial businesses, which left to themselves might work against the public interest. The analysis of NGO advocacy therefore also brings us back to the liberal conception of 'civil society' in which organized groups of citizens challenge and check the excesses of state and market. It also brings us into other areas of research on social change, such as the concept of 'social movement organizations'. Some NGOs can be seen as organizational components of such social movements which seek connections with institutionalized systems of decision making (McCarthy and Zald 1977; Dechalert 1999). On the other hand, NGOs may become advocates of issues which have yet to generate a wider social movement, such as child rights or consumer rights, by acting as the 'advance guard' for the sentiments on behalf of a certain part of the population.

For the past decade or so, development NGOs have attempted to try and widen their effectiveness away from merely implementing projects and managing partnerships and towards influencing the formation of policies. For example, in 1993 ActionAid India outlined six possible strategies for advocacy work with its partners that have come to illustrate the advocacy 'toolkit' for NGOs more or less everywhere: negotiations, lobbying (i.e. influencing key individuals), gaining membership of government bodies, building networks and coalitions, using the media and conducting campaigns. Bratton (1990) was one of the first researchers to assess systematically in the African context the record of NGOs that were seeking to carry out an advocacy agenda and achieve policy influence. Analysing case studies from Zimbabwe and Kenya, where NGOs have tried to represent the 'voice' of the rural poor to policy makers, Bratton focuses on the Savings Development Movement (SDM) in Zimbabwe, the National Farmers' Association of Zimbabwe (NFAZ) and Voluntary Agencies Development Assistance (VADA) in Kenya. He finds that policy advocacy is most likely to be effective if NGOs have the following characteristics:

- a homogeneous membership, which gives a clear policy platform
- a federated structure such as a coordinated network of community-based organizations
- a focused programme with clear and simple objectives (VADA was tempted by donor ideas and tried to be all things to all people)
- a set of informal ties with political leaders by NGO leaders (this was found to be a main predictor of impact)
- a solid domestic funding base, since dependency on foreign funding tends to be negatively related to NGO effectiveness at influencing policy because such work requires funds with 'no strings attached'.

The study showed the important range of contextual factors that an NGO needs to appreciate and react to: in Zimbabwe during the 1980s, after independence, there was a new government in place that appeared far more ready to work with NGOs on poverty issues than the entrenched Kenyan regime of the time that remained more interested in protecting privilege and controlling NGOs. In a study of NGO advocacy work around land rights in Kenya and Mozambique, advocacy strategies by NGOs are also found to be significantly influenced by contextual factors such as the continuing periodic hostility to NGOs from the Kenyan government and the struggle by a new NGO sector in Mozambique to absorb relatively large amounts of donor funds very quickly (Kanji *et al.* 2002).

Advocacy organizations may involve the use of routine political channels or more confrontational direct actions such as marches or demonstrations. Bratton argues that NGOs gaining a 'voice' for the poor in policy making through non-confrontational means is a more useful strategy for NGOs in Africa than 'empowerment' against the power structure (which may be too confrontational) because it allows the NGO leaders 'to identify openings in the administrative system and to cultivate non-adversarial working relationships with the politically powerful' (Bratton 1990: 95–6).

Bratton's model gives NGOs the task of articulating many of the underrepresented demands and needs of the poor to policy makers more effectively. In this way, the policy environment can be 'influenced' even if it cannot be 'controlled'. But in order to be successful at advocacy in achieving policy impact, NGOs need both technical and managerial competence on the one hand, and political clout (i.e. a mobilizable political constituency) on the other (Bratton 1990: 93). This is born out by work in Kenya and Mozambique (Kanji *et al.* 2002). The experience of the PDI in the Philippines within the agrarian reform process (Box 5.3) shows the way in which an NGO can make progress if it is able to combine service delivery and community organizing with an advocacy strategy that is based on carefully negotiated and managed partnerships with both government and local organizations.

Networks of advocacy

In a systematic review of NGO advocacy networks in the environmental sector, Covey (1995) analyses four case studies (three from the Philippines and one from Mexico) and examines both national and transnational alliances. Covey asks two sets of questions:

1   What factors increase the effectiveness of NGO alliances in achieving policy outcomes and strengthening civil society?
2   What factors enable alliances to be accountable to their members, especially grassroots groups?

She found that the main factors affecting success or failure could be analysed in terms of both 'policy effectiveness' (i.e. did the alliance achieve its policy goals through direct or indirect influence on decision makers?) and the 'civil society dimension' (i.e. did the alliance strengthen local institutions and change the nature of community participation in the process of policy influence?). In the case of the first criterion the case studies show that total victories are extremely rare but that a level of success can be achieved by a process of compromise in which the original goals are modified to take account of new opportunities, such as moving from a position of confrontation to influencing a new piece of legislation in favour

The work of PDI in the Philippines: an SNGO combining advocacy and service delivery

The Project Development Institute (PDI) was founded in 1990 with a vision of building and strengthening local people's organizations (POs) in support of poverty-focused agrarian reform. The government of the Philippines has been committed in principle since the late 1980s through the Department of Agrarian Reform (DAR), to redistribute agricultural land from rich to poor. However, the process has so far been slow, its procedures top-down and little progress has been made, particularly in relation to indigenous people who are often the most marginalized section of the rural population. The Rural Empowerment through Agrarian/Asset Development (READ) programme has been developed to follow PDI's policy of securing 'genuine' land reform through combining provision of social and economic support services to farmers alongside active lobbying and negotiations with DAR and the government to maintain pressure to secure asset redistribution. At the forefront of this process are the POs of peasants and indigenous people, which PDI has helped to strengthen and build through provision of organizational and financial support services. For example, the institutionalization of regular negotiation meetings between public officials and POs has helped to reduce the gap between bureaucrats and farmers in the area. By the time of an independent evaluation undertaken in late 2003, the READ programme was found in two years to have established 59 POs in the Central Luzon area and PDI to have built a credible partnership with DAR in the implementation of agrarian reform. By October 2003, 2,953 hectares of agricultural land had been successfully transferred to 985 low-income peasant households, with another 2,000 hectares soon to follow. Furthermore, PDI had also managed to build a stronger understanding amongst the POs of the agrarian reform law and of their rights under it.

Source: evaluation of the READ programme, PDI, Manila, January 2004.

of the poor. If there are 'multiple policy goals', the case studies show that some may be won while others are lost. Policy outcomes can be achieved at 'different levels' such that local change may be effected, while the national level remains resilient to NGO influence, and while the need to influence 'multiple actors' is also difficult to achieve. In one case, some strong grassroots groups left the alliance in protest over compromises in the original objectives:

> Because the ebb and flow of a successful campaign must match the rhythm of the political process, it often appears that trade-offs must be made, at least in the short term, between policy gains and strengthening grassroots organizations.
>
> (Covey 1995: 861)

One of Covey's case studies showed that effectiveness in both dimensions is possible by educating and involving grassroots groups in campaign decisions and by strengthening alliance capacity to achieve policy outcomes. There were three simultaneous parts of the strategy: increasing the commitment of the poor to support legislation through mass action; expanding their understanding of political decision-making processes; and increasing their confidence and skills for dealing with the government. Another showed that neither policy goal nor civil society impact was achieved: the national NGOs were unable to forge an alliance with grassroots groups and could not combine 'livelihood' and 'environmental issues'.

In terms of the strategic management of NGO advocacy, there are a number of lessons which emerge from Covey's work. In order to achieve success in changing policy, a coherent campaign strategy must be combined with adequate resources, and it is necessary for NGOs to 'frame' the issue in such a way that it must appeal to grassroots groups and also limit the opposition's ability to organize. For example, in one case a ban on logging was portrayed effectively by opponents as a threat to local jobs and livelihoods. In order to achieve impact at the civil society level, the case studies reveal the value of building international support networks among a range of different kinds of third sector organizations, and the need for local grassroots groups to have voice within the alliance, without which they will 'exit', as did a group of Mexican Indians in one case when they found that they were not being listened to by more powerful environmental NGOs.[9]

Organization of advocacy

What are the organizational implications of advocacy work for NGOs? This is an area in which there has so far been very little research. Norrell (1999) analysed the tendency among some UK NGOs to drift from service delivery into advocacy work, bringing a range of organizational tensions and problems, including tensions between operational and policy staff, and an inadequate appreciation of resource allocation issues for undertaking advocacy work.

Young (1992) examined the activities of a group of international NGOs based in the United States. The study suggests that an increase at the international level in advocacy as opposed to service delivery has been facilitated by, first, the growth in perceptions of the global nature of problems such as pollution, disease and poverty, which therefore require cooperation across national boundaries; and second, the emergence of improved communications and transportation technology.[10] Organizations need to react organizationally to achieve success and are increasingly opting for decentralized and federated structures as the most viable for international advocacy work. Young therefore argues that, as with other types of international organization facing similar global contextual change (such as multinational corporations), international advocacy NGOs are increasingly grappling with the transnational issues of distance, language and culture. Young (1992) discusses three international NGO case studies: Nature Conservancy, International Physicians for the Prevention of Nuclear War and the Institute of Cultural Affairs. All have their roots in the USA but work internationally, and each has formed a loose 'federal structure' with networks of relatively autonomous units (analogous to a 'multi-headed hydra') rather than a formal, monolithic hierarchy. This is proving the most appropriate structure to accommodate competing demands, such as having to manage tensions between the need for coherence and unity while at the same time building and maintaining local autonomy and diversity.

Each NGO was found to depend heavily on a 'charismatic leader' at the early stages of its formation, but to be moving towards the replication of dynamic and visionary leadership at the local level in order to carry on the work. The organizations relied on a set of common values and beliefs about conservation, development and peace as the 'glue' which binds the organization together, and an organizational culture which values collegiality rather than material reward as the main incentive for staff performance. The levels of internal democracy in these organizations in terms of membership was found to be not particularly high, with quite low levels of participation and a certain amount of 'free-riding'. Instead, the NGOs tend to have 'privileged member' groups upon whom they rely for a disproportionate amount of support and work. Two at least are moving towards a decentralized structure with greater emphasis on local and regional concerns and autonomy.

Edwards (1993) has raised concerns that the advocacy work of Northern NGOs in achieving influence with powerholders and in educating their publics has been somewhat patchy. In Edwards's view, Northern NGO advocacy is a distinctive activity with ambitious aims and objectives which is tied in with these agencies' efforts to build partnerships in the countries where they work and change the 'rules of the game' in their own countries:

> [advocacy] . . . is an attempt to alter the ways in which power, resources and ideas are created, consumed and distributed at global level, so that people and their organizations in the South have a more realistic chance of controlling their own development.

> (Edwards 1993: 164)

This action may have two forms: first, influencing global processes such as world trade, or bringing about lifestyle changes among their own supporters and constituents; and second, influencing specific policies or projects. The former may be relatively public and confrontational – and therefore quite difficult to achieve – while the latter is less so and may be based on dialogue and information provision. Both of these activities are complementary, according to Edwards, but he suggests that many NGOs have failed to realize this and have been unable to build on available opportunities to combine local, national and international work. Clark (1992) points out that Northern NGOs have found some success with efforts to establish a baby milk marketing code, drafting a list of essential drugs and removing restrictions on trade for some items in favour of poor producers in developing countries. But according to Edwards (1993), many of the results have been disappointing and the potential has not been fulfilled due to the absence of clear strategy, a general failure to build on strong alliances, an inability to develop suitable alternatives to current orthodoxy, and the problem of 'room for manoeuvre' created by the relations with official donors which exist for many Northern NGOs. Such problems are also very real ones for NGOs elsewhere too. For example, in Armenia the PRSP process has been a reasonably inclusive one at the formal level, but since most participating NGOs remain heavily dependent on the major international bilateral and multilateral donors it is not surprising that they do not choose to voice critical views (Ishkanian 2006).

The Jubilee 2000 campaign arguably tells a brighter story, since this multi-sectoral alliance of church groups, NGOs, trade unions and other civil society groups has succeeded in generating considerable awareness among policy makers and publics about the problem of Third World debt, but ultimately failed to generate more than a small impact on the overall scale of the problem, which remains vast. Nevertheless, it created momentum built upon by the Make Poverty History campaign which secured further commitments to debt reduction. Edwards (1999b) later became more optimistic about NNGO advocacy work around the success of campaigns dealing with subjects such as 'sex tourism' and landmines because, unlike subjects such as environmentalism and women's rights, it has become possible to present these subjects powerfully both to the public and to policy makers, and link them to practical solutions.

Assessing advocacy progress

An important part of this advocacy effort has been directed towards the World Bank and other international institutions. Kardam's (1993) study examined progress in bringing about change towards policy reform within international organizations such as the World Bank, and identifies four factors as being crucial: the degree of relative independence of the organization within the context in which it functions; the amount and nature of external pressure for the new issue to be taken on board; the consistency of the new ideas with the target's organizational goals; and the extent of internal advocacy taking place within the international organization itself.

As we saw in Chapter 2, there has also been a growth of NGO participation at the series of global United Nations summits on issues such as the environment, social development, population and gender, both at the formal meetings (which have grown more open to NGO participation) and in the establishment of 'shadow summits' occurring alongside the main meeting which seek to influence what takes place. Van Rooy's (1997) influential analysis of two such summits seeks to analyse the impact of NGO efforts to influence processes and outcomes, at the 1974 World Food Conference and the 1992 Earth Summit. The findings are encouraging in that they show that NGO influence is possible, but they also highlight the need for NGOs to be realistic about what can and cannot be achieved through advocacy and lobbying work at these kinds of fora, which remain dominated by governments. Van Rooy suggests that NGO advocacy impact tends not surprisingly to be circumscribed by the sensitivity of the policy issue under discussion: for so-called 'high-salience' issues such as human rights, which may have major resource or security implications for governments, NGOs must wait until such issues are actually on an agenda for review if they wish to try to influence them, and will be unable to bring to bear power which will persuade governments to address them if no such process for review is yet in place. It is with what Van Rooy terms 'low policy' issues which do not threaten national security, are relatively cheap and easy to administer and are non-controversial (such as gender, social development, environment, changes to development practice) that NGOs can expect to achieve more impact on the policy process through lobbying.

There are therefore some important limitations to the NGO advocacy strategy. First, as Jenkins (1987: 314) acknowledges from the US context, it is difficult for not-for-profit advocacy efforts to counteract the influence of special interest groups such as the large corporations, which have enormous power in any capitalist society, and suggests instead that

'At best they can set up roadblocks that ensure consideration of a broader range of interests'. Rather it is the ability of NGOs to forge wider links with broad-based social movements or grassroots organizations that is likely to contribute to securing change. The campaigning in Europe by NGOs such as Greenpeace and Friends of the Earth in the late 1990s against corporations such as Monsanto (that sought the introduction of genetically engineered food crops) forged links with a wide range of community groups, NGOs and social movements at local and international levels, and presented a serious challenge to what might once have seemed to be an unproblematic moment of technological 'progress'.[11] Nevertheless, as Brown and Fox (2001) have shown, while these types of transnational civil society coalitions may be able to extract promises of reform from certain powerful interests, the challenge of securing lasting change and compliance will require NGOs to develop techniques for monitoring and imposing sanctions on non-compliance in the longer term.

Second, there is the question of NGO accountability and the problem of legitimacy – exactly whose views are NGOs representing, by what authority, and how accurate is the information that they are presenting? Doubts have been raised as to the ability of NGOs to convey complex scientific and technical issues which can easily be distorted to fit a particular ideological position, such as the environmentalist argument that biotechnology is harmful (*The Economist*, 29 January 1999). Third, there is the conceptual problem of developing a model of NGO advocacy solely in terms of the workings of Western liberal democratic states. In Peru, Diaz-Albertini (1993: 331) argues that Western theories about NGO and government relations regarding advocacy tend to assume a stable democracy and an 'institutionalized' state. The challenge for NGOs in many Latin American countries is not to improve services or challenge privatization, but to get the state to even accept that it has responsibility for welfare in the first place – the prevailing conditions of debt, political and bureaucratic corruption and inefficiency all combine to make even this basic acceptance of responsibility a rather remote possibility.

Finally, there is in the area of NGO advocacy a serious problem in judging effectiveness and impact. Covey's (1995) case study of an NGO advocacy alliance in Mexico revealed that in the end it was macro-economic issues which eventually made the proposed World Bank-funded forestry project unattractive to the government, rather than the NGO advocacy alliance which was secondary in its impact. In the case of the 1999 'Battle of Seattle', which some NGOs have claimed as a notable success in securing the abandonment of the World Trade Organization (WTO) trade liberalization negotiations, it has been argued with some plausibility by NGO insiders and commentators that the real reasons for failure lay elsewhere, for example with the inability of the United States and the European Union to agree with each other on the terms of trade reform.

We have seen from several examples discussed in this chapter, such as the work of Covey (1995) and Van Rooy (1998), that there can be different levels of impact from advocacy work. Developing a new approach to assess the impact of advocacy work was explored by Lewis and Madon (2003), drawing on case study material from an NGO in Bangladesh that has long been involved in advocacy work. A framework was generated during discussions with NGO staff and other stakeholders through which different levels of impact from advocacy work could be assessed according to a set of criteria (Table 5.1). Four types of impact were identified in this study: (1) the immediate outcome in terms of whether the overall

Table 5.1 *A framework for assessing NGO campaign impacts*

Activity	Immediate policy outcomes	Process policy outcomes	Organizational learning outcomes	Civil society outcomes
Campaign to remove dangerous illegally imported pesticides from the market	High	Low	Medium	High
Campaign to introduce wider consultation into national budgetary planning	Medium	Medium	High	High
Campaign to change forestry policy in favour of the rights of minority forest dwellers	High	High	Medium	Medium
Participation within a donor employment and business support project to try to shift the project towards a stronger poverty focus	Low	Low	High	Low
Participation within a civil society initiative to examine the poverty impact of World Bank structural adjustment policy and thereby influence the bank	High	Medium	Medium	Medium

Source: Lewis and Madon 2003.

aim of the campaign was met; (2) whether there were deeper rooted changes in the process of policy making over the longer term (such as a commitment to consult more broadly) or whether the result achieved was merely 'one-off' in nature; (3) the results in terms of an NGO's own learning about approaching its future advocacy work; and (4) whether wider relationships for future action amongst civil society actors have been strengthened, regardless of whether the campaign had been a success in terms of meeting its immediate goals.

This framework aims to disaggregate different kinds of advocacy impacts in the attempt to judge success, and could be developed further in many ways depending on the specifics of organization and context. However, its successful use will naturally depend upon the quality of the information systems that an NGO is able to build (see Chapter 7).

ROLE OF INNOVATION IN NGO MANAGEMENT

An ability to innovate is often claimed as a special quality, or even as an area of comparative advantage of NGOs over other kinds of organization, especially government agencies.

Innovation is arguably a central component of one of the key justifications of NGOs as purveyors of development alternatives (Mitlin *et al.* 2005). While there are many NGOs which do not see innovation as part of their activities, there is certainly ample evidence to support the claim that certain NGOs have been able to develop alternative approaches to poverty reduction. Innovation may be linked to the development of new technologies (such as the SALT technology in the Philippines referred to earlier in the chapter), creating new management practices (such as the Grameen Bank's credit model with its tightly structured village-based group system), or devising new planning and research methods (such as participatory rural appraisal or PRA).

How are some NGOs able to manage an innovative approach? Clark (1991: 59) argues that NGOs may be less constrained by orthodox ideas and structures than are mainstream aid agencies and governments. In an influential review of NGO activity around the world, he found evidence that their staff have considerable flexibility to experiment, adapt and try out new approaches to problem solving. There are several reasons for this in Clark's view: they may be smaller in scale, with fewer staff and formal structures, which can mean that decision making is a relatively straightforward process; local officials will not be very involved, which can reduce the level of administrative red tape; the level of outside scrutiny and regulation may be very low; and the ethos of 'voluntarism' may encourage individuals to develop their own ideas, experiment and take risks. In many of the 'reluctant partner' series case studies (Farrington and Lewis 1993) collected among agricultural NGOs in South Asia, it became apparent that NGO innovations are rooted in a problem- or issue-oriented approach to agricultural change: responding to opportunities and constraints identified by the rural poor. The case study in Box 5.4 highlights the continuing role of NGOs in supporting innovation systems that can address local development challenges in poor communities.

Aside from the availability of case study material which provides evidence for innovation by NGOs, there is comparatively little conceptual work around the issue of NGO innovation.[12] For such conceptual discussions, it is necessary to turn to the business and non-profit literatures. In the wider organizational literature, Amendola and Bruno (1990: 419) argued that innovation was 'a learning process which concerns both the firm and its environment and that results in deep changes for both of them'. In the non-profit literature, the British writer Perri 6 (1993) defines innovation as 'the introduction of changes in the production of goods and services' and presents a framework which distinguishes invention, innovation and diffusion as distinct parts of the innovation process. Drawing on the US literature on non-profits, Kanter and Summers's (1987) classic paper explored innovation in organizational terms:

> Innovation is a crucial element of an organization's effectiveness because it addresses the organization's potential to meet future demands, to take advantage of opportunities and resources within the environment, and to use resources (both human and material) to generate new products and services.
>
> (Kanter and Summers 1987: 161–2)

The authors present a case study of a US non-profit healthcare service organization, and show that innovation within an organization can be measured by conducting an audit of the

---

An NGO innovates a post-harvest processing system for small-scale Indian hill farmers

One form of innovation undertaken by an NGO working in India has involved combining research and intervention in ways that seek to combine continuous organizational learning with a recognition of institutional change in order to build improved sustainability. International Development Enterprises (IDE) was established in the late 1970s as an NGO with an interest in appropriate technology. However, what made it different was that it remained dedicated not just to developing appropriate technology but also to combining it with a business approach that would ensure users were able to adopt it sustainably within viable livelihood systems. Farmers in the North Indian state of Himachal Pradesh were searching for ways to market their tomato crop in high-value urban markets and identified post-harvest packaging as a key constraint. IDE was able to play a flexible role in researching potentially useful alternative packaging forms both internationally and locally through its partners and contacts, a trail that led to both public research institutes, a local NGO and private companies. A successful project was able to replace inappropriate wooden boxes with a locally produced cardboard packaging system in a way that has provided a sustainable low-cost solution to the farmers' business problem. IDE played 'a role that falls somewhere between the conventional mandate of public and private sectors, creating the initial conditions needed for the market to take over and provide services to rural households' (p. 1856). IDE's approach is therefore to try to support the emergence of new 'innovation systems' through a process of trust building and exhange within the wider system in which farmers and NGOs operate. IDE seeks to bring to the table skills in critical reflection and learning, facilitation and trust building, as well as team building and relationship-creating capacities.

Source: Clark *et al.* 2003.

---

organization's capacity to develop and implement new policies, new services, new organizational structures and new working methods. They also suggest a number of organizational factors which are likely to either encourage or constrain innovation, such as: support of middle managers by senior managers and the existence of appropriate rewards and incentives for experimentation and risk taking; collaborative mechanisms which can facilitate exchange and learning with other organizations; support from experts and other contacts outside the organization; and systems which can facilitate participation from beneficiaries and the wider community. Factors which discourage innovation within a non-profit organization were found to be active or passive resistance from colleagues, powerlessness in the form of an inability to command the necessary resources or technical information, and lack of reward for experimentation, such as performance-related pay.

This has led to a strong emphasis on innovation as a management challenge and to a set of high expectations about what NGOs can achieve. Hudson (1995), in his introduction to management in the UK voluntary sector, sees the encouragement of innovation as a key task

155

for managers, going almost far enough to suggest that successful innovation is the key to third sector survival:

> Chief executives have to encourage innovation: they have to ensure that the organization is constantly moving forward and finding ways to campaign and deliver services that meet new circumstances. It means searching for new ideas, sometimes from other countries, sometimes from local branches and sometimes from organizations in other fields. It means putting staff time and money into new ideas and acknowledging that while many will fail, a few will become the engine for the organization's future development.
>
> (Hudson 1995: 238)

Stern (1992) makes the point from the UK perspective that voluntary organizations become caught between the government's contracting and privatization policy and a range of pressing social needs, such that their room for manoeuvre is heavily circumscribed: in this situation innovation helps organizations to avoid becoming simply agents of service delivery for the state, and it is therefore crucial for their survival. This brings a distinctive view of voluntary sector evaluation in the current policy climate: rather than trying to develop new approaches and techniques, as voluntary organizations did in the earlier pioneering days of welfare state development in Britain, the challenge now is to innovate in order to ensure the continuing existence of a healthy voluntary sector as part of 'civil society', which is considered socially desirable as an end in itself.

The idealism of the 'NGOs as innovators' approach has inevitably generated scepticism in some quarters. As Clark (1991) points out, the claimed special strengths of NGOs in innovation capacity, such as voluntaristic style and small scale, is really doubled-edged, because the same points can be used to make the case for NGO amateurism, since it 'fosters idiosyncrasy, lack of continuity and poor learning abilities. It should also be said that many NGOs are far from innovative, but prefer to apply well-tested approaches to new constituencies' (Clark 1991: 59).

Some analysts have argued that far from being inherent, NGO innovativeness may derive instead from an organization's relationships with other agencies and with professionals working in other institutions (Kaimowitz 1993). Perhaps it is 'alliances' rather than 'products' which we need to examine with reference to NGO innovation. Biggs and Neame (1995) suggest that we must view with caution claims that NGOs have an inherent capacity to innovate: it is through building constructive links and networks that most innovations take place. NGOs therefore need to take care that their multiple linkages are maintained, since they are a source of strength.

It is clear therefore that innovation is not a prerequisite for success, and nor can it be regarded in any general sense as an innate characteristic of all NGOs. There are many cases of inept, amateurish NGOs which struggle on with out-of-date or discredited approaches to poverty reduction and welfare, while at the same time there are many NGOs doing perfectly useful work using tried and tested – though hardly innovative – methods. There are also problems associated with the policy pressures on some NGOs to come up with novel solutions to what amount to complex problems. In an article based on Zimbabwe and sustainable development in agriculture, Vivian (1994) identifies the problem of unrealistic donor and NGO supporter expectations leading to what she calls the 'magic bullet syndrome'. She sees the emphasis on simplicity and success as potentially counterproductive, since problems of poverty and development are not new problems and many individuals and agencies have long struggled with them. So keen have we been to find alternatives to the dismal record of development work overall that we have seized upon NGOs as an all-purpose solution.

Biggs and Neame (1995: 36) go further than Clark in casting doubt upon the idea that NGOs are especially good at innovating, and argue that the conventional wisdom simply does not stand up to scrutiny. In their view, the history of innovations by NGOs in agricultural research often relies on the professional involvement of universities, government research institutes and international agencies, or on individual practitioners in the field with little or no organizational affiliation to either governments or NGOs. It is the collaborative process which drives the appearance of innovation, rather than any inherent capability of NGOs themselves.

A key indicator of successful innovation is whether ideas and practices are taken up elsewhere, spread or replicated (Chambers 1992). For example, PRA has been adapted and further developed by NGOs such as MYRADA in India by inviting people from government and other NGOs to participate in field training meetings. Good ideas and experiences, says Chambers, tend to travel very fast, such as the idea of using farmers as extension agents which was pioneered by the US NGO World Neighbors (Bunch 1985) and has been adopted very widely across the world by a variety of agencies:

> This points to methodological innovation and the sharing of innovations as NGO activities which can have a very wide impact indeed. An NGO which develops an approach and method which then spreads can count that spread among the benefits from its work. A small NGO can, in such a manner, have a good impact vastly out of proportion to its size, especially if it shares open-handedly and builds in self-improvement. Indeed where small NGOs have successful innovations, they should consider their strategies to stress dissemination.
>
> (Chambers 1992: 46)

Chambers (1992: 46) argues that the scope for innovation and spreading innovations is also crucially linked to the organizational cultures of NGOs. Some remain 'bounded, possessive and territorial' and less likely to share, spread, adopt and improve than those which are 'open and undefended'. Although the process of spreading innovations and ideas can be 'degenerative' (such that innovations can become institutionalized and lose much of their power), if NGOs can manage the spreading process using careful monitoring and quality control then a measure of 'self-improving spread' can be achieved.

In more recent work, there has been an acknowledgement that for NGOs to play stronger roles within the broader and highly contested landscape of development ideas it is increasingly difficult, and simply not enough, for NGOs to just focus on generating new ideas. Instead, as Mitlin et al. (2005) argue, there is a pressing need for NGOs to focus more strongly on building relationships with other progressive actors such as political parties and social movements in order to maintain pressure for alternative outcomes in the face of an increasingly orthodox policy environment.[13] The relationships that NGOs need to build and manage are discussed in more detail in Chapter 6.

The discussion of innovation leads us on to consider the issues of evaluation, performance and 'scaling up'.

EVALUATION, IMPACT AND 'SCALING UP'

Despite the increased profile of the NGO sector and the growing resources it consumes and generates, the overall NGO contribution to reducing global poverty through service delivery and advocacy remains small and largely unproved. This section discusses the ways in which NGOs have attempted to improve their performance and effectiveness, and focuses on using the techniques of performance evaluation and the challenge of increasing impact through what has become known as strategies for 'scaling up' (Edwards and Hulme 1992). Yet of all the areas of NGO management, this remains one of the least developed and the least researched. As Lindenberg and Bryant (2001: 237) state regretfully in their detailed analysis of twelve prominent international NGOs' engagement with organizational transformation: 'In researching the NGOs on the topics covered in this chapter – more than on any other – it was striking to see how little is actually known about monitoring and evaluation systems in NGOs.'

There is a long history of approaches which seek to measure the effectiveness of development projects, from the mainstream planning tool of traditional cost – benefit analysis long used by the public and private sectors to the more recently fashionable 'stakeholder analysis' approach developed by some development institutions (Eade and Williams 1995; Gosling and Edwards 1995).[14] Yet there are arguably two quite surprising features of the NGO evaluation scene which become apparent from a reading of the literature. The first is the relative lack of attention which has been paid among NGOs in general, until quite recently, to the importance of evaluation as a tool for improving performance through learning and as a means of ensuring accountability. Instead, evaluation is frequently viewed as something which has been imposed upon NGOs by a funder or a government agency and therefore undertaken with reluctance or even resisted. As Smillie (1995) points out, many NGOs in the North and South have been reluctant to undertake evaluations because they lack the necessary tools or time, because they are not secure enough to face up to negative outcomes, or because evaluations are imposed by donors. The result has been a frequent 'failure to learn from failure' among the NGO community. The second is the fact that when NGOs have either undertaken or been subjected to evaluations, the information about their performance which has emerged has often been rather less flattering to the NGOs than many would assume from current received wisdom and public perceptions.

Evaluation is the term usually given to describe the process of assessing performance against objectives, and it can be contrasted with the activities of monitoring, which usually refers to the regular collection and analysis of data about the organization's ongoing activities, and the process of appraisal, which is the assessment of a proposed project or programme. As Riddell and Robinson (1995: 44) point out:

At their best, evaluation techniques should be able to assess performance results against objectives, and benefits against costs, and in so doing identify strengths and weaknesses in a way which can have a positive impact on the effectiveness of projects and programmes.

There are two main trends in the growth of interest in evaluation of NGOs. The first might be described as the technocratic, managerialist approach, in which evaluation is seen primarily as a means of control which can ensure accountability for the responsible management of donor funds and to confirm that the agreed activities have actually been undertaken. Such evaluations are frequently undertaken by donors as part of the funding relationship, or by the government which needs to know what it is that NGOs are doing. The tools which are deployed within such evaluations may include cost–benefit analysis, staff and beneficiary interviews, detailed financial audit, and the use of logical framework analysis which allows the measurement of progress by charting indicators against the objectives agreed before the beginning of the project or programme. The overall purpose may be the need to confirm that funds have been used properly, or to make a decision as to whether funding should be renewed for another period. This perspective on evaluation seeks to form an objective view of events which have taken place and tends to assume that given the 'right' approach to gathering information a relatively clear picture can emerge.

The second trend is the growth of the participatory evaluation tradition which has emerged from the wider growth of participatory development approaches associated with Chambers (1994, 2005) and others (Box 5.5). This approach tends to see evaluation in less objective, factual terms than as a 'combined judgement' which reflects the different perspectives of the different stakeholders involved and which requires a relatively long-term process view instead of a 'snapshot' of a particular moment. The second approach is the one which has more recently gained favour. However, the new participatory approaches lend themselves to criticism in two main areas: the first is that they are easily abused or co-opted into the top-down paradigm, while the second is the conceptual contradictions which can arise when distinctions are made between different kinds of knowledge, and the problem that these techniques can all too often mask differences of power, class and status (e.g. in the use of the term 'community').

Pressure for improved evaluation comes from internal and external sources. As bilateral and multilateral donors have increasingly funded development NGOs since the 1980s (Fowler 1997), there have been more stringent contractual demands placed upon NGOs for financial accountability and for the realization of agreed impacts. There is also a set of pressures which come from inside the NGO. Riddell and Robinson (1995) argue that evaluation is in the interests of NGOs because practical lessons can be fed back into decision making in order to improve future performance, and because by showing that funds are well spent, support can be strengthened and funding can be made more secure. Evaluation is the key to the 'learning organization' approach favoured by Korten (1990) and other writers on organizations (see Chapter 4).

Evaluations can operate at three different levels, as Marsden and Oakley (1990: 12–13) have outlined. The first is at the level of the donor agency (an NNGO or a funding agency), which is usually an 'external evaluation' in which evaluators are not themselves involved in

The rise of participatory monitoring and evaluation (PM&E)

The importance of taking local people's perspectives into account, the rise of organizational learning and the pressures for greater accountability have all contributed to the rise of PM&E as a means to improve the effectiveness of development intervention.

Advocates of this approach suggest a radical rethinking of conventional monitoring and evaluation work based on four broad principles:

1   opening up design and implementation to those affected (participation);
2   discussions with all stakeholders about data collection and analysis (negotiation);
3   using the evaluation as the basis for improvement and course correction (learning);
4   responding to changes in the overall group of stakeholders and the environment (flexibility).

An extensive toolbox exists for doing this, ranging from the use of conventional questionnaires and mapping techniques to the more open-ended and experimental collection of personal histories and the use of video for the presentation and discussion of ideas and viewpoints. Indicators for identifying and monitoring change are essential to PM&E, and this is a complex task which needs to balance local relevance with wider comparability, the involvement of stakeholders with the time available, and tangible with intangible changes (e.g. increased income as well as increased self-esteem). There are many problems which arise, such as the different interests between stakeholders which can lead to conflicts, and the need for managers and community members to be open to different points of view. In this approach, it is often necessary to work with informal forms of data collection and imperfect information, based on the idea that information only needs to be 'good enough' for the task at hand. In some situations, PM&E can be used alongside more conventional forms of M&E in order to supplement it.

Source: Guijt and Gaventa 1998.

the project implementation. The second is undertaken by the implementing rather than the funding agency (such as an SNGO) and this may take the form of a 'joint evaluation' involving both external evaluators and project staff. The third is the idea of the 'self-evaluation' which is undertaken by the so-called 'beneficiaries' themselves, usually with the participation of project staff, and perhaps drawing upon the services of an outside facilitator (Sen 1987).

According to Riddell and Robinson (1995: 50) judging NGO performance is more an 'art' than an exact science. The main reasons for this are, first, the difficulty of measuring 'social development' as opposed to economic development in that qualitative achievements cannot be evaluated objectively (Marsden and Oakley 1990; Harding 1991); second, the difficulty of building into evaluations the idea of 'process', because there is no 'correct' time at which assessment should be made (during the project, five years after?); and third, the attribution problem created by the fact that the changing wider social and economic context in which NGO activities take place can make it difficult to make an objective judgement about whether the NGO or some other factor has brought about an observed change. Fowler

(1997) therefore suggests a way forward by assessing NGO performance as 'combined social judgement' in which the uniting principle can be the structural engagement of multiple 'stakeholders'. Evaluation should therefore be seen as part of the NGO learning process, not as an externally imposed burden, and as part of a continuous process, not as an isolated event (Marsden and Oakley 1990).

Even when an NGO is improving its performance and accountability through the use of evaluation, it may be achieving little impact beyond the immediate community in which it works. Some NGOs have been content to take a 'small is beautiful' approach to their work, but awareness both of the limitations of a piecemeal approach to large-scale problems, and of the vulnerability of NGOs to criticism from development policy makers of simply tinkering around the edges of the problem of poverty, has led to the discussion of 'scaling up' strategies. This is a somewhat vague term, but Uvin (1995: 927) argues that it refers to attempts at 'increasing the impact of grassroots organizations and their programs'. A conceptual framework is provided by Edwards and Hulme (1992), who argue that there are three main types of scaling up which can be observed; the first is 'additive', in which an organization seeks simply to increase its size and the overall coverage of its programmes; the second is 'multiplicative', in which an organization attempts to gain more leverage and influence by ensuring that its ideas are put into practice by other development actors and therefore reach a greater number of the target population; and the third is 'diffusive', in which the NGO tries to transfer or spread its approaches beyond the organization's own immediate sphere of influence. There are four main strategies for achieving scaling up, and these are working with government (e.g. Parry-Williams 1992); linking the grassroots with lobbying and advocacy efforts in order to move beyond mere service delivery (Constantino-David 1992); advocacy work in the North in order to change the broad institutional and public frameworks in which resource allocations are made (Clark 1992); and finally the strategy of organizational growth which has seen a few NGOs grow rapidly in size and scope (Howes and Sattar 1992).

Just as the debates about the management of evaluation by NGOs have focused on cases of the imposed nature of NGO evaluation, there are also hazards on the road to scaling up. Dichter (1989b) has discussed the dangers for NGOs of what he terms the 'replication trap' – unrealistic pressure from donors or governments to develop easily replicable projects – and he emphasizes long-term institutional learning as the prerequisite for a scaling-up strategy. One of the best documented examples of NGO scaling up is Bangladesh's Grameen Bank, which is discussed widely in the literature. Rather than growing any larger as an implementing organization, it has instead encouraged replication and adaptation of its original micro-credit delivery model around the world. Hulme (1990) likens this to 'institution breeding', rather than replication, since it has worked best when the model has been carefully adapted by users to suit local conditions, rather than simply transferred wholesale from one context to another.

CONCLUSION

This chapter has reviewed the main activities undertaken by NGOs and has discussed some of the key management challenges raised, focusing selectively on two main types of activity which for many NGOs need not only to be managed singly but often in combination. A study from Peru by Dawson (1993) well illustrates the management challenges facing NGOs seeking to combine service delivery, policy advocacy and innovation. Each NGO in her study tried to set up an innovative model of community service provision which might, by example, influence policy making. Although there were some notable successes, there were a number of factors which hindered successful policy influence: local authorities undergoing expenditure reductions and therefore unable to assume new expenses incurred in the NGO proposals; the tendency of government to view NGOs and their efforts to strengthen community participation and organizations as political opposition. As well as internal organizational factors, the environment in which the NGOs operate proved to be a crucial variable. For these innovations to influence wider policy, they needed to be consistent with national or regional tendencies, in an environment which is relatively stable, peaceful and free from natural disasters. Another prerequisite was found to be a stable government with an interest in long-term development rather than in short-term electioneering. From the point of view of NGOs themselves, the study found that to be successful, NGOs require a broad level of recognition in society, and they must be able to analyse and disseminate results from their work.

The service delivery and advocacy roles each require NGOs to develop appropriate structures which both 'get the work done' as well as conforming with the NGOs' own values and priorities. NGO management is also concerned with the question of improving performance, which requires evaluation and increasing impact, and which has led to the new strategies for 'scaling up'. For example, the Bangladesh Rural Advancement Committee (BRAC) has developed a 'flat organizational structure', as Lovell (1992) has outlined, as well as striving to put in place structure and culture which will facilitate a process of organizational learning. The Grameen Bank has developed a model of service delivery which innovates both at the level of the grassroots group (which builds strong peer group accountability in order to ensure loan repayment) and at the organizational level, using a combination of controlled values and vision, but with a looser, more decentralized approach to implementation which allows considerable autonomy at the field level (Holcombe 1995). As a relatively new area of professional activity, NGO management therefore requires both the evolution of distinctive new approaches to problem-solving as well as the borrowing and adaptation of techniques and ideas from other areas of management. Issues of scaling up and evaluation have become central to NGO management, and draw on a combination of internal innovation and external learning and adaptation.

REVIEW QUESTIONS

- Is Fowler fair in his criticism of NGOs that stick to service delivery as against seeking strategies for advocacy?
- How can advocacy NGOs address critics who complain that it is not clear on whose behalf or in whose interests such NGOs are campaigning?
- How can NGOs combine the need for effective evaluation to judge their own performance with the demands from outside stakeholders for information?

Chapter 6

NGOs and the management of relationships

LEARNING OBJECTIVES

After considering this chapter, the reader will be able to describe and analyse:

- Key relationships that are vital to NGO management, along with the challenges of accountability
- Main areas of recent and current changes within the wider environment in which NGOs operate
- A set of critical perspectives on the concept of 'partnership' between NGOs and with other types of organization

KEY TERMS

- Strategic management
- Accountability
- Community
- Social capital
- Partnership
- Active/dependent partnership
- Fair trade
- Corporate social responsibility

INTRODUCTION

This chapter examines the issue of managing relationships as the second main area of NGO management. In keeping with the conceptual framework presented in Chapter 1 (Figure 1.1), these relationships also need to be understood in relation to a broader context. Fowler (1997) argues that NGOs are not closed systems with clear boundaries around them, but are instead part of 'open systems'. This makes NGOs highly dependent on events and resources in their environment, so that they cannot be viewed in isolation from what goes on around them. As we saw in Chapter 5, Biggs and Neame (1995: 39) highlighted the danger of viewing NGOs simply as 'sources' of innovation or improved service delivery. Instead, we should pay close attention to the fact that whatever creativity NGOs may bring to the table can derive in large part from the relationships which they seek to maintain with a wide range of other actors and agencies through their participation in 'formal and informal networks and coalitions involving other NGOs, government agencies and the private sector'. This insight implies that it will be useful to review the range, nature and purposes of such relationships. We will therefore examine each relationship in turn by briefly discussing NGO relationships with local communities, with government, with business and with other development agencies.

It is first necessary to establish a conceptual framework in which such relationships can be analysed. As we saw in Chapter 1, the concept of the triangle of state, market and civil society is one useful tool for understanding the management of NGO relationships (Brown and Tandon 1994; Turner and Hulme 1997; Wood 1997). Yet this triangle can only be usefully conceived as being located within a specific political, institutional and historical context. The civil society space in say, China, where the state is dominant and strong, is a far smaller and more constrained one than that say in Brazil or India. Contextual analysis is an essential element in de Graaf's (1987) 'strategic management' framework. De Graaf draws upon ideas from organization theory developed by Smith *et al.* (1980) to show that NGOs, in addition to managing events and processes within the boundaries of their own organizational set-up, need also to understand and influence the wider organizational environment which lies beyond their immediate field of operation:

> The environment is crucial for NGOs because unlike commercial organizations which can measure their success in terms of activities and their immediate results (i.e. production, sales and profits) NGOs must perceive and assess the implementation of their plans within the context of external dimensions.
>
> (de Graaf 1987: 285)

The NGO environment can therefore be seen as having two dimensions: one which consists of factors which lie largely within the span of an NGO's control, while the other consists of processes shaping the wider environment over which an organization has proportionately less control.

A FRAMEWORK FOR MANAGING RELATIONSHIPS

We can represent some of these ideas in diagrammatic form in terms of the three concentric circles set out in Figure 6.1. The first circle contains factors which can be *controlled* by the NGO, in terms of staffing, budgeting, planning specific activities, setting objectives or choosing an organizational structure. The second circle encapsulates elements of the environment which can be *influenced* or even changed by an NGO, by processes of persuasion, lobbying, patronage, co-option and collaboration. These include, for example, elements of government policy, the activities of an international donor or the agenda of a UN summit meeting. The third circle contains aspects which can – at a particular moment – only be *appreciated* by the NGO, such as wider political structures, the macro-economic system, the technological environment and the international dimensions of context. There is no assumption made here that the elements found in the third circle are never open to change by an NGO (or by a movement in which an NGO may take part), but the model expresses the idea that NGOs need to prioritize strategies based on opportunities and constraints if they are to be effective. This final circle can also be understood to include the process and relationships which may need to be 'read' but which cannot easily be predicted (Kaplan 1999). The value of this framework is that it allows an NGO to develop a strategic approach to management in which priorities can be set and resources allocated, while still keeping a watchful eye on the 'big picture' within which the NGO operates. Furthermore, it is a

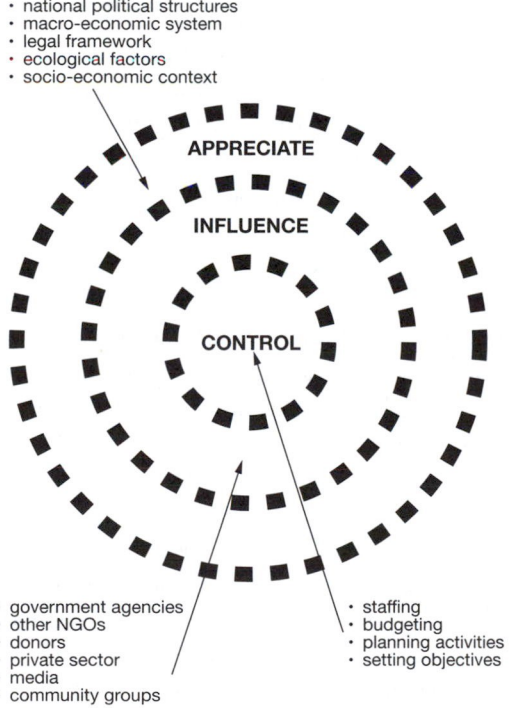

- national political structures
- macro-economic system
- legal framework
- ecological factors
- socio-economic context

APPRECIATE

INFLUENCE

CONTROL

- government agencies
- other NGOs
- donors
- private sector
- media
- community groups

- staffing
- budgeting
- planning activities
- setting objectives

Figure 6.1 *A framework for strategic NGO management*

Source: adapted from de Graaf 1987.

dynamic framework in which NGOs can both seek out opportunities to influence change, as well as react to shifts in wider economic and political processes. For example, an NGO which is normally engaged in service delivery may, based on its reading of the environment, decide at a particular moment – such as after a change of government, the appointment of a new minister or during a period of media publicity relating to a particular issue – that an opportunity to lobby the government over a particular issue should be exploited. NGOs both influence, and are influenced by, their wider environment.

The boundaries around these three areas are neither permanent nor clear-cut, but will change from time to time as an organization gains more influence over parts of an environment, such as when the NGO increases its lobbying work, manages to attract more funds or when it enters a new coalition with other organizational actors. At other times, the environment itself may alter as a result of wider political or economic processes, which may then allow more opportunity for an NGO that is alert to begin to exercise greater influence or, conversely, the 'closing off' of the organizational and political space in which NGOs work. The case given in de Graaf's paper is that of newly independent Zimbabwe in 1980, which brought political changes that gave more opportunities for NGOs to work with the government than they had had before, but at the same time tightened the laws and rules concerning the regulation of NGO activities. Dramatic changes of a similar nature took place in 1986 in the Philippines after the fall of the Marcos dictatorship, and in many countries of the former Soviet bloc which have undergone rapid changes in their wider political and economic frameworks. The NGO environment does not stand still for long, however. At the time of writing in early 2006, one of the oldest NGOs established in Russia in 1990 immediately after the fall of the Soviet Union, the Russian Human Rights Research Centre, was facing a crackdown by the government which fears that human rights NGOs have become a front for political opposition and foreign interests.[1]

De Graaf's critique of the common NGO management approach is that organizations concentrate disproportionately on the factors under their control – such that leaders and managers tend to prioritize deciding and implementing internal plans, personnel, budgets and procedures – at the expense of monitoring and considering the factors which have enormous importance for NGO programmes and activities, but over which they have only the weaker power of influence or the need for appreciation. The success or failure of a development NGO therefore depends largely on its ability to influence its environment and appreciate outside forces correctly, and NGOs are more dependent on these external factors than most other organizations. Some NGOs can ignore the outside world and may begin to turn inwards, seeking to bring beneficiaries under their control rather than supporting people's efforts to gain access to wider resources and build greater levels of self-sufficiency and autonomy. De Graaf sees the way forward in terms of a 'strategic management' perspective which can increase NGO awareness of the importance of combining and balancing its control, appreciation and influence of its environment. In terms of our original conceptual framework on NGO management that was presented in Chapter 1 (Figure 1.1), de Graaf's perspective draws attention back to the crucial interrelationship between activities, organization and relationships undertaken by an NGO and the wider context in which all three take place.

For example, an expansion of an NGO's appreciative capacity can be achieved through a better focus on the economic, social, political and cultural contexts which shape the lives of its clients, and this may bring a greater realism to NGO programmes. Linkages with specialized institutions such as universities can prove useful in this regard. The need to improve influence (what Fowler (1997) calls 'leverage') has obvious benefits in terms of reducing an organization's 'romantic isolation', so that it can learn from other lessons and experiences, seeking a new resource base which may lead it to reduce its dependence upon its funders, and improved levels of impact through synergies with other NGOs, with government agencies and selective lobbying. The model of strategic NGO management emphasizes the organization, its environment and its intended product as three interrelated entities:

> The essential challenge in NGO management lies in maintaining and exploring the fine balance between recognition and change, between sufficient integration with its environment to be efficient and sufficient distance from it to be effective.
>
> (de Graaf 1987: 297)

The second key element to a discussion of NGO relationships is that of accountability, a relational concept which has been presented as both a potential strength and a source of weakness for NGOs. One widely used definition is: 'Accountability is generally interpreted as the means by which individuals and organizations report to a recognised authority (or authorities) and are held responsible for their actions' (Edwards and Hulme 1995:9). It is a source of strength because, as Biggs and Neame (1995) have shown, it is precisely the wide range of relationships and contacts which NGOs maintain and must respond to which allows them to generate a creativity based on multiple perspectives and a balance of different interests. Yet as Hulme and Edwards (1997) also show, the lack of attention paid by NGOs to questions of accountability and the dangers of over-accountability to government or donors at the expense of 'downward' or 'sideways' accountability to clients and beneficiaries, and other third sector organizations, can also be understood to be the 'Achilles heel' of the NGO movement. Furthermore, the understanding of accountability provided in the definition above does not adequately explain the need for NGOs to ensure that they are accountable to the people on whose behalf they are working – the idea of a 'recognised authority' suggests only official mechanisms.

As NGOs have grown in scale and scope there has been a growing debate concerning the question of accountability. In a sense this is a fairly straightforward technical question because most NGOs are accountable to some kind of voluntary body (a board of trustees or governors) who derive no financial gain from the organization and have no ostensible financial interest. NGOs which are membership organizations are directly accountable to their members, who elect a governing body. All NGOs are also accountable under the relevant laws of a particular country where they operate, and, in theory at least, the state has powers to intervene if they transgress laws relating to accounting, rules of bureaucratic procedure and registration obligations. The reality is rarely so simple for NGOs because they have multiple stakeholders and are accountable in different and complex ways to a variety of different groups and interests. Edwards and Hulme (1995) show that NGOs face demands for two principal types of accountability, the first being functional accountability (short term,

167

such as accounting for resources, resource use and immediate impacts), and the second strategic accountability (accounting for the impacts that NGO actions have more widely and on other organizations). This makes accountability a complex challenge for NGOs. Rochester (1995) has suggested that voluntary organizations in the UK have far more complex problems of accountability than do private sector or public sector agencies, and this observation can be applied to development NGOs more widely.

Leat (1988) outlines three levels of third sector accountability. In the case of 'full accountability' there is a right to demand an account from an NGO and then impose a penalty if it is not forthcoming, such as the withdrawal of funding. This type of accountability has become a dominant feature of the NGO world because it has been associated with the growing concerns of funders to ensure that NGOs use resources efficiently and for the purposes agreed. This trend has also drawn criticism, however, because financial accountability of this kind is only one element of the complex 'bundle' of accountabilities to which an NGO must respond. The second category is that of 'explanatory accountability', which means that an organization needs to respond to a call for account with information and explanation, but the only sanction applicable if this is not forthcoming is one of disapproval. This is the type of accountability which an NGO might face when it seeks to work with local authorities within a loose framework of informal cooperation and coordination. The third type is that of 'responsive accountability', where there is no formal sanction at all but which runs instead on trust and good faith. When, for example, an NGO claims to be accountable to the wishes of a particular section of the community, the truth of such a claim depends on the willingness of the agency to take this into account, rather than on any real ability of the community to exercise effective power over the organization. Accountability is important at the level of the organization because an NGO's legitimacy depends upon it. Without this accountability, for example, Southern NGOs will find it difficult to mobilize funds from within their own societies and reduce dependency on international funding channels, and Northern NGOs will find it hard to win the support of official donors who may wish to fund them. NGO claims to legitimacy are often based on the strength of their accountability to 'the poor', but the reality for many NGOs is that this area of 'responsive accountability', which lacks sanctions or accountability mechanisms, may be the weakest link of all.

There may never be perfectly accountable NGOs or other organizations. Fox (1992), for example, has shown that in many public and private agencies both leaders and subordinates seek generally to avoid accountability. But when accountability falls below a certain level, the likelihood of ineffectiveness or illegitimate actions is likely to increase (Edwards and Hulme 1995). According to Jan Pronk (in Hellinger *et al.* 1988), the main danger for NGOs in the future is that of 'corruption', defined not just narrowly in terms of financial scandal, but in broad terms of the drift away from NGOs' mission for social transformation. The wider policy environment of the 'new policy agenda' may have offered considerable opportunities to NGOs, but there may also be the dangers of co-optation and goal deflection. This danger has become arguably more acute in the post 9/11 era of 'the war on terror' where Western governments may demand specific loyalty to foreign policy objectives as a condition of funding (Howell 2006b).

Accountability, like evaluation (discussed in Chapter 5), is often seen by NGOs themselves as something unwillingly imposed upon them from outside. While this may sometimes be the case (and is of course necessary), the establishment of strong internal accountability systems are vital for the health of any third sector organization. These are needed for their own sake because, as Edwards and Hulme (1995) point out: 'Performing effectively, and accounting transparently, are essential components of responsible practice, on which the legitimacy of development intervention ultimately depends.' Essential to this process is the need for NGOs to manage their 'multiple accountabilities' rather than to have these account-abilities eroded by allowing only one line of accountability – such as to funders – to dominate within the accountability 'bundle'. In the balancing of multiple accountabilities, every NGO faces organizational tensions which require effective management if over- or under-accounting is to be avoided in key areas of NGO relationships.

There have been several efforts in the direction of improved NGO self-regulation in recent years in the form of 'codes of conduct'.[2] The Philippines Caucus of Development NGO Networks (CODE-NGO) network established in 1991 was one of the first attempts to create a development NGO code of practice at the national level, setting out a clear set of principles for NGO accountability and transparency (Sidel 2005). Other initiatives of this kind have come from the NGO humanitarian context, such as the *Code of Conduct for International Red Cross and Red Crescent Movement and NGOs in Disaster Relief* (IFRC 1997), the *People in Aid Code of Best Practice in the Management and Support of Aid Personnel* (ODI 1997), and the Sphere Project 'Humanitarian Charter and Minimum Standards' document (IFRC 1999). These codes are considered by many governments, donors and NGOs as a valuable step forward, but it remains difficult for such codes to be enforced across all organizations. The development of appropriate sanctions mechanisms is one possible response to this problem. For example, Box 6.1 summarizes an initiative by One World Trust which explores the need for complaints procedures systems as a mechanism of last resort for accountability within NGOs, for the benefit of staff and clients.

There have also been larger-scale attempts to regulate organizations, such as the American Competitiveness and Corporate Accountability Act of 2002, commonly known as the Sarbanes-Oxley Act, which was passed partly in response to corporate scandals in the United States such as that of the Enron energy company. The act sets out strengthened measures to safeguard auditors' independence from their clients and creates a new entity that can enforce audit standards. It also makes it a crime to destroy litigation-related documents, and affords new protection to whistleblowers. Although this act is primarily concerned with the regulation of for-profit businesses and only applies to publicly traded corporations, some argue that its principles of new governance standards may also serve as 'a wake-up call to the entire nonprofit community'.[3] According to the GuideStar website (www.guidestar.org), there are already non-profit organizations in the USA who have voluntarily begun implementing elements of Sarbanes-Oxley by creating new audit committees and procedures.

Sidel (2005) warns in a wide-ranging review of self-regulation initiatives around the world that there are dangers both from over-zealous self-regulation by NGOs, and from the more intrusive forms of government regulation such as schemes for certification or accreditation. Meeting a heavy level of bureaucratic top-down accountability criteria could easily draw NGO energies away from their work and sap their potential for innovation and creativity:

Improving accountability through self-regulation: complaint and redress mechanisms for NGOs

Work at One World Trust to establish a Global Accountability Framework has identified four main areas of NGO accountability: transparency, participation, evaluation and 'complaints and redress' (C&R). This latter dimension has to date received very little attention in the NGO world. While other more familiar mechanisms will ensure accountability under normal circumstances, C&R is identified as an important mechanism of 'last resort' which can ensure that both internal and external stakeholders can ensure that any complaints about an NGO's operations are reviewed and acted upon. As such it is an important element of NGO self-regulation. But a review of existing procedures found that even in NGOs where there was a C&R mechanism there was a lack of clarity on what constituted a complaint 'against whom' or 'against what standards', and on the procedure for filing and processing such complaints. The resulting guidelines developed by One World Trust for this purpose suggest a new framework for a workable C&R policy. Five principles are set out: (1) the need for complaints to be made confidentially, (2) assurance that the complainant will not be retaliated against, (3) making information about the procedure readily available to all stakeholders, (4) making it straightforward for a complaint to be filed and (5) ensuring that any learning from the complaint is fed back into the organization. Significant challenges include the capacity to determine relevant or valid complaints, making the mechanism as independent as possible from the organization and ensuring access to the mechanism for the weakest and most vulnerable stakeholders.

Source: Commonwealth People, published by the Commonwealth Foundation, April 2005. Further details of the initiative can be found at www.oneworldtrust.org

best practices or 'weak codes' may in fact be all that is needed to keep most nonprofits on a straight and narrow path, along with a stronger backbone on the part of key nonprofit and philanthropic umbrella organizations to criticize clearly inappropriate activities of their peers, and perhaps a stricter set of rules reserved for those organizations receiving substantial government funding or those engaged in clearly quantifiable and rankable activities. In seeking to forestall or ameliorate government's occasionally strong impulses towards stricter regulatory plans, we must take care that the harder forms of self-regulatory solutions do not do nearly as much damage as well.

(Sidel 2005: 835)

NGO RELATIONS WITH COMMUNITIES

This section looks at the different ways in which NGOs need to manage relationships with people, and takes as its starting point the discussions in Chapter 5 about empowerment and participation, through which NGOs have tried to build sustainable development interventions.

Many NGOs form direct relationships with sections of local communities, as in the case, for example, of an organization which delivers services to a marginalized group of people (such as landless rural women) or one which attempts to build the organizational capacity of a neighbourhood organization. Some NGOs seek a less direct relationship with local communities but attempt to represent their interests in undertaking advocacy work, or attempt to work within broader definitions of the public interest. Other NGOs seek to influence sections of the community, such as those working for development education in the North. Whichever the approach, most NGOs claim to be accountable to wider communities, and claim legitimacy on the basis of this accountability.

One of the main problems with the concept of community is its impreciseness, and there are those who find the frequency with which community is invoked by NGOs deeply suspicious. In the 1980s the Bangladeshi NGO BRAC undertook research on the power structure of ten local villages and produced its influential study of *The Net*, which exploded the myth that villages were socially cohesive and relatively egalitarian communities (BRAC 1983). This myth had been embodied in earlier development efforts by the government to organize 'farmers' cooperatives' in rural areas that had quickly become dominated by the rich and which excluded the poor. BRAC found that NGO efforts (including their own) to provide material and organizational resources for low-income households were systematically undermined by local elites who captured these resources and imposed powerful constraints on efforts to bring about changes with the poor. Division and conflict between landowners and landless villagers, men and women and patrons and clients, all added up to a complex working environment which NGOs needed to negotiate with care and with the use of detailed local knowledge. The 'myth of community' has come under attack from feminist scholars and activists who argue that the concept is unhelpful because it masks in most societies important areas of difference in gender and power (Guijt and Shah 1998). *The Net* has remained an influential analysis for those seeking to analyse and intervene in rural Bangladesh, although there are signs that more room for manoeuvre for action may be appearing as older elites lose power to emerging middle classes (Lewis and Hossain 2004).

In addition to the debates about empowerment and participation which have been evident in relation to NGOs, interest among policy makers in the concept of 'social capital' has potentially useful implications for NGO management. The concept of social capital can be related to the efforts of some NGOs to work towards the strengthening of local organizational structures in the form of group building, and to the efforts of sections of the community to organize themselves into membership NGOs. Cross-cutting ties based on trust and reciprocity between organized individuals can offer a challenge to the relationships of subordination, exploitation and oppression highlighted in studies such as *The Net*, which illustrated how village-level resources in Bangladesh were appropriated by a powerful local elite (BRAC 1983). Yet social capital is understood differently by different social scientists, as we saw in Chapter 2. In the context of the present discussion, Coleman's view is useful because it refers to changing relationships between people which make possible forms of action:

> Just as physical capital is created by changes in materials to form tools that facilitate production, human capital is created by changes in persons that bring about

> skills and capabilities that make them able to act in new ways . . . social capital is less tangible yet, for it exists in the relations between persons. . . . For example, a group within which there is extensive trustworthiness and extensive trust is able to accomplish much more than a comparable group without that trustworthiness and trust.
>
> (Coleman 1988: 19)

Apart from the basic delivery of services, NGO roles in supporting local sustainable development initiatives centre on the attempt to strengthen social capital. For example, traditional rotating credit groups exist in many societies, in which trust between members makes possible the undertaking of group savings and loan schemes as a form of self-help initiative by small, locally formed membership NGOs (Chhetri 1995). These may in turn be supported by outside NGOs and can be used as the basis for new work, such as skills training or Freirean 'conscientization'. There are many NGOs, such as the Grameen Bank or BRAC, which seek to build new groups, forms of social capital, which will provide a stable and accountable set of local structures for micro-credit provision and other services.

There is a whole raft of problems which have been raised in connection with the ways in which NGOs have attempted to build relationships at the community level. Carroll (1992) highlights the dangers of overstatement among NGOs and their supporters regarding the scale and extent to which NGOs have managed to build sustainable structures among communities of the poor. In another study from Latin America, Arellano-Lopez and Petras (1994) have argued that in Bolivia, where outside NGOs have linked with local free-standing grassroots groups and movements, NGOs may have actually weakened the structures for local action and autonomy by bringing people into conventional donor-funded 'poverty alleviation' activities. Another frequent area for criticism is the tendency for some NGOs to 'hold onto' groups for too long without withdrawing so that there can be sustainable, autonomous group action (Carroll 1992: 113; Lewis and Siddiqi 2006). Howes (1997) demonstrates the need for NGOs to promote membership organizations which can be self-sustaining after NGO withdrawal, but notes the rareness of this actually taking place. Finally, the 'dark side of social capital' (Putzel 1997) has been documented by those who argue that organized local action is not always a force for 'good', and may reflect precisely the kinds of subordination, narrow self-interest or intolerance that an NGO programme may be seeking to challenge. Nevertheless, the value of the social capital concept, as Bebbington (2004: 348) has suggested, is that it represents 'an attempt to understand the social and cultural dimensions of development processes'.

NGO RELATIONS WITH GOVERNMENT

We have already touched on the importance of managing relationships with government in the discussion of service delivery and advocacy in Chapter 5. There have been a number of approaches to understanding the state with the study of social policy. The 'public interest' view of the state which was prevalent in the 1950s and the 1960s, in which it was believed that society has a set of common interests which can be identified and served by the state, has gradually been discredited, as Mackintosh (1992) has argued. The critique of this view from the left argues that there is a lack of identifiable common interest in society due to the fragmentation of interests produced by class, ethnicity, gender and age, and that the state mainly exists to serve the interests of the middle class and of commerce. The neo-liberal critique of the state centres instead on the likelihood of officials to act in their own, rather than common, interests, and the tendency of bureaucratic structures to obstruct rather than facilitate development initiatives.

The work of Chambers (1994) advances a reformist view of the state based on the need to 'reverse' the conventional relationships that exist between professionals and clients, age and authority, and masculinity and femininity. Chambers's view is one of building the 'enabling' state, such that the government carries out the essential tasks of maintaining peace and the rule of law, basic infrastructure and services, and manages the economy effectively. Generalizations about the nature of states are probably unwise, since most states are not monolithic and, as some have argued, may be losing power and influence under the processes of globalization. Indeed, some argue that NGOs are part of a wider process of the neo-liberal restructuring of governance relationships in which states also see NGOs as flexible tools for maintaining or extending their power (Fisher 1997). As Ferguson and Gupta (2002: 990) have suggested:

> The outsourcing of the functions of the state to NGOs and other ostensibly nonstate agencies, we argue, is a key feature, not only of the operation of national states, but also of an emerging system of transnational governmentality.[4]

It is clear that most NGOs are faced with a set of difficult questions in managing their relationship with the government. A collection of writing on NGOs in Africa characterizes African NGOs including in Kenya, Tanzania and Zimbabwe as being caught 'between a rock and a hard place': between the governments that feel threatened by their activities on the one hand, and by the development donors with their changing priorities and unrealistic expectations on the other (Igoe and Kelsall 2005).

Most NGOs realize that their impact will be limited unless they form wider links, with one important option being a link with government. As de Graaf (1987) has shown in his conceptual framework, the management of relationships with the state is an important element of overall strategy for most NGOs. Although there are cases of NGOs avoiding any kind of relationship at all with the state by 'lying low', or through working with communities in remote localities, Clark's (1991) assertion that NGOs can oppose, complement or reform the state but they cannot ignore it, remains an important insight. As we saw in Chapter 3, some analysts have made the point that NGOs themselves cannot be effectively understood without reference to the governments which they seek to work with or to struggle against, and the very label 'non-governmental organization' may lead us to examine what it is about the state that the NGOs are so keen to dissociate themselves from.

There are therefore major challenges for NGOs in developing strategy in relation to government. Many NGOs have an ambivalent attitude to the state, and those organizations which were formed under conditions of political repression may find it difficult to trust or work with government, even when it has changed. On the other hand, NGOs which have their roots in struggles against repressive states, such as in South Africa or in Palestine, may

173

then find that their roles are less clear once a more accountable, democratic government has been installed. NGOs may indeed be perceived by government as a threat or as competitors. Even when democracy is in place it may be fragile, and government may still be bureaucratic and inefficient, which can make formal contact hazardous for the NGO. If NGOs decide to work together actively with the state, the risk is that they could themselves become less effective (because they may enter into more bureaucratic ties and arrangements) and that the relationships 'downwards' to their community-level groups will be damaged.

NGOs adopt several strategies in relation to government. First, they can seek to maintain a low profile by working in the 'spaces' which exist in government provision, sometimes with tacit government acknowledgement or letting government take credit for what is achieved by the NGO. This gap-filling role may bring short-term benefits, as we saw in Chapter 5, particularly when resources are severely limited, but can raise problems of sustainability and accountability in the longer term. Second, NGOs can engage in selective collaboration with certain government agencies, which may be restricted to a particular sector, or may be based on individual relationships between personnel or local-level links which may not have formal government backing. This strategy has the merit of pragmatic thinking, but may lead to haphazard inconsistencies in policy and implementation. The final stance which NGOs may take is that of policy advocacy, in which the organization acts as a pressure group in support of the interests of certain groups, or demonstrates alternatives to the government's own approaches along the lines suggested by Najam and discussed earlier.

NGOs' efforts to try to improve the accountability of government to citizens has taken an interesting turn in parts of India with the rise of the 'right to information' movement. For example, the potential for NGOs to strengthen accountability between communities and public officials is well illustrated by an unusual group in the state of Rajasthan. A small and well-connected activist group known as Mazdoor Kisan Shakti Sangathan (MKSS) has been working to improve the right of access of ordinary citizens to information held by public officials in rural areas. In particular, the organization began to address problems in the public distribution system that prevented government-subsidized essential goods and public works schemes benefiting the people for whom they were intended. By gaining access to some public records through petitioning a small number of sympathetic public officials, MKSS was able to begin to match stated resource allocations with actual sales and distribution, and uncovered levels of fraud ranging from $2,500 to $12,500 per village in 'missing' resources. The group has successfully organized 'public hearings' in which detailed information is read out to villagers and elected government officials are invited to attend and account for any discrepancies. In a few cases, resources have been returned to villagers by shamed officials. More significantly, by involving sympathetic members of the Indian administrative service in exposing corruption in this way, the pressure for state government reforms to provide better access to information in order to improve transparency and accountability in relation to public goods is gaining momentum (Jenkins and Goetz 1998). An example from Delhi is presented in more detail in Box 6.2.

However, a close relationship with the state can also bring identity problems and organizational tensions within the NGO, if it has grown up with opposition to government as a key plank of strategy. In Chile, Bebbington and Thiele (1993) describe how some NGOs have moved from an opposition stance to the roles of constructive critic and innovator, and

Confronting corruption: an NGO uses the Delhi Right to Information Act

In 2001, the State Government of Delhi passed the Right to Information Act, which made it incumbent upon government departments to publicly account for their actions and policies. Satark Nagrik Sangathan (SNS), a citizens group disseminating information about food security entitlements in slum settlements of South Delhi, began actively using the act to gain access to public records pertaining to the distribution of state-subsidized food and fuel meant for low-income households.

SNS concentrated their activities in five slum areas where low-income residents had not received their food and fuel rations for over five years. The government-appointed distribution shops had refused to sell rations to designated ration card holders on the pretext that they had not received the rations from the state. Most of these card holders were from households who could not afford two square meals a day, let alone buying food and fuel in the open market.

SNS repeatedly approached the State Food and Civil Supplies Department at various levels, from the local public distribution system inspector, whose job it was to ensure ration distribution in the area, to the food commissioner, who sat at the head of the department. When no action was taken, SNS applied for access to the records of two distribution shops under the act, on behalf of the local residents. These records revealed that despite having regularly received highly subsidized foodgrain intended for sale to poor households, the shop owner had been selling it on the market for the past five years! Not only were the most vulnerable being deprived of their food entitlements, it was a loss to the system to the tune of several million rupees.

SNS therefore organized a *jan sunvai* (public hearing) to address the various issues they had uncovered. About 400 largely women slum dwellers gathered at a local community centre. The hearing was attended by the shop owners, the departmental officials, other NGOs and the press, and was presided over by a panel comprising members of the National Campaign for People's Right to Information and the adviser to the Supreme Court on Food Security. The shop owner apologized publicly, but the people demanded legal action against him. They also demanded a departmental inquiry and that action be taken against the PDS (public distribution system) inspector and other officials concerned. The residents called for systemic changes such as the availability of rations at the beginning of the month, when salaries had been received, as well as the setting up of local vigilance groups to ensure proper distribution of rations.

This hearing was important because it voiced the concerns of vulnerable and marginalized people, and highlighted the positive role played by women in securing the household's food entitlements. Further, it provided a viable urban model for the *jan sunvai*, with a tightly knit and focused agenda and a time-bound schedule. Previously, such hearings in rural settings had often been lengthy and rambling affairs, involving multiple issues. Above all, the *jan sunvai* brought together antagonistic parties on a common platform and engaged them in a dialogue for systemic change.

Source: personal communication, Yaaminey Mubayi.

they have shown how the contracting relations which emerged between NGOs and the demilitarizing state led NGOs to take on many new staff, some of whom did not share the ideological commitment of the founders or supporters recruited during the years of repression. Even when the state is democratic, social and economic work by NGOs implies criticism of the state's own shortcomings, which can continue to generate tension between government and NGOs.

From the perspective of governments, it has on the whole been political factors in many developing countries which have influenced state attitudes to NGOs, according to Bratton (1989): not the analysis of NGOs' actual or potential social and economic contribution. Indeed, the growth of NGOs can pose a dilemma for the state, since private institutional initiatives can challenge the state's legitimacy if it shows that it is unable to deliver what it has promised to the population, or undermine its power base if discontent is fostered among certain sections of the population. The state is interested in NGOs if it sees the potential for NGOs to broaden development services under an overall guiding hand from government, and of course the government may benefit from resulting public gratitude and approval.

The state also tends to take an interest in NGOs from the perspective of ensuring financial control and accountability, particularly if there are foreign funds being channelled to the NGO sector. As Bratton shows, the state can use at least four different strategies to define its relationships with NGOs: monitoring (keeping track of what NGOs are doing and, if necessary, restricting registration of organizations it does not like); coordination (seeking to spread NGO activities more evenly across geographical areas and sectors in order to avoid duplication); co-optation (in which it seeks to 'capture' NGOs and steer them away from potentially threatening roles into the kind of work it wants); and finally dissolution (in which it develops mechanisms that give it absolute control over NGOs, enabling it to delay approval for their activities, limiting their scope or ultimately closing down NGOs if considered necessary). Fowler (1997) also highlights a further strategy which government can use – the creation of quasi-governmental organizations or government-organized NGOs (GONGOs) which take the form of NGOs but are ultimately the tools of government. Overall, Bratton (1989) suggests from his work in Africa that:

> Government–NGO relations are likely to be most constructive where a confident and capable government with populist policies meets an NGO that works to pursue mainstream development programmes . . . and most conflictual where a weak and defensive government with a limited power base meets an NGO that seeks to promote community mobilisation.
>
> (Bratton 1989: 585)

Rather than seeing government and NGOs as being in competition, Evans (1996) has instead pointed to the need for building synergies between different kinds of public and private agency. Meanwhile Tendler (1997: 146) observed that successful development in north-east Brazil was based on a three-way dynamic between central government, local government and civil society, and noted the movements of key individuals between different sectors such that 'the assumed clear boundary between government and non-government is actually quite blurred'.

NGOs AND THE BUSINESS SECTOR

Moving on from state and civil society, this section examines the management of relationships between NGOs and the market. This relationship is as yet less widely explored in the NGO literature than that with the state, yet it is one which is attracting growing interest. For example, in 1999 the Resource Centre for the Social Dimensions of Business Practice was established in the UK with DFID funding to explore ways to strengthen links between business and poverty reduction, and included among its partners NGOs, businesses and researchers. The Ethical Trading Initiative, established in 1999, is an alliance of NGOs, trade unions and companies concerned with improving labour standards within international supply chains (Forstater *et al.* 2002).[5]

There are now an increasing range of points of contact between NGOs and business. At the most extreme level, there are companies which have set up their own NGOs, just as governments have sometimes created their own GONGOs (Clarke 1998). However, there have always been philanthropic links between business and the third sector in many countries. Examples include the Ford Foundation in the United States, which owes its endowment to the famous car company and which now funds a range of third sector activities (among other types of organizations), and the Tata Foundation, which was funded by a large Indian industrialist family. It has also been fairly common practice to invite representatives from the business sector to serve on the governing bodies of some NGOs, either to lend respectability to the organization or to provide specialized skills and knowledge that can contribute to strengthening the NGO's work.

Newer types of relationships which are emerging are social action partnerships in which a private company works with an NGO as part of a government-initiated multi-agency development programme on a social or environmental issue, or a problem-based alliance in which a partnership develops where a business brings in an NGO with specialized skills, such as the initiation of an ecotourism venture in an area known to the NGO. An example from Brazil, in which a small voluntary NGO seeks to form developmental exchanges between urban tourists and low-income communities in the Amazon, is presented in Box 6.3. There are also emerging relationships, with varying levels of success, between NGOs and businesses seeking to harness 'win–win' outcomes in relation to trade and social or environmental justice. An overview of the links that have developed between some NGOs and the Starbucks coffee company around forms of corporate partnership for 'fair trade' are presented in Box 6.4.

There are also growing 'service ties' between NGOs and business, in which a company engages an NGO to carry out a certain social function, an example of which is the way in which oil companies in Nigeria have used NGOs to provide water and healthcare services to remote communities living in oilfield areas. Finally, the market has become a potential source of income for NGOs seeking to reduce or eliminate their dependence on foreign donors or the government. For example, NGOs have developed relationships with local businesses in order to gain not just financial resources in the form of donations or sponsorship, but also information and advice as well as donations in kind, such as the use of office furniture or equipment. Some NGOs have formed their own businesses, such as BRAC in Bangladesh, which established a printing press, the profits from which are ploughed back

Projeto Bagagem: NGOs and community-based tourism in Brazil

Projeto Bagagem – roughly translated as 'Project Backpack' – is a small Brazilian NGO set up in 2002 by two Brazilian university friends after organizing an expedition to visit river communities in Santarém, Pará, in the heart of Brazilian Amazonia. It promotes community-based tourism in areas where local development initiatives are taking place with community-based NGOs and government. Small groups of people – including families, students and professionals from different walks of life – are taken for a week 'off the beaten track' for an unconventional travel holiday. Projeto Bagagem runs on volunteer labour and activities are self-financing through participant fees.

Rather than simply visiting tourist attractions, the idea is to enable visitors to gain a wider experience of community life and observe achievements and challenges, as well as exchanging ideas and experiences through a learning process in which both visitors and community members can benefit. Recreational activities, including educational trekking in the jungle, swimming in rivers, sunset watching and traditional fishing, are combined with structured learning about community organization and development. These include practical sessions on recent innovations such as solar energy systems, improved sanitation, traditional medicine and new forms of income-generation activities. All participants sleep in hammocks on the boat or in the settlement and have the opportunity to live like a *caboclo* ('mestizo') for a few days.

Before each trip, Projeto Bagagem works closely with both visitors and communities so that their mutual expectations can be constructively managed. Organizers negotiate with host communities about the kind of contribution visitors might make, whether a financial or material donation, or volunteering time or talent, depending on context. For example, in one community a portion of a new multipurpose community building was constructed with funds from the tours; in another, a medical doctor taught a traditional healer how to measure blood pressure; also, participants from all groups have contributed to community schools by bringing school materials, books, toys and games. Visitors are encouraged to share their own culture with the host communities by bringing things such as photos, stories, recipes, dances and songs. As a result, the Projeto Bagagem experience helps to build understanding among people from different backgrounds.

Since the projects do not require much start-up funding, it has so far been possible to create a sustainable NGO initiative, the crucial factor being building good relationships with local organizations. The simplicity of the idea has made it easily replicable to other sites, and a second itinerary was launched in July 2005 in the north-eastern state of Ceará. Nevertheless, more resources are needed since the coordination team still works on a voluntary basis and fund-raising efforts will be required if a planned expansion of operations is to take place. More work is also needed to familiarize community members with the visitors' interests and needs, to ensure that both parties benefit from the experience as much as possible.

Source: Mônica Mazzer Barroso (more information and photos from the expeditions available at: www.projetobagagem.org).

NGOs and corporate coffee partnerships

In 1991 CARE convinced Starbucks to undertake policies of social responsibility in countries where Starbucks purchased its coffee – Guatemala, Ethiopia, Kenya. The initial partnership had a philanthropic focus. During the Christmas season of 1992, Starbucks began sales of coffee from the three countries where CARE conducted its activities. From each sample sold, CARE received US$2. Two years later the relationship had begun to take a more transactional shape. Starbucks began to donate directly to CARE projects in water and sanitation as well as micro-credit programmes. CARE staff, on the other hand, provided Starbucks management an insight to the developing world and particularly its labour practices. In the late 1990s, the cooperation deepened further as CARE staff were offered opportunities for training in Starbucks corporate units, human resources and marketing in particular. Starbucks staff took part in CARE development seminars, voluntary activities and began to serve on CARE board committees. In June 2000, Starbucks was the first major corporation to sell Fair Trade coffee in its stores. According to material available in Starbucks' stores, to date it has also contributed $1.8 million to CARE, in support for literacy and education programmes in coffee-growing regions of Indonesia, Ethiopia, Kenya and Guatemala.

Oxfam has also established links. In a pilot venture, Starbucks UK is contributing £100,000 to Oxfam's rural development programme in the East Hararge region of Egypt, where farmers producing high-quality Arabica coffee struggle with poverty and frequent drought. Oxfam decided Starbucks was a suitable collaborator because it had been building long-term contracts with some of its producers and had expanded its Fair Trade coffee commitment. However, in 2004 this still only accounted for just 1–2 per cent of all the coffee Starbucks buys. Starbucks has also put in place purchasing guidelines that stipulate a set of quality, social and environmental standards that farmers must meet in return for these improved terms. The company pays them an average of US $1.20 (56p) a pound, which is about twice the market price for high-quality Arabica beans.

Sources: Lindenberg and Bryant 2001; 'Why are Starbucks and Oxfam sharing the same table?', *Developments*, 2004, issue 28: http://www.developments.org.uk/data/issue28/coffee-for-two.htm

---

into the NGO.[6] This preserves the status of the organization as a 'not-for-profit' organization, even though a part of the organization is engaged in profit-making activity, and this and other business ventures, along with the service charges administered, has helped to reduce the NGOs' reliance on foreign funding to less than one-third of the overall budget.[7]

Many NGOs have moved significantly towards the private sector in the current trend towards micro-credit programmes, because financial services require both a sound knowledge of banking management practices and a close understanding of local business opportunities in the community.[8] For some analysts who see support to local business as the means for NGOs to address poverty through an engagement with the market, these are taken as very positive developments, with micro-finance represented as one of the few conspicuous development 'success stories' of recent decades. The success of the Grameen Bank has been linked with the emerging concept of the 'social economy', which according to Reifner and Ford (1992) can be defined as 'a market economy in which asocial market forces have been socialized'. This concept has its roots in the work of Karl Polanyi (1957), which analysed the social embeddedness of the economies of pre-industrial societies, and highlighted the norms of social reciprocity and mutual aid that dominated earlier social and economic life but which became weakened by modern industrial consumer capitalism.

The Grameen Bank and other micro-finance approaches have focused particularly on the power of women as effective borrowers. Dignard and Havet (1995) present a series of case studies to show that the funding of micro- and small-scale enterprises carried out by women has become a popular development strategy, because these activities can accelerate overall levels of economic activity and can contribute a more equitable distribution of development benefits than male borrowers. At the household level, gendered management and invest-ment strategies often mean that women expand their enterprises to kin networks (i.e. social priorities) rather than growth and profits, by creating 'multiple enterprises' (Downing 1991). For other analysts, such as Dichter (1997), the apparently irresistible drive among NGOs to move into the micro-finance field is a factor sapping the diversity and the creativity of the sector, by pulling organizations away from their social origins and values and slowly turning them into private sector organizations.

We turn now to consider two areas of interaction between NGOs and the business world. The first is the growth of campaigning by NGOs to improve accountability and social respon-sibility among the corporate sector, such as the campaigning work undertaken by UK NGOs and their partners in the South around business, for example child labour (Stichele and Pennertz 1996). Zadek (2000) has analysed the efforts of NGOs to influence the behaviour of corporations through potential damage to their reputations brought about by civil action by NGOs. This 'civil regulation' model has been observed in campaigns against high-profile companies such as Nike, Monsanto, Shell and Nestlé which appear to have made a differ-ence and where a potential 'win–win' situation emerges because staff are more motivated and work harder under a more ethical regime, consumers buy more products and govern-ments provide more 'enabling' services. Zadek is careful to point out that there is little detailed evidence to prove that this civil regulation model is effective in practice. He outlines the twin challenges faced by NGOs to explore strategies for leverage in the short term, and to maintain pressure on governments and global institutions to ensure that business policy frameworks reflect concerns about sustainable development. The Starbucks case highlighted in Box 6.4 also shows the hazards faced by NGOs engaging with big business, as well as the potential shifts that can take place.

The second area of interaction between NGOs and the business sector is the growth of the concept of 'fair trade', which serves the multiple purposes of securing better prices for developing country producers, educating consumers to demand social, economic and environmental business standards, and generating revenue for an NGO from the market (Box 6.5). Yet fair trade is an ambiguous concept, and this ambiguity creates both oppor-tunities and constraints for NGO management strategies. In this case, new opportunities and creative ideas were found to be highly vulnerable to the changing tastes of Western consumers and difficult to sustain. The concept of ambiguity in organizations explains

International and local private sector support to an NGO in Nepal through 'fair trade'

In Nepal during the 1990s, a major UK company (the Body Shop) built a trading relationship with a local socially and environmentally aware paper business and a local NGO, funded through profits generated by this 'fair trade' link. The small family-owned enterprise makes handmade paper for the local market, and like the Body Shop sees itself as a socially aware business with a set of environmental, social and economic objectives. Under the trade link, the size and scale of its operations increased considerably. From a turnover of only a few thousand pounds in the mid-1980s based only on domestic sales, a move into exports through the Body Shop increased turnover to over 250,000 pounds by 1995 and the local market was abandoned. Staff quadrupled in number, working conditions were improved way beyond local standards, and paper production was made environmentally sustainable through the use of innovative recycling, renewable energy and organic dyes. A local community-based NGO (established by managers and friends of the local business) was able to fund itself using the innovative method of taking a share of the trade profits, made possible by the payment of a 10 per cent premium by the Body Shop, over and above the agreed price paid for the paper products. The NGO initially worked on credit and literacy programmes with the local community around the factory, including employees and their families, but later broadened its activities to include other nationally identified priorities such as HIV/AIDS awareness raising and education work. However, rapidly changing consumer tastes in the North had led to falling sales by 1995, creating a funding problem for the NGO and difficulties for the paper company itself. With renewed efforts at diversification, and a late re-entry into the local market, many problems have been solved and the NGO and the business remains active. Expectations, which became confused by the ambiguities between 'business' and 'social' objectives, have now been scaled down to a more realistic level on both sides.

Source: Lewis 1998a.

problems which emerge whenever activities take place on the boundary between the for-profit and non-profit sectors. The concept of ambiguity has long been identified by anthropologists as a source of both creativity and danger. Within organizational theory, the management of ambiguity has also been seen as key to understanding the challenges faced by organizations in the postmodern world, in contrast to earlier 'rational scientific' theories of management (Peters and Waterman 1982; Morgan 1997). Martin and Meyerson (1988) show how ambiguity can bring both paralysis and innovation within organizational culture. The emphasis on the management of shared meanings in current organization theory highlights the need for managers to clarify and project the desired future organizational identity and image in order to guide organizational change (Gioia and Thomas 1996).

In the non-profit literature – drawing upon the work of the anthropologist Edmund Leach – Billis (1993a) has argued that organizations may exhibit a set of organizational problems created by the existence of an ambiguous zone between the bureaucratic and associational 'worlds' which operates through very different sets of rules. For example, the bureaucratic world relies upon hierarchy and role specialization, while the world of associations is characterized by face-to-face, egalitarian relationships and multifaceted, informal roles. Following from this approach, the idea has also been applied to analysis of the boundaries between sectors (Billis 1993b).

An ambiguous zone exists between the for-profit and the NGO sectors around 'business' and 'development' objectives, which creates distinctive problems for organizations of both types engaged in fair trade partnerships. This is because fair trade explicitly mixes profit-making with the objective of social or environmental development and change. While profit-making has traditionally been associated with the business sector, these other activities have been associated with the non-governmental or non-profit sectors in which NGOs and other civil society organizations operate. Fair trade may have the potential to generate more sustainable alternatives to conventional development assistance and project-based interventions, but it blurs further the boundaries set out by the three-sector model as organizations within fair trade partnerships are forced to operate beyond the rules of their usual 'known' environments.

NGOs AND INTERNATIONAL DEVELOPMENT AGENCIES

As we saw in Chapter 2, what might be loosely termed the 'aid industry' is a set of institutions and organizations concerned with the funding of international development, and includes multilateral agencies such as the World Bank, bilateral donors such as the UK Department for International Development (DFID), Northern NGOs such as Oxfam, and foundations such as Ford (Robinson 1997). NGOs have always been players in development processes, but it is only since the late 1980s that the aid industry has invested NGOs with major significance. This was, as we saw in Chapter 1, due to a variety of factors, including disillusionment with the apparent inefficiency of state-centred development paradigms, and the growing voice of the third sector in parts of the South. However, data on the precise levels of funding going to NGOs are notoriously difficult to come by, because of the large numbers of donors and funding channels involved, and of course the matter is complicated further by the importance of funding from governments and the resources to NGOs provided by public donations and volunteer labour.[9] Figures quoted by Van Rooy (1997), based on statistics collected by the Development Assistance Committee (DAC) of the OECD, indicate that more than US$1 billion of aid globally is now channelled through NGOs, and that while bilateral donors such as Denmark spend less than 0.5 per cent of their overall development assistance on NGOs, other countries such as the Netherlands and Switzerland spend more than 10 per cent via NGOs. The pace of the increase in official funding of NGOs has been quite dramatic. For example, in the UK, figures presented by ODI (1995) indicate that between 1983/4 and 1993/4 there was an increase of almost 400 per cent to £68.7 million as the total share of British aid going to NGOs rose from 1.4 per cent to 3.6 per cent.

Aside from raising the profile of NGOs, these increases in official funding have impacted on some organizations in a variety of important ways. All non-profit organizations tend to be highly resource-dependent and may require diverse sources of funds for their survival (Bielefeld 1994), and it has been argued convincingly that the 'resource dependency perspective' developed by the influential organizational theorists Pfeffer and Salancik (1978) can be usefully applied to NGOs in seeking explanations for their relationships and activities (Hudock 1995). In some cases, the rapid growth and organizational expansion of NGOs has created structural pressures such as the transition from the associational world of informal face-to-face organizational styles to the bureaucratic world of formal structures and hierarchies, thus creating a new set of administrative problems (Billis and MacKeith 1992). For other NGOs there has been the hazard of what organization theorists term 'goal deflection', as funders have favoured certain approaches such as service provision over earlier empowerment-centred activities (Hashemi and Hassan 1999). Some observers have argued that the rapid increases in official funding for short-term humanitarian emergency funding has deflected some NGOs from longer-term development work (Fowler 1994). An NGO may also become more vulnerable to changing donor fads and fashions (Smillie 1995) or may face decreased legitimacy in the eyes of some of its other stakeholders (Bratton 1989).

At the same time, NGO approaches and concerns are now also beginning to influence official aid policy in a number of ways, which Riddell (in ODI 1995) has termed the 'reverse agenda'. For example, the concept of participatory concerns in general and participatory planning in particular has been taken on board by most donors, and part of the credit for this lies arguably in pressure brought to bear by NGOs. The same is true of the increasing interest in the gender dimensions of development in which the ideas of NGOs played a part. Brown and Covey (1983) show the need for NGOs to deal with the tensions inherent in their external relations, and there is no doubt that NGOs have begun to develop distinctive techniques for managing the donor dimensions of their relationships more effectively. For example, the evolution of the 'donor consortium' idea, in which NGOs receive funding from a number of different donors (each of which may have different disbursal methods and reporting criteria), is one such response (Smillie 1988; Wright 1996). In this model an NGO works with the donors to form a group which can standardize procedures and timetables and establish a single point of contact and communication working with donor consortia. Some of the major NGOs such as BRAC in Bangladesh have found this an improved way to organize relations with donors, although in the case of Sarvodaya in Sri Lanka in the 1980s, a donor consortium led to unnecessary administrative centralization, an increased workload for staff and the loss of the bottom-up culture of participation within the organization (Perera 1997).

Some donors are also now considered to be looking beyond mere funding relationships. According to Bebbington and Riddell (1995), donors can work towards helping to create an enabling environment which would assist the work of NGOs – for example, building bridges between non-membership NGOs, membership organizations and wider political structures such as the state and international donors. This strategy too can be hazardous. Schmidt and Zeitinger (1996) argue that donors often still do not know enough about many of the NGOs they support, and that a more genuine partnership is needed, rather than just instinctive trust.

The increasing numbers and scale of NGOs have also highlighted the need for NGOs to coordinate more effectively with each other, which has not proved a straightforward challenge. Carroll (1992) has argued that coordination between NGOs is a key to improving performance, but that in practice 'competition' is more common, which brings us back to the subject of resource dependence, since NGOs may wish, due to limited funding sources, to protect their funding source information and to maintain a distinct activity niche which they can then use to maintain access to resources. The attempt to coordinate NGOs may come from NGOs themselves, which is more likely to succeed, or it may be imposed from outside, usually by government or donors. Coordination may take the form of a formal structure, such as the national NGO council which was established and documented in Simukonda's (1992) case study from Malawi, which was ultimately an unsuccessful venture, or it may be informal in nature, such as the flexible grassroots network in Thailand discussed by Korten (1980), in which NGOs came together around a specific campaign, in this case against a proposed dam project.

One of the main issues in the management of NGO relationships within the 'aid industry' is the changing balance of power which is emerging between Northern NGOs and Southern NGOs. Many Northern NGOs have moved in broad terms from an approach in which they implemented projects themselves in developing country contexts, to one in which most now seek to form 'partnerships' with local organizations which they fund and support in other ways, such as 'capacity building' support. Overlaid onto this changing scenario is the growth of what is often termed 'direct funding' of Southern NGOs by Northern bilateral donors, in place of an earlier funding model in which 'indirect funding' took place through Northern NGO intermediaries.

These changes may have profound implications for the Northern NGO community, which has increasingly found itself in the midst of a rapidly changing aid environment and Southern institutional context. For some observers this has been evident in a sharpening of purpose and a productive new questioning of roles, while others have suggested that there may be a growing 'crisis of identity' among Northern NGOs (Smillie 1994).[10] One study has analysed these changing relationships in the context of Swedish NGO assistance in Bangladesh, which has worked to support Bangladeshi NGOs over the years (Lewis and Sobhan 1999). The study compared the effectiveness of the new 'direct' route via the SIDA office in Dhaka with the more familiar 'indirect' route in which SIDA funds Swedish NGOs that then work with Bangladeshi NGO partners. The study found the two routes essentially complementary, since direct funding can cut out the costs of the Northern 'intermediary' NGO and allow a direct dialogue with local leaders and organizations, while indirect funding can maintain a link and a dialogue between the government's aid programme and the Swedish public, and create opportunities for Swedish NGOs to undertake development education work at home informed by their work overseas.

However, the research suggested that in general the arguments for direct funding were more compelling as a means for identifying and channelling resources to the most effective and innovative Bangladeshi NGOs. There was some evidence that many Swedish NGOs (particularly those from the more conservative missionary backgrounds) tended to be involved in routine, operational, less sustainable NGO activities (such as running clinics and schools) rather than the more challenging activities carried out by some of SIDA's more innovative NGO partners.

184

THE DISCOURSE OF 'PARTNERSHIP'

This chapter concludes with a discussion of 'partnership', a key policy concept which is currently deployed in relations between NGOs and other institutional actors. For example, the 1997 UK White Paper on international development contained numerous references to building partnerships: between rich and poor countries, between NGOs and governments, between development agencies and the business community, and between Northern and Southern NGOs. Calls for partnership (along with other related terms used around the world such as 'collaboration', 'accompaniment', 'coordination', 'cooperation' and 'complementarity') are now a regular and important part of the development discourse (and policy implementation).

However, inter-agency partnership arrangements in practice are rarely subjected to detailed scrutiny (see Box 3.6 on Afghanistan for an exception). In many aid-dependent contexts it is common for partnerships involving NGOs to have a *passive* character, often because the idea of partnership has been 'forced' in some way or because agencies have brought themselves into partnerships in order to gain access to external resources. Partnerships are usually formed between unequal development actors. Passive partnerships may not add much value to ongoing activities; nor are they likely to generate the learning which often comes from joint discussion and action. Such 'dependent' partnerships are also likely to be unsustainable. Many partnerships may begin this way – the challenge is to transform them into something more worthwhile.

Based on research undertaken within an inter-agency project in Bangladesh (Lewis 1998b), it is possible to suggest an outline of guidelines which might be used for generating and maintaining creative or 'active' partnerships. The process monitoring which was undertaken during the research focused on the differing perceptions and expectations of agency staff engaged in the project. It also attempted to identify what value, if any, partnership had added to the project's work. Partnership was found to be an evolving process which had both passive and active elements over time and at different levels of the project. In some cases (although not by any means all) partnership linkages had contributed to useful changes of approach within the project, with benefits to the project's 'target group', in this case low-income rural households engaged in small-scale aquaculture.

Table 6.1 presents a set of criteria for identifying and building active partnerships based on the findings of the research. Active partnership is seen here very much in terms of a process. While respective roles between agencies and individuals need to be clearly agreed in advance, project actors also renegotiate and reassess their roles where necessary. Linkages should not be premised on an over-rigid notion of 'comparative advantage', such as one which requires NGOs to deliver inputs while government carries out research. Synergies may result in unintended outcomes, some of which may be useful, others not. For example, some forms of dependent partnership also run the risk of 'agency creation' by powerful NNGOs who seek to use partnerships as a vehicle for their own interests, a fact rarely considered in the partnership literature (Box 6.6).

Partnership also needs to embody the sharing of risks across collaborating agencies and persons, otherwise there is little chance of efficiency, innovation or creativity. Discussion concerning progress needs to be open and honest, with mistakes acknowledged and failures faced up to. The free exchange of information between agencies and individuals in partnership is a

Table 6.1 Contrasting characteristics of 'active' and 'dependent' partnerships

Active partnerships	Dependent partnerships
Process	Blueprint, fixed term
Negotiated, changing roles	Rigid roles based on static assumptions about 'comparative advantage'
Clear purposes, roles and linkages but an openness to change as appropriate	Unclear purposes, roles and linkages
Shared risks	Individual interests
Debate and dissent	Consensus
Learning and information exchange	Poor communication flows
'Activity-based' origins – emerging from practice	'Resource-based origins' – primarily to gain access to funds

Source: adapted from Lewis 1998b.

prerequisite for learning within the project or programme. Dependent partnership, on the other hand, is characterized by blueprint thinking and a superficial clarity about the purposes of the partnership which may obscure the need to face up to creativity, risk taking and learning. These criteria are set out in Table 6.1, which can be used as a checklist or a set of guidelines in the planning of partnership ventures.

It is important therefore for NGOs to see partnership as a process, and its form may need to be constantly reworked in the light of ongoing experience and there will be many unintended outcomes, some useful, some not. Partnerships are also diverse, varying from sector to sector and country to country, and it may be difficult to 'replicate' successful ones. Partnerships are also highly sensitive to external factors, including economic conditions, political climate, culture and ecology, and may be strongly influenced by support or obstruction from key individuals in positions of power and authority. For example, sudden changes in key government personnel (such as the director of the government's NGO unit moving to another post) can alter the balance of NGO/government relationships at a stroke in a particular country context.

The process view of partnership therefore helps to increase the likelihood that sustainable inter-agency linkages can be built. Active partnership can only be achieved if agencies define and agree principles of 'appropriate practice'. Active partnerships are one way for NGOs to open up space for themselves so that they can move out of purely instrumental service delivery roles and into the areas of networking, campaigning and policy advocacy and entrepreneurship. They may also be a way in which government can increase its effectiveness through the generation of private/public synergies. However, partnership cannot usefully be viewed in purely instrumental terms. Arguing against the rise of complex bureaucratic forms of inter-agency relationship, Mawdsley *et al.* (2005) suggest that a greater level of personal interaction in the form of face-to-face visits and relationships is an essential ingredient for the formation of effective North–South partnerships. Each specific partnership will require new definition and adaptation and continuous review. Partnerships cannot be replicated in any

The pursuit of partnership by NNGOs: power, funding and the dilemmas of 'agency creation'

NNGOs increasingly work 'through' SNGOs to undertake development activities within partnership arrangements. A recent study examined relationships between four NNGOs and five SNGOs working on urban poverty in Nairobi, Kenya. The study found that NNGOs followed a number of strategies to secure their own objectives, such as encouraging SNGOs to try new approaches and activities through simple requests or on occasion as a requirement for the continuation of funding. A further strategy that emerged in the course of the study was that of 'agency creation'. Three of the NNGOs had been directly involved in founding new organizations and two others had sponsored local activities that resulted in new organizations being formed. These Northern-sponsored Southern agencies have Kenyan board members (for the most part) and employ Kenyan staff.

A number of reasons for agency creation emerged. In one case, an NNGO initiated the establishment of a network to share information and lobby for policy change. Whilst the members of the network included both Northern and Southern agencies, the network promoted a Southern identity but was managed and funded by the instigating NNGO. The second case of agency creation occurred when an NNGO withdrew from an area of work that it had supported within its own operational activities, and its programme staff then decided to go ahead and form a local NGO to carry on their work. Staff of the Northern NGO provided informal support. A third example occurred when a local voluntary group providing professional legal services formalized and modified their work and created a specialist SNGO. This followed an offer of funds from an official development assistance agency (which was rejected) and then from an NNGO. A further reason for establishing new agencies that occurred in two cases was to promote areas of development work that the NGOs considered not to be taking place; and in a further case it was to replicate work that was not judged to be done to an adequate standard.

NNGO influence remains strong in these newly created development agencies. One staff member for the network noted that: 'All proposals have to be approved by [the NNGO] in Kenya and the head office'. A second donor agreed that the founding agency 'has a strong direction on the programme'. An NNGO staff member, reflecting on one more such effort, argues that the Northern NGO is 'likely to be too prescriptive'. But others are more supportive of such work. Two of the Southern board members of one 'created' organization spoke of their appreciation of Northern NGO support: 'it was good for [the Northern NGO] to give it direction in the early phase or it might not have got off the ground.' The strategy of agency creation has wider implications for relationships between NNGOs and SNGOs. First, it demonstrates the ways NNGOs use their power to modify the nature of the SNGO sector. Second, in creating new SNGOs, NNGOs may reduce solidarity and create more competition between SNGOs. Third, the strategy may enable NNGOs to pursue agendas with less consideration given to the perspectives of the South.

Source: Diana Mitlin, IIED/University of Manchester, personal communication.

straightforward way from one setting to another. The first step is to identify the goals of partnership, the second is to design mechanisms for achieving the necessary linkages and communication channels, while the third is to review purposes and progress regularly. Active partnership is only likely to emerge as a result of shared risk, joint commitment and negotiated roles which are linked to a clear set of purposes.

CONCLUSION

This chapter has discussed the management of the relationships which NGOs need to maintain with people and with other development actors if they are to do effective work. The work of development NGOs depends on the successful management of interactions with communities, government, business and development donors, though the environment in which NGOs operate is an increasingly turbulent and uncertain one. De Graaf's (1987) framework is discussed as a useful way in which to analyse these relationships, which helps illustrate the need for NGOs to balance internal management with the management of relationships in the NGO's wider environment. As Bratton (1990: 115) points out (in the African context, but relevant more widely) there is a need for NGOs:

> to strengthen their internal management procedures with reference to planning, programming, budgeting and financial control. . . . But there is even greater need for NGO managers to concentrate on strategic issues of programme scope and external organizational relations.

The difficult concept of 'partnership', which is the prescribed process through which NGOs are increasingly expected by policy makers to manage these external relationships, has also been critically analysed in this chapter, which has identified the need for 'active' partnership in which NGOs can add value to their work through managing relationships effectively, but has also analysed the considerable pressures placed on NGOs to form partnerships which are instead more 'dependent'. The growing importance of global and local networks in the maintenance of their relationships, and the increasing role and sophistication of information technology are likely to become increasingly important for the management of activities beyond the formal boundaries of the organization.

REVIEW QUESTIONS

- Outline the main relationships that need to be understood and managed in an NGO known to you.
- Do you agree with the claims that accountability is the 'Achilles heel' of NGOs?
- How can accountability be strengthened within an organization with which you are familiar?
- Is 'partnership' a useful term for policy and practice, or should more attention be paid to questions of unequal power in inter-organizational relationships?

Chapter 7

The dynamics of internal management

LEARNING OBJECTIVES

After considering this chapter, the reader will be able to describe and analyse:

- Key areas of third sector management research that have applicability to development NGOs
- Organizational characteristics of NGOs and their importance in determining NGO performance
- Different ways of understanding organizational change in relation to development NGOs and their work

KEY TERMS

- Third sector management
- Leadership
- Governance
- Strategy
- Human resources
- Information management
- Capacity building
- Internationalization
- Organizational change theory
- Complexity

INTRODUCTION

This chapter takes us inside the non-governmental organization and examines the internal management issues which have led some people to argue that NGOs face distinctive challenges which make general management prescriptions difficult. One of the earliest academic discussions of third sector management can be found in a special issue of the US journal *Public Administration Review* published in 1975, which argues that while the writings of Levitt and Etzioni in 1975 usefully identified the roles and relevance of third sector organizations and brought their existence to the attention of policy makers and scholars, they 'reveal little about the internal workings of third sector organizations' (McGill and Wooton 1975: 447).

Despite being more than thirty years old, this paper remains a useful introduction to the field of third sector management research. The key management problems which these authors identify for third sector organizations (despite their acknowledged diversity of structures and purposes) are those of 'goal ambiguity' and 'conflicting performance standards', based on an original idea by Frank (1959). In an environment of goal ambiguity and conflicting standards, managers in third sector organizations may develop approaches to decision making which are different to those found in public or private sector organizations, where ambiguous goals lead organizations to define their future in terms of general directions or thrusts and not by formally stated, definable goals. For NGOs, the process of setting goals becomes highly politicized by a range of external stakeholder pressures, leading to a frequent confusion between means and ends. It becomes difficult, therefore, to make use of formal rational management planning tools. It also becomes likely that there will be a wide gap between the formal public statements made by the organization about what it is doing, and the unofficial goals which are being pursued on a day-to-day level by people within the organization – what Perrow (1967) calls the 'official' and the 'operative' goals. Following from this is the observation that the evaluation of performance for third sector organizations is also more complex because they tend to plan their work on the basis of contingency and incremental learning, which is based on a general sense of 'organizational direction' rather than on clearly defined, achievable goals. They tend to use informal management procedures rather than the clearly defined and relatively stable roles and hierarchies set out in the German sociologist Max Weber's work on bureaucracy.

The managerial system of the third sector organization in this early model is one which was evolving a 'process' approach towards management, which acknowledges the importance of 'open systems', due to the need to respond to contingencies, in contrast to the goal-oriented, task-specific procedures which lend themselves to techniques such as 'management by objectives' in the private sector. Instead:

> many third sector organizations attempt to create a highly flexible management system built around temporary project groups, collegial management, etc. The widespread use of organization development, particularly the action research model of OD, are examples of this trend and are very popular in the third sector.
>
> (McGill and Wooton 1975: 451)

In this model, there is a constant threat to the legitimacy of the third sector organization because the goals of the organization may be constantly under challenge from within and from outside in the organization's environment, and because the very existence of the organization is called into question regularly through unstable funding conditions and through the possibility that the need which the organization is trying to meet can change. The people who work in third sector organizations, according to McGill and Wooton, may also have some distinctive characteristics. In contrast to the Weberian model of the functional executive who works towards the completion of hierarchically devolved, goal-specific tasks, the third sector manager is:

> a facilitator, an information gatherer, a person who thrives on giving and receiving feedback. This type of executive operates effectively in unstructured environments where policy making and implementation are constantly linked in a decentralised organization. A key theme for the existential executive is enabling others throughout the organization to exercise a high degree of choice and responsiveness.
>
> (McGill and Wooton 1975: 452)

The authors acknowledge that they have drawn an over-rigid distinction between third sector management and management in the private and public sectors in order to highlight the emerging arena of third sector management more clearly. But their points are as relevant today as they were in the 1970s. They suggest that third sector management is influencing other areas of management more widely, where organizations in the other sectors are beginning to take on some of the characteristics of the third sector management approach.

In the UK third sector, organizations have tended to display a rather ambiguous attitude to the idea of management, as we saw in Chapter 1. Organizations in the UK which had their roots in radical activism in the 1960s and 1970s were prone to see the whole idea of 'management' as linked essentially to capitalist, and therefore undesirable, ideologies, and preferred to use the term 'coordination' as one more suitable to describe what went on within their organizations. Landry *et al.* (1992: 23) point out in their 'analysis of radical failure' that this was a wholly inadequate response, given the challenges such organizations set out to undertake and the growing weight of expectations raised about the possibilities for change, and that it was like 'concentrating on swabbing the decks of the *Titanic* while failing to look out for ice-bergs'. Dartington (1992: 30–1) makes the point that third sector organizations have tended to build management skills on a rather ad hoc basis as and when they were needed. They shunned the formal management training and techniques found elsewhere, and instead developed their management skills through 'the experience of doing and through peer support'. This generated a set of strongly expressive (rather than instrumental) management priorities, which focused on mission rather than objectives and on roles rather than job descriptions. Now that there has been a change in attitude among many third sector organizations, and 'management' is no longer a dirty word, the question then arises as to what *kind* of management skills are required and from where these might be drawn. Now that third sector organizations are happy to work with 'professional managers', there may be a danger that:

> some professional management, with its emphasis on management by objectives rather than mission, on job descriptions rather than roles, on financial sophistication

rather than political will, could lead to the development of static and uncreative organizations, which cannot sustain the creative tension between entrepreneurship and corporatism.

(Dartington 1992: 31)

Smillie and Hailey (2001) recount how management fads and fashions from the business world have impacted upon the third sector at regular intervals during recent decades, with management by objectives (MBO) in the 1970s, total quality management (TQM) in the 1980s and results-based management in the 1990s, often in the case of development NGOs via their donors who had learned about these new ideas from the business sector. There is an irony here because at the same time as NGOs are looking to 'management' ideas and seeking to formalize the diffuse and complex spirit of voluntary action, the private sector is rediscovering the positive values of 'amateurism', the value of participatory management and leadership, the importance of 'flatter' organizational structures and the need for organizational learning systems. For example, in a text on global management, Parker writes of the decline of the top-down management style and of the overriding importance of the top-level manager in the private sector:

In a rapidly changing global world where flexibility is a critical variable, resources are less than abundant, and learning and thinking at all levels have become important, lower level employees also have become involved in all aspects of organizational change and development.

(Parker 1998: 146)

From the vantage point of the present, the prediction made by McGill and Wooton (1975) that third sector management issues and concerns could point the way to new directions for mainstream management can now be seen to be coming true, in the sense that the most up-to-date management thinking stresses many of the characteristics associated with the ideal type of third sector management – open systems thinking, flexibility, reduced hierarchy and decentralized structures. The interesting question, perhaps, is the fact that while many businesses are now practising aspects of a participatory management approach, there are still many NGOs which remain stuck in outmoded or inappropriate models, half-borrowed from the business sector of old, or haphazardly evolved 'on the hoof' within a rapidly changing environment. For example, strategic planning is still regarded by many US third sector organizations as an example of 'best practice' despite the 'waning confidence' of business theorists in the approach (Mulhare 1999).[1]

THIRD SECTOR MANAGEMENT RESEARCH

Today there is a richer field of research on third sector management, particularly in the United States, than there was when McGill and Wooton were writing in 1975 (e.g. Anheier 2005). While much of the early interest in the 1970s came from public administration researchers (the concepts of capacity building, participation and empowerment which have formed part of the language of NGOs all have their origins in the field of public administration), in the 1980s and 1990s business management writers also began to contribute to the growing discussion of third sector management. Charles Handy, for example, who has written extensively on the business world, published a book on voluntary organizations in 1988 and has been described by Davis Smith (1996: 186) as 'the management guru of the voluntary sector'. It was the US business guru Peter Drucker (1990) who argued that third sector organizations lack a clear bottom line and therefore face distinctively complex management challenges. Hudson (1995) develops this idea in his argument that third sector organizations differ from organizations in the public and private sectors because there is no clear link between the providers of funds and the users of the services. In the private sector, customers pay for goods and services at a market price, and if the organization fails to provide these at the 'right' quality and price, either the organization improves its performance or it goes out of business. In the public sector, if people within a democratic political system are not receiving an acceptable level or quality of services then they can, at least in theory, vote officials out of office. For third sector organizations, this lack of clear accountability through markets or political process creates an unusually complex set of management challenges and problems.

Handy (1988) argues that the important difference is that third sector organizations are 'value-driven' organizations, and this poses distinctive management challenges, because people work in these voluntary organizations from a variety of public and private motives – such as altruism, an escape from dominant ideologies, increasing public status from being on an NGO board, or simply for experience, friendship and to add something new to their CVs. How does one manage such multiple interests and objectives? The emphasis on values is, however, criticized by researchers such as Paton (1999), who argues that there is a new voluntary sector variant of 'managerialism' evolving. This is based on the idea of the centrality of third sector values, which can lead to management 'solutions' based on static or rigid notions of values instead of the evolving, often conflictual processes of value-based action within the third sector. Talk of values, Paton points out, can sometimes mask the realities of confusion and rhetoric in many third sector organizations. Furthermore, there is considerable emphasis on the building of shared values within corporations as a precondition for successful business enterprise (Parker 1998: 206). Perhaps the key point is not the importance of values in third sector management, but the nature of those values. Clashes over different values are common in the NGO sector, for example between NGOs which come from a Christian missionary tradition and take a 'charity' approach to tackling problems of poverty and those which are motivated by the political ideas of Paulo Freire and seek the mobilization of the poor.

Hudson (1995) outlines the common problems for third sector organizations as the tendency for vague organizational objectives, the difficulties of monitoring performance effectively, the need to balance multiple accountabilities of a range of stakeholders inside and outside the organization, the resulting evolution of intricate management structures designed to do this, the centrality of the difficult concept of 'voluntarism' to many third sector organizations, and the need to maintain organizational 'values' over time in addition to demonstrating effective actions. Anheier (2000) argues that Drucker is not actually correct in suggesting that there is no bottom line for third sector organizations, and suggests instead that the problem is that there are too many bottom lines. This reflects the complex pattern of stakeholders in each organization, and, coupled with the high level of diversity of structure and purpose, gives rise to the distinctive complexity of third sector management. This view moves much closer to a view of third sector management as a process of choice and balance which takes place around a particularly complex set of themes, which cannot usefully rely on the simple importation of 'one size fits all' business models.

There has also been work on third sector management which has tried to develop new concepts and models based on an ongoing research programme undertaken with third sector organizations. Billis (1993a) developed a model of third sector organization based on work on service delivery organizations in the British voluntary sector, in which he analysed the roots of organizational problems within a framework of change from loose 'associational' structures and single purposes which frequently shift over time, driven by the logic of organizational growth and change and pressures from the wider policy environment, towards more hierarchical 'bureaucratic' structures and changing purposes. The essence of Billis's 'worlds theory' is that one common source of management problems for third sector organizations lies in the difficult and ambiguous positioning of many organizations on the boundaries between the associational and the bureaucratic worlds. For example, having begun as a small-scale organization providing a service to its members, organized around face-to-face relationships and relying mainly on volunteers, an organization may become a victim of its own success and grow beyond the point where informal structures are sufficient into one which requires more formal bureaucratic structures, such as the introduction of paid staff. The danger is that the new formalized organization may lose touch with its earlier values and goals. Unless growth and change take place with a proper sense of awareness and accountability, Billis argues, there will be profound tensions between the different parts of the organization, such as between volunteers and paid staff, people with formal job descriptions and those without, and between the head of the organization and other stakeholders such as the governing body. Change is neither inevitable nor necessarily bad, argues Billis, but the organizational consequences of 'sliding into change' will cause management problems which will be highly significant in terms of accountability and effectiveness.

Third sector management research has generated a wide-ranging subject matter relating to internal organizational issues, as is apparent from the collection of papers edited by Billis and Harris (1996) on the field in the UK, which explores a wide range of increasingly familiar themes, such as the confusion which arises over roles and internal structures in the form of 'fragmented accountability', tensions between organizational aims and structures, and issues of governance such as the relationships between headquarters and local organizations and between staff and management committees.

The subject of leadership in the third sector is one such area of research, a concept which has at times fallen from fashion in the wider management literature, and which has sometimes simply been used interchangeably with that of 'management'. Kay (1996: 131) suggests that interpretative approaches have begun again to favour a definition of leadership: 'as a multi-dimensional process of social interaction, creating and sustaining acceptable meanings of issues, events and actions. Leaders are conceptualized as those who have involvement and influence in this leadership process.' In this way, leadership is seen as a process of sense-making rather than as a measurable aspect of individual human behaviour, and one which is characterized by the creation and sustaining of acceptable meanings of issues and actions rather than simply as the responsibility of a particular individual in a formal leadership position. In Kay's research it was found that in the UK third sector the role of chief executive was an important one in shaping such processes, but that there was activity throughout the organization which also played a part. The pattern of leadership which was identified was therefore seen in terms of an essentially participatory ideal rather than the heroic leader model:

> It is therefore seen as important that all staff and volunteer members at all levels of voluntary organizations, *and* service users, need to be enabled to exercise leadership and to develop the skills to participate in this process.
>
> (Kay 1996: 145)

However, it is not always clear in the study how frequently this form of leadership is found among third sector organizations in the UK, where there is also anecdotal evidence that the problem of over-dominant 'charismatic' leaders is also to be observed.

Harris's (1996) work on governing bodies in the UK has drawn upon her own research as well as literature from the USA to consider the ways in which these structures are supposed to function in theory, and then to compare these 'assumed' roles with the realities encountered in the messy world of real organizations. In the UK 'charity' world there are, she argues, five main functions which are usually claimed for the board, in the organization's own public statements or which are required by English charity law:

1   to act as the point of final accountability for the organization, such that it is answerable for the organization's conduct to government, clients and regulatory bodies, and responsible for the action of the agency's staff and its use of resources;
2   to act as the employer of the third sector organization's staff, whether paid or voluntary, such that it takes the final decision on such issues as appointments, promotion and disciplinary action (even though these may be handled by paid staff on a day-to-day basis within the organization);
3   to formulate and develop the organization's policy in terms of its overall mission and purposes, and to set priorities and plan monitoring activities;
4   to take responsibility for ensuring the availability of resources, from financial to the more material needs of office space, vehicles and personnel, and in this sense the governing body is ultimately responsible for the organization's continuation and survival;
5   to mediate between the organization and its environment, representing the organization to outside actors and bringing information and ideas back into the organization from the outside world.

What is apparent from Harris's research is that there is a gulf between the assumed and the manifest functions of the governing body. There are several reasons for this, one of them being a simple ignorance among agency governing bodies that they have been allocated certain duties, and instead seeing the executive director of the agency as being in charge, in the way that the chief executive officer of a commercial business organization operates. Another reason for this lack of awareness may be that unless there is a crisis of some kind, the day-to-day management of a reasonably stable and successful organization will be taken care of by its professional paid staff without much involvement by the governing body. The gap between theory and practice may also result from the relationship which evolves between the governing body and the paid staff, which is vulnerable to tensions and communication difficulties unless both sides are committed to making the relationship work. Finally, the structure of service-providing organizations offers a third area of explanation, and Harris outlines an 'entrepreneurial model', common among newer agencies in Britain, in which the power of the governing body is curtailed by the existence of energetic staff and guardians (the people who have set up the organization and care about its future) who take care of many of the prescribed functions of the governing body and leave it without a clear role or purpose.

The people who make up the governing body of a third sector organization are usually volunteers, and even if the organization does not make use of volunteer staff, these people may constitute the 'voluntary' element of a third sector organization which gives it its distinctive character (Salamon and Anheier 1992). However, many third sector organizations do involve volunteers at other levels, and this is another distinctive area of management which has received considerable attention in the research literature. Davis Smith (1996) has analysed the trend towards formalizing the activities of volunteers within agencies, and the overtones of 'managerialism' which threaten the complex bundle of motivations which make up the volunteer 'ethos' in the UK. Since the 1960s there has been a questioning of the idea that volunteers can be left to themselves in third sector organizations as well-meaning amateurs if their work has important social consequences, and a gradual move towards professionalization can be detected, a combination of pressure from government and from inside many third sector organizations, where both paid staff and volunteers themselves have urged greater levels of professional support. This has led to the managerialist view that volunteers should be treated as 'unpaid professionals' with parity with paid staff in every other respect, a trend which has met with considerable resistance in some quarters of the third sector.

It has been argued that – and this takes us back to the ambiguous position of the third sector agency in Billis's (1993a) model, where both personal informality and bureaucratic systems may coexist within a single agency – such changes are out of step with the essentially heterogeneous motivations and needs of volunteers in which formal training and job descriptions only appeal to one section of the volunteer community. Instead, Davis Smith makes the case that many third sector organizations will therefore require a management style which is closer to the enabling model than the controlling one (see Chapter 2): 'For some this will mean the workplace model of individual job descriptions and the like; for others it will mean a much more informal and flexible approach (Davis Smith 1996: 198).

The growth of third sector management, despite its focus on Northern contexts, has profound implications for understanding NGO management, because it represents a starting body of knowledge which can be approached, adapted or rejected when considering organizations concerned with development work in different cultures and contexts. There is very little, for example, which has been written on governance or staffing within development NGOs, particularly in the South, yet these are subjects explored in comparative detail in relation to the Northern third sectors.

While discussions about NGO management have generally been relatively slow to take shape, there have been lively debates taking place in some of the wider third sectors of the North. In a book which examines current trends in non-profit management reform in the United States (Light 2000), there is much that also has relevance for development NGOs. Light's work is based on large-scale surveys of non-profit organizations in nineteen states, and identifies a set of pressures on organizations to reform their management practices, which include pressure from funders and clients, higher levels of public scrutiny arising from legitimacy problems generated by recent public scandals, the growth of specialized consultants and advisers to the sector, and the growth of increasingly similar, professionalized non-profit organizations seeking uniqueness in a competitive marketplace. Light goes on to identify four 'tides of reform', each of which is based on different assumptions about non-profit organizations and their roles, and each of which has distinctive strengths and weaknesses:

1   *Scientific management*: this model seeks to establish a set of core best practices which all organizations should follow, based on developing standards and codes of conduct. Taking its cue from the 'patron saint' of scientific management F. W. Taylor, the approach requires organizations to work towards improving their internal systems and structures over time, but it can be costly to implement and runs the risk of placing emphasis on relatively unimportant elements of organizational performance.

2   *Liberation management*: rather than focusing on the rules, systems and structures of organizations, this approach argues that an assessment of outcomes (in relation to an organization's mission statement) should be the ultimate indicator of non-profit effectiveness. The model stresses employee empowerment, deregulation and entrepreneurialism, but runs the risk that an organization might lose internal discipline or lose sight of its original target group.

3   *War on waste*: this model draws on ideas from the corporate sector to improve efficiency through mergers, strategic alliances and shared administrative costs. Placing an emphasis on re-engineering and downsizing, the main assumption is that by reorganizing the non-profit organization, gains in efficiency can be achieved. The strengths of the approach lie in its ability to reduce duplication and allocate funds more efficiently, but the danger is that an emphasis on uniformity will lead to a reduction in the diversity of the non-profit sector, and that it may impact negatively on staff morale within organizations.

4   *Watchful eye*: this approach stresses the need for public scrutiny of non-profit organizations in order to promote management discipline. Focusing on the concept of transparency, it assumes that the availability of financial and performance information will create competition and reduce inefficiency, and while its openness is a key strength, there are fears that the model is also open to manipulation and the use of inaccurate information to maintain a good public image.

All four 'tides of reform' were found to be active in the United States, but there is little consensus emerging as to whether one model is more ideal than any other, partly because of the diversity of organizations and perspectives on non-profit organization roles. The study, however, suggests that some trends are apparent, with 'scientific management' seen as suitable for small emergent non-profits seeking to improve their capacity, while larger established organizations have been drawn into the 'watchful eye' model as the government increases financial reporting regulations. While the 'liberation management' idea has been found attractive to many organizations, it has generated debates about the practice of effective evaluation and the definitions of 'success' among different stakeholders. While (1) and (2) are based on the assumption that the organization can undertake reforms from within and regulate itself, (3) and (4) instead place an emphasis on the need for outside pressure. The study concludes that what is needed is for organizations to set their own priorities and avoid either being drawn by management reform fashions or simply importing practices from the government or business sectors, and instead to build capacity to improve their performance.

However, this third sector literature does have certain weaknesses, such as the context-specific assumptions which inform the research approaches of some of its exponents. For example, many Southern NGOs see themselves in professionalized terms and do not identify with the ethos of 'voluntarism', while the governing body model, though common in many countries, is not universal, and it is possible to find NGOs which do not operate in this way (Fowler 1997, for example, outlines a non-governing body structure common in Latin America). Smillie and Hailey (2001: 108) argue from their study of South Asian NGOs that the much-observed tensions between staff and board in the third sector literature is actually quite rare in Southern NGOs, simply because 'many NGO boards act more as rubber-stamp cheering sections than as the policy formulation bodies so beloved of nonprofit management literature'. Third sector research is also strongly focused on service delivery organizations, and engages far less with organizations concerned with advocacy and social change. As we have seen, development NGOs are a diverse group and NGO management needs to go much further than this in examining the full range of NGO organizational forms and development approaches.

INTERNAL MANAGEMENT

Although there is a considerable literature written by academic researchers and reflective practitioners on NGOs and development, there is little work which examines what actually goes on inside these organizations. There was some interest in NGO management during the mid-1980s, with the formation of the NGO management network by the International Council for Voluntary Agencies (ICVA) which set in motion a fascinating debate (summarized in Chapter 1) about how to generate a discussion about management within the NGO world. Many of the writers referred to in this volume, such as Campbell and Fowler, were key participants in this discussion, which was concerned with advocating that NGOs take management concerns more seriously. In the pages of the *NGO Management Newsletter* (which was published between 1986 and 1992) NGO analysts and practitioners began sketching out the possible terrain of NGO management.

One of the earliest – but arguably still relevant – studies from this period was that of Stark Biddle (1984), who gathered data from more than one hundred senior staff of

US international development NGOs through interviews and questionnaires, in order to outline their specific management needs. He identifies a series of important factors which influence NGO management, which include the general public lack of interest in the North in issues of development and consequently low and unpredictable levels of funding for US NGOs; the tendency for dependence on government funding to develop; the lack of leadership capacity in the NGO sector due in part to problems of over-dominant, charismatic NGO leaders; and the issue of communication problems due to the geographical separation of headquarters and field offices. The resultant pattern of distinctive NGO management problems are identified as weak approaches to financial and institutional planning, poor fund-raising management, problems in the governance relations and the functioning of boards, and the management of human resources within NGOs. Stark Biddle found that most of these NGOs saw themselves as 'different' from other kinds of organization, since they placed a high priority on being flexible and idealistic, rather than highly organized and hierarchical.

The difficulties of maintaining a level of flexibility during processes of growth and change are a recurring concern. There has been some work on the issue of bureaucratization and NGOs, however. Max Weber's analysis of bureaucracy linked both the organizational and the political within one frame of reference, and connected bureaucracy with politics and society. Most discussions of bureaucracy start with Weber. On the one hand, it has negative connotations of red tape, slowness and corruption, while on the other, it is the foundation stone of administrative practice – precision, speed and impartiality can all be optimized in the Weberian 'ideal type'. Narayana (1992: 135) writes about the bureaucratization of NGOs in India and finds that though many NGOs have not taken on 'bureaucratic' characteristics, some are becoming increasingly bureaucratic in terms of 'structure, process and behaviour'. For example, in the Indian context some older 'Gandhian' NGO leaders are being replaced by new professionals who may be more interested in maximizing resources and economic incentive systems. This process of bureaucratization is of course being conditioned by external factors such as sources of funding and government control bodies. These demands all produce pressures which can lead NGOs to formulate and adhere to bureaucratic procedures such that there was a general observed tendency for 'NGOs to adjust to their complex environment by becoming increasingly bureaucratic'. This finding is also born out by Wallace *et al.*'s (2006) study of NGOs in Uganda and South Africa.

After the ICVA activity, less was written on the subject of NGO management until the late 1990s, when two major books on this theme emerged, one by Alan Fowler (1997), who pulled together many of his previous writings into a vast, detailed text, and Suzuki (1997), whose work with a Japanese NGO in Africa had provoked a major research study which he later wrote up. Both books therefore merit summary and discussion in some detail. Fowler (1997) begins by defining the aims of NGOs as reducing poverty and increasing social justice, which requires a management style which prioritizes 'humility, leverage and deflection'. This style reflects the fact that most NGOs are restricted to working on a relatively small scale, but may create a wider impact by seeking to redirect development aid policies towards a greater poverty focus, and by attempting to strengthen the position of poor people within markets by promoting fair trade or lobbying for reforms of international trade regulations.

199

Fowler goes on to outline what he terms the 'capacities approach' to understanding NGO management issues. This approach has five dimensions. The first is the organizational 'set-up' in which an NGO needs to link vision, mission and role clearly and use strategic planning to turn strategy into programmes. He suggests that an emphasis on reflection and learning is necessary for effectiveness, and discusses the importance of linking micro- and macro-level activity for maximum impact. Within the organization Fowler (1997: 61) argues that effective management requires a combination of the 'participatory' and the 'instrumental' dimensions of management, pointing out that 'decision-making must be consultative enough for shared ownership of the outcomes and directive enough to be timely'. The second set of issues relates to the improvement of leadership and human resources (see Box 7.1). Here, he discusses the need for the organization culture of the NGO to reflect its values and approach, and the fact that the organization will reflect the wider gender balance of power. The problem of leadership and succession is discussed and there is a useful section on the use of expatriate staff. Moving on to the third set of issues, Fowler discusses the importance to an NGDO of managing external relationships with 'primary stakeholders' (i.e. beneficiaries or clients) and with other NGOs. The concept of 'authentic partnership' is outlined in relation to changing relations between Northern and Southern NGOs in which

---

NGOs IN ACTION 7.1

Contrasting organizational characteristics of two NGOs in South Asia

Edwards (1999a) contrasts the organizational characteristics of two NGOs in South Asia. The first organization, which was the more successful, had 'inspirational but not overbearing' leadership, which was respected both by staff within the organization and by members of the disadvantaged communities within which the NGO was active. However, a shared organizational culture had been built up through long-term education and dialogue about the causes of poverty and the appropriate response to it, which created a high level of commitment, selflessness and 'a determination to hand over power at every opportunity' during the course of the NGO's development work. This had the result that local community groups, rather than the NGO itself, were gradually strengthened through the NGO's work. By contrast, another NGO, which was judged less successful in the study, was characterized by a strong director whose personal influence shaped the work undertaken to the detriment of middle-level and junior staff further down the hierarchy, who found themselves with very little opportunity to influence decisions or events. For example, a new credit scheme was introduced from the top without consultation, despite the fact that local staff had learned from their own informal efforts that such a design could not work properly. Consultation at the country-office level took place not with country staff, but with the headquarters in London, which led not only to missed opportunities for learning, but also to extremely high overheads. Important preconditions for success such as risk-taking, communication and initiative were all discouraged by this excessive centralization and bureaucracy.

Source: Edwards 1999a.

the latter struggle towards freeing themselves from an unequal donor–recipient relationship in favour of broader working coalitions. Finally, the task of influencing government is discussed, with the need for NGDOs to provide distinctive development inputs which avoid duplicating government efforts. The fourth area of NGO capacities concerns the mobilization of funds, which Fowler insists should be of sufficient 'quality' to allow the NGO to pursue its work properly. The author distinguishes 'hot' from 'cold' money (in terms of its conditionality levels) and reviews three sources of funding in the form of gifts, taxes and market-based transactions, and points out that sustainable development is neither cheap nor quick. The fifth and final set of capacities involves 'managing through achievement'. This section discusses the problems of the complexity of the development task, the blunt tools available for the measurement of success, and the dominant NGO culture of action over reflection which often inhibits organizational learning.

Fowler favours moving from an emphasis on measurement of development impact towards one of 'interpretation', mainly through working with different 'stakeholders' and incorporating their feedback and perspectives on progress, rather than seeking to develop quantitative evaluation tools. This allows an NGO to build its legitimacy through achievement and accountability. The final parts of the book are concerned with improving NGDO effectiveness by developing the five capacities through both 'organizational development' as well as strengthening wider 'civil society', a process which Fowler distinguishes as 'institutional development'. He is careful to characterize this as a process, not a means or an end. Ending the book with a set of future choices for NGOs, Fowler mixes a clear sympathy with NGOs with a sense of realism about the future. He sees the priority as creating NGO distinctiveness (building people's capacities rather than providing global welfare, linking with wider social movements) as well as learning from practice in order to gain leverage on aid, states and markets. The author suggests that NGO leaders need to think carefully about the future, because they need to improve their effectiveness and reduce their dependence upon foreign aid, which is in decline:

> It seems to me that this is a moment in NGDO history when leaders have to [be] . . . motivators charting future directions for development and then mobilising followers . . . the ball is in the court of NGDO leaders and followers to generate a vision of the future they want *beyond aid*.
>
> (Fowler 1997: 234)

Despite the vast amount of ground covered, there are some limitations to this approach. The first is in the narrowness of the NGO definition used by the author. The idea of 'nongovernmental development organizations' is slanted firmly towards organizations promoting social change, and Fowler (1997: 223) is somewhat dismissive of NGOs which deliver services or provide 'welfare', which as we saw in Chapter 6 is a key NGO activity. In practice, the boundaries between service delivery and advocacy can be blurred, and the tone of the book is rather prescriptive in the way that it makes judgements about certain kinds of NGOs. The second is that NGOs are characterized throughout the book as being part of the 'aid industry', but there are many kinds of organizations – such as small-scale campaigning groups or self-help community organizations – which play a developmental role and which form part of the broader NGO sector. If the author is right about the imminent future decline of international development assistance, then perhaps it is to the non-dependent parts of the third sector that we must look for a more sustainable contribution to social development.

Suzuki's (1997) book is very different and takes as its focus the world of Northern development NGOs. It concentrates on the internal management questions rather than on programmatic issues for NGOs. Suzuki argues that these NGOs are characterized by a series of organizational tensions which generate a set of specific management dilemmas. He locates the key dimension of NGO management in terms of a struggle between headquarters and field offices, in which the different roles and activities of the two create a basic tension: the headquarters office tends to be physically distant and concerned with fund-raising efforts, while the local office is concerned with relationships with the local community and the implementation of poverty reduction programmes. This study is based on detailed interviews with NGO staff, and one of its strengths is the ability to examine NGO management through the stories told by staff themselves.

Three sets of tensions are revealed within NGOs. The first is between 'organizational maintenance and project implementation', in the sense that NGOs which are funded by donors must always prioritize the provision of reports and information to these donors, but at the same time the organization must maintain a focus on the implementation of projects and the maintenance of effective relationships with the beneficiaries. The second is the tension between 'diversity and similarity', in which staff within the same organization must undertake potentially contradictory tasks while still seeking to work together to achieve common goals. The third tension which is highlighted is that 'between flexibility and consistency', such that on the one hand donors may impose a set of systematic rules and regulations about performance and accountability, but for the field office the local realities of development work are inevitably 'messy' and difficult to build systems around. Both Fowler (1997) and Suzuki (1997) advance understanding of the field of NGO management in important ways, but both also present a selective view of what is a very large subject. Fowler balances internal and external aspects of NGO management and links it very strongly with the aid industry, while Suzuki examines specific problems for international NGOs working across space and culture.

One of the problems apparent within the NGO literature (but one which both the above authors largely avoid) is that there is in general very little effort made to link the concerns of the third sector literature and the NGO literature around organization and management issues, a point explored by the various papers in Lewis (1999a). While there is a lively discussion around a variety of management themes in the third sector literature, there is very little of this in the NGO literature, which has focused more strongly on the external aspects of NGO relationships and action.

A common area of internal NGO weakness is that of governance structure and process, which is rarely discussed in the NGO literature. One exception is a useful paper by Tandon (1995) on NGO board relationships in India. A key reason for the importance of this theme is the current emphasis on social capital, which suggests that internal democracy within the associations of civil society (of which development NGOs are an important part) is a precondition for democratic politics and prosperous communities in the wider sense. Fulfilling these roles and providing informal structures and relationships necessary for democracy to flourish increasingly falls on the shoulders of non-profit boards. Tandon argues that in the West, at its best board membership is seen as a means of civil engagement, such that it can strengthen the networks of trust and collaboration which can contribute to healthy communities and democratic process. Well-organized boards have the potential to cut across class, race and gender lines, with members bringing their own skills as well as the perspectives of the communities which they serve.

Tandon (1995) sees these questions as relevant to many South Asian NGOs legally registered (under colonial legislation which is still in use) as societies and trusts, which dictates that there should be an executive council and committee or governing board, and a chief executive officer (CEO) such as a secretary, president, director or coordinator. In his study Tandon identifies a range of strategies pursued in South Asia, which he calls 'board games'. For example, in the case of 'family boards' NGO boards may operate like a small family business based on kinship, informality and trust, which provides a supportive structure in the early stages of an NGO but which over time leads to patriarchal governance structures and few entrances for new staff. In the case of 'invisible boards', there is a small group of family and friends brought together by the founder from time to time simply as a 'rubber stamp' in order to meet the legal requirements of NGO registration, with the result that governance and management are clearly separated. Also common is the 'staff board', in which the NGO's staff also act as the board. While this can be effective in the short term, the lack of separation of the governance function from the demands of day-to-day management can prove an inadequate system for dealing rationally with senior staff conflicts, and rarely allows for fresh perspectives to enter the organization. Finally, for 'professional boards', in which competent people are brought together formally (and sometimes remunerated), it may be difficult to generate a shared vision and a sustained commitment.

Each of these NGO boards, while displaying certain strengths, nevertheless contains important weaknesses which limit the organizational capacity of the NGO in important ways. The importance of the charismatic founder-leader (a reality which is somewhat different to the leadership picture painted by Kay (1996) in the previous section) in shaping the vision and perspective of the NGO tends to limit the autonomy of the board such that the leader builds up 'sweat equity' by continually providing the bulk of the ideas and energy. As the NGO moves through its life cycle from the early days of defining its vision and mission and building its programmes (during which time the dominant leader model can prove effective) towards a second period of growth and expansion, the board is needed more and more but performs less and less well. For NGOs which are 'internationalizing', there are a further set of distinctive organizational issues (Box 7.2).

There has been much less research into issues of NGO leadership than in the wider third sector literature. Carroll (1992: 92) found that NGOs which were good at service delivery and participation were headed by strong, charismatic single leaders or managers with 'extraordinary vision and personal commitment'. What has been termed the 'Lawrence of Arabia

Issues in the 'internationalization' of NGO management

The growth of international NGOs (as distinct from Northern and Southern NGOs) is an increasingly important trend, existing alongside the world of intergovernmental organizations such as the UN agencies. There are two main trends: there are INGOs which began in one country but which have expanded to new ones in a process of 'going international' (such as ActionAid); and there are new transnational NGOs specifically formed with representatives from more than one country (such as CIVICUS). This brings a distinctive set of organizational problems, and two structural forms are emerging: 'ethnocentric' structures based on tight control of subsidiary offices by centralized headquarters, and 'polycentric' structures with a high degree of decentralized local control and interconnectedness. The structure which an INGO adopts needs to maximize proximity of decision-making processes to its constituent groups wherever they are. It needs to balance structures with members' and core values, to sensitize structures to cultural and regional diversities, and to create communication methods to allow participation. One strategy is that of the rotating headquarters: the International Association for Volunteer Effort's (IAVE's) original HQ was in the USA, but moved to Colombia for four years when its president was from that country, and then to Australia. An additional range of skills is needed by staff at all levels. For example, board members' competencies need to be different within an INGO as compared to a national NGO. They require a global perspective, not just their own national one; they need to fund-raise through their own community links which may not be accessible to professional staff; they must be sensitive to language and culture, for example during board meetings where discussions must be inclusive to all; they can identify specific local issues which can then be fed into common public relations themes for the INGO; they need visionary leadership skills which can build internationalism rather than nationalism. There are also new demands on professional staff within INGOs, who need to have an international outlook, multicultural sensitivities and the ability to remain as neutral or objective as possible in discussions based on cultural, national and political difference.

Source: Koenig 1996.

syndrome' has been deplored by some of the donor agencies (such as the Inter-American Foundation, which funded his study) but Carroll (1992: 140) focuses on its strengths as well as its weaknesses: 'strong central leadership has been essential to the survival and strength of these organizations and has generally not spawned the autocratic, paternalistic relationships often attributed to it'. Carroll finds that central strong leadership is very important, especially in the early years of an NGO's existence. In Sri Lanka, Zadek and Szabo (1994: 30) considered the issue of the charismatic NGO leader in connection with the NGO Sarvodaya, which was established by a leader who sought to combine participatory decision making with his personal abilities to inspire, but created a decision-making structure that at times showed signs of paternalism and ultimately left an organization that was weakened by subsequent leadership transition.

Since the key works by Fowler and Suzuki already discussed emerged in the late 1990s, a third text by Smillie and Hailey (2001) on management and leadership in South Asian development NGOs has contributed useful knowledge in relation to the internal workings of NGOs, based on detailed interviews with a range of NGO leaders in India, Pakistan and Bangladesh and case studies produced by local researchers. A key strength of the book is the way that each of the organizations described is located firmly within its organizational history, showing how these NGOs emerged and changed over time. Among the more surprising conclusions from the study is the relatively heavy investment in training and research observed in these SNGOs as compared to what the authors see as the relative neglect of such investment by many NNGOs: 'This failure to invest in their own learning and self-reflection stands in marked and odd contrast with their willingness to build the same capacities in their Southern counterparts, (Smillie and Hailey 2001: 79). This leads us neatly into another key area of NGO management, one that links – in our original conceptual framework in Figure 1.1 – the circle of organization with that of relationships. This is the complex issue of 'capacity building'.

CAPACITY BUILDING

Despite the lack of profile of management issues within the literature on NGOs, there has been a considerable amount of writing devoted to the issue of 'capacity building' since the 1990s in connection with NGOs and development. Like many of the terms employed in relation to NGOs (such as 'participation' and 'empowerment') the term 'capacity building' is somewhat imprecise, but is usually used to refer to the strengthening of the organizational dimensions of NGOs, and it is therefore of crucial importance for NGO management. The term 'capacity building' is frequently used with reference to the public sector in developing countries (Polidano and Hulme 1999). It has long been used in relation to outside efforts to strengthen government's capacity to carry out various tasks from service delivery to policy analysis, and it arose as a reaction against the tendency for development projects to generate dependency and an inability to sustain performance beyond the end of the project:[2] 'the process of identifying and developing the management skills necessary to address policy problems; attracting, absorbing and managing financial, human and information resources; and operating programmes effectively' (Umeh 1992: 58).

In the NGO field, the discourse of capacity building has emerged mainly in the context of the changing and unequal relationship between Northern and Southern NGOs (Lewis 1998c). During the past decade or so there has been a gradual shift among Northern NGOs from the transfer of resources and skills towards the idea of building structures for self-reliance and sustainability within the communities in which they work. Rather than implementing projects, there has been a shift towards working with local 'partner' organizations as we saw in Chapter 6, along with a search by Northern NGOs for new 'enabling' roles in relation to SNGOs. For example, Egeland and Kerbs (1987), in a survey of eight international NGOs and their Southern partners, have argued that many Northern NGOs tend to see their own effectiveness in terms of the development of their Southern partners. These NNGOs may put pressure on their partners to demonstrate their effectiveness and by considering their longer-term needs in terms of organizational strengthening. At the same time, there has been pressure from bilateral and multilateral funders under the 'new policy agenda' to ensure that

NGOs are made more effective if they are to play expanded roles in the private service delivery and active civil society approaches which are now in vogue (Sahley 1995). This Northern approach to 'capacity building' in the NGO world has led definitions of capacity building to centre on efforts by Northern NGOs and donors to 'strengthen' Southern NGOs.[3]

As a result of many of the negative experiences from the perspective of Southern NGOs, Fisher (1994) points out that much of the discourse on capacity building has been tinged with a 'subtle paternalism', and the term has been associated with the growing instrumentalist view of NGOs as delivery systems for donor funds. Despite the problems, Fowler (1997) argues that the capacity-building debate can provide an opportunity for reflection on development approaches and organization, and for a possible renegotiation of Northern NGO roles, perhaps leading to a move beyond the simple rhetoric of 'partnership'.

An INTRAC study of Northern NGOs' capacity-building efforts offers the following definition: 'an explicit outside intervention to improve an organization's effectiveness and sustainability in relation to its mission and context' (James 1994: 5).

The survey found that the term was understood in different ways by different NGOs, few of which had a clearly defined idea about what 'capacity building' was. It tended to be seen as an 'add on' to other activities, and few NGOs were found to evaluate the effectiveness of their capacity-building efforts. Some NGO writers have pointed out that capacity building is often understood by NGOs as a form of 'organization development', or OD as it is known in the business sector, where it emerged some years ago. Fowler *et al.* (1992) distinguish organization development from the wider concept of institutional development, by defining institutions as stable sets of widely recognized rules such as laws, markets or civil society, and organizations as structures bringing together people to work towards a common purpose, such as NGOs or businesses, such that OD generally refers to activities such as the strengthening the board or training staff of an NGO, while ID in relation to NGOs is concerned with efforts to improve the performance of the wider context in which NGOs operate, such as network building between organizations, the reform of the legal environment in which NGOs operate, and efforts to influence the policy environment. OD is defined by Fowler *et al.* (1992: 18) as 'an ongoing process that optimises an organization's performance in relation to its goals, resources and environments'. Cooke (1996) has distinguished different approaches to OD, which he terms 'development organization development' (DOD), which tends to be flexible and experiential, and 'managerialist organization development' (MOD), which is planned and systematic in nature.

The importance of the 'capacity-building' idea for NGOs is, as Fowler points out, the recognition that factors both inside *and* outside the NGO are important for effectiveness, since any comparative advantage that NGOs may have over governments is only 'potential' and needs to be 'realized'. One study on NGO capacity building which has been strongly influenced by organization development is that carried out by Sahley (1995), who identifies three groups of NGO capacities:

1 identity, culture and purpose, such as the capacity for a clear ideology of development, good staff/management relations and effective conflict resolution mechanisms;
2 management systems and structure in relation to the existence within the NGO of clear procedures, roles and responsibilities, effective decision making and financial management;

3 programme and technical capacity, which refers to the ability of the NGO to deliver services effectively and develop strategies based on understanding the social, political and economic contexts.

This has led to many different forms of support under the general heading of 'capacity building'. The first is technical assistance, which is usually concerned with basic operation issues of the NGO and can include technical resources such as a monitoring system or computer software, specialized advice, or exchange or secondment of staff in order to strengthen certain skills. The second is provision of organizational assistance as a response to overall organizational needs, and may take the form of management training or short-term consultancy inputs designed to build capacity in an area such as strategic planning in a problem-solving approach. The third type of intervention is termed by Sahley as 'organizational development intervention', in which a longer-term view is formed of organizational capacity overall, leading to a facilitative programme over a number of years of interventions designed to help the organization diagnose and solve present and future challenges itself.

Eade's (1997) study of capacity building – built in part on Oxfam's long experience – is one of the most comprehensive reviews of the subject, but the author wisely resists the temptation to offer a single definition of what is often understood differently by different individuals and agencies. Instead, Eade (1997: 35) distinguishes three views of capacity building within an NGO – which she distinguishes from other forms of capacity building, such as building the capacity of wider civil society, i.e. institutional development – and points out that while these are clearly interrelated, they are often muddled and can usefully be separated out. First, capacity building can be understood as a 'means' through which an organization is strengthened to perform specific activities. Second, it can be viewed as a 'process' of searching for greater coherence within an organization based on reflection and leadership in relation to mission, structure and activities. Third, it can be understood as an 'end', which is to provide an organization with the means to survive and fulfil its mission and objectives. Kaplan (1999) argues that there has been too much attention given to a 'simplistic delivery' view of capacity building, which instead needs to be rooted in the specifics of an individual organization's history and distinctive processes, rather than 'one size fits all' solutions. The debate on capacity building has brought NGO organization and management issues into focus more sharply than ever. The shifts away from the more traditional models of North–South capacity building are illustrated by the case material in Boxes 7.3 and 7.4.

Challenging the North/South conventions of 'capacity building'

There are currently some interesting examples of NGOs which move beyond the rhetoric of capacity building towards radical organizational support and change. For example, the Katalysis approach involves a small NGO in the United States which works long term with just five partners in Central America. This is not a conventional North/South partnership, but one in which the six agencies exchange members of their boards in order to facilitate joint decision making, undertake strategic planning exercises together so that the Southern

NGOs IN ACTION 7.3 *continued*

NGOs are not simply responding to the Northern NGO's agenda, and make available to each other all financial information which relates to each NGO and its programmes (James 1994). Details of Katalysis's latest work can be found at www.katalysis.org.

The NGO Resource Centre in Karachi is an example of capacity building which moves beyond the conventional North/South model. Established with the support of the Aga Khan Foundation in 1990, the centre provides capacity-building support in the form of training, information provision and linkage support to local NGOs in Pakistan. More information can be found at www.ngorc.org.pk.

Finally, the Transform Programme began in the UK as a capacity-building programme for the Southern partners of a group of UK NGOs including Christian Aid, CAFOD, World University Service and Oxfam. Over time, it has evolved into a network of NGOs and consultants in Southern and East Africa which aims to strengthen the capacity of organizations and businesses to build organizational support locally and reduce dependence on Northern organizations and resource channels. It has now become Transform Africa, an independent organization. For more details, see www.transformafrica.org.

NGOs IN ACTION 7.4

Government-sponsored NGO capacity building in Mexico

As part of the ongoing process of democratic change in Mexico, relations between government and NGOs are changing. When a new government took office in 2000 after seventy years of unbroken rule by a single party, a number of former NGO managers crossed over into the new government to take charge of INDESOL (El Instituto National de Desarrollo Social), a public institution dedicated to funding and promoting NGOs in social development. They found that grant-making to NGOs had often been motivated more by political logic than by systematic criteria. They began reforming the system in line with more professional proposal evaluation criteria, but also realized that in order to meet these, many NGOs would also need organizational strengthening. The result was the organization of a new diploma course for NGO capacity building.

There was initial scepticism about the idea of government officials training NGOs, in relation to motives behind curriculum design and opportunities for political co-optation. So INDESOL set up a fund that allowed selection of suitable NGOs to be used as trainers and counterparts to run the diploma locally and manage NGO selection for the training. The topics covered included project formulation, financial and human resource management, strategic planning, information technology, evaluation, and history and identity of NGOs. A second, more advanced level adds social policy and development, public policy advocacy, visibility and relations with media, internal transparency and accountability, and best practices documentation. More than a thousand NGO participants in twenty cities have now been trained in the last three years. An evaluation indicated high levels of satisfaction among participants and is now following these participants as they try to apply the knowledge and skills they have acquired. ➤

One of the NGOs participating in providing training was Alternativas y Capacidades (Alternatives and Capacities), which designed and taught the module on public policy advocacy. The first challenge was to translate concepts such as the policy process, public policy, law making and public accountability into accessible language and provide locally relevant examples. The second was to offer participants practical tools that they could use in their dealings with the government in pursuit of policy change. The main training exercises – which took a highly participatory form – drew upon examples such as Oxfam's international Fair Trade campaign as well as local NGO efforts to improve municipal accountability.

The hope is that NGOs will gradually gain a broader and more constructive view of politics, policy and public affairs and the potential for change. Politics has for many years been characterized by clientelism, co-optation and repression, and so this is a particularly difficult challenge. But many in NGOs and INDESOL believe that a democratic transition can only make progress if it is supported by NGO roles in helping to construct a stronger local civic and political culture. This is a slow process that goes well beyond mere electoral changes. As the diploma participants draw up their policy advocacy plans, we are observing seeds that may soon grow, which would not have been possible without a change of government and efforts of NGO activists within INDESOL.

Source: Mónica Tapia A., Alternativas y Capacidades A.C.

ORGANIZATIONAL CHANGE AND NGOs

One of the key themes of the third sector literature is that of rapid change and the struggle for appropriate organizational response. Can NGOs learn how to manage change better? A brief review of the extensive literature on organizational change indicates that no one agrees about how planned change is achieved in business organizations, and it seems logical to suppose that there is no reason why NGOs should be any different. The standard textbook view of organizational change is explained by Robbins (1990) who uses the ideas of a three-step change process for organizations in unfreezing, moving and refreezing, which recognizes that change does not occur simply because a decision has been taken that it will occur, and engineering change needs to be seen as a process, especially if that change is to be lasting. This view also shows how change within an organization can be resisted for many different reasons: people with power fear losing what they have, the bureaucratic structures of an organization tend to favour the status quo, cultures resist pressures to change and organizations often work hard to 'manage' the environment in order to protect themselves from the need for any change. Recognition of the need to confront the tendencies within all organizations that can lead to postponement of dealing with problems and weaknesses lay, for example, at the heart of a learning exercise undertaken by IIED on participation (Box 7.5).

If we briefly examine prevailing ideas about organizational change in the business world, we find agreement that the ways in which organizations change is likely to be influenced by two main types of factor. Both the context and the environment impel changes to take place and constrain the changes which are possible, as well as the efforts made by managers within organizations who may struggle to understand the need for change, to work consciously to

Internal processes and participation: learning within IIED

The International Institute for Environment and Development (IIED) is a non-governmental research organization which works extensively with a range of partners in the South on research and advocacy. In 2001 IIED undertook a review of its internal systems and structures and external project relationships in order to stimulate learning and increase IIED's transparency to its partners. While the review found plenty of evidence to indicate that IIED remained at the forefront of using and promoting participatory approaches and methods, it was also agreed that – like many NGOs – IIED also needed 'to draw out, disseminate and incorporate lessons from our work much more systematically than we do' (p. 33). Issues raised by the study included the need to: (a) recognize the demands on the time of staff and partners and ensure that there are adequate incentives in place to encourage learning and exchange; (b) understand that there can be trade-offs between interesting processes and useful high-quality products, so that judgements sometimes need to be made in cases where time and/or resources are tight; (c) ensure that dissemination and influencing strategies are better planned and budgeted for with partners; and (d) recognize that there are several different understandings of participation that exist and that it is necessary to negotiate these clearly with staff and partners. The authors concluded that the experience of doing the review 'illustrates the complexities involved in "practising what we preach" and reminds us how difficult it is to keep to the values that underpin "participation" in a demanding and competitive environment' (p. v).

Source: Kanji and Greenwood 2001.

achieve it, to develop capacities of organizations to change and to learn. For example, the view of DiMaggio and Powell (1991) is that organizations tend to change primarily in order to be more like each other – pressured, for example, by the state and other institutions to conform to accepted practice – and they term this process 'isomorphism'. The work of Pettigrew (1987) argues that securing strategic change is extremely complex and requires understanding of context, content and process by managers often over a long period. In Senge's (1990) work there is an emphasis on the need for organizations to have a systems approach to change, in which they seek to build a 'learning organization' which can change effectively – this requires new disciplines in thinking by managers. Peters (1994) argues that the most important thing for managers to do is not to think consciously about change processes but instead to seek out unusual new challenges and make their organization an exciting place to work in – by building the 'curious corporation' – and success will automatically follow. Finally, G. Morgan (1994) argues that change has a symbolic dimension and that managers need to apply appropriate 'images' to conceive of possible changes, e.g. the spider plant, which grows and changes simultaneously through multiple centres and strands in more complex ways than linear models of change may allow.

From the public administration field, research has shown that efforts to change are often unsuccessful, and emphasizes the problem of power and resistance. Some organizational change is merely a relabelling exercise, and we need to understand the role of dominant elites and the power of ideology in the change process. From the institutional perspective, it is argued that the adoption of new structures is often a legitimization device to maintain outside support and funding, rather than signifying underlying change to values and purpose, that is, values get decoupled from purposes. On the other hand, change may be top-down, power-driven change and may take real effect. For example, the growth of the new public management has been associated with widespread organizational change based on changes in the response to funding and resources, and to changes in the realm of ideas and ideology. Both of these may contribute to organizational change.

In the UK third sector, there are similar preoccupations with organizational change, as we have seen from Osborne's (1996) outline of the new management demands on the sector brought about by the growth of contracting for service delivery. In the NGO field there have been two sets of pressures. The donor interest in NGOs as service providers has helped to establish the use by NGOs of formal management tools such as the logical framework, while the donor emphasis on NGOs as actors in civil society has prompted questions about levels of participation and hierarchy *within* NGOs. Management, as we have seen, is difficult on account of a range of factors, such as the lack of markets, which means that NGOs can ignore poor service delivery to beneficiaries because there is no market mechanism to carry any message of customer satisfaction; because of the vague and difficult-to-measure 'objectives' of many NGOs; and because of the overall context of 'resource' scarcity and unpredictability.

It becomes possible to untangle two basic approaches to organizational change, as Tassie *et al.* (1996) have shown. First, there are what might be termed programmatic or 'rational change' models. These tend to draw upon predominantly Western mechanistic models of transition and change followed by periods of calm. An example of this are models of strategic planning which began with Mintzberg, and this perspective is based on the assumption that rational, top-down restructuring of organizations is possible.[4] This is the dominant post-1960s Western model of organizational change, which uses military language of 'planning', 'scenarios' and 'objectives' and identifies definable problems which need to be overcome in organizations. There are many approaches which fit this general model, and variants which add different ideas to the basic package. For example, there is an 'incremental' variant which acknowledges the role of politics, power, incremental change and feedback (Quinn 1980). There are also interpretative variants which place a more central importance on the role of people within the organization – Senge's (1990) ideas about 'learning' organizations and Weick's (1979) sense-making concept are good examples of this.

The second group of perspectives are non-linear, with a focus on self-organization as well as externally directed change. In chaos theory, for example, causes and effects are unclear and multi-directional, and change process patterns emerge from apparent disorder through a process of self-organization. For example, an organization takes a decision to acquire a computer in order to improve its record keeping, but this generates unexpected discussions within the organization about which records are to be kept, and the ripples from this change eventually feed into wider negotiations about changing the mission of the organization.

Chaos and complexity theory is at the heart of some of these new debates. For example, CMC (n.d.) reviews how the central issue facing managers today is increasing rapidity of change and turbulence in the environment, which then creates more complexity and ambiguity for managers. There is growing dissatisfaction about how planned change does not yield results, leading to more and more 'new recipes for success' which repeatedly disappoint. The reasons for this are that organizations are not in equilibrium with their environments as some 'open systems' theories suppose, that there is no linear cause and effect operating, and that managers' realities may often be quite different within an organization, such that understandings and representations are open to question within organizations. These ideas about complexity theory are leading researchers to refine earlier models such as 'organizational learning' in order to emphasize and understand such features of organizations (a) as the existence of informal spontaneous networks among staff which 'shadow' formal structures (e.g. resistance, favouritism, etc.); (b) the need to encourage 'spontaneous self-control' during periods of organizational change which does not tip over into an 'unstable zone' in which change becomes impossible to guide.

This latter view was apparent in the work of DiBella (1992) who brings a postmodern perspective to a study of an organizational change programme within a Northern NGO and its field offices. DiBella's study found that change was perceived very differently by staff in different parts of the organization, with a particular discrepancy between the headquarters and the field offices overseas. Although the organizational change which was being promoted was ostensibly designed to promote regionalization, with a devolution of many powers to the local offices (with overall control retained by the centre), this was perceived by the field offices as a concentration of power by the centre. DiBella concludes by suggesting that the process of organizational change in the NGO was closer to 'organized anarchy' than planned change, and that there can be no shared vision across an NGO in which goals are ambiguous, technologies are unclear and structures are loosely coupled.

Writing from the third sector perspective, Tassie *et al.* (1996) argue that both of these views on change can be reconciled, because each has a validity in certain circumstances. The change model which is realistic is one in which efforts are made to secure the right fit between the level of unpredictability in the environment (which brings us back to de Graaf's (1987) ideas about control and influence), the links between means and ends in terms of assessing whether a given process will produce a given outcome, and the level of 'programmability' possible in the change process if parts of it are to be managed:

> the failure of most change initiatives in . . . [third sector organizations] . . . can be attributed to an inability to match the adopted approach to change (programmatic or self-organized) with the situation (external environment or means/ends relationships orientated).
>
> (Tassie *et al.* 1996: 144)

Lindblom's (1959) ideas about the implementation of public policy which he called 'the science of muddling through' demonstrate the importance of emergent, incremental change based on a series of small but significant policy changes – negotiations of multiple demands and competing values along with a process of mutual adjustments. He suggests that formal techniques such as strategic planning are beyond the capacities of real people because both technique and organization are so complex, and that a longer process of 'successive limited comparison' can produce change through small, incremental steps. The art of change management for Tassie *et al.* (1996) is therefore one in which managers try to create a 'context for change' which allows for both patterns, rather than trying simply to impose a top-down master plan. Once a leader realizes that they cannot easily predict or control change, then it is better to build a context by articulating a commitment to the process and to the core vision and values of the organization, and then to leave the precise trajectory of different parts of the change process to managers, who are then free to pursue diverse initiatives as long as they fall within the overall context domain.

NGOs AND INFORMATION MANAGEMENT

NGOs can be seen as being increasingly concerned in their work with 'linkages and information flows with national and international development agencies' (Madon 1999: 253) and with the people they work with. However, as Powell (1999: 12) points out in one of the few studies so far to examine the role of information in development organizations, while most NGOs are conscious of the need to collect and manage information, the problem is that not all information is actually useful: 'Even the best-constructed information has no value if it is not used. It is the flow and exchange of information which help to create its value.' The challenge for NGOs is therefore that of distinguishing between, gathering and utilizing different kinds of information for different purposes including *data* (which are quantitative or qualitative facts), *information* (data and other objective facts which have been given meaning) and *knowledge* (the product of people giving some kind of significance or value to this information). This can be seen as 'a chain of increasing value, whereby data can become information, which can then be transformed into knowledge' (Powell 1999: 11).

It is almost self-evident that good information management can improve an organization's efficiency, effectiveness and creativity. But as Powell argues, it is the current high speed of technological change and the growing complexity of tasks which causes many NGOs problems:

> Everyone is agreed that information and knowledge are of vital importance. However, no one knows which knowledge, applied to which information, in which way, will prove to be the most effective way in shaping the new realities.
>
> (Powell 1999: 21)

This produces and reinforces conceptual uncertainty among NGO managers and managing information is clearly getting more difficult. Turning the mass of information into 'useable knowledge' is difficult for NGOs, because it requires well-developed analytical skills, especially to link the micro and the macro levels. This is particularly apparent for NGOs engaging with markets, where there is rapid change and a high economic cost to out-of-date or inadequate information. For example, in an initiative by NGOs such as Technoserve working in Mozambique to support emerging entrepreneurship among small producers in the recently privatized cashew nut industry, it was found that learning to manage information was a key constraint in building and supporting successful businesses in conditions in which global markets can change rapidly (Artur and Kanji 2005).

213

Edwards (1994) highlights some of the barriers that operate to impede information management within NGOs. Internally, NGOs may develop an organizational culture which restricts information exchange. For some activists, information gathering may simply be seen as a luxury the organization cannot afford. At the level of structure, NGO staff may be geographically scattered and compartmentalized and this too may restrict the generation of useful knowledge. Most important of all is the need to acknowledge the role of power within organizations and between stakeholders. In practice, many NGOs are vulnerable and therefore defensive organizations that have strong incentives to reject information that does not fit with their existing practices or which they feel some stakeholders will not wish to hear.

The generation of knowledge from information, argues Powell, while increasingly relying on technology, is therefore an essentially human process since reaction to information necessarily draws upon peoples' experience, judgement, values and insights, and therefore is not necessarily 'objective'. And yet the reality for many NGOs, and the aid system within which many are embedded, is one in which information is often used to limit and control more than it is to unlock creativity and challenge the realities of poverty. This point is made forcefully by Wallace and Kaplan (2003: 61) in their heartfelt study of the process of organizational change which ActionAid Uganda has been undertaking in recent years:

> ActionAid Uganda has achieved far more than we could have hoped for. . . . On the other hand, the entire system in which ActionAid Uganda is embedded relies on the kind of thinking which revels in lists, which insists upon logical frameworks, quantitative analysis and reporting, boxes, compartments, tables. The tendency is towards reduction of complexity and nuance and contradiction to lowest common denominators of facts and numbers which can be perused and assessed in the quickest possible time, with the least amount of effort. This remains the ActionAid centre's main expectation, as it does the expectations of the aid world generally. Uncertainty, ambiguity, nuance, complexity – all these are to be avoided. They demand high levels of emotional and thinking ability, and they don't easily bring in the money.

With this reflection, we are brought back firmly to the issues of power and information raised in Chapter 4 by Ebrahim (2003) and set out in Box 4.3. It raises questions about culture and the types of information that are valued. It also bears out the common finding that formal quantitative data tend to be valued within dominant information systems over the informal or local types of information that may be valued by people in less powerful positions in the community or NGO.

Information is ultimately linked to power, since participation in the new 'informational economy' remains highly uneven, as the influential work of Manuel Castells (1996) shows. The well-known idea of the 'digital divide' is apparent to most NGOs and raises important issues of exclusion and inclusion in relation to the new technologies that are available. These problems are also related to organizational culture. Within organizations, managers' own behaviour often reveals them to be deploying power – sometimes consciously, sometimes unconsciously – at various levels to control information. The informal networks that result may exclude certain people and create knowledge cliques. For example, issues of representation are an important component of NGO information management. Bebbington (2005) shows how dominant NGO representations of Andean people by Dutch and Peruvian NGOs have often served to perpetuate a largely out-of-date picture of these people as primarily depending upon agrarian livelihoods, which the very poor no longer did. This misrepresentation resulted in development interventions that were biased towards the less poor groups and that ignored the needs of those most marginalized.

CONCLUSION

This chapter has examined some of the issues which emerge in the internal management of NGOs, focusing on aspects of both the third sector and the wider management literature. On the whole there is surprisingly little written on the internal management of NGOs. Starting with the wider third sector literature, it is possible to identify a set of distinctive management issues which apply to most third sector organizations, such as leadership, governance and volunteerism. However, development NGOs have differences in terms of context and approach and, for example, work on governing bodies in India reveals a related though potentially distinctive set of challenges and issues. Much of the work on NGOs has taken the form of a discussion about 'capacity building', though this was narrowly focused on North/South NGO relationships until quite recently. Ideas from business management relating to organizational change can be seen to have relevance to NGOs, particularly in relation to chaos and complexity theory, which fits the unstable world of NGOs quite well.

There are important hazards which can damage the practice and understanding of NGO management. One is the ideology of 'managerialism', which exists both in a wider form and in the form of a specialized third sector variant. A second is the danger of a 'one size fits all' management prescription, which results from a lack of understanding of the diversity of NGO forms, approaches and contexts. A third and final danger is the idea that the values of the business sector are being imposed on NGOs through the new interest in management. This can seem attractive to NGOs which are already moving in the direction of becoming businesses (such as those running cost-recovery service provision or micro-credit banking facilities), but is unlikely to suit organizations with a more radical, non-market agenda, and ultimately runs the risk of homogenizing the NGO sector.

REVIEW QUESTIONS

- Should we distinguish between the internal management challenges found in third sector organizations working in 'developed' country contexts from those of development NGOs working in poorer or less stable areas of the world? If so, on what grounds?
- Why has NGO management raised different challenges for managers than those found within other types of organization such as those within the business world?
- How well have capacity-building efforts towards NGO management strengthening engaged with wider questions of organizational change within NGOs?

Conclusion

Understanding NGO management

INTRODUCTION

In the chapters that precede, an attempt has been made to provide an overview of the diverse management issues confronting development NGOs, and the task for us now is to pull together the various themes which have been explored.

In Part I of the book, 'The theory of NGO management', Chapters 2, 3 and 4 each examined a different area of the NGO management context set out in the conceptual framework outlined in Chapter 1 (Figure 1.1). In this framework, NGO management is encapsulated in the interlinked realms of activities, organization and relationships – all of which take place against a complex, changing context or operating environment. Chapter 2 set development NGOs within the context of theory and history, while Chapter 3 introduced the field of international development in which NGOs operate. Chapter 4 explored areas of organization theory and anthropology that have particular relevance to the management challenges development NGOs face. In Part II, 'The practice of NGO management', our challenge was to examine the three main sets of challenges NGOs face in their work. Chapter 5 covered the activities of service provision and advocacy, Chapter 6 examined the management of relationships, while Chapter 7 focused on the ways in which NGOs direct their own organizational systems and structures.

THREE APPROACHES TO NGO MANAGEMENT

It is possible to untangle three main schools of thought in relation to NGO management. The first of these is the generic management view, which assumes that 'management is management' and places a strong emphasis on a 'one size fits all' approach. According to this view, there is no particular reason why NGOs should not seek to strengthen and improve their management by drawing strongly on mainstream business thinking. One practical implication of this perspective is that NGOs should consider sending their staff to the established management training courses along with colleagues from the worlds of business and government. This is the line of thinking which emerges, at least in part, from Dichter's (1989a) discussion of the common failure of many development NGOs to engage with the 'nuts and bolts' of basic management due to a preoccupation with what he terms 'fancy' alternative, value-driven management ideas.

The second broad school of thought is the 'adaptive' view of NGO management. Within this perspective, it is argued that while generic or mainstream management ideas may be useful and relevant to development NGOs, these cannot be applied in any simple, straightforward way. Instead, they will need to be adapted in the light of NGO distinctiveness in terms of organizational structure and culture, and in terms of the complex forms of work which development NGOs seek to undertake. This view emerges broadly from the work of Korten (1990) and Fowler (1997), who place an emphasis on the need for development NGOs to learn from other sectors, as well as to build innovative management approaches which both get the work done more effectively *and* remain appropriate to an NGO's core principles and values.

A third view of NGO management pushes this point further by arguing that a 'distinctive' view of NGO management may be needed. Billis and MacKeith (1992: 44) state that

NGO management is 'a massive uncharted territory awaiting exploration' and hypothesize that NGO management may embody a unique 'combination of challenges' for managers, which will need to be explored through further investigative research. This position is an extension of that taken by some third sector management researchers who, frustrated at the neglect that third sector management received until comparatively recently, have argued that new management models and concepts need to be developed based on the distinctive, specific experiences of third sector managers (Billis 1993a; Harris 1996).

Each of these perspectives has something to recommend it. There has been so little systematic research on NGO management to date that it remains difficult at this point to draw definite conclusions. The 'composite' model of NGO management which is presented below therefore acknowledges both the currently uncertain grasp which exists of the subject field, and the probability that NGO management is an emerging synthesis of various management perspectives which shift over time and across the many different types of development NGO which exist. The subject of NGO management can therefore best be approached from four perspectives simultaneously: business management, public management, third sector management and development management. As they carry out their day-to-day work NGO managers are – in addition to learning by doing – engaged in the complex task of synthesizing and distilling ideas from other sources in the hope that some will fit their needs. While improvisation is important to all kinds of management, there is a distinctive and deep-rooted 'improvisational quality' at the heart of NGO management. In the process of building appropriate practice, an NGO manager needs to draw upon different combinations of ideas, approaches and techniques from various sources, and the precise mix adopted will depend on an NGO's own mission, culture and values, as well as on the forces in its wider operating environment, such as the demands of donors or the requirements of government.

Both sets of factors may also shift an NGO's overall identity and position within the three-sector model presented in this book. While it may be useful to conceive of an NGO as being part of the third sector, it is just as important to understand its position in relation to the other two sectors. For example, an NGO which moves into not-for-profit trading activity in order to reduce its dependence on donors may find itself increasingly drawing upon private sector business management thinking, but an NGO which undertakes contract work within a government-run service provision system may need to engage with and take on many of the public sector management traditions.

THE COMPOSITE MODEL

Back in the late 1980s when the NGO management debate was first ignited, the argument was made by Campbell (1987) that NGOs needed to take management more seriously if they were to improve their performance and build a more solid reputation. In response to the suspicion of management expressed by some development NGOs, he suggested that there was nothing inherently 'good' or 'bad' about the concept of management per se, and pointed out that management was simply 'the process of mobilizing resources towards a given purpose'. At a more conceptual level, Campbell showed that one way of seeking to understand NGOs – as with other types of organization – was to view them in terms of both their organizational characteristics and the wider context in which they operated. What

Table 8.1 *A composite framework for understanding NGO management*

	Contextual features	Organizational features
All organizations	Environment (culture, context, institutions)	Generic management (mainly from the 'for-profit' business world
Development NGOs	Development management (from 'Southern' projects and programmes)	Third sector management (mainly from 'Northern' voluntary/non-profit sectors)
		Public sector management (from government in 'North' and 'South')

Source: adapted from Campbell 1987.

makes development NGOs different, he argued, were certain distinctive aspects of their work, their structure and their environment, and he suggested that an ongoing synthesis of generic management, development management and third sector management was needed. Table 8.1 develops this line of thinking further and sets out a conceptual framework, based on Campbell's earlier work but adding public sector management as another potentially useful source of ideas and skills, that illustrates the 'composite' nature of NGO management based on at least *four* different 'sources' of management thinking.

First, what might be termed *generic management* is important because development NGOs like any other organization need to give priority to well-established 'nuts-and-bolts' management principles. Second, *third sector management* ideas are potentially useful to development NGOs because, as we have seen in Chapter 7, third sector organizations – of which NGOs are a subset – face distinctive challenges of structure and context which may go beyond the scope and competence of theories developed within the generic management field. There is little in mainstream management theory which would equip an NGO for the difficult tasks of managing the demands of different funding agencies, or balancing its accountabilities simultaneously to both a formal governing body and its large numbers of geographically remote, impoverished users; yet these are the kinds of questions which the emerging field of third sector management theory is seeking to address. Third, some relevant principles drawn from *public sector management* – such as the need to empower users of services, to improve the level of public participation in choice and decision making and the need to ensure that equal opportunities policies are in place to prevent discrimination by race or gender – will be drawn upon by development NGOs, particularly those which are engaged in the delivery of public services. Fourth, the concept of *development management* seeks to achieve a good fit between both the outcomes of activities undertaken and the manner in which such work is carried out (Thomas 1999). This becomes a vital area for development NGOs seeking to build distinctive values into their work – 'to walk the talk', as the expression goes.

Campbell's work outlined the importance of an organization's operating environment as being crucial to its management systems and choices. This includes the institutional context, the level of political stability, the resource availability and the cultural norms which exist

Table 8.2 *The sectoral origins of selected concepts relevant to NGO management*

Public sector	Private sector	Third sector
Accountability	Strategic planning	Volunteer management
Empowerment	Management by objectives	Fund-raising management
Capacity building	Social audit	Governance and governing bodies
Participation	Stakeholder analysis	Participatory evaluation
Equal opportunities	Organizational learning	Advocacy

both within and beyond an organization's boundaries. This contextual component of NGO management has been emphasized throughout the previous chapters in order to counter the somewhat inward-looking, technocratic and apolitical tendencies which occasionally surface in some writings on 'NGO management science' which have been critiqued by Stewart (1997).

The sectoral origins of the management concepts central to NGO management may therefore have roots outside the immediate experience of development NGOs – in the worlds of business or government organizations, or among the non-profit or voluntary sectors of the industrialized countries of Europe and North America. Table 8.2 shows how many of the key issues of NGO management have their origins in concepts and techniques from within these other sectors. For example, it has recently been common for development NGOs to experiment with the technique of 'strategic planning' in response to perceived planning weaknesses. The idea originated in the business sector in the 1970s, but it is now believed to have had mixed results and limited conceptual value (Mintzberg 1994). At the same time, strategic planning was taken up enthusiastically by many non-profit organizations in the USA during the 1990s, but while it sent signals of 'professionalization' to certain key stakeholders, there have been questions raised as to its practical value and concerns voiced about its overall effects on the diversity of non-profit organizations (Mulhare 1999). There are many other examples of this hidden history, of which NGOs need to be aware if they are to avoid risks of 'reinventing the wheel'. Current interest in the 'social audit' as a method for improving performance and accountability revisits previous debates from the commercial sector about business practice and social responsibility, and the term was first coined four decades ago (Goyder 1961). The concept of public accountability, which remains a hot issue for NGO supporters and critics alike (and for the wider third sector), can be traced back to much older debates within the field of public administration. For example, Selznick's (1966) influential study of the Tennessee Valley Authority examined the constraints to public participation in a large public sector development project.

It is often surprising – though perhaps ultimately reassuring – to discover that many of the key management challenges with which NGOs currently grapple are far from new, and have long institutional histories. But as we have seen, there are new ideas in management theory and practice that also resonate with development NGO work, such as the growth of interest in complexity (Stacey *et al.* 2000) and critical management (Grey and Willmott 2005).

At the same time, there are areas in which NGOs are themselves innovating in the management field. Some are developing new management approaches, such as the concept of 'accompaniment' in Latin America as a reaction against largely discredited Northern forms of inter-agency 'partnership' in which the SNGO found itself a subordinate player (Hoyer 1994). However, these innovations frequently go undocumented, and more systematic research will be needed in order to understand the emerging, distinctive features of NGO management, particularly in Southern contexts. Such models need to be based on new research and related to the specific needs of development NGOs, and not simply 'recycled' from other sectors. They will also need to be context-specific and context-sensitive, and Chapter 4 has argued that a comparative approach to the analysis of NGO management practice in different cultural contexts is an important priority. One example of the type of further research that is needed is the book by Wallace et al. (2006) on the ways in which partnerships with NGOs in the South have played out in practice, undertaken as a multi-country study over a long period involving a partnership between Northern and Southern researchers and organizations.

MUDDYING THE WATERS: HYBRIDITY AND AMBIGUITY

We have seen that for reasons of organizational diversity and change, NGOs increasingly need to draw upon management approaches taken from a combination of different sources. As the environment in which NGOs operate becomes more complex and uncertain, as we saw in Chapters 1 and 2, it seems probable that this state of affairs will continue to be the case. Development NGOs are increasingly setting themselves tougher and more complex challenges, as Clark (2003b: 147) points out:

> Twenty years ago most NGOs concentrated on what they thought they did best, whether relief, self-help, conservation, micro-credit or advocacy. Now leading NGOs are seeing the need to do all these things and take a holistic view of development.

At the same time, development as an idea has once again become more and more connected with broader debates. NGOs that were previously content to try to make a difference at the local project level, perhaps combined with some national-level advocacy work are finding themselves participating in more wide-ranging debates and forms of action. NGOs at the international level have themselves become part of a changing system of world politics within increasing levels of globalism and interdependence, in which more and more issues that were previously debated nationally are now 'up for grabs internationally', such as pharmaceutical testing, accounting standards, multilateral trade negotiations and financial regulation (Keohane and Nye 2003).

The vast diversity of NGOs and issues means that the 'mix' will be different for each NGO, and that this mix may also change as the organization evolves, takes new decisions and develops new strategies. Over time, some NGOs may move closer towards the market sector and sell services in order to become sustainable, while others may choose to rely on a more value-based, voluntaristic motivation to their work and remain true to founding

221

principles. Some NGOs may decide that entering into contracting arrangements with government for service delivery is appropriate to their objectives, and these organizations may then grow to take on more of the characteristics of government agencies.[1]

These trajectories will each have a set of advantages and disadvantages in terms of the work NGOs undertake and the management implications of these activities. A dynamic model of NGO management therefore needs to encapsulate organizational diversity, learning and change. The model reflects a 'process' view of management which recognizes that NGOs are adaptive, constantly changing organizations within increasingly uncertain and unpredictable contexts, and that there is therefore no single 'blueprint' for managing NGOs. It also acknowledges that there are increasingly many management issues – such as information technology – with which all three kinds of organization may be simultaneously grappling.

Within these change processes, there are three conceptual issues which need to be considered. The first is *organizational hybridity*: we are seeing new combinations of organizational structures and objectives, from the rise of the socially aware or ethical business organization to the increasingly businesslike and commercialized world of NGO micro-credit provision. This makes a composite model of NGO management necessary for understanding the ways in which NGO organizational universes are changing. While the conventional organizational choices, such as self-management systems, decentralized structures and classic bureaucracies, can all be found amongst the NGO sector, mixed organizational forms are also becoming increasingly common. For example, some NGOs which run micro-credit programmes now draw upon private sector financial management techniques and practices in calculating and recovering administrative costs, yet many seek to do so within the overall framework of the not-for-profit form, and may combine this work with community development work which draws upon radical empowerment approaches. In a study of women's organizations in the US third sector, the initial hypothesis was that the more politically radical women's organizations would increasingly adopt collectivist, non-hierarchical forms, while apolitical, professionalized women's organizations would take on more traditional formal bureaucratic structures. Instead, a hybrid organizational form was found to be most common, in which organizations tried in novel ways to get the 'best of both worlds': 'Women's nonprofits in New York City that adopt a feminist ideology are not only thriving with the formal bureaucratic form but are also innovating by combining aspects of both bureaucratic and collectivist structures' (Bordt 1997: 80).

In Bordt's study, the principles associated primarily with top-down management were found to have been successfully incorporated into third sector organizations concerned with radical, participatory social change and with a consciously 'alternative' orientation. This example also suggests another important priority for further NGO management research: the field of gender and organization. As Howell (2006a: 60) has highlighted, more empirical work and theory building is needed to understand differences between men's and women's organizing, in terms of the psychological, discursive and material resources that each deploy, the patterns of leadership that emerge and the organizational forms that are preferred.

A second important concept is that of *ambiguity*, which as we have seen is crucial to an understanding of NGO management in a number of ways. For example, Billis (1993a) has shown how third sector organizations may contain elements of both the associational and the bureaucratic worlds, creating both danger and opportunity. As we saw in Chapter 6, the growth of development NGOs which work in the area of 'fair trade' can easily lead to tensions between charitable and business management styles, raising a very specific set of management challenges. In his overview of non-profit management, Anheier (2005) also highlights four sets of tensions that arise from the common ambiguities that exist within non-profit organizations: between structures that allow predictability but that also need to be able to improvise and be creative; between a technocratic culture that emphasizes perfor-mance and outputs, and one that focuses on people; between the structures of hierarchy and centralization, as opposed to ones that facilitate bottom-up decision making and decen-tralized networks; and finally between 'outer-directedness' (reacting to and adapting to events and opportunities in the outside environment) and 'inner-directedness' (focusing on the organization's own objectives, values and world view as the main source of strategy).

Hulme (1994) has shown that in Africa and Asia there are different NGO strategies which are increasingly in use at the same time, such as 'empowering' transformational approaches and modernizing 'income generation'. This is often justified by short-term practicalities such as the shortage of members or staff time and the need to demonstrate individual benefits, as well as by long-term goals of structural change. Hulme calls this the 'double-headed strategy' and it allows NGOs to present different sides to their various supporters and clients under shifting conditions of uncertainty and change. This allows SNGOs to respond to donors and governments with a non-threatening face, and allows NGOs to expand their membership, while offering ideological attractions to NNGOs and people's organizations and to supporters from radical backgrounds. It may also allow NGOs to adapt to working within a repressive political environment while working towards longer-term change. But there is a contradiction which emerges from being all things to all people:

> the income generation activities operated by SNGOs commonly integrate members more deeply into the processes that their consciousness-raising and dialogical activities identify as causes of poverty – profit maximisation, competition among the poor reducing group solidarity and the acquisition of the assets of the poor by entrepreneurs.
>
> (Hulme 1994: 260)

The fact that many development NGOs can construct a non-political image for state approval, but then project the language of political action locally, can confuse its member-ship and may also bring conflicts with charity laws or with suspicious governments. Yet as Mitlin *et al.* (2005) argue in support of the idea of NGOs as development actors producing development alternatives, the need to build linkages more broadly with social movements and political parties in order to support political change processes will require NGOs to build skills that will allow them to negotiate more effectively in this difficult area.

This ambiguity is becoming more and more apparent as global changes bring into sharper focus the contradictions faced by many NGOs within the larger framework of development assistance and economic change. For NNGOs in particular we have seen the growth of a confused identity, the consequences of which Edwards (1999b: 198) sums up in terms of two divergent trends: 'some NGOs are moving further into the global service-providing

223

marketplace, while others see themselves as part of international social movements'.[2] These two trajectories are not new, and reflect in part the long-running dichotomy which has often been observed within the wider third sector between service providing and advocacy organizations, and there is every reason to suppose that both types of agencies will remain important within development work. But it is, as Edwards points out, the organizations which remain caught in the middle of these changes which are a cause for concern. While it may be possible to combine both trends effectively within a single, flexible organization, there are increasing numbers, particularly of NNGOs, which lack a clear strategy and structure and whose disorientation is apparent from the continuing crises of reorganization involving efforts at decentralization, regionalization and even 'indigenization'. There may come a point at which ambiguity becomes more clearly a source of weakness than a source of strength.

GROWTH OF ORGANIZATIONAL AND POLICY COMPLEXITY

Some mainstream management theory sees the growth of complexity as linked to the increasingly dispersed spatial dimension of business practices and the multicultural character of business practice (Harzing 1995). For example, the use of familiar management techniques may not work in unfamiliar contexts, and it becomes more difficult for organizations to implement uniform personnel practices and performance standards. For NGOs, work may be located in particularly difficult areas – in places where there is continuous conflict and instability or in remote, isolated communities. Kelleher and McLaren (1996) emphasize the turbulent context in which many development NGOs tend to work, and use the phrase 'grabbing the tiger by the tail' to encapsulate the challenge of taking control of organizational change under difficult circumstances.

These wider contextual changes are taking place at various levels. Hinton and Groves (2004: 5) write of 'the new complexity of inclusive aid' and suggest that the new dynamic and logic of the international development environment requires an abandonment of linear thinking in favour of a complex systems approach that can help NGOs and other actors to negotiate difficult choices and make sense of an increasingly complex environment. At the political level there are changes in the regulatory frameworks operated by governments, with a shift towards enablement and competition. The millennium development goals signal a set of important commitments at the international level to poverty reduction, but are also a sign of new forms of 'targeting' managerialism within development administration. Since the 9/11 attacks on the United States, the so-called 'war on terror' has changed the priorities and contexts of international development assistance. There are at the same time continuing and growing areas of political instability and violence in many parts of the world, and a growing number of what it has become fashionable to call 'failed states'. At the economic level, market reforms and changing international trade rules currently raise more questions than ever about economic winners and losers, while the growing interest in the social accountability of the business community may bring new opportunities for NGOs to influence business practice (Zadek 2000; Forstater *et al.* 2002). At the social level, there are heightened public expectations about development participation and about improving the ways in which development work is undertaken (Jenkins and Goetz 1998).

224

At the technical level, the rapid growth in communications technology is transforming the ways in which organizations can approach their work (Scott Morton 1996). These technologies may make it possible for NGOs to react more quickly to events, and make it easier for information to be deployed for advocacy purposes. New technology also makes an impact on the ways in which NGOs relate with actors in their external environment, making coordination efforts potentially more effective, and bringing new dimensions to the tasks of internal management. The increase in quantity and quality of information available generates complex challenges for NGO managers, but it could also allow better 'sensing' by organizations of events within their external environment. An abuse of human rights in a country can be signalled around the world in seconds so that NGOs can immediately take action. Yet, as Clark and Themudo (2006: 70) point out, the new technology allows smaller, more flexible network structures to react far more quickly to rapidly changing events and issues than the traditional NGOs with their unwieldy systems and structures:

> Most established NGOs are hobbled by elaborate management and board processes that must approve major policy statements; dotcauses do not have such constraints. Hence, we find that, today, there are strong advantages to being small, flexible, and dependent primarily on web-based communications.

An important way in which NGOs have responded has been through the forging of alliances, the construction of networks, and what Brown has termed the 'bridging' role – between local community organizations and government, between consumers and producers, between constituents in rich countries and those in poor countries. The result has been the rise of inter-organizational and inter-sectoral partnerships (Lindenberg and Bryant 2001). Information technology also potentially brings increases in the controlling dimension of management work, such as in terms of performance measurement (Scott Morton 1996), and these may be an unwelcome trend for NGOs if it adds to pressures for technocratic forms of evaluation at the expense of more participatory learning-based approaches.

Indeed, there is evidence that these technocratic pressures in the wider aid environment are making life much more difficult for NGO managers, particularly in the South, where small under-resourced organizations struggle with increasingly complex demands for bilateral or non-governmental funders. In Wallace *et al.*'s (2006: 165) study of organizations in Uganda and South Africa:

> Many staff in both north and south complained that they felt more like bureaucratic aid administrators than development workers and that more time was spent on paperwork than development. . . . The disjuncture between the paper-based plans, objectives, activities and indicators and the day-to-day realities that poor people and NGO staff try to grapple with in a wide range of contexts and cultures is too great to be bridged. The paper-based plans and timetables are left in the office, while NGO staff try to find ways – many innovative, others very inappropriate – to work with poor communities, marginalized groups and the neglected. They then revert to the written tools again when it comes to reporting and accounting for donor aid money.

The present political climate is an increasingly difficult and turbulent one for development NGOs. But while aid policy remains dominated by neo-liberal policy ideas, it also remains open to a range of NGO identities and roles – as deliverers of humanitarian relief goods, as social service providers contracted by governments and donors, and as advocates of human rights, democracy and social justice. But it is an environment that seems likely to continue the long-standing pressures that limit the 'room for manoeuvre' available to development NGOs to pursue diverse strategies, and to experiment with alternatives to the mainstream:

> The third sector is being encouraged to restructure itself from a source of innovation, organizational pluralism, alternative knowledge creation and 'new' political force into a contractor for national governments and international aid agencies.
>
> (Hulme 1994: 257)

Since writing the first edition of this book, the context in which NGOs operate has become more complex, as the post-2001 US-led 'war on terror' has become overlaid on the neo-liberal framework that was intensifying in the period since the end of the Cold War. Reflecting on the impact of the war on terror on civil society, Howell (2006b: 126–7) writes:

> the global war on terror has led to the constriction of civil society space, a clampdown on NGOs with a concomitant othering of Muslim organizations, the unsettling of an overzealous embrace of civil society by donor agencies, and the undermining of the principles of neutrality, impartiality and independence amongst humanitarian agencies.

At the organizational level, development NGOs need to be able to manage change either by being clear enough about their goals and purposes to resist pressures to grow or change, or else by building change strategies that allow structures and practices to evolve that are in keeping with the organization's own values and ethics. Yet this is an increasingly difficult challenge, as development funders such as the DFID combine the provision of ever-larger quantities of aid (in keeping with the UK government's stated commitment to UN targets of 0.7 per cent of GDP) with ever more stringent controls on its disbursal and use. Another contradiction in the world of aid is one that is highlighted by Wallace *et al.* (2006: 168) in that funding processes appear to be becoming more and more complex and bureaucratic despite the more flexible language of development discourse, ironically involving the use of unwieldy and inflexible management tools and traditions in reporting and accounting that have long been left behind within the public and private sectors:

> In some ways it was hard for the researchers to understand why a set of tools based on approaches to planning, development and change that have been so questioned and discredited over decades, has come to dominate aid funding processes.

An increasingly observable trend is that of convergence. One dimension of this is the trend of organizational isomorphism in which, either by design or accident, NGOs evolve to become more like each other, for example by placing micro-finance programmes at the heart of their work. Another dimension is the fact that boundaries between the three sectors of government, business and the third sector are arguably becoming more blurred, with important implications for NGO management. An emerging set of issues – such as the use of information technology and the need to manage transnationally under conditions of growing global interdependence – will increasingly be common challenges faced by all three institutional sectors. For example, the growing demand for accountability and social responsibility is beginning to impact upon mainstream management practice, and higher standards are increasingly being asked of government, business and the third sector (Parker 1998). NGO management needs to be seen primarily in terms of process rather than blue-print. As Kaplan (1999: 54) has argued, 'while every organization may share similar features, nevertheless each organization is unique'.

LOOKING FORWARD

How will the management of NGOs evolve over the coming decade? Will there be a trend towards strength through a diversity of structures and approaches, or will there be a process of standardization – what Foreman (1999), writing about the influence of Northern or inter-national over Southern organizations, has termed the 'McDonaldization of NGOs' – in which NGOs tend towards a unidirectional isomorphism? What is clear from our discussion is that there are just as many pitfalls for NGOs if they simply rely upon 'high moral purpose, good will, hard work, and common sense' (Korten 1987: 155) as there are if they respond unthinkingly to pressures from the environment to professionalize. As Smillie (1995: 147) puts it rather eloquently: 'Criticised by governments for their lack of professionalism, NGOs are then accused of bureaucratisation when they do professionalise.'

Ultimately these are political choices which development NGOs in the North and South and their stakeholders will need to make, rather than technocratic questions. How NGOs in the end relate to the issue of management will depend upon the type of organization an NGO wants to be, the values it seeks to express and the approach it takes to the pursuit of social and economic change. The 'strategic management' framework which was developed in Chapter 6, which was adapted from the work of de Graaf (1987) and Smith et al. (1980), represents one way of conceptualizing NGO choices in this area: between expressing core values, getting the work done and shaping and reacting to wider contextual forces. The model highlights the need for NGOs to distinguish between shifting zones of control, influ-ence and appreciation; and this can serve as a guiding framework for all types of development NGOs. Organizations both shape, and are shaped by, this wider context. At the same time, the different 'tides' of management reform currently being experienced by non-profit organ-izations in the United States (Light 2000, discussed in Chapter 7) may find echoes in NGO sectors in other parts of the world.

The concept of ambiguity has been central to our argument, because development NGOs face difficult questions about their structures (such as the associational versus the bureaucratic form), their approach to the work (such as whether to attempt to meet short-term needs or to undertake long-term 'sustainable' development) and their response to the contradictory pressures coming from their environment (acting as 'contractors' for governments or responding to bottom-up pressures for change). This ambiguity, as we have seen, is at times a source of weakness and confusion, but it also lies at the heart of some of the creativity which some NGOs are able to display as organizations. The challenge for development NGOs remains one of maintaining an ability to think and act creatively, while maintaining a high level of commitment and operating in their chosen field of activities as effectively as possible.

Whether or not one agrees that 'NGO management' is a new field, the debates under way about the management needs of development NGOs are important. The days of the 'reluctant manager' seem to be over for many NGOs, but the danger now is that professionalization and mainstream development delivery approaches may also lead to fewer NGOs of the 'committed activist' type. Dichter (1999: 54) argues that there has been a general global shift among development NGOs towards the commercial sector such that:

> To survive, today's NGO has been forced to become more corporation-like and less church-like. Its primary concern, though rhetorically still to actualise social visions, is also to cater to a marketplace (of ideas, funders, backers, supporters).

Dichter's concept of the current 'global marketplace of altruism', in which professionalized NGOs now operate, leads him to argue that development NGOs may need to rethink the implications of their recent growth and return to their roots – of working for change 'quietly, locally, and modestly' – although there is also a danger in idealizing small, informal NGOs. The more corporate NGO model such as BRAC in Bangladesh has arguably evolved into a key player in that country's struggle against poverty, while thousands of smaller, less bureaucratized organizations remain active in a range of fields at local and national levels. The NGO universe will be a poorer place without diversity and pluralism.

CONCLUSION

Whichever way NGOs choose to move over the next decade (and it seems unlikely that any single trend will be discernible amongst such a diverse family of organizations) the current interest in the subject of NGO management will continue. Along with improving the ways NGOs conceptualize and go about their work, such attention also serves a useful purpose by bringing prevailing images and expectations of NGOs – among both advocates and detractors – down to more realistic proportions. There is now the danger that, just as NGOs were idealized by many people in the development industry during the 1990s, a counter-reaction is setting in during the current decade in which NGOs are 'written off' as having failed to live up to expectations. The growing backlash against NGOs was outlined in Chapter 1. A critical approach to NGO management can help to build a stronger focus on what development NGOs can achieve and what they cannot, and on improving their effectiveness. It may also enrich our wider understanding of management by bringing to light new ideas and alternative approaches – ones rooted in different values and cultures, and in a genuinely developmental approach to overcoming obstacles to positive social change.

Many would agree that the development industry and the NGOs which have associated themselves with it have achieved far less than was once expected in terms of poverty reduction and social justice. Yet as the work of people like Edwards (1999a), Tendler (1997) and Kaplan (1999) indicates, there is a considerable amount known about what – in Edwards's phrase – 'breeds success'. In Brazil, Tendler shows how improved health services resulted from highly motivated and well-organized public sector workers who were kept on track by suitable incentives and the watchful eye of organized citizens, while in India Edwards (Box 7.1) shows that success was derived from a facilitating role which assisted local organizations to identify anti-poverty strategies, and supported them in their struggle against structural obstacles and interests. In development work, both 'enabling' and 'controlling' management have their uses.

The challenge – as Fowler (1997) points out – is for development NGOs to clarify their vision and goals, balancing a range of internal and external factors and keeping a clear eye on 'what is to be managed'. Management for NGOs can be seen as having both an instrumental purpose (i.e. achieving the desired results) as well as an expressive quality, that is a certain organizational style or culture which is both appropriate to the task at hand as well as in keeping with the values of those involved. For development NGOs the expressive side of management remains a priority, but NGOs cannot afford to lose sight of the practical. The challenge for such organizations is therefore to build appropriate management models which will improve management performance without losing sight of core values.

Finally, NGOs also constitute an important subject for mainstream management research, which has given little attention to the third sector. Mainstream management theory is now paying close attention to the idea of hybridity as a post-bureaucratic organizational form, and Parker (1998: 236) sees 'expanding choices for organizations' which 'involve more complex, hybrid structures and processes capable of surviving and thriving in the global marketplace'. Others have begun to turn their attention to the ways in which NGOs as organizations may be challenging some of the assumptions and theories held more widely in management circles. Fisher (1994) suggests that NGOs in the South are developing organizational forms that challenge Michels's (1962) 'iron law of oligarchy' in which grassroots membership organizations' commitment to democracy is gradually replaced over time by the rule of oligarchic officials whose views prevail over those of the rank and file. More attention to the ways in which the diverse range of development NGOs are managed could enrich the theory and practice of organizations of all types.

REVIEW QUESTIONS

- What are the main features of NGO management that are likely to become more important in the future?
- What kinds of political choices might development NGOs need to make over the coming decade to ensure their continuing relevance?
- How are changes in the external environment in which NGOs operate influencing current and future management strategies?

Appendix: some useful NGO management websites

AccountAbility

This is an organization dedicated to strategies for promoting improved accountability and stakeholder involvement in relation to civil society, business and public sector organizations.

www.accountability.org.uk

Capacity.org

Capacity.org describes itself as a 'gateway on capacity development' and offers a quarterly newsletter as well as a platform for access and exchange for materials and ideas on capacity development. Its materials are available in French and English.

www.capacity.org

INTRAC

The International NGO Training and Research Centre (INTRAC) has undertaken research, consultancy and training on NGO management for more than fifteen years. Its triannual newsletter *OnTrac* provides a wealth of useful information for the NGO manager.

www.intrac.org

Keystone

Formed in 2001, this group is working for improved measurement and reporting practices for organizations engaged in social change.

www.keystonereporting.org

Management Accounting for Non-Governmental Organizations (Mango)

Founded in 1999, Mango is a UK-registered charity which aims to strengthen the financial management of NGOs.

www.mango.org.uk

Management Help

A good general site with access to basic information on key management ideas and tools, with a useful section that covers non-profit organizations.

www.managementhelp.org

Most Significant Change (MSC) monitoring and evaluation

MSC is a technique aimed at organizations and individuals who wish to monitor and evaluate their social change programmes and projects. By 2004, the MSC technique had been used both by NGOs and governments in Africa, Asia, Latin America, Europe and Australasia.

www.mande.co.uk/docs/MSCGuide.htm

NGO Manager

Formed by former participants of the LSE's NGO Management MSc course as a site run by NGO managers for NGO managers, this initiative has grown to include a wide range of resources relating to all aspects of NGO management, including management tools, training and education and upcoming jobs.

www.ngomanager.org

RAPID Programme

The Research and Policy in Development (RAPID) programme is an initiative at the Overseas Development Institute that aims to improve the use of research and evidence within development policy and practice through research and debate. The site has useful materials on the link between research and policy that NGOs will find useful.

www.odi.org.uk/rapid

Glossary

Accountability a process in which an organization builds and maintains a relationship with stakeholders based on transparency and influence.

Advocacy an activity in which an NGO seeks changes in policy, and ultimately in the allocation of power, through political influence based on representing members' and supporters' interests to policy makers.

Association an organizational form based around membership, usually but not necessarily informal in structure.

Capacity building originally a public sector term that became widely used in relation to NNGO/SNGO relationships during the 1990s, usually referring to processes of organization development (OD), but sometimes used more generally.

Civil society a complex term with many different definitions, but which usually refers to the set of organizations and institutions situated between the state, the business world and the household, and to the 'space' in which various kinds of organized entities (religious groups, NGOs, social movements, the media, professional associations, etc.) negotiate and pursue diverse (and sometimes contradictory) social interests.

Community-based organization local, 'grassroots' membership organizations which often form part of the 'coping strategies' of low-income households (also sometimes known as 'people's organizations').

Dotcause a flexible civil society network that draws on new information technology to organize campaigning and protest.

Empowerment an imprecise term which refers to a transformative process in which individuals and groups move from insight to action in pursuit of changes in the exercise of power.

Global civil society a diverse collection of non-state actors (including associations, organizations and networks) operating transnationally within civil society spaces.

Governance the ongoing process within organizations by which guidelines for decision making, mission and action are developed and compliance with them is monitored.

Legitimacy a term which refers to the credibility of an organization, based on perceived moral justifications for its social and political actions.

NGO non-governmental organization, a highly imprecise term which usually refers to the subset of 'third sector' organizations involved in poverty reduction, human rights and environmental concerns.

Non-profit organization the term commonly used in the United States for 'third sector organization', so labelled because it is distinguished from the culturally dominant model of profit-making organization.

'The North' the group of rich countries that used to be generally referred to as 'developed'.

Not-for-profit a term which has tended to replace 'non-profit', meaning that an organization may engage in profit-making activities (such as selling goods or services) but that the proceeds are ploughed back into the organization's activities rather than distributed to shareholders as in the case of a for-profit company.

Participation a somewhat imprecise term which refers to the complex political process of increasing people's involvement in decision making which can sometimes result in greater 'voice', but may simply legitimize existing decision making.

People's organization a term often used to refer to local, membership organizations. These can be contrasted with non-membership forms of NGO sometimes called 'intermediary organizations' or 'grassroots support organizations' which provide support and services to POs.

Philanthropy the ethical notion of giving and serving to people beyond one's own family, a term which is common particularly in the United States.

PVO a term commonly used in the United States to describe its development NGOs working in the 'third world'.

Scaling up the process in which NGOs seek to move beyond transitory or localized activities to achieve greater impact through a variety of possible strategies.

Service delivery public provision by government agencies, private sector organizations or NGOs of services such as education, healthcare, agricultural extension, etc.

Social economy economic activities which serve social rather than primarily economic aims such as profit maximization; a term commonly used in continental Europe.

Social entrepreneur creative individuals in the civil society, public or business sector who seek to put underutilized resources to use to satisfy unmet social needs.

Social movements loosely organized groups of organizations and individuals around pressing problems of a local, national or global nature, such as environment, identity, poverty or human rights.

'The South' a term which has been recently used in preference to earlier terms such as 'third world' or 'developing countries' (but which excludes Australia and New Zealand).

Stakeholder any person or group that is able to make a claim on an organization's attention, resources or output, or that may be affected by the organization.

Third sector a term referring to the collection of institutions and organizations that, particularly in the West, are seen as separate from state and market (which are said to form the other two sectors) and that has emerged to challenge this 'two sector' view of the world. Also refers to the institutional 'space' between state and market.

Transition country an area of the former Soviet bloc in transition from a planned socialist economy towards free-market capitalism.

TSO an organization, such as a trade union, religious group, NGO or community organization, that is neither formally part of government nor a for-profit organization.

VO a term used commonly in Britain to refer to a third sector organization; effectively a synonym for non-profit organization or non-governmental organization. Sometimes it is misleadingly used to refer to organizations composed of volunteers (as opposed to more professionalized third sector organizations).

Voluntarism the tradition of organized voluntary action, but also the philosophical idea that the will dominates the intellect.

Volunteer a person who enters into a service or a transaction of their own free-will without an expectation of remuneration.

Notes

1 THE NGO MANAGEMENT DEBATE

1   However, as we will see in Chapter 3, it is also recognized that development can be defined broadly to include elements of these fields. For example, the rise of 'right-based approach' within development – as practised by many of the NGOs that make up the Save the Children alliance of organizations – makes an explicit link between human rights and development.

2   The terms 'development NGO' and 'non-governmental development organization' (NGDO) are both used in the literature, but the first term is used throughout this book, as explained in the Introduction.

3   Despite the volume of publications on NGOs that has emerged, writers such as Najam (1996b), Clarke (1998), Stewart (1997), Hilhorst (2003), DeMars (2005) and Lewis (2005) all draw attention to important limitations in much of this 'NGO literature'. It has often tended to be either donor-driven (and therefore with a tendency not to confront political complexity) or written by NGO activists (which has lent it something of a 'feelgood' quality in which positive rather than negative experiences have been emphasized). These factors have contributed to literature on NGOs that can sometimes be seen as analytically weak and normative in its tone.

4   Some writers who are basically sympathetic to NGOs nevertheless have argued that unless NGOs pay more attention to key issues of accountability, probity and effectiveness they will face a backlash against NGOs (e.g. Slim 1997). More recent writings by Bond (2000) and Mallaby (2004) suggest that such a backlash is, in some quarters at least, already underway.

5   BRAC's website, which contains a wealth of information about this large influential NGO, is at www.brac.net

6   Vetwork's website can be found at www.vetwork.org.uk

7   There are some exceptions in Stark Biddle (1984), Billis and MacKeith (1992), Fowler (1997) and Suzuki (1997).

8   The one-year MSc in Management of NGOs began in 1995 at the London School of Economics' Centre for Civil Society in the Department of Social Policy. A wide variety of experienced practitioner students from all over the world (but mostly from the 'South') have now graduated from the course. Some current and former students have contributed to this book in the form of case study material illustrating some of the NGO challenges they have faced since graduating.

9   The 'management guru' phenomenon is one in which charismatic individuals claim to have all-purpose, novel answers to important management questions. A lively and provocative overview of the world of the management gurus can be found in Micklethwait and Wooldridge (1996). The authors conclude that while management theory is a commercially successful industry which acts as a 'magnet to charlatans', it does offer some general lessons and is 'not entirely devoid of intellectual context'!

10 Further information about INTRAC's work and publications can be found at www.intrac.org

11 The UNDP Human Development Reports can be found at www.hdr.undp.org/reports/

12 The selection and management of specific poverty reduction activities – such as making choices between campaigning versus service delivery work, or 'participatory' versus 'top-down' interventions – is of course critical to any discussion of NGO management. See Thomas (1996) for a useful overview.

13 The influential bundle of approaches and ideas previously known by different names such as participatory rural appraisal (PRA) or rapid rural appraisal (RRA) and associated with the work of Robert Chambers and others.

14 Kiggundu (1989: 30), however, suggests that too much emphasis has frequently been placed on 'cultural variables' within organization and management studies of non-Western cultures, and not enough on the process of managing task, performance and technology.

2 CONTEXTS, HISTORIES AND CONCEPTS

1 In a comment on the frequent reinvention of new policy approaches – and terms – in relation to poverty reduction, Maxwell's reference point is with the earlier New Poverty Agenda generated by ideas in the 1990 *World Development Report*.

2 'Moscow asks court to close down civil rights group: first sign of long-awaited crackdown, say critics', *The Guardian*, 28 January 2006.

3 The term third sector can be confusing because it is sometimes used differently by some authors in relation to NGOs. For example, Uphoff (1995) argues that only membership-based, self-help organizations can be seen as part of the third sector. He states that public benefit NGOs which provide services to third parties should more properly be considered part of the not-for-profit *private* sector.

4 This can be downloaded from www.jhu.edu/%7Ecnp/

5 Vakil (1997) suggests that the 'voluntary' element of the structural/operational definition be dropped to reflect the growing professionalization of NGOs. Although this may be appropriate in some cases, it would arguably close off a key element of most third sector organizations. Even BRAC, perhaps the largest NGO in the world, and one which now sports a strong private – even corporate – image, still has a voluntary board of directors and still relies on village-level volunteers for aspects of its work. However, Fowler (1997) notes the existence of NGOs in Latin America which do not follow the governing body structure but are managed and governed by an executive director.

6 See for example Horton Smith's (1997) passionate case for arguing that informal grass-roots groups are perhaps best seen as the 'true' third sector, a position closer to that of Uphoff.

7 For a short and clearly written introductory overview of the main issues and complex debates around the concept of social capital, see Bebbington (2004).

8 Kaldor (2003) sees the emergence of the 'anti-globalization movement' in the late 1990s as a sign that other less progressive streams within civil society, such as certain NGOs which represent 'tamed social movements' and those which embody nationalist or fundamentalist interests, are under an increased challenge.

9 There are different views about where the third sector term came from, with Etzioni (1972) usually credited as the originator. Levitt (1975), however, writing around the same time in the 1970s, does not refer to Etzioni's work. Another possible contender for the originator of the term is Daniel Bell who refers to the third sector in his 1976 book *The Coming of Post-Industrial Society* (Martin Albrow, personal communication). Fisher (1998) seems to attribute the origins of the term to Nielsen's 1979 book *The Endangered Sector*, but this would appear to be a later derivative usage.

10 An interesting parallel can be found in the participatory development movement embodied in the work of Robert Chambers (1994, 1995, 2005) whose ideas also centre on a critique of 'normal professionalism'.

11 There are increasing numbers of 'hybrid' organizations existing around the alliances and networks which spring up within changing institutional environments (Kramer 1995). This increasing hybridization of the third sector is discussed further in Chapter 8.

12 While Nerfin (1986) asserts the moral superiority of the citizen, Najam (1996b) makes no judgements at all about the relative values of these three different sectors, merely that they are different.

3 NGOS AND DEVELOPMENT

1 In many developing countries, the donor fashion for NGOs which emerged at this time greatly enlarged the size and numbers of the NGO community. In some areas, this led to the creation of new NGOs specifically for the purpose of receiving the funds that were being made available. NGOs can sometimes merely be the product of a supply of international aid resources from outside. This has led in many cases to the highly uncomplimentary view of NGOs simply as vehicles for unscrupulous entrepreneurial individuals to 'get rich quick' (Lofredo 1995).

2 For example, while Educare Trust in Nigeria has chosen to remain very much a 'one person' NGO, relying on the support of a few local volunteers in order to provide new learning resources to local schools and campaign for education policy change (despite numerous offers of funding), the Bangladesh Rural Advancement Committee (BRAC) has grown. However, BRAC has massively reduced its earlier dependency on foreign aid by charging for services and establishing a range of social enterprises, including a bank and a university. BRAC's 2004 Annual Report states that of its annual budget of US$245 million, around 77% is now self-financed.

3 The official donor scruples about core costs rarely seem to apply to consulting firms, which receive overheads from donors, often multiplying by three- or fourfold the salary component (Brown and Korten 1989).

4 Some organizations such as Oxfam GB have responded to this problem by starting a poverty programme in the UK (Lewis 1999a).

5 This replaced the old Joint Funding Scheme which was DFID's main means of funding UK NGOs.

6 For a general introductory review, see Gardner and Lewis (1996).

7 This is not the place to discuss ongoing critiques of development as a concept, which now include the concept of 'post-development'. But it is worth noting that such critiques, despite many useful ideas, at times can appear perverse and surprising. For example, one radical 'post-development' writer is opposed to the idea of development because it can involve the destruction of 'noble forms of poverty' and 'arts of suffering' (Rahnema 1997: x).

8 Korten's argument is that although public service contractors may be well managed and efficient, NGOs which move away from more complex agendas towards service provision tend to lose autonomy by becoming more dependent on others, and can become simply a proxy for government under privatization agendas. The reasons why NGOs change in this way is given as: becoming tired of surviving at the financial margins; or of fighting against established interests; a sense of obligation to improve job security for staff; a belief that contracting will eventually bring more funding and opportunities to go back to earlier approaches. It also brings greater susceptibility to Northern policy priorities of shifting public to private responsibility; and Korten points out that more than 50 per cent of US non-profits now receive more than 50 per cent of their funds from public sources.

9 Empowerment is also used widely within business and management as well as in development (Wright 1994). Many NGOs now speak of an 'empowering' or 'participatory' management

style. In this type of perspective, operating staff are seen as the starting point for action, as a source of skills and capacities, encouraged to take the initiative in solving problems (e.g. Holcombe (1995) on the Grameen Bank model).

10 Despite the high profile achieved by the Make Poverty History campaign, there were critics who remained disappointed by the lack of coordination among organizations and the tangible changes on the trade reform agenda, e.g. 'We achieved next to nothing', Noreena Hertz, *New Statesman*, 12 December 2005.

4 CULTURE, AMBIGUITY AND NGO MANAGEMENT

1 Many of these ideas have strongly influenced work in the non-profit literature on organization and management (e.g. Billis 1993a), which is discussed in Chapter 7.

2 For example, Billis and MacKeith (1992) using the three organizational 'worlds' theory, show how NGOs are agencies which may find themselves located in an ambiguous zone between associations and bureaucracies. They face specific management challenges as a result, such as the dilemmas of choosing participatory or hierarchical management approaches, or dealing with the tensions produced by priorities of awareness raising as opposed to fund-raising (MacKeith 1992).

3 For example, in the discussion of inter-agency partnership in Chapter 6, the role of power in the creation of weak or 'dependent' partnerships between unequal organizations is analysed. (Table 6.1) In a study of NGOs in Bangladesh, Foucauldian ideas about 'discourse' were used to show the ways in which power is exercised through the policy language of partnership (Lewis 1998b).

4 There is a wide literature on social movements (e.g. McAdam *et al.* 1996; Canel 1997) which has only rarely been linked with the literature on NGOs (Dechalert 1999; Norrell 1999; Morris-Suzuki 2000). One tradition which emerged from the United States argues that movements such as the civil rights and women's movements rely on the availability of resources to turn grievances into action and protest, and this has become known as the 'resource mobilization' approach (McCarthy and Zald 1977). Another radical tradition has been strongly associated with European and Latin American contexts, and has become known as 'new social movement' theory, which examines the ways in which social movements constitute local responses and resistance to processes of globalization and cultural imposition (Escobar and Alvarez 1992).

5 The currently fashionable concept of the 'social entrepreneur' can provide a potentially useful insight into NGO leadership. In the UK, the term implies taking the economic concept of the entrepreneur and applying it to creative individuals engaged in value-driven social change processes (Leadbeater 1997). In this sense, NGO founders can be viewed as types of social entrepreneurs. According to Leadbeater, social entrepreneurs are innovators who frequently draw on business ideas and methods. They may also operate on the margins of the third and the public sectors: for example, A. H. Khan in Pakistan was originally a civil servant who initiated the public sector Pakistan Academy for Rural Development in the 1960s (now BARD in Bangladesh) and later established the influential NGO Orangi Pilot Project in Karachi during the 1980s (Khan 1999).

6 The most authoritative and theoretically informed study of organizational change and learning in relation to NGOs is that by Ebrahim (2003). Drawing on work by James March and others, he distinguishes three ways of learning: *learning by doing*, as a trial-and-error process; *learning by exploring* which involves a more open-ended process of search and experimentation; and *imitation*, which involves mimicking the behaviour of another organization.

7 Management by objectives (MBO) is the basis for a methodology familiar to those working in international development, where a similar planning tool has become known as Logical Framework Analysis (LFA), currently used by most project planners and many NGOs.

8   An important postmodern critique of cross-cultural training work within multinational corporations – which partly draws on Hofstede's ideas – is made by Leggett (1999: 2), who argues that despite its admirable integrative goals, such training rests on the misguided modernist universalizing assumption that trainees from other cultures are seeking to participate in emerging global systems 'without quite understanding the rules' and need therefore to be 'helped up the ladder'.

9   However, we must bear in mind that there is also a danger in always simply assuming the appropriateness of South–South learning. In a presentation by the author in China, NGO case study examples were presented from both Northern and Southern contexts, but every question received from the participants indicated a desire to learn from the Northern examples rather than the Southern ones.

10   One of the problems of such an approach is that it assumes that differences between large national groups are stronger than those within populations, which of course runs the risk of stereotyping cultural characteristics.

11   A study on this theme by Mukasa (1999) carried out in the context of an international NGO's work in Uganda raises a fascinating set of preliminary issues and questions. Kaufman (1997) provides some interesting insights into the career paths of some UK NGO staff, while Biggs (1997) examines the 'coping strategies' of development agency personnel.

12   This is not to imply that the discipline of anthropology has any more relevance to the study of NGOs than say political economy or geography, but simply that anthropological ideas interact in potentially useful ways with some current themes in organization theory. This chapter also reflects my own personal interest and training in social anthropology.

5 SERVICE DELIVERY AND ADVOCACY

1   There are of course many different ways of conceptualizing the 'policy process'. Some emphasize the technical and instrumental dimensions of the policy process, while others highlight the role of politics and power. NGO managers will find a useful and concise overview of these different perspectives in Sutton (1999).

2   Freire's ideas were politically radical, envisaging class empowerment as the outcome, and he later became critical of the use of the term 'empowerment' in the USA as a form of individual self-improvement. Within Freire's framework, the idea of groups is important, supported by facilitative, non-directive external professional help.

3   Thomas (1992) suggests that there are two approaches to empowerment: providing tools for self-reliance – organizational innovations and technical and training solutions to local problems (e.g. cooperatives, village cereal banks) and participatory action research (PAR) – animators work with local groups who decide on their own forms of action after analysing their situation.

4   Participation also has a political meaning, such that liberal theory sees participation as a crucial element of democratic responsive government by providing a voice for ordinary people in decision making, and the UNDP *Human Development Report* (1993) saw participation as the key to innovation and the creation of more democratic and just societies.

5   This point is not intended here as a criticism of credit as a developmental service provided by NGOs – though there are those such as Rogali (1996) who are critical of the microfinance movement – but to illustrate the isomorphic pressures on NGOs that diminish the creativity and diversity of the NGO sector as a source of ideas and alternatives (cf. Mitlin *et al.* 2005).

6   Interestingly, there may also be pressures from other parts of the NGO environment, such as the NGO beneficiaries themselves, who may demand certain services from the NGO. For example, one NGO known to the author in Bangladesh reported that while it had originally been its policy to go into communities with a consciousness-raising approach rather than

delivering material resources, pressure from local clients gradually persuaded the NGO to operate a credit delivery service. (Of course, from another perspective, this could be seen as an example of an NGO responding in a participatory way to community needs.)

7   I recall a conversation with a landless rural woman in Bangladesh, who explained that she knew about the Grameen Bank but considered that its repayment criteria were far too strict for her to be viable, and had gone instead for credit to another NGO operating in the area. In areas of the country where many NGOs operate credit schemes, this has the effect of creating a market for NGO services among not-for profit service providers.

8   As Charnovitz (1997) has shown, NGO advocacy has a very long history, which is discussed in more detail in Chapter 2.

9   Many of these findings are echoed by the research study on NGOs engaged in advocacy for land reform in Mozambique and Kenya (Kanji *et al.* 2002). In Mozambique NGOs were found to have made a 'significant contribution' to the formulation and the dissemination of a new national land law established in 1997, though it has proved difficult to maintain the momentum in the implementation stage.

10 Annis (1992) reflects on the idea of 'informational empowerment' as a tool for evolving greater connectedness among environmental networks in Central America.

11 The Monsanto company was forced to rethink its approach to winning support for its biotechnology programme in the face of considerable opposition in Europe.

12 In the agricultural development sector, a series of case studies can be found drawn from Asia (Farrington and Lewis 1993), Latin America (Bebbington and Thiele 1993) and Africa (Wellard and Copestake 1993).

13 These authors suggest two new and memorable metaphors for thinking about NGOs: 'as jelly' – the NGO focuses on the process of building relationships, becomes pushed and pulled in different directions, but manages to hold a coherent policy agenda together; and as 'microchip' – the NGO is more proactive and seeks to convene relationships based around an intellectual contribution which gives it a 'convening legitimacy' among other actors. This is achieved by NGOs that can add value by bringing a broader perspective to discussions and creating a specific space for discussion (Mitlin *et al.* 2005).

14 Private sector techniques include the 'social audit', first outlined in Goyder (1961) and outlined in the NGO context in Zadek and Gatwood (1995); and the idea of 'developmental market research', which adapts conventional market research for development work, and has been pioneered in this context by S. Epstein (Marsden *et al.* 1995).

6 THE MANAGEMENT OF RELATIONSHIPS

1   *The Guardian* newspaper, 28 January 2006.

2   One of the outcomes of the UK's Commission on the Future of the Voluntary Sector in 1997 was a Code of Practice for the UK voluntary sector. Its main points included stating an organization's purpose clearly and keeping it relevant to current conditions; being explicit about the needs an organization intends to meet and the ways this will be achieved; managing and targeting resources effectively and 'doing what we say we will do'; evaluating effectiveness of work, tackling poor performance and responding to complaints fairly and promptly; agreeing and setting out all those to whom an organization is accountable and how it will respond to those responsibilities; being clear about the standards to which work is undertaken; being open about arrangements for involving users; having an open and systematic process for appointing to the governing body; setting out the role and responsibilities of the governing body; having clear arrangements for involving, supporting and training volunteers; ensuring policies and practices do not discriminate unfairly; and recruiting staff openly and remunerating them fairly (Ashby 1997).

3 http://guidestar.org/news/features/sarbanes_oxley.jsp (accessed 27 May 2006). See the guidestar.org website for more detailed information about the act and its implications for non-profit organizations.

4 The concept of 'governmentality' was coined by Michel Foucault to encapsulate the multiple ways in which the conduct of a population is governed, through organizations and institutions of the state, through norms and identities and through individual self-regulation.

5 More details can be found at www.eti.org.uk

6 The efforts by BRAC to develop its social business has at times met with resistance from established interests that accuse the NGO of unfair or inappropriate trading practices. This became clear when BRAC was challenged in the courts in 1999 by a local academic economist when it sought to expand into commercial banking as being inappropriate for a charitable, non-profit organization. The Supreme Court upheld BRAC's right to establish a bank as long as its profits were ploughed back into development activities, but required that tax be paid on commercial revenues arising from banking (Sidel 2004).

7 This type of arrangement has led to the preference in some quarters for the term 'not-for-profit' to be used rather than 'non-profit', which embodies the issue of primary purpose more clearly.

8 Interestingly, the Grameen Bank – despite its third sector origins as a university-based action research project – has let it be known in recent years that it does not wish to be considered an 'NGO' but instead regards itself as a specialized financial institution incorporated by statute into the public banking sector. Perhaps this terminological anxiety is also a response to the negative associations of the 'NGO' label among some sections of the public in Bangladesh.

9 The picture is complicated further by the fact that there are many NGOs in both the North and South which do not receive funds at all from the 'aid industry' and rely instead on selling services, local fund-raising from the public or the private sector, or on voluntary commitment and activism.

10 The current preoccupation of many of the main UK development NGOs with ongoing processes of restructuring, regionalization and decentralization is arguably one indication of this crisis of identity.

7 THE DYNAMICS OF INTERNAL MANAGEMENT

1 Bryson (1994: 155) writes that strategic planning is 'a disciplined effort to produce fundamental decisions and actions that shape and guide what an organization (or other entity) is, what it does, and why it does it'.

2 It is interesting to note that 'capacity building' is not a term which has been used very much in the third sector management literature, despite its popularity in the development industry. The same can also be said for 'scaling up'.

3 As we saw in Box 6.6, this capacity building effort can sometimes result not in changes to an existing organization but even in the actual creation of new organizations in the South.

4 Strategic planning is a process for deciding what an organization wants to be and do; and how it will therefore proceed. It is intended to provide a framework of directions and priorities within which an organization's members can make long-term decisions, and also operate effectively on a day-to-day basis, towards common goals and a shared vision (Eade and Williams 1995). Mintzberg (1994), who was one of its originators, traces the history of strategic planning and argues that claims for its usefulness have been greatly exaggerated since then. It assumes that organizational events can be predicted and controlled, but by doing this has separated strategies from operational activities. In practice the two are closely linked. Planning is linked to analysis, strategy is linked to synthesis. If it is linked with a wider, processual approach to organizational learning, it can be a useful tool. As Bryson

(1988) says, 'strategic thinking and acting are what count, not strategic plans in and of themselves'.

8 CONCLUSION: UNDERSTANDING NGO MANAGEMENT

1   Government organizations, of course, are not static either, and take a variety of forms, some of which may gradually evolve into more 'NGO-like' agencies. In the UK, the frequent public hostility to what are termed QUANGOs (quasi-non-governmental organizations) created by the government is because these are perceived to represent the worst of both organizational worlds – bureaucratic and unaccountable.
2   Kaldor (2003) suggests that some NGOs can best be understood as co-opted social movements in the sense that they represent domesticated, institutionalized forms of formerly radical movements.

Bibliography

Abdel Ati, H. A. (1993) 'The development impact of NGO activities in the Red Sea province of Sudan: a critique', *Development and Change*, 24: 103–30.

Abramson, D. M. (1999) 'A critical look at NGOs and civil society as means to an end in Uzbekistan', *Human Organization*, 58, 3: 240–50.

Abzug, R. and Forbes, D. (1997) 'Is civil society unique to nonprofit organizations?', paper presented at Association for Research on Nonprofit Organizations and Voluntary Action (ARNOVA) conference, Indianapolis.

ActionAid India (1993) 'Understanding advocacy: report of the first ActionAid India Advocacy Workshop', unpublished report, ActionAid, Banglalore.

Alley, K. D., Faupel, C. E. and Bailey, C. (1995) 'The historical transformation of a grassroots group', *Human Organization*, 54, 4: 410–16.

Alvesson, M. (1993) *Cultural Perspectives on Organizations*, Cambridge: Cambridge University Press.

Amendola, M. and Bruno, S. (1990) 'The behaviour of the innovative firm: relations to the environment', *Research Policy*, 19: 419–33.

Anderson, K. and Rieff, D. (2005) 'Global civil society: a sceptical view', in H. Anheier, M. Glasius and M. Kaldor (eds) *Global Civil Society 2004/5*, London: Sage.

Anheier, H. K. (1987) 'Indigenous voluntary associations, non-profits and development in Africa', in W. W. Powell (ed.) *The Nonprofit Sector: A Research Handbook*, New Haven, CT: Yale University Press.

—— (1990) 'Private voluntary organizations and the Third World: the case of Africa', in H. K. Anheier and W. Seibel (eds) *The Third Sector: Comparative Studies of Non-profit Organizations*, Berlin and New York: Walter de Gruyter.

—— (2000) 'Managing nonprofit organizations: towards a new approach', Civil Society Working Paper 1, Centre for Civil Society, London School of Economics.

—— (2005) *Nonprofit Organizations: Theory, Management, Policy*, London: Routledge.

Anheier, H., Glasius, M. and Kaldor, M. (2001) *Global Civil Society 2001*. Oxford: Oxford University Press.

Annis, S. (1987) 'Can small-scale development be a large-scale policy? The case of Latin America', *World Development*, 15 (supplement): 129–34.

—— (1992) 'Evolving connectedness among environmental groups and grassroots organizations in protected areas of Central America', *World Development*, 20, 4: 587–95.

Archer, R. (1994) 'Markets and good government', in A. Clayton (ed.) *Governance, Democracy and Conditionality: What Role for NGOs?*, Oxford: INTRAC.

Arellano-Lopez, S. and Petras, J. F. (1994) 'Non-governmental organizations and poverty alleviation in Bolivia', *Development and Change*, 25: 555–68.

Argyris, C. and Schon, D. (1978) *Organizational Learning: A Theory of Action Perspective*, New York: Addison-Wesley.

Artur, L. and Kanji, N. (2005) 'Satellites and subsidies: learning from experience in cashew processing in Northern Mozambique', project report, London.

Ashby, J. (1997) *Towards Voluntary Sector Codes of Practice: A Starting Point for Voluntary Organizations, Funders and Intermediaries*, York: Joseph Rowntree Foundation.

Ashworth, G. (1996) 'Gender, culture and NGOs', in A. Clayton (ed.) *NGOs, Civil Society and the State*, Oxford: INTRAC.

Atack, I. (1999) 'Four criteria of development NGO legitimacy', *World Development*, 27, 5: 855–64.

Avina, J. (1993) 'The evolutionary life-cycles of non-governmental development organizations', *Public Administration and Development*, 13: 453–74.

Avritzer, L. (2004) 'Civil society in Latin America: uncivil, liberal and participatory models', in M. Glasius, D. Lewis and H. Seckinelgin (eds) *Exploring Civil Society: Political and Cultural Contexts*, London: Routledge.

Badalt, C. (1997) 'Entrepreneurship theories of the non-profit sector', *Voluntas*, 8, 2: 162–78.

Baig, Q. (1999) 'NGO governing bodies and beyond: a Southern perspective on third sector governance issues', in D. Lewis (ed.) *International Perspectives on Voluntary Action: Reshaping the Third Sector*, London: Earthscan.

Banfield, E. (1958) *The Moral Basis of a Backward Society*, Chicago, IL: Free Press.

Bate, S. P. (1997) 'Whatever happened to organizational ethnography?', *Human Relations*, 50, 9: 1147–75.

Batsleer, J., Cornforth, C. and Paton, R. (eds) (1992) *Issues in Voluntary and Non-Profit Management*, Milton Keynes: Open University Press/Wokingham: Addison-Wesley.

Beall, J. (2005) *Funding Local Governance: Small Grants for Democracy and Development*, Rugby: ITDG Publishing.

Bebbington, A. (1991) 'Sharecropping agricultural development: the potential for GSO–government collaboration', *Grassroots Development*, 15, 2: 20–30.

—— (2004) 'Social capital and development studies 1: critique, debate, progress?', *Progress in Development Studies*, 4, 4: 343–9.

—— (2005) 'Donor–NGO relations and representations of livelihood in nongovernmental aid chains', *World Development*, 33, 6: 937–50.

Bebbington, A. and Riddell, R. (1995) 'The direct funding of Southern NGOs by donors: new agendas and old problems', *Journal of International Development*, 7, 6: 879–94.

Bebbington, A. and Thiele, G. (eds) (1993) *Non-Governmental Organizations and the State in Latin America: Rethinking Roles in Sustainable Agricultural Development*, London: Routledge.

Bebbington, A., Guggenheim, S., Olson, E. and Woolcock, M. (2004) 'Exploring social capital debates at the World Bank', *Journal of Development Studies*, 40, 5: 33–64.

Bell, D. (1976) *The Coming of Post-Industrial Society: A Venture in Social Forecasting*, London: Harper.

Bennett, J. (ed.) (1995) *Meeting Needs: NGO Coordination in Practice*, London: Earthscan.

Benthall, J. (2003) 'Humanitarianism, Islam and 11 September', HPG Briefing no. 11, July, London: Overseas Development Institute.

Bhalla, A. and Lapeyre, F. (1997) 'Social exclusion: towards an analytical and operational framework', *Development and Change*, 28, 3: 413–34.

Bielefeld, W. (1994) 'What affects nonprofit survival?', *Nonprofit Management and Leadership*, 5, 1: 19–36.

Biggs, S. (1997) 'Livelihood, coping and influencing strategies of rural development personnel', *Project Appraisal*, 12, 2: 101–6.

Biggs, S. and Neame, A. (1995) 'Negotiating room for manoeuvre: reflection concerning NGO autonomy and accountability within the new policy agenda', in M. Edwards and D. Hulme (eds) *Beyond the Magic Bullet: NGO Performance and Accountability in the Post-Cold War World*, London: Earthscan.

Biggs, S. and Smith, G. (1998) 'Beyond methodologies: coalition building for participatory technology development', *World Development*, 26, 2: 239–48.

Billis, D. (1993a) *Organizing Public and Voluntary Agencies*, London: Routledge.

—— (1993b) 'What can nonprofits and businesses learn from each other?', in D. C. Hammack and D. R. Young (eds) *Nonprofit Organizations in a Market Economy*, San Francisco, CA: Jossey-Bass.

Billis, D. and Harris, M. (eds) (1996) *Voluntary Agencies: Challenges of Organization and Management*, London: Macmillan.

Billis, D. and MacKeith, J. (1992) 'Growth and change in NGOs: concepts and comparative experience', in M. Edwards and D. Hulme (eds) *Making a Difference: NGOs and Development in a Changing World*, London: Earthscan.

Billis, D. and MacKeith, J. (1993) *Organizing NGOs: Challenges and Trends in the Management of Overseas Aid*, London: LSE Centre for Voluntary Organization.

Black, J. K. (1991) *Development in Theory and Practice: Bridging the Gap*, Boulder, CO: Westview Press.

Blackburn, J. (2000) 'Understanding Paulo Freire: reflections on the origins, concepts and possible pitfalls of his educational approach', *Community Development Journal*, 35, 1: 3–15.

Blair, H. (1997) 'Donors, democratization and civil society: relating theory to practice', in D. Hulme and M. Edwards (eds) *Too Close for Comfort? NGOs, States and Donors*, London: Macmillan.

Bond, M. S. (2000) 'Special report: the backlash against NGOs', *Prospect*, April: 52–5.

Booth, D. (1994) 'Rethinking social development: an overview', in D. Booth (ed.) *Rethinking Social Development: Theory, Research and Practice*, London: Longman.

Bordt, R. L. (1997) *The Structure of Women's Nonprofit Organizations*, Bloomington IN: Indiana University Press.

Borg, M. and Harzing, A.-W. (1995) 'Internationalisation and the international division of labour', in A.-W. Harzing and J. van Ruysseveldt (eds) *International Human Resource Management*, London: Sage.

BRAC (1983) *The Net: Power Structure in Ten Villages*, Rural Study Series, Dhaka: Bangladesh Rural Advancement Committee.

—— (2004) *Annual Report 2004*, Dhaka: Bangladesh Rural Advancement Committee.

Bratton, M. (1989) 'The politics of NGO–government relations in Africa', *World Development*, 17, 4: 569–87.

—— (1990) 'Non-governmental organizations in Africa: can they influence public policy?', *Development and Change*, 21: 87–118.

—— (1994a) 'Civil society and political transitions in Africa', in J. W. Harbeson, D. Rothchild and N. Chazan (eds) *Civil Society and the State in Africa*, Boulder, CO: Lynne Rienner.

—— (1994b) 'Civil society and political transition in Africa', *IDR Reports*, 11, 6, Boston, MA: Institute for Development Research.

Brett, E. A. (1993) 'Voluntary agencies as development organizations: theorising the problem of efficiency and accountability', *Development and Change*, 24: 269–303.

Britton, B. (1998) 'The learning NGO', Occasional Papers Series no. 17, Oxford: INTRAC.

Brodhead, T. (1987) 'NGOs: in one year, out the other?', *World Development* 15 (supplement): 1–6.

Brown, L. D. (1987) 'Development organizations and organization development: towards an expanded paradigm', *Research in Organizational Change and Development*, 1: 59–87.

—— (1991) 'Bridging organizations and sustainable development', *Human Relations*, 44, 8: 807–31.

—— (1994) 'Creating social capital: nongovernmental development organizations and intersectoral problem solving', *IDR Reports*, 11, 3, Boston, MA: Institute for Development Research.

Brown, L. D. and Ashman, D. (1996) 'Participation, social capital and intersectoral problem-solving: African and Asian cases', *World Development*, 24, 9: 1467–79.

Brown, L. D. and Covey, J. (1983) 'Organizational microcosms and ideological negotiation', in M. H. Bazerman and R. J. Lewicki (eds) *Negotiating in Organizations*, Newbury Park: Sage.

Brown, L. D. and Covey, J. (1987) 'Organizing and managing private development agencies: a comparative analysis', Boston, MA: Institute for Development Research/Newhaven, CT: Yale Program on Non-profit Organization (PONPO) Working Paper no. 129.

Brown, L. D. and Covey, J. (1989) 'Organization development in social change organizations: some implications for practice', in W. Sikes, A. Drexier and J. Grant (eds) *The Emerging Practice of Organization Development*, San Diego, CA: University Associates.

Brown, L. D. and Fox, J. (2001) 'Transnational civil society coalitions and the World Bank', in M. Edwards and J. Gaventa (eds) *Global Citizen Action*, Boulder, CO: Lynne Rienner.

Brown, L. D. and Korten, D. C. (1989) 'Understanding voluntary organizations: guidelines for donors', Working Paper 258, Country Economics Department, Washington DC: World Bank.

Brown, L. D. and Tandon, R. (1994) 'Institutional development for strengthening civil society', *Institutional Development (Innovations in Civil Society)*, 1, 1: 3–17.

Bryman, A. (1992) *Charisma and Leadership in Organizations*, London: Sage.

Bryson, J. (1988) *Strategic Planning for Public and Non-Profit Organizations*, San Francisco, CA: Jossey-Bass.

—— (1994) 'Strategic planning and action planning in nonprofit organizations', in Robert D. Herman and Associates (eds) *The Jossey-Bass Handbook of Nonprofit Leadership and Management*, San Francisco, CA: Jossey-Bass.

Buchanan-Smith, M. and Maxwell, S. (1994) 'Linking relief and development: an introduction and overview', *IDS Bulletin*, 25, 4: 2–16.

Bunch, R. (1985) *Two Ears of Corn: A Guide to People-Centred Agricultural Improvement*, Oklahoma, OK: World Neighbors.

Campbell, P. (1987) 'Management development and development management for voluntary organizations', Occasional Paper no. 3, Geneva: ICVA.

—— (1988) 'Relations between Northern and Southern NGOs in the context of sustainability, participation and partnership in development', mimeo, Geneva: ICVA.

—— (1994) 'Alternative financing strategies for Southern NGOs', mimeo, Geneva: ICVA.

Canel, E. (1997) 'New social movement theory and resource mobilisation theory: the need for integration', in M. Kaufman and H. D. Alfonso (eds) *Community Power and Grassroots Democracy*, London: Zed Books.

Carroll, T. F. (1992) *Intermediary NGOs: The Supporting Link in Grassroots Development*, Hartford, CT: Kumarian Press.

Castells, M. (1996) *The Rise of the Network Society*, Oxford: Blackwell.

Cernea, M. M. (1988) 'Non-governmental organizations and local development', World Bank Discussion Papers, Washington, DC: World Bank.

Chambers, R. (1983) *Rural Development: Putting the Last First*, Harlow: Longman.

—— (1987) 'Sustainable livelihoods, environment and development: putting poor rural people first', Discussion Paper no. 240, Brighton: Institute of Development Studies.

—— (1992) 'Spreading and self-improving: a strategy for scaling up', in M. Edwards and D. Hulme (eds) *Making a Difference: NGOs and Development in a Changing World*, London: Earthscan.

—— (1994) *Challenging the Professions*, London: Intermediate Technology Publications.

—— (1995) 'Participatory rural appraisal (PRA): challenges, potentials and paradigm', *World Development*, 22, nos. 7, 9, 10 (in three parts).

—— (2005) *Ideas for Development*, London: Earthscan.

Charnovitz, S. (1997) 'Two centuries of participation: NGOs and international governance', *Michigan Journal of International Law*, 18, 2: 183–286.

Chhetri, R. (1995) 'Rotating credit associations in Nepal: dhikuri as capital, credit, saving and investment', *Human Organization*, 54, 4: 449–54.

Clark, J. (1991) *Democratizing Development: The Role of Voluntary Organizations*, London: Earthscan.

—— (1992) 'Policy influence, lobbying and advocacy', in M. Edwards and D. Hulme (eds) *Making a Difference: NGOs and Development in a Changing World*, London: Earthscan.

—— (1997) 'The state, popular participation and the voluntary sector', in D. Hulme and M. Edwards (eds) *Too Close for Comfort? NGOs, States and Donors*, London: Macmillan.

—— (ed.)(2003a) *Globalizing Civic Engagement: Civil Society and Transnational Action*, London: Earthscan.

—— (2003b) *Worlds Apart: Civil Society and the Battle for Ethical Globalization*, Hartford, CT: Kumarian Press.

Clark, J. and Themudo, N. (2006) 'Linking the web and the street: internet-based "dotcauses" and the "anti-globalization" movement', *World Development*, 34, 1: 50–74.

Clark, N., Hall, A., Sulaiman, R. and Naik, G. (2003) 'Research as capacity building: the case of an NGO facilitated post-harvest innovation system for the Himalayan Hills', *World Development*, 31, 11: 1845–63.

Clarke, G. (1998) 'Nongovernmental organizations and politics in the developing world', *Political Studies*, 46: 36–52.

CMC (n.d.) 'A brief survey of complexity science and how it is being used in relation to organizations and their management', Paper 8, Complexity and Management Centre, University of Hertfordshire.

Coleman, J. (1988) 'Social capital in the creation of human capital', reprinted in P. Dasgupta and I. Seargeldin (eds) (1999) *Social Capital: A Multifaceted Perspective*, Washington, DC: World Bank.

—— (1990) *Foundations of Social Theory*, Cambridge, MA: Harvard University Press.

Comaroff, J. L. and Comaroff, J. (2000) *Civil Society and the Critical Imagination in Africa: Critical Perspectives*, Chicago, IL: University of Chicago Press.

Commonwealth Foundation (1995) *Nongovernmental Organizations: Guidelines for Good Policy and Practice*, London: Commonwealth Foundation.

Constantino-David, K. (1992) 'The Philippine experience in scaling-up', in M. Edwards and D. Hulme (eds) *Making a Difference: NGOs and Development in a Changing World*, London: Earthscan.

Cooke, B. (1996) 'Organization development and institutional development', mimeo, Manchester Institute for Development Policy and Management.

—— (1997) 'Participation, "process" and management: lessons for development in the history of organization development', *Journal of International Development*, 10, 1: 35–54.

Cooke, B. and Kothari, U. (2001) (eds) *Participation: The New Tyranny?* London: Zed Books.

Cooprider, D. L. and Srivastva, S. (1987) 'Appreciative enquiry in organizational life', *Research in Organizational Change and Development*, 1: 129–69.

Cornwall, A. and Brock, K. (2005) 'Beyond buzzwords: "poverty reduction", "participation" and "empowerment" in development policy', paper no. 10, Geneva: UNRISD.

Covey, J. (1995) 'Accountability and effectiveness in NGO policy alliances', *Journal of International Development*, 7, 6: 857–67.

Cox, T. (1994) *Cultural Diversity in Organizations: Theory, Research and Practice*, San Francisco, CA: Berret-Koehier.

Curtis, D. (1994) 'Owning without owners, managing with few managers: lessons from Third World irrigators', in S. Wright (ed.) *Anthropology of Organizations*, London: Routledge.

Cushing, C. (1995) 'Humanitarian assistance and the role of NGOs', *Institutional Development (Innovations in Civil Society)*, 2, 2: 3–17.

Dale, R. (2004) *Development Planning: Concepts and Tools for Planners, Managers and Facilitators*, London: Zed Books.

Dartington, T. (1992) 'Professional management in voluntary organizations: some cautionary notes', in J. Batsleer, C. Cornforth and R. Paton (eds) *Issues in Voluntary and Non-profit Management*, Milton Keynes: Open University Press/Wokingham: Addison-Wesley.

Davies, R. (1997) 'Donor information demands and NGO institutional development', *Journal of International Development*, 9, 4: 613–20.

Davis Smith, J. (1996) 'Should volunteers be managed?', in D. Billis and M. Harris (eds) *Voluntary Agencies: Challenges of Organization and Management*, London: Macmillan.

Davis Smith, J., Rochester, C. and Hedley, R. (eds) (1995) *An Introduction to the Voluntary Sector*, London: Routledge.

Dawson, E. (1993) 'NGOs and public policy reform: lessons from Peru', *Journal of International Development*, 5, 4: 401–14.

de Berry, J. (1999) 'Exploring the concept of community: implications for NGO management', Centre for Civil Society International Working Paper 8, London: London School of Economics.

de Graaf, M. (1987) 'Context, constraint or control? Zimbabwean NGOs and their environment', *Development Policy Review*, 5: 277–301.

de Haan, A. and Maxwell, S. (1998) 'Poverty and social exclusion in North and South', *IDS Bulletin*, 29, 1: 1–9.

de Waal, A. and Omaar, R. (1993) 'Doing harm by doing good? The international relief effort in Somalia', *Current History*, 92, 574: 198–202.

Deacon, B., Hulse, M. and Stubbs, P. (1997) *Global Social Policy: International Organizations and the Future of Welfare*, London: Sage.

Dechalert, P. (1999) 'NGOs, advocacy and popular protest: a case study of Thailand', Centre for Civil Society International Working Paper 6, London: London School of Economics.

—— (2002) 'Non-governmental organizations and resources: case studies of four NGOs in Thailand', unpublished PhD thesis, London School of Economics.

DeMars, W. E. (2005) *NGOs and Transnational Networks: Wild Cards in World Politics*, London: Pluto Press.

Denning, S. (2000) *The Springboard: How Storytelling Ignites Action in Knowledge-Era Organizations*, Boston, MA: Butterworth-Heinemann.

Desai, U. and Snavely, K. (1998) 'Emergence and development of Bulgaria's environmental movement', *Nonprofit Management and Leadership*, 27, 1: 32–48.

DFID (Department for International Development) (1997) *Eliminating World Poverty: A Challenge for the 21st Century*, London: The Stationery Office.

Diaz-Albertini, J. (1991) 'Non-government development organizations and the grassroots in Peru', *Voluntas*, 2, 1: 26–57.

—— (1993) 'Nonprofit advocacy in weakly institutionalized political systems: the case of NGDOs in Lima, Peru', *Nonprofit and Voluntary Sector Quarterly*, 27, 4: 317–37.

DiBella, A. (1992) 'Planned change in an organized anarchy: support for a postmodernist perspective', *Journal of Organizational Change Management*, 5, 3: 55–65.

Dichter, T. W. (1989a) 'Development management: plain or fancy? Sorting out some muddles', *Public Administration and Development*, 9: 381–93.

—— (1989b) 'NGOs and the replication trap', *Technoserve Findings 89*, Norwalk CT: Technoserve Inc.

—— (1996) 'Questioning the future of NGOs in micro-finance', *Journal of International Development*, 8, 2: 259–70.

—— (1997) 'Appeasing the gods of sustainability: the future of international NGOs in micro-finance', in D. Hulme and M. Edwards (eds) *Too Close for Comfort? NGOs, States and Donors*, London: Macmillan.

—— (1999) 'Globalization and its effects on NGOs: efflorescence or a blurring of roles and relevance?', *Nonprofit and Voluntary Sector Quarterly* (supplement), 28, 4: 38–86.

—— (2003) *Despite Good Intentions: Why Development Assistance to the Third World Has Failed*, Boston: University of Massachusetts Press.

Dignard, L. and Havet, J. (1995) *Women in Micro- and Small-Scale Enterprise Development*, London: Intermediate Technology Publications.

DiMaggio, P. and Powell, W. W. (1991) 'The iron cage revisited: institutional isomorphism and collective rationality in organizational fields', in P. DiMaggio and W. W. Powell (eds) *The New Institutionalism in Organizational Analysis*, Chicago, IL: University of Chicago Press.

Downing, J. (1991) 'Gender and the growth of micro-enterprises', *Small Enterprise Development*, 2, 1: 4–12.

Drabek, A. G. (1987) 'Development alternatives: the challenge for NGOs', *World Development*, 15 (supplement): ix–xv.

Drucker, P. (1990) *Managing the Nonprofit Organization*, New York: Collins.

Duffield, M. (1993) 'NGOs, disaster relief and asset transfer in the Horn: political survival in a permanent emergency', *Development and Change*, 24, 1: 131–57.

—— (2002) 'Social reconstruction and the radicalization of development: aid as a relation of global liberal governance', *Development and Change*, 33, 5: 1049–71.

Dunleavy, P., Margetts, H., Bastow, S. and Tinkler, J. (2005) 'New public management is dead – long live digital-era governance', *Journal of Public Administration and Theory*, 16, 3: 1–28.

Eade, D. (1997) *Capacity Building: An Approach to People-Centred Development*, Oxford: Oxfam Publications.

Eade, D. and Williams, S. (1995) *The Oxfam Handbook of Development and Relief*, Oxford: Oxfam Publications.

Ebrahim, A. (2003) *NGOs and Organizational Change: Discourse, Reporting and Learning*, Cambridge: Cambridge University Press.

The Economist (1999) 'NGOs: sins of the secular missionaries', 29 January: 25–8.

Edoho, F. (1998) 'Management capacity building: a strategic imperative for African development in the twenty-first century', in V. Udoh James (ed.) *Capacity Building in Developing Countries: Human and Environmental Dimensions*, New York: Praeger.

Edwards, M. (1993) 'Does the doormat influence the boot? Critical thoughts on UK NGOs and international advocacy', *Development in Practice*, 3, 3: 163–75.

—— (1994) 'NGOs in the age of information', *IDS Bulletin*, 25, 2: 117–24.

—— (1996) 'International development NGOs: legitimacy, accountability, regulation and roles', discussion paper prepared for the Commission of the Future of the Voluntary Sector and the British Overseas Aid Group (BOAG), London.

—— (1998) 'Nailing the jelly to the wall: NGOs, civil society and international development', unpublished draft mimeo.

—— (1999a) 'NGO performance: what breeds success?', *World Development*, 27, 2: 361–74.

—— (1999b) *Future Positive: International Co-operation in the 21st Century*, London: Earthscan.

Edwards, M. and Gaventa, J. (eds) (2001) *Global Citizen Action*, Boulder, CO: Lynne Rienner.

Edwards, M. and Hulme, D. (eds) (1992) *Making a Difference: NGOs and Development in a Changing World*, London: Earthscan.

Edwards, M. and Hulme, D. (eds) (1995) *Beyond the Magic Bullet: NGO Performance and Accountability in the Post-Cold War World*, London: Earthscan.

Edwards, M., Hulme, D. and Wallace, T. (2000) 'Increasing leverage for development: challenges for NGOs in a global future', in D. Lewis and T. Wallace (eds) *New Roles and Relevance: Development NGOs and the Challenge of Change*, Hartford, CT: Kumarian Press.

Egeland, J. and Kerbs, T. (eds) (1987) *Third World Organizational Development: A Comparison of NGO Strategies*, Geneva: Henry Dunant Institute.

Ellis, G. (1984) 'Making PVOs count more: a proposal', in R. F. Gorman (ed.) *Private Voluntary Organizations as Agents of Development*, Boulder: Westview Press.

Escobar, A. (1995) *Encountering Development: The Making and Unmaking of the Third World*, Princeton, NJ: Princeton University Press.

Escobar, A. and Alvarez, S. E. (eds) (1992) *The Making of Social Movements in Latin America: Identity, Strategy and Democracy*, Boulder, CT: Westview Press.

Escobar, J. S. (1997) 'Religion and social change at the grassroots in Latin America', *Annals of the American Academy of Political and Social Science*, 554: 81–103.

Etzioni, A. (1961) *A Comparative Analysis of Complex Organizations: On Power, Involvement and their Correlates*, New York: The Free Press of Glencoe.

—— (1972) 'The untapped potential of the third sector', *Business and Society Review*, 1, Spring: 39–44.

—— (1973) 'The third sector and domestic missions', *Public Administration Review*, 33, 4: 314–23.

Evans, P. (1996) 'Government action, social capital and development: reviewing the evidence for synergy', *World Development*, 24, 6: 1119–32.

Evers, A. (1995) 'Part of the welfare mix: the third sector as an intermediate area', *Voluntas*, 6, 2: 159–82.

Farrington, J. and Bebbington, A., with Wellard, K. and Lewis, D. (1993) *Reluctant Partners?: NGOs, the State and Sustainable Agricultural Development*, London: Routledge.

Farrington, J. and Lewis, D. with Satish, S. and Miclat-Teves, A. (eds) (1993) *NGOs and the State in Asia: Rethinking Roles in Sustainable Agricultural Development*, London: Routledge.

Ferguson, J. and Gupta, A. (2002) 'Spatializing states: towards an ethnography of neoliberal governmentality', *American Ethnologist*, 29, 4: 981–1002.

Ferlie, E., Ashburner, L., Fitzgerald, L. and Pettigrew, A. (1996) *The New Public Sector Management in Action*, Oxford: Oxford University Press.

Fernando, J. L. (1997) 'Nongovernment organizations, micro-credit and the empowerment of women', *Annals of the American Academy of Political and Social Science*, 554, November: 150–77.

251

Fernando, J. L. and Heston, A. (eds) (1997) 'The role of NGOs: charity and empowerment', introduction to *Annals of the American Academy of Political and Social Science*, 554, November: 8–20.

Fisher, J. (1993) *The Road from Rio: Sustainable Development and Nongovernmental Movement in the Third World*, New York: Praeger.

—— (1994) 'Is the iron law of oligarchy rusting away in the third world?', *World Development*, 22, 4: 129–44.

—— (1998) *Nongovernments: NGOs and the Political Development of the Third World*, Hartford, CT: Kumarian Press.

Fisher, W. F. (1997) 'Doing good? The politics and anti-politics of NGO practices', *Annual Review of Anthropology*, 26: 439–64.

Foreman, K. (1999) 'Evolving global structures and the challenges facing international relief and development organizations', *Nonprofit and Voluntary Sector Quarterly*, 28, 4 (supplement): 178–97.

Forstater, M., MacDonald, J. and Raynard, P. (2002) *Business and Poverty: Bridging the Gap*, Resource Centre for the Social Dimensions of Business Practice, Prince of Wales International Business Leaders Forum, London.

Fowler, A. (1993) 'Non-governmental organisations as agents of democratisation: an African perspective', *Journal of International Development*, 5, 3: 325–39.

—— (1994) 'Capacity building and NGOs: a case of strengthening ladles for the global soup kitchen?', *Institutional Development (Innovations in Civil Society)*, 1, 1: 18–24.

—— (1997) *Striking a Balance: A Guide to Enhancing the Effectiveness of NGOs in International Development*, London: Earthscan.

—— (1999) 'Advocacy and third sector organizations', in D. Lewis (ed.) *International Perspectives on Voluntary Action: Reshaping the Third Sector*, London: Earthscan.

—— (2000) *The Virtuous Spiral: A Guide to Sustainability for NGOs in International Development*, London: Earthscan.

Fowler, A. and Biekart, K. (1996) 'Do private agencies really make a difference?', in D. Sogge, K. Biekart and J. Saxby (eds) *Compassion and Calculation: The Business of Private Foreign Aid*, London: Pluto Press.

Fowler, A. and Edwards, M. (eds) (2002) *The NGO Management Reader*, London: Earthscan.

Fowler, A., Campbell, P. and Pratt, B. (1992) *Institutional Development and NGOs in Africa: Policy Perspectives for European Development Agencies*, NGO Management Series no. 1, Oxford: INTRAC.

Fox, J. (1992) 'Democratic rural development: leadership accountability in regional peasant organizations', *Development and Change*, 23, 2: 1–36.

Frank, A. G. (1959) 'Goal ambiguity and conflicting standards: an approach to the study of organization', *Human Organization* (Winter 1958/9): 8–13.

Freeman, J. (1973) 'The tyranny of structurelessness', *Berkeley Journal of Sociology*, 17: 151–64.

Friedmann, J. (1992) *Empowerment: The Politics of Alternative Development*, Oxford: Blackwell.

Fry, R. (1995) 'Accountability in organizational life: problem or opportunity for nonprofits?', *Nonprofit Management and Leadership*, 6, 2: 181–96.

Fyvie, C. and Ager, A. (1999) 'NGOs and innovation: organizational characteristics and constraints in development assistance work in the Gambia', *World Development*, 27, 8: 1383–96.

Gardner, K. and Lewis, D. (1996) *Anthropology, Development and the Postmodern Challenge*, London: Pluto Press.

Gardner, K. and Lewis, D. (2000) 'Dominant paradigms overturned or business as usual? Development discourse and the White Paper on international development', *Critique of Anthropology*, 20, 1: 15–29.

Gaventa, J. (1999) 'Building links and learning between NGOs and community-based organizations in North and South', in D. Lewis (ed.) *International Perspectives on Voluntary Action: Reshaping the Third Sector*, London: Earthscan.

Geertz, C. (1973) *The Interpretation of Cultures*, New York: Basic Books.

Gioia, D. A. and Thomas, J. B. (1996) 'Identity, image and issue interpretation: sensemaking during strategic change in academia', *Administrative Science Quarterly*, 41: 370–403.

Glasius, M., Lewis, D. and Seckinelgin, H. (eds) (2004) *Exploring Civil Society: Political and Cultural Contexts*, London: Routledge.

Glasius, M., Kaldor, M. and Anheier, H. (eds) (2006) *Global Civil Society 2005/6*, London: Sage.

Gledhill, J. (1994) *Power and its Disguises: Anthropological Perspectives on Politics*, London: Zed Books.

Goetz, A. M. (ed.) (1997) *Getting Institutions Right for Women in Development*, London: Zed Books.

Goetz, A. M. and Sen Gupta, R. (1996) 'Who takes the credit? Gender, power and control over loan use in rural credit programmes in Bangladesh', *World Development*, 24: 1.

Gosling, L. and Edwards, M. (1995) *Toolkits: A Practical Guide to Assessment, Monitoring, Review and Evaluation*, London: Save the Children Fund Development Manual no. 5.

Goyder, G. (1961) *The Responsible Company*, Oxford: Blackwell.

Grey, C. and Willmott, H. (2005) *Critical Management Studies: A Reader*. Oxford: Oxford University Press.

Grint, K. (1995) *Management: A Sociological Introduction*, Cambridge: Polity Press.

Guareschi, P. and Jovchelovitch, S. (2004) 'Participation, health and the development of community resources in Southern Brazil', *Journal of Health Psychology*, 9, 1: 303–14.

Guha, R. (1989) *The Unquiet Woods: Ecological Change and Peasant Resistance in the Himalaya*, Oxford: Oxford University Press.

Guijt, I. and Gaventa, J. (1998) 'Participatory monitoring and evaluation: learning from change', IDS Policy Briefing no. 12, Brighton: Institute of Development Studies.

Guijt, I. and Shah, M. K. (1998) 'General introduction: waking up to power, process and conflict', in I. Guijt and M. K. Shah (eds) *The Myth of Community*, London: Intermediate Technology Publications.

Hadenius, A. and Uggla, F. (1996) 'Making civil society work, promoting democratic development: what can states and donors do?', *World Development*, 24, 10: 1621–39.

Hadjipateras, A. (1997) 'Implementing a gender policy in ACORD: strategies, constraints, and challenges', *Gender and Development*, 5, 1: 28–34.

BIBLIOGRAPHY

Hailey, J. (1999) 'Charismatic autocrats or development leaders? Characteristics of first generation NGO leadership', draft presented to the UK Development Studies Association Conference, University of Bath, September.

—— (2000) 'Learning for growth: organizational learning in South Asian NGOs', in D. Lewis and T. Wallace (eds) *New Roles and Relevance: Development NGOs and the Challenge of Change*, Hartford, CT: Kumarian Press.

—— (2006) 'NGO leadership development: a review of the literature', Praxis Paper no. 10, Oxford: INTRAC.

Hamada, T. (1992) 'Anthropology and organizational culture', in T. Hamada and W. E. Sibley (eds) *Anthropological Perspectives on Organizational Culture*, Lanham, MD: University Press of America.

Handy, C. (1988) *Managing Voluntary Organizations*, Harmondsworth: Penguin.

—— (1995) 'Trust and the virtual organization', *Harvard Business Review* (May–June): 40–50.

Hanlon, J. (1991) *Mozambique: Who Calls the Shots?*, London: James Currey.

Hann, C. and Dunn, E. (eds) (1996) *Civil Society: Challenging Western Models*, London: Routledge.

Harding, P. (1991) 'Qualitative indicators and the project framework', *Community Development Journal*, 26: 4.

Harmer, A. and L. Cotterrell (2005) 'Diversity in donorship: the changing landscape of official humanitarian aid', Humanitarian Policy Group Report 20, September, London: Overseas Development Institute.

Harmer, A. and Macrae, J. (2003) 'Humanitarian action and the global war on terror: a review of trends and issues,' HPG Briefing no. 9, July, London: Overseas Development Institute.

Harris, M. (1996) 'Do we need governing bodies?', in D. Billis and M. Harris (eds) *Voluntary Agencies: Challenges of Organization and Management*, London: Macmillan.

—— (1999) 'Voluntary sector governance: problems in practice and theory in the United Kingdom and North America', in D. Lewis (ed.) *International Perspectives on Voluntary Action: Reshaping the Third Sector*, London: Earthscan.

Harriss, J. (1997) 'Social capital: missing link or analytically missing?', *Journal of International Development*, 9: 7.

Harzing, A.-W. (1995) 'Internationalization and the international division of labour', in A.-W. Harzing and J. van Ruysseveldt (eds) *International Human Resource Management*, London: Sage.

Hashemi, S. M. (1989) 'NGOs in Bangladesh: development alternative or alternative rhetoric?', mimeo, Jahangirnagar University, Bangladesh.

—— (1995) 'NGO accountability in Bangladesh: beneficiaries, donors and the state', in M. Edwards and D. Hulme (eds) *Beyond the Magic Bullet: NGO Performance and Accountability in the Post-Cold War World*, London: Earthscan.

Hashemi, S. M. and Hassan, M. (1999) 'Building NGO legitimacy in Bangladesh: the contested domain', in D. Lewis (ed.) *International Perspectives on Voluntary Action: Reshaping the Third Sector*, London: Earthscan.

Hatch, M. J. (1997) *Organization Theory: Modern, Symbolic and Postmodern Perspectives*, Oxford: Oxford University Press.

Hellinger, D. (1987) 'NGOs and the large aid donors: changing the terms of engagement', *World Development*, 15 (supplement): 135–43.

Hellinger, S., Hellinger, D. and O'Regan, F. M. (1988) *Aid for Just Development: Report on the Future of Foreign Assistance*, London: Lynne Rienner.

Hickey, S. and Mohan, G. (eds) (2004) *Participation: From Tyranny to Transformation*, London: Zed Books.

Hickey, S. and Mohan, G. (2005) 'Relocating participation within a radical politics of development', *Development and Change*, 36, 2: 237–62.

Hilhorst, D. (2003) *The Real World of NGOs: Discourses, Diversity and Development*, London: Zed Books.

Hinton, R. and Groves, L. (2004) 'The complexity of inclusive aid,' in L. Groves and R. Hinton (eds) *Inclusive Aid: Changing Power Relationships in International Development*, London: Earthscan.

Hirschmann, A. (1970) *Exit, Voice and Loyalty*, Cambridge, MA: Harvard University Press.

Hofstede, G. (1991) *Cultures and Organizations: Software of the Mind – Intercultural Cooperation and its Importance for Survival*, London: HarperCollins.

Hoksbergen, R. (2005) 'Building civil society through partnership: lessons from a case study of the Christian Reformed World Relief Committee', *Development in Practice*, 15, 1: 16–27.

Holcombe, S. (1995) *Managing to Empower: The Grameen Bank's Experience of Poverty Alleviation*, London: Zed Books.

Honey, R. and Okafor, S. (1998) *Hometown Associations: Indigenous Knowledge and Development in Nigeria*, London: Intermediate Technology Publications.

Hood, C. (1998) *The Art of the State: Culture, Rhetoric and Public Management*, Oxford: Clarendon Press.

Horton Smith, D. (1997) 'Grassroots associations are important: some theory and a review of the impact literature', *Non-Profit and Voluntary Sector Quarterly*, 26, 3: 269–306.

Howell, J. (2006a) 'Gender and civil society', in M. Glasius, M. Kaldor and H. Anheier (eds) *Global Civil Society Yearbook 2005/6*, London: Sage.

—— (2006b) 'The global war on terror, development and civil society', *Journal of International Development*, 18, 1: 121–35.

Howell, J. and Pearce, J. (2000) 'Civil society: technical instrument or force for change?', in D. Lewis and T. Wallace (eds) *New Roles and Relevance: Development NGOs and the Challenge of Change*, Hartford, CT: Kumarian Press.

Howell, J. and Pearce, J. (2001) *Civil Society and Development: A Critical Exploration*, London: Lynne Rienner.

Howes, M. (1997) 'NGOs and the institutional development of membership organizations: the evidence from six cases', *Journal of International Development*, 9, 4: 597–604.

Howes, M. and Sattar, M. G. (1992) 'Bigger and better? Scaling-up strategies pursued by BRAC 1972–1991', in M. Edwards and D. Hulme (eds) *Making a Difference: NGOs and Development in a Changing World*, London: Earthscan.

Hoyer, H. J. (1994) 'Reflections on partnership and accompaniment', *Institutional Development*, 1, 1.

Hudock, A. (1995) 'Sustaining Southern NGOs in resource-dependent environments', *Journal of International Development*, 7, 4: 653–67.

—— (1997) 'Institutional interdependence: capacity-enhancing assistance for intermediary NGOs in Sierra Leone and the Gambia', *Journal of International Development*, 9, 4: 589–96.

Hudson, M. (1995) *Managing Without Profit: The Art of Managing Non-Profit Organizations*, Harmondsworth: Penguin.

Hulme, D. (1990) 'Can the Grameen Bank be replicated? Recent experiments in Malaysia, Malawi and Sri Lanka', *Development Policy Review*, 8: 287–300.

—— (1994) 'NGOs and social development research', in D. Booth (ed.) *Rethinking Social Development: Theory, Research and Practice*, London: Longman.

Hulme, D. and Edwards, M. (eds) (1997) *Too Close for Comfort? NGOs, States and Donors*, London: Macmillan.

Hulme, D. and A. Shepherd (2003) 'Chronic poverty and development policy: an introduction', *World Development*, 31, 3: 399–403.

IDS (Institute of Development Studies) (2003) 'The rise of rights: rights-based approaches to international development', IDS Policy Briefing, Issue 17, May. www.ids.ac.uk

IFRC (1997) *Code of Conduct for International Red Cross and Red Crescent Movement and NGOs in Disaster Relief*, Geneva: International Federation of the Red Cross.

—— (1999) *World Disasters Report 1999*, Geneva: International Federation of the Red Cross and Red Crescent Societies.

Igoe, J. and Kelsall, T. (eds) (2005) *Between a Rock and a Hard Place: African NGOs, Donors and the State*, Durham, NC: Carolina Academic Press.

Ilchman, W. F., Katz, S. N. and Queen, E. L. (eds) (1998) *Philanthropy in the World's Traditions*, Indianapolis: Indiana University Press.

Ishkanian, A. (2006) 'From inclusion to exclusion: Armenian NGOs' participation in the PRSP', *Journal of International Development*, 18, 5: 729–40.

Jaeger, A. M. and Kanungo, R. N. (eds) (1990) *Management in Developing Countries*, London: Routledge.

Jain, P. S. (1996) 'Managing credit for the rural poor: lessons from the Grameen Bank', *World Development*, 24, 1: 79–90.

Jalali, R. (2002) 'Civil society and the state: Turkey after the earthquake', *Disasters*, 26, 2: 120–39.

James, R. (1994) 'Strengthening the capacity of Southern NGO partners: a survey of current NNGO approaches', Occasional Papers Series no. 5, Oxford: INTRAC.

—— (2003) 'Exploring OD in Africa', *Nonprofit Management and Leadership*, 14, 313–24.

Jenkins, J. C. (1987) 'Nonprofit organizations and policy advocacy', in W. W. Powell (ed.) *The Nonprofit Sector: A Research Handbook*, New Haven, CT: Yale University Press.

Jenkins, R. and Goetz, A. M. (1998) 'Accounts and accountability: theoretical implications of the right-to-information movement in India', unpublished mimeo, Brighton: Institute of Development Studies.

Jones, B. D. (1995) '"Intervention without borders": humanitarian intervention in Rwanda 1990–94', *Millennium: Journal of International Studies*, 24, 2: 225–49.

Jones, F. E. (1996) *Understanding Organizations: A Sociological Perspective*, Toronto: Copp Clark.

Kaijage, F. J. (ed.) (1993) *Management Consulting in Africa: Utilizing Local Expertise*, Hartford, CT: Kumarian Press.

Kaimowitz, D. (1993) 'The role of NGOs in agricultural research and technology transfer in Latin America', *World Development*, 21, 7: 1139–50.

Kaldor, M. (2003) *Global Civil Society: An Answer To War*, Cambridge: Polity Press.

Kanji, N. and Greenwood, L. (2001) *Participatory approaches to research and development in IIED: learning from experience*. International Institute for Environment and Development (IIED). Available at www.iied.org

Kanji, N., Kapiriri, M., Hearn, J. and Manyire, H. (2000) 'An assessment of DFID's engagement with civil society in Uganda: past work and current shifts', Department for International Development office, Uganda.

Kanji, N., Braga, C. and Mitullah, W. V. (2002) *Promoting land rights in Africa: how do NGOs make a difference?* International Institute for Environment and Development (IIED). Available at www.iied.org

Kanter, R. M. and Summers, D. (1987) 'Doing well while doing good: dilemmas of performance measurement in nonprofit organizations and the need for a multiple constituency approach', in W. W. Powell (ed.) *The Nonprofit Sector: A Research Handbook*, New Haven, CT: Yale University Press.

Kaplan, A. (1999) 'The development of capacity', Non-Governmental Liaison Service (NGLS) Development Dossier, Geneva: United Nations Organization.

Kardam, N. (1993) 'Development approaches and the role of advocacy', *World Development*, 21, 11: 1773–86.

Karim, M. (2000) 'NGOs, democratization and good governance: the case of Bangladesh', in D. Lewis and T. Wallace (eds) *New Roles and Relevance: Development NGOs and the Challenge of Change*, Hartford, CT: Kumarian Press.

Karsten, M. F. (1994) *Management and Gender: Issues and Attitudes*, London: Praeger.

Kaufman, G. (1997) 'Watching the developers: a partial ethnography', in R. D. Grub and R. L. Stirrat (eds) *Discourses of Development: Anthropological Perspectives*, Oxford: Berg.

Kawashima, N. (1999) 'The emerging non-profit sector in Japan', Centre for Civil Society International Working Paper 9, London School of Economics.

Kay, R. (1996) 'What kind of leadership do voluntary organizations need?', in D. Billis and M. Harris (eds) *Voluntary Agencies: Challenges of Organization and Management*, London: Macmillan.

Keane, J. (1998) *Civil Society: Old Images, New Visions*, Cambridge: Polity Press.

Keck, M. and Sikkink, K. (1998) *Activists Beyond Borders: Advocacy Networks in International Politics*, Ithaca, NY: Cornell University Press.

Kelleher, D. and McLaren, K. (1996) *Grabbing the Tiger by the Tail: NGOs Learning for Organizational Change*, Ottawa: Canadian Council for International Cooperation.

Kendall, J. (2003) *The Voluntary Sector: Comparative Perspectives in the UK*, London: Routledge.

Kendall, J. and Knapp, M. (1999) 'Evaluation and the voluntary (non-profit) sector: emerging issues', in D. Lewis (ed.) *International Perspectives on Voluntary Action: Reshaping the Third Sector*, London: Earthscan.

Keohane, R. O. and Nye, J. S. (2003) 'What's new? What's not? (And so what?)', in D. Held and A. McGrew (eds) *The Global Transformations Reader*, second edition, Cambridge: Polity Press.

Khan, T. A. (1999) 'The Muslim Buddhist: Akhtar Hameed Khan (1914–1999)', *Himal*, 12, 11: 49–50.

Kiggundu, M. N. (1989) *Managing Organizations in Developing Countries: An Operational and Strategic Approach*, Hartford, CT: Kumarian Press.

Knight, B. (1993) *Voluntary Action*, London: Home Office.

Koenig, B. (1996) 'The management of international non-governmental organizations in the 1990s', *Transnational Associations*, 2: 66–72.

Korten, D. C. (1980) 'Community organization and rural development: a learning process approach', *Public Administration Review*, 40: 480–511.

—— (1987) 'Third generation NGO strategies: a key to people-centred development', *World Development*, 15 (supplement): 145–59.

—— (1988) 'NGOs and the future of Asian development'. Mimeo, Insititute for Development Research (IDR), Boston, USA, April.

—— (1990) *Getting to the 21st Century: Voluntary Action and the Global Agenda*, Hartford, CT: Kumarian Press.

Korten, F. F. and Siy, R. Y. (1989) *Transforming a Bureaucracy: the Experience of the Philippines National Irrigation Administration*, Hartford, CT: Kumarian Press.

Kramer, R. (1994) 'Voluntary agencies and the contract culture: dream or nightmare?', *Social Service Review*, 63, 1: 33–60.

—— (1995) 'Is the third sector concept obsolete?', *Inside ISTR*, 4, 4: 6–7 (International Society for Third Sector Research).

Kramsjo, B. and Wood, G. (1992) *Breaking the Chains: Collective Action for Social Justice Among the Rural Poor in Bangladesh*, London: Intermediate Technology Publications.

Kubicek, P. (2002) 'The earthquake, civil society, and political change in Turkey: assessment and comparison with Eastern Europe', *Political Studies*, 50: 761–78.

Kumar, S. (1996) 'Accountability: what is it and why do we need it?', in S. P. Osborne (ed.) *Managing in the Voluntary Sector: A Handbook for Managers in Charitable Organizations*, London: Thomson.

Landry, C., Morley, D., Southwood, R. and Wright, P. (1985) 'What a way to run a railroad', in J. Batsleer, C. Cornforth and R. Paton (eds) *Issues in Voluntary and Non-profit Sector Management*, Milton Keynes: Open University Press/Wokingham: Addison-Wesley.

Landry, C., Morley, D., Southwood, R. and Wright, P. (1992) 'An analysis of radical failure', in J. Batsleer, C. Cornforth and R. Paton (eds) *Issues in Voluntary and Non-profit Sector Management*, Milton Keynes: Open University Press/Wokingham: Addison-Wesley.

Leadbeater, C. (1997) *The Rise of the Social Entrepreneur*, London: Demos.

Leat, D. (1988) *Voluntary Organizations and Accountability*, London: National Council for Voluntary Organizations.

—— (1993) *Managing Across Sectors: Similarities Between For-Profit and Voluntary Non-Profit Organizations*, London: City University Business School.

—— (1995) *Challenging Management: An Exploratory Study of Perceptions of Managers who have Moved from For-profit to Voluntary Organizations*, London: City University Business School.

Leggett, W. H. (1999) 'Tensions of business: processes of identification in a transnational corporate office', unpublished draft conference paper, American Anthropological Association Conference, Chicago.

Legrain, P. (2002) *Open World:/The Truth About Globalization*, Harmondsworth: Penguin.

Lehmann, D. (1990) *Democracy and Development in Latin America*, Cambridge: Polity Press.

Levitt, T. (1975) *The Third Sector: New Tactics for a Responsive Society*, New York: AMACOM, American Management Association.

Lewis, D. (1992) 'Catalysts for change? NGOs, agricultural technology and the state in Bangladesh', Agricultural Administration (Research and Extension) Network paper 38, London: Overseas Development Institute.

—— (1997) 'NGOs and the state in Bangladesh: donors, development and the discourse of partnership', *Annals of the American Academy of Political and Social Science*, 554: 33–45.

—— (1998a) 'Nonprofit organizations, business and the management of ambiguity: case studies of "fair trade" from Nepal and Bangladesh', *Nonprofit Management and Leadership*, 9, 2: 135–52.

—— (1998b) 'Inter-agency partnerships in aid-recipient countries: lessons from an aquaculture project in Bangladesh', *Nonprofit and Voluntary Sector Quarterly*, 27, 3: 323–38.

—— (1998c) 'Development NGOs and the challenge of partnership: changing relations between North and South', *Social Policy and Administration*, 32, 5: 501–12.

—— (ed.) (1999a) *International Perspectives on Voluntary Action: Reshaping the Third Sector*, London: Earthscan.

—— (1999b) 'Revealing, widening, deepening? A review of the existing and potential contribution of anthropological approaches to "third sector" research', *Human Organization*, 58, 1: 73–81.

—— (2002a) 'Civil society in African contexts: reflections on the "usefulness" of a concept', *Development and Change*, 33, 4: 569–86.

—— (2002b) 'Organization and management in the third sector: towards a cross-cultural research agenda', *Nonprofit Management and Leadership*, 13: 67–83.

—— (2004) 'On the difficulty of Studying "civil society": reflections on NGOs, state and democracy in Bangladesh', *Contributions to Indian Sociology*, 38, 3: 299–322.

—— (2005) 'Actors, ideas and networks: trajectories of the non-governmental in development studies', in Uma Kothari (ed.) *A Radical History of Development Studies*, London: Zed Books.

—— (2006) 'Non-governmental organizations and international politics', in N. Tate (ed.) *Governments of the World*, Farmington Hills, MI: Macmillan Reference USA.

Lewis, D. and Hossain, A. (2004) 'Beyond the Net?: the changing rural power structure in Bangladesh', Report to Swedish International Development Agency. Stockholm: Sida.

Lewis, D. and Madon, S. (2003) 'Information systems and non-governmental development organizations (NGOs): advocacy, organizational learning and accountability in a Southern NGO, *Information Society*, 20, 2: 117–26.

Lewis, D. and Mosse, D. (eds) (2006) *Development Brokers and Translators: The Ethnography of Aid and Agencies*, Bloomfield, CT: Kumarian Press.

Lewis, D. and Opoku-Mensah, P. (2006) 'Moving forward research agendas on international NGOs: theory, agency and context', *Journal of International Development*, 18: 1–11.

Lewis, D. and Siddiqi, M.S. (2006) 'Social capital from sericulture?', in A. Bebbington, M. Woolcock and S. Guggenheim (eds) *Social Capital and the World Bank*, Bloomfield, CT: Kumarian Press.

Lewis, D. and Sobhan, B. (1999) 'Routes of funding, roots of trust? Northern NGOs, Southern NGOs and the rise of direct funding', *Development in Practice*, 9, 1 and 2: 117–29.

Lewis, D. and Wallace, T. (eds) (2000) *New Roles and Relevance: Development NGOs and the Challenge of Change*, Hartford, CT: Kumarian Press.

Lewis, D., Bebbington, A., Batterbury, S., Shah, A., Olson, E., Siddiqi M. S. and Duvall, S. (2003) 'Practice, power and meaning: frameworks for studying organizational culture in multi-agency rural development projects', *Journal of International Development*, 15: 1–17.

Light, P. C. (2000) *Making Nonprofits Work: A Report on the Tides of Nonprofit Management Reform*, Aspen, Washington, DC: The Aspen Institute/Brookings Institution Press.

Lindblom, C. (1959) 'The science of muddling through', *Public Administration Review*, 19: 79–88.

Lindenberg, M. and Bryant, C. (2001) Going Global: Transforming Relief and Development NGOs, Bloomfield, CT: Kumarian Press.

Little, D. (2003) *The Paradox of Wealth and Poverty: Mapping the Ethical Dilemmas of Global Development*, Boulder, CO: Westview Press.

Lofredo, G. (1995) 'Help yourself by helping the poor', *Development in Practice*, 5: 4.

Long, N. and Long, A. (eds) (1992) *Battlefields of Knowledge: The Interlocking of Theory and Practice in Social Research and Development*, London: Routledge.

Lovell, C. (1992) *Breaking the Cycle of Poverty: The BRAC Strategy*, Hartford, CT: Kumarian Press.

Lyman, S. M. (1995) *Social Movements: Critiques, Concepts and Case-Studies*, London: Macmillan.

McAdam, D., McCarthy, J. D. and Zald, M. N. (1996) *Comparative Perspectives on Social Movements*, Cambridge: Cambridge University Press.

McCarthy, J. D. and Zald, M. N. (1977) 'Resource mobilisation in social movements: a partial theory', *American Journal of Sociology*, 82: 1212–34.

McClelland, D. C. (1961) *The Achieving Society*, New Jersey: Van Nostrand.

MacDonald, L. (1994) 'Globalizing civil society: interpreting international NGOs in Central America', *Millennium: Journal of International Studies*, 23, 2: 267–85.

McGill, M. E. and Wooton, L. M. (1975) 'Management in the third sector', *Public Administration Review*, 35, 5: 444–56.

McGregor, J. A. (1989) 'Towards a better understanding of credit in rural Bangladesh', *Journal of International Development*, 1: 467–86.

MacKeith, J. (1992) 'Raising money or raising awareness? Issues and tensions in the relationship between fundraisers and service providers', Centre for Voluntary Organization Working Paper 12, London School of Economics.

—— (1993) *NGO Management: A Guide Through the Literature*, London: Centre for Voluntary Organization, London School of Economics.

Mackintosh, M. (1992) 'Questioning the state', in M. Wuyts, M. Mackintosh and T. Hewitt (eds) *Development Policy and Public Action*, Milton Keynes: Open University Press/Oxford: Oxford University Press.Macrae, J. and Zwi, A. (eds) (1994) *War and Hunger: Rethinking International Responses to Complex Emergencies*, London: Zed Books/Save the Children Fund.

McSweeney, B. (2002) 'Hofstede's model of national culture differences and their consequences: a triumph of faith and a failure of analyusis', *Human Relations*, 55, 1: 89–118.

Madon, S. (1999) 'International NGOs: networking, information flows and learning', *Journal of Strategic Information Systems*, 8 : 251–61.

Mallaby, S. (2004) 'NGOs: fighting poverty, hurting the poor', *Foreign Policy*, September/October.

Marsden, D. (1994) 'Part I: Indigenous management (Introduction)', and 'Indigenous management and the management of indigenous knowledge', in S. Wright (ed.) *Anthropology of Organizations*, London: Routledge.

Marsden, D. and Oakley, P. (1990) *Evaluating Social Development Projects*, Oxford: Oxfam Publications.

Marsden, D., Oakley, P. and Pratt, B. (1995) *Measuring the Process: Guidelines for Evaluating Social Development*, Oxford: INTRAC.

Martens, K. (2006) 'NGOs in the United Nations system: evaluating theoretical approaches', *Journal of International Development* , 18, 5: 691–700.

Martin, J. and Meyerson, D. (1988) 'Organizational cultures and the denial, channeling and acknowledgement of ambiguity', in L. R. Pondy, R. J. Boland and H. Thomas (eds) *Managing Ambiguity and Change*, New York: Wiley.

Mathews, J. (1997) 'Power shift', *Foreign Affairs*, 76, 1: 50–66.

Mawdsley, E., Townsend, J. and Porter, G. (2005) 'Trust, accountability, and face-to-face interaction in North–South NGO relations', *Development in Practice*, 15, 1: 77–82.

Maxwell, S. (1997) 'Implementing the World Food Summit Plan of Action', *Food Policy*, 22: 6.

—— (2003) 'Heaven or hubris?: reflections on the new "New Poverty Agenda"', *Development Policy Review*, 21, 1: 5–25.

Messer, J. (1998) 'Agency, communion and the formation of social capital', *Nonprofit and Voluntary Sector Quarterly*, 27, 1: 5–12.

Meyer, C. (1997) 'The political economy of NGOs and information sharing', *World Development*, 25, 7: 1127–40.

Michels, R. (1962) *Political Parties*, New York: Free Press.

Micklethwait, I. and Wooldridge, A. (1996) *The Witch Doctors: What the Management Gurus Are Saying – Why it Matters and How to Make Sense of it*, London: Heinemann.

Midgley, J. (1995) *Social Development: The Development Perspective in Social Welfare*, London: Sage.

Millard, E. (1996) 'Appropriate strategies to support small community enterprises in export markets', *Small Enterprise Development*, 7, 1: 4–16.

Minogue, M., Polidano, C. and Hulme, D. (eds) (1998) *Beyond the New Public Management: Changing Ideas and Practices in Governance*, Cheltenham: Edward Elgar.

Mintzberg, H. (1994) 'The fall and rise of strategic planning', *Harvard Business Review*, January–February: 107–14.

Mitlin, D., Hickey, S. and Bebbington, A. (2005) 'Reclaiming development: NGOs and the challenge of alternatives', background paper presented at conference on Reclaiming Development: Assessing the Contribution of NGOs to Development Alternatives, University of Manchester, UK, 27–29 June.

Molyneux, M. and Lazar, S. (2003) *Doing the Rights Thing: Rights-based Development and Latin American NGOs*, London: Intermediate Technology Development Group (ITDG) Publishing.

Moore, H. (1988) *Feminism and Anthropology*, Cambridge: Polity Press.

Moore, M. and Stewart, S. (1998) 'Corporate governance for NGOs?', *Development in Practice*, 8, 3: 335–42.

Morgan, G. (1994) *Imaginization*, London: Sage.

—— (1997) *Images of Organization*, second edition, London: Sage.

Morgan, T. (ed.) (1994) *Women in Management: A Developing Presence*, London: Routledge.

Morris, S. (1999) 'Defining the nonprofit sector: some lessons from history', Centre for Civil Society International Working Paper 3, London School of Economics.

Morris-Suzuki, T. (2000) 'For and against NGOs', *New Left Review*, March/April: 63–84.

Moser, C. O. (1989) *Gender Planning and Development: Theory, Practice and Training*, London: Routledge.

Mosse, D. (2005) 'Global governance and the ethnography of international aid', in D. Mosse and D. Lewis (eds) *The Aid Effect: Giving and Governing in International Development*, London: Pluto Press.

Mukasa, S. (1999) 'Are expatriate staff necessary in international development NGOs? A case study of an NGO in Uganda', Centre for Civil Society International Working Paper 4, London School of Economics.

Mulhare, E. M. (1999) 'Mindful of the future: strategic planning ideology and the culture of nonprofit organizations', *Human Organization*, 58, 3: 323–30.

Najam, A. (1996a) 'NGO accountability: a conceptual framework', *Development Policy Review*, 14: 339–53.

—— (1996b) 'Understanding the third sector: revisiting the Prince, the Merchant and the Citizen', *Nonprofit Management and Leadership*, 7, 2: 203–19.

—— (1999) 'Citizen organizations as policy entrepreneurs', in D. Lewis (ed.) *International Perspectives on Voluntary Action: Reshaping the Third Sector*, London: Earthscan.

Narayana, E. A. (1992) 'Bureaucratisation of non-governmental organizations: an analysis of employees' perceptions and attitudes', *Public Administration and Development*, 12: 123–37.

Naschold, F. (2002) 'Aid and the Millennium Development Goals', ODI Opinions Number 4, London: Overseas Development Institute.

Nelson, P. (2006) 'The varied and conditional integration of NGOs into the aid system: NGOs and the World Bank', *Journal of International Development*, 18, 5: 701–13.

Nerfin, M. (1986) 'Neither prince nor merchant: citizen – an introduction to the Third System', in K. Ahooja-Patel, A. G. Drabek and M. Nerfin (eds) *World Economy in Transition*, Oxford: Oxford University Press.

Nielsen, W. (1979) *The Endangered Sector*, New York: Columbia University Press.

Norrell, A. (1999) 'Bridging gaps or "a bridge too far"? The management of advocacy within service providing NGOs in the UK', Centre for Civil Society International Working Paper 3, London School of Economics.

North, L. (2003) 'Rural progress or rural decay?: an overview of the issues and case studies', in L. North and J. D. Cameron (eds) *Rural Progress, Rural Decay: Neoliberal Adjustment Policies and Local Initiatives*, Bloomfield, CT: Kumarian Press.

Norton, M. (1996) *The Worldwide Fundraiser's Handbook: A Guide to Fundraising for Southern NGOs and Voluntary Organizations*, London: International Fundraising Group.

Nyland, J. (1995) 'Like ships in the night: feminist theory and third sector theory', *Third Sector Review*, 1.

Obadare, E. (2003) 'White collar fundamentalism: youth, religiosity and uncivil society in Nigeria'. Unpublished ongoing PhD research paper.

ODI (Overseas Development Institute) (1995) 'NGOs and official donors', Briefing Paper no. 4, August, London: Overseas Development Institute. www.odi.org.uk

—— (1997) *The People in Aid Code of Best Practice in the Management and Support of Aid Personnel*, Relief and Rehabilitation Network, February, London: Overseas Development Institute. www.odi.org.uk

—— (1999) 'What can we do with a rights-based approach to development?', Briefing Paper no. 3, September, London: Overseas Development Institute. www.odi.org.uk

Olie, R. (1996) 'The culture factor in personnel and organization policies', in A.-W. Harzing, and J. van Ruysseveldt (eds) *International Human Resource Management*, London: Sage.

Onis, Z. and Senses, F. (2005) 'Rethinking the emerging post-Washington Consensus', *Development and Change*, 36, 2: 263–90.

Osborne, M. and Homer, L. (1996) 'Managing equal opportunities and anti-oppressive practice', in S. P. Osborne (ed.) *Managing in the Voluntary Sector*, London: Thomson.

Osborne, S. P. (ed.) (1996) *Managing in the Voluntary Sector: A Handbook for Managers in Charitable Organizations*, London: Thomson.

Owusu, C. (2004) 'An international NGO's staff reflections on power, procedures and relationships', in L. Groves and R. Hinton (eds) *Inclusive Aid: Changing Power Relationships in International Development*, London: Earthscan.

Parker, B. (1998) *Globalization and Business Practice: Managing Across Boundaries*, London: Sage.

Parry-Williams, J. (1992) 'Scaling up via legal reform in Uganda', in M. Edwards and D. Hulme (eds) *Making a Difference: NGOs and Development in a Changing World*, London: Earthscan.

Paton, R. (1991) 'The social economy: value-based organizations in the wider society', in J. Batsleer, C. Cornforth and R. Paton (eds) *Issues in Voluntary and Non-profit Management*, Milton Keynes: Open University Press/Wokingham: Addison-Wesley.

—— (1999) 'The trouble with values', in D. Lewis (ed.) *International Perspectives on Voluntary Action: Reshaping the Third Sector*, London: Earthscan.

Paton, R., Clark, G., Jones, G., Lewis, J. and Quintas, P. (1996) *The New Management Reader*, London: Thomson/Milton Keynes: Open University Press.

PDI (2004) *Evaluation of the Program Rural Empowerment Through Agrarian/Asset Development*, Federal Ministry for Economic Cooperation and Development Department 120/Project Development Institute (PDI), Manila, The Philippines.

Pearce, J. (1997) 'Between co-option and irrelevance? Latin American NGOs in the 1990s', in D. Hulme and M. Edwards (eds) *Too Close for Comfort? NGOs, States and Donors*, London: Macmillan.

Perera, J. (1997) 'In unequal dialogue with donors: the experience of the Sarvodya Shramadana Movement', in D. Hulme and M. Edwards (eds) *Too Close for Comfort? NGOs, States and Donors*, London: Macmillan.

Perri 6 (1993) 'Innovation by non-profit organizations: policy and research issues', *Nonprofit Management and Leadership*, 3, 4: 397–414.

Perrow, C. (1967) 'The analysis of goals in complex organizations', *American Sociological Review*, April: 194–208.

Peters, T. J. (1994) *The Tom Peters Seminar*, New York: Vintage Books.

Peters, T. J. and Waterman, R. H. (1982) *In Search of Excellence*, New York: Harper and Row.

Pettigrew, A. M. (1987) 'Context and action in the transformation of the firm', *Journal of Management Studies*, 24, 6: 649–70.

Pfeffer, J. and Salancik, G. (1978) *The External Control of Organizations: A Resource Dependence Perspective*, New York: Harper and Row.

Polanyi, K. (1957) *The Great Transformation: The Political and Economic Origins of our Time*, Boston, MA: Beacon Press.

Polidano, C. and Hulme, D. (1999) 'Public management reform in developing countries', *Public Management*, 11, 1: 121–32.

Pollitt, C. (1993) *Managerialism and Public Services*, Oxford: Blackwell.

Pondy, L. R., Boland Jr, R. J. and Thomas, H. (eds) (1988) *Managing Ambiguity and Change*, London: Wiley.

Poole, N. (1994) 'The NGO sector as an alternative delivery system for agricultural public services', *Development in Practice*, 4, 2: 100–11.

Postma, W. (1998) 'Capacity building: the making of a curry', *Development in Practice*, 8, 1: 54–63.

Powell, M. (1999) *Information Management for Development Organizations*, Oxford: Oxfam Publications.

Powell, W. W. (ed.) (1987) *The Nonprofit Sector: A Research Handbook*, New Haven, CT: Yale University Press.

Pugh, D. (ed.) (1997) *Organization Theory: Selected Readings*, fourth edition, Harmondsworth: Penguin.

Putnam, R. D. (1993) *Making Democracy Work: Civic Traditions in Modern Italy*, Princeton, NJ: Princeton University Press.

Putzel, J. (1997) 'Accounting for the "dark side" of social capital: reading Robert Putnam on democracy', *Journal of International Development*, 9, 7: 939–50.

Quinn, J. B. (1980) *Strategies for Change: Logical Incrementalism*, Homewood, IL: Irwin.

Rahman, M. (1995) 'Development of people organization through NGOs: a study of RDRS support to its federations', *Grassroots*, 16, April–June.

Rahnema, M. (1992) 'Participation', in W. Sachs (ed.) *The Development Dictionary: A Guide to Knowledge as Power*, London: Zed Books.

—— (1997) *The Post-Development Reader*, London: Zed Books.

Rao, A. and Kelleher, D. (1995) 'Engendering organizational change: the BRAC case', *IDS Bulletin*, 26: 3.

—— (1998) 'Gender lost and gender found: BRAC's gender quality action-learning programme', *Development Practice*, 8, 2: 173–85.

Reifner, U. and Ford, J. (eds) (1992) *Banking for People*, Berlin and New York: Walter de Gruyter.

Ridde, V. (2006) 'Performance-based partnership agreements for the reconstruction of the health system in Afghanistan', *Development in Practice*, 15, 1: 4–15.

Riddell, R. (1999) 'Evaluation and effectiveness in NGOs', in D. Lewis (ed.) *International Perspectives on Voluntary Action: Reshaping the Third Sector*, London: Earthscan.

Riddell, R. C. and Robinson, M. (1995) *NGOs and Rural Poverty Alleviation*, Oxford: Clarendon Press.

Robbins, S. P. (1990) *Organization Theory: Structure, Design and Applications*, New York: Prentice-Hall.

Robinson, M. (1993) 'Governance, democracy and conditionality: NGOs and the new policy agenda', in A. Clayton (ed.) *Governance, Democracy and Conditionality: What Role for NGOs?*, Oxford: INTRAC.

—— (1995) 'Strengthening civil society in Africa: the role of foreign political aid', in M. Robinson (ed.) *Towards Democratic Governance, IDS Bulletin*, 26, 2.

—— (1997) 'Privatizing the voluntary sector: NGOs as public service contractors', in D. Hulme and M. Edwards (eds) *Too Close for Comfort? NGOs, States and Donors*, London: Macmillan.

Robinson, M. and White, G. (1997) 'The role of civic organizations in the provision of social services', Research for Action Papers no. 37, Helsinki: United Nations University/World Institute for Development Economics Research.

Rochester, C. (1995) 'Voluntary agencies and accountability', in J. D. Smith, C. Rochester and R. Hedley (eds) *An Introduction to the Voluntary Sector*, London: Routledge.

Rogali, B. (1996) 'Microfinance evangelism, "destitute women" and the hard selling of a new anti-poverty formula', *Development in Practice*, 6, 2: 11–112.

Rondinelli, D. (1993) *Development Projects as Policy Experiments*, London: Routledge.

Rotberg, R. I. (ed.) (1996) *Vigilance and Vengeance: NGOs Preventing Ethnic Conflict in Divided Societies*, Washington, DC: Brookings Institution Press.

Rowlands, J. (1995) 'Empowerment examined', *Development in Practice*, 15, 2: 101–7.

Sahley, C. (1995) 'Strengthening the capacity of NGOs: cases of small enterprise development agencies in Africa', Management and Policy Series no. 4, Oxford: INTRAC.

Salamon, L. (1994) *Partners in Public Service: Government-Nonprofit Relations in the Modern Welfare State*, Baltimore, MD: Johns Hopkins University Press.

Salamon, L. and Anheier, H. (1992) 'In search of the non-profit sector: in search of definitions', *Voluntas*, 13, 2: 125–52.

Salamon, L. and Anheier, H. (1994) *The Emerging Sector: The Nonprofit Sector in Comparative Perspective – An Overview*, Baltimore, MD: Johns Hopkins University Press.

Salamon, L. and Anheier, H. (1996) *The Emerging Nonprofit Sector*, Manchester: Manchester University Press.

Salamon, L. and Anheier, H. (1997) *Defining the Nonprofit Sector: A Cross-National Analysis*, Manchester: Manchester University Press.

Salamon, L. and Anheier, H. (1999) 'The third sector in the Third World', in D. Lewis (ed.) *International Perspectives on Voluntary Action: Reshaping the Third Sector*, London: Earthscan.

Salamon, L.E., Wojciech Sokolowski, S. and List, R. (2003) *Global Civil Society: An Overview*, Baltimore, MD: Centre for Civil Society Studies, The Johns Hopkins University.

Sanyal, B. (1991) 'Antagonistic cooperation: a case study of NGOs, government and donors' relationships in IG projects in Bangladesh', *World Development*, 19, 10: 1367–79.

Satish, S. and Prem Kumar, N. (1993) 'Are NGOs more cost-effective than government in livestock service delivery? A study of artificial insemination in India', in J. Farrington and D. J. Lewis (eds) *NGOs and the State in Asia: Rethinking Roles in Sustainable Agricultural Development*, London: Routledge.

Satterthwaite, D. (2005) 'Introduction: Why local organizations are central to meeting the MDGs', in T. Bigg and D. Satterthwaite (eds) *How To Make Poverty History*, London: IIED.

Saxby, J. (1996) 'Who owns the private aid agencies?', in D. Sogge, K. Biekart and J. Saxby (eds) *Compassion and Calculation: The Business of Private Foreign Aid*, London: Pluto Press.

Schaffer, B. (1969) 'The deadlock in development administration', in C. Leys (ed.) *Politics and Change in Developing Countries*, Cambridge: Cambridge University Press.

Schmidt, R. H. and Zeitinger, C. P. (1996) 'Prospects, problems and potential of credit granting NGOs', *Journal of International Development*, 8, 2: 241–58.

Schuurman, F. J. (1993) 'Modernity, post-modernity and the new social movements', in F. J. Schuurman (ed.) *Beyond the Impasse: New Directions in Development Theory*, London: Zed Books.

Scott, C. and Hopkins, R. (1997) 'The economics of non-governmental organizations', mimeo, Queen Mary and Westfield College, London.

Scott, M. J. O. (2001) 'Danger – landmines! NGO–government collaboration in the Ottawa process', in M. Edwards and J. Gaventa (eds) *Global Citizen Action*, Boulder CO: Lynne Rienner.

Scott Morton, M.S. (1996) 'Information and communication technologies', in R. Paton, G. Clark, G. Jones, J. Lewis and P. Quintas (eds) *The New Mangement Reader*, London: Routledge/Open University Press.

Seckinelgin, H. (2006) 'The multiple worlds of NGOs and HIV/AIDS: rethinking NGOs and their agency', *Journal of International Development*, 18: 715–27.

Seligman, A. (1993) 'The fragile ethical vision of civil society', in B. Turner (ed.) *Citizenship and Social Theory*, London: Sage.

Selznick, P. (1966) *TVA and the Grassroots*, New York: Harper and Row.

Semboja, J. and Therkildsen, O. (1995) *Service Provision Under Stress in East Africa: State, NGOs and People's Organizations in Kenya, Tanzania and Uganda*, London: James Currey.

Sen, A. (1981) *Poverty and Famines: An Essay on Entitlement and Deprivation*, Oxford: Oxford University Press.

—— (1983) 'Poor, relatively speaking', *Oxford Economic Papers*, 35: 153–69.

Sen, B. (1987) 'NGO self-evaluation: issues of concern', *World Development*, 15 (supplement): 161–7.

Sen, S. (1992) 'Non-profit organizations in India: historical development and common patterns', *Voluntas*, 3, 2: 175–93.

Senge, P. M. (1990) *The Fifth Discipline: The Art and Practice of the Learning Organization*, New York: Doubleday.

Senillosa, I. (1998) 'A new age of social movements: a fifth generation of non-governmental organization in the making?', *Development in Practice*, 8, 1: 40–53.

Sethi, H. (1993) 'Action groups in the new politics', in P. Wignaraja (ed.) *New Social Movements in the South: Empowering the People*, London: Verso.

Shaw, M. (1994) 'Civil society and global politics: beyond a social movements approach', *Millennium: Journal of International Studies*, 23, 3: 647–67.

Sidel, M. (2004) 'States, markets and the nonprofit sector in South Asia: judiciaries and the struggle for capital in comparative perspective', *Tulane Law Review*, 78, 5: 1611–69.

—— (2005) 'The guardians guarding themselves: a comparative perspective on non-profit self-regulation', *Chicago-Kent Law Review*, 80: 803–35.

Simbi, M. and Thom, G. (2000) '"Implementation by proxy"?: the next step in power relationships between Northern and Southern NGOs', in D. Lewis and T. Wallace (eds) *New Roles and Relevance: Development NGOs and the Challenge of Change*, Hartford, CT: Kumarian Press.

Simukonda, H. P. M. (1992) 'Creating a national NGO council for strengthening social welfare services in Africa: some organizational and technical problems experienced in Malawi', *Public Administration and Development*, 12: 417–31.

Skloot, E. (1987) 'Enterprise and commerce in non-profit organizations', in W. W. Powell (ed.) *The Nonprofit Sector: A Research Handbook*, New Haven, CT: Yale University Press.

Slim, H. (1997) 'To the rescue: radicals or poodles?', *World Today*, August/September: 209–12.

Smillie, I. (1988) 'Northern "donors" and Southern "partners": arguments for an NGO consortium approach', mimeo, Development Assistance Committee (DAC) Paris NGO meeting.

—— (1994) 'Changing partners: Northern NGOs, Northern governments', *Voluntas*, 5, 2: 155–92.

—— (1995) *The Alms Bazaar: Altruism Under Fire – Non-Profit Organizations and International Development*, London: Intermediate Technology Publications.

—— (1998) 'NGOs in their dotage', *Appropriate Technology*, 25, 1: 21–2.

Smillie, I. and Hailey, J. (2001) *Managing for Change: Leadership, Strategy and Management in Asian NGOs*, London: Earthscan.

Smith, B. (1987) 'An agenda of future tasks for international and indigenous NGOs: views from the North', *World Development*, 15 (supplement): 87–93.

Smith, C. and Friedmann, A. (1972) *Voluntary Associations: Perspectives on the Literature*, Cambridge, MA: Harvard University Press.

Smith, G. (2002) 'Faith in the voluntary sector: a common or distinctive experience of religious organizations?' Centre for Institutional Studies, University of East London.

Smith, S. R. and Lipsky, M. (1993) *Nonprofits for Hire: The Welfare State in the Age of Contracting*, Cambridge, MA: Harvard University Press.

Smith, W. E., Lethem, F. and Thoolen, B. A. (1980) 'The design of organizations for rural development projects: a progressive report', Washington, DC: World Bank Staff Working Paper no. 375.

Sogge, D., Biekart, K. and Saxby, J. (eds) (1996) *Compassion and Calculation: The Business of Private Foreign Aid*, London: Pluto Press.

Solomon, B. B. (1976) *Black Empowerment: Social Work in Oppressed Communities*, New York: Columbia University Press.

Stacey, R. (1992) *Managing Chaos*, London: Kogan Page.

Stacey, R., Griffin, D. and Shaw, P. (2000) *Complexity and Management: Fad or Radical Challenge to Systems Thinking?* London: Routledge.

Stark Biddle, C. (1984) *The Management Needs of Private Voluntary Organizations*, Washington, DC: USAID.

Staudt, K. (1991) *Managing Development: State, Society and International Contexts*, London: Sage.

Stern, E. (1992) 'Evaluating innovatory programmes: an external evaluator's view', in J. Batsleer, C. Cornforth and R. Paton (eds) *Issues in Voluntary and Non-Profit Management*, Milton Keynes: Open University Press/Wokingham: Addison-Wesley.

Stewart, S. (1997) 'Happy ever after in the marketplace: non-government organizations and uncivil society', *Review of African Political Economy*, 71: 11–34.

Stichele, M. V. and Pennertz, P. (1996) *Making it Our Business: European NGO Campaigns on Transnational Corporations*, CIIR Briefing, London: Catholic Institute for International Relations.

Stoddard, A. (2003) 'Humanitarian NGOs: challenges and trends', HPG Briefing no. 12, July, London: Overseas Development Institute.

Stremlau, C. (1987) 'NGO coordinating bodies in Africa, Asia and Latin America', *World Development*, 15 (supplement): 213–25.

Sutton, R. (1999) 'The policy process: an overview', Working Paper no. 118, London: Overseas Development Institute.

Suzuki, N. (1997) *Inside NGOs: Learning to Manage Conflicts Between Headquarters and Field Offices*, London: Intermediate Technology Publications.

Tandon, R. (1995) 'Board games: governance and accountability in NGOs', in M. Edwards and D. Hulme (eds) *Beyond the Magic Bullet: NGO Performance and Accountability in the Post-Cold War World*, London: Earthscan.

—— (1997) 'Organizational development and NGOs: an overview', *Institutional Development*, 4, 1: 3–19.

Tandon, Y. (1996) 'An African perspective', in D. Sogge, K. Biekart and J. Saxby (eds) *Compassion and Calculation: The Business of Private Foreign Aid*, London: Pluto Press.

Tassie, B., Zohar, A. and Murray, V. (1996) 'The management of change', in S. P Osborne (ed.) *Managing in the Voluntary Sector*, London: Thomson.

Tayeb, M. H. (1988) *Organizations and National Culture: A Comparative Analysis*, London: Sage.

Tembo, F. (2004) 'NGDOs' role in building poor people's capacity to benefit from globalization', *Journal of International Development*, 16: 1023–37.

Temple, D. (1997) 'NGOs: a Trojan horse', in *The Post-Development Reader*, compiled and introduced by M. Rahnema with V. Bawtree, London: Zed Books.

Tendler, J. (1982) 'Turning private voluntary organizations into development agencies: questions for evaluation', Program Evaluation Discussion Paper 12, Washington, DC: USAID.

—— (1997) *Good Governance in the Tropics*, Baltimore, MD: Johns Hopkins University Press.

Themudo, N. (2003) 'Managing the paradox: NGOs, resource dependence, and independence in environmental NGOs – case studies from Portugal and Mexico', Unpublished PhD dissertation, University of London.

Therkildsen, O. and Semboja, J. (1995) 'A new look at service provision in East Africa', in J. Semboja and O. Therkildsen (eds) *Service Provision Under Stress in East Africa: The State, NGOs and People's Organizations*, London: James Currey.

Thomas, A. (1992) 'NGOs and the limits to empowerment', in M. Wuyts, M. Mackintosh and T. Hewitt (eds) *Development Action and Public Policy*, Oxford: Oxford University Press.

—— (1996) 'What is development management?', *Journal of International Development*, 8, 1: 95–110.

—— (1999) 'What makes good development management?', *Development in Practice*, 9, 1 and 2: 9–17.

Turner, M. and Hulme, D. (1997) *Governance, Administration and Development: Making the State Work*, London: Macmillan.

Tvedt, T. (1998) *Angels of Mercy or Development Diplomats? NGOs and Foreign Aid*, Oxford: James Currey.

—— (2006) 'The international aid system and the non-governmental organisations: a new research agenda', *Journal of International Development*, 18: 677–90.

Udoh James, V. (ed.) (1998) *Capacity Building in Developing Countries: Human and Environmental Dimensions*, New York: Praeger.

Umeh, O. J. (1992) 'Capacity building and development administration in Southern African countries', *International Review of Administrative Sciences*, 58, 1: 57–70.

UNDP (United Nations Development Programme) (1993) *Human Development Report*, New York: UNDP.

Uphoff, N. (1995) 'Why NGOs are not a third sector: a sectoral analysis with some thoughts on accountability, sustainability and evaluation', in M. Edwards and D. Hulme (eds) *Beyond the Magic Bullet: NGO Performance and Accountability in the Post-Cold War World*, London: Earthscan.

Uvin, P. (1995) 'Fighting hunger at the grassroots: paths to scaling up', *World Development*, 23, 6: 927–39.

Vakil, A. (1997) 'Confronting the classification problem: toward a taxonomy of NGOs', *World Development*, 25, 12: 2057–71.

Van Rooy, A. (1997) *Civil Society and the Aid Industry*, London: Earthscan.

—— (1998) 'The frontiers of influence: NGO lobbying at the 1974 World Food Conference, the 1992 Earth Summit and beyond', *World Development*, 25, 1: 93–114 (offprint P5031).

Velloso de Santisteban, A. (2005) 'The poor will always be with us – and so will NGOs', *Development in Practice*, 15, 2: 200–9.

Vivian, J. (1994) 'NGOs and sustainable development in Zimbabwe', *Development and Change*, 25: 181–209.

Vivian, J. and Maseko, G. (1994) 'NGOs, participation and rural development: testing the assumptions with evidence from Zimbabwe', Geneva: UN Research Institute for Social Development.

Wallace, T. (1998) 'Institutionalizing gender in UK NGOs', *Development in Practice*, 8, 2: 159–72.

Wallace, T. and Kaplan, A. (2003) 'The taking of the horizon: lessons from ActionAid Uganda's experience of changes in development practice', Working Paper Series no. 4, Kampala: ActionAid Uganda.

Wallace, T., Crowther, S. and Shepherd, A. (1997) *Standardizing Development: Influences on UK NGOs' Policies and Procedures*, Oxford: Worldview Press.

Wallace, T., Bornstein, L. and Chapman, J. (2006) *Coercion and Commitment: Development NGOs and the Aid Chain*, Rugby: Practical Action/Intermediate Technology Development Group (ITDG).

Watson, H. and Laquihon, W. (1993) 'The MBRLC's Sloping Agricultural Land Technology (SALT) research and extension in the Philippines', in J. Farrington and D. Lewis (eds) *NGOs and the State in Asia: Rethinking Roles in Sustainable Agricultural Development*, London: Routledge.

Weick, K. E. (1979) *The Social Psychology of Organizing*, Reading, MA: Addison-Wesley.

Wellard, K. and Copestake, J. (eds) (1993) *Non-Governmental Organizations and the State in Africa: Rethinking Roles in Sustainable Agricultural Development*, London: Routledge.

White, G. (1994) 'Civil society, democratization and development', *Democratization*, 1, 3: 375–90.

White, J. and Morton, J. (2005) 'Mitigating impacts of HIV/AIDS on rural livelihoods: NGO experiences in sub-Saharan Africa', *Development in Practice*, 15, 2: 186–99.

White, S. (1995) 'Depoliticizing development: the uses and abuses of participation', *Development in Practice*, 6, 1: 6–15.

Willets, P. (ed.) (1996) *The Conscience of the World*, Washington, DC: Brookings Institution.

Wood, G. D. (1997) 'States without citizens: the problem of the franchise state', in D. Hulme and M. Edwards (eds) *Too Close for Comfort? NGOs, States and Donors*, London: Macmillan.

World Bank (1990) *World Development Report*, Washington, DC: World Bank.

—— (1996) *Pursuing Common Goals: Strengthening Relations between Government and NGOs in Bangladesh*, Dhaka: World Bank.

—— (1999) 'Turkey Marmara Earthquake Assessment', Turkey Country Office, Ankara, September.

—— (2002) *Empowerment and Poverty Reduction: A Sourcebook*, Washington DC: World Bank.

Wright, D. (1996) 'The perils and pleasures of donor consortia', *Small Enterprise Development*, 7, 4: 32–8.

Wright, S. (ed.) (1994) *Anthropology of Organizations*, London: Routledge.

Wuthnow, R. (1991) *Between States and Markets: The Voluntary Sector in Comparative Perspective*, Princeton, NJ: Princeton University Press.

Young, D. (1992) 'Organizing principles for international advocacy associations', *Voluntas*, 3, 1: 1–28.

Young, D., Koenig, B., Najam, A. and Fisher, J. (1999) 'Strategy and structure in managing global associations', *Voluntas*, 10, 4: 323–44.

Zadek, S. (2000) 'The future of non-government organizations in a world of civil corporations', in D. Lewis and T. Wallace (eds) *New Roles and Relevance: Development NGOs and the Challenge of Change*, Hartford, CT: Kumarian Press.

—— (2001) *The Civil Corporation: The New Economy of Corporate Citizenship*, London: Earthscan.

Zadek, S. and Gatwood, M. (1995) 'Social auditing or bust?', in M. Edwards and D. Hulme (eds) *Beyond the Magic Bullet: NGO Performance and Accountability in the Post-Cold War World*, London: Earthscan.

Zadek, S. and Szabo, S. (1994) *Valuing Organization: The Case of Sarvodaya*, London: New Economics Foundation.

Index

Aarong 13
Abdel Ati, H.A. 10, 99
Abramson, D.M. 63
Abzug, R. 63
accompaniment 221
accountability 10, 14, 21, 23–4, 26, 29;
    advocacy 147, 152; businesses 180; capacity
    building 208; communities 171; complexity
    224, 227; contexts 39, 42, 46, 53, 55, 61,
    64–5; definition 167; development 78–80,
    83, 89–90, 98; evaluation 158–61;
    government 175–6; internal management
    193–5, 200, 202; management approaches
    220; relationships 167–8, 170, 173–4;
    service delivery 130, 133–4, 142, 162
accreditation 169
ACORD 114
action research 190
ActionAid India 146
ActionAid Uganda 214
active partnership 94–5, 185–6, 188
adaptive management 217
administration 1, 25, 31, 42; complexity 220,
    222, 224–5; contexts 48; culture 104, 113,
    117; development 77, 93; internal
    management 192–3, 197, 199; organizational
    change 210; relationships 183; service
    delivery 134, 147
advocacy 3, 7, 10, 41, 46; ambiguity 221, 224;
    assessment 151–3; capacity building 208;
    complexity 225, 229; contexts 53, 55–7, 60,
    64, 66; culture 116; development 83, 87–8,
    92–3; evaluation 158; government 172;
    internal management 201; life cycles 109;
    networks 147–9; organizations 149–51, 210;
    relationships 171; service delivery 129–62;
    structural change 143–53

advocates 130
Afghanistan 8, 10, 12, 41, 84, 86, 94, 119,
    185
Africa 1–2, 10, 15–16, 41, 49; contexts 52,
    55–6, 61–2, 64; culture 123; development
    81, 84, 90, 98; internal management 199,
    207; relationships 173, 176, 188; service
    delivery 131–2, 134, 142, 146–7;
    understanding 223
African Union 82
Aga Khan Foundation 207
age 173
agency creation 187
agenda setting 130
Agrarian Reform Law 148
agriculture 38, 50, 85, 88–9; innovation
    154–5, 157; service delivery 132–3, 136,
    141–2, 147–8
aid agencies 42, 44, 154, 229
aid architecture 80
aid industry 7, 11, 47, 51, 71; development
    74–8, 86, 98; internal management 201;
    relationships 182, 184; service delivery
    134, 145
alibis 114
alienation 68, 103
alliances 145, 147–50, 156, 177, 197
Alternativas y Capacidades 209
alternatives 7–8, 18, 20, 23–4; ambiguity 125,
    222; complexity 229; contexts 38–40, 43,
    49, 55, 66; culture 104, 109; debates 30;
    development 91, 93; empowerment 136,
    138; innovation 158; relationships 182;
    service delivery 140–1
altruism 20, 29, 44, 103, 193, 228
Alvesson, M. 113
Amazon 177–8

ambiguity 102–26, 180–2, 190, 194, 196, 212, 214, 221–4, 227–8
Amendola, M. 154
American Competitiveness and Corporate Accountability Act 169
American Enterprise Institute (AEI) 10
Amnesty International 66, 111
Andean people 215
Anderson, K. 67
Anheier, H.K. 47, 52, 117, 193, 223
animals 14
Annis, S. 53
anthropologists 61, 70, 106
anthropology 38, 103, 121–6, 181
Anti-Corn Law League 50
anti-globalization movement 67
anti-performativity 18
appropriate practice 186, 218
appropriate technology 51, 155
aquaculture 185
Arama Kurtarma Dernegi (AKUT) 87
Archer, R. 55
Arellano-Lopez, S. 97, 98, 172
Argentina 61
Argyris, C. 115
Armenia 63–4, 150
arms flows 144
arts 4, 7, 47
Ashman, D. 93
Ashworth, G. 114
Asia 1–2, 16, 49, 52, 64, 76, 82, 84, 223
Association of Sarva Seva Farms (ASSEFA) 51, 91, 136–7
Association of South East Asian Nations (ASEAN) 82
assumptions 18–19, 23, 32, 94–6; anthropology 122; culture 103, 110, 119–21; future trends 229; information management 118, 214; internal management 197–8
audits 81, 169, 220
Atack, I. 91
Australia 204
authoritarianism 53, 123
Avina, J. 110
Avritzer, L. 61

baby milk 92, 150
Baig, Q. 29
Banda, President 123
Banfield, E. 58

Bangladesh 13, 15–16, 28, 44, 49; contexts 51, 63; culture 111, 119; development 82, 91–3, 98–9; internal management 205; relationships 171, 177, 183–5; service delivery 131, 133, 137, 140, 142–3, 152, 161; understanding 228
Bangladesh Rural Advancement Committee (BRAC) 13, 22, 46, 49, 114–15, 119, 162, 171–2, 177, 183, 228
banks 108, 134, 179, 215
Baptist Rural Life Centre (BRLC) 89, 132
Bate, S.P. 122
Batsleer, J. 20
Beall, J. 79
Bebbington, A. 172, 174, 183, 215
Beijing Women's Conference 144
benchmarks 97–8
Benin 61
Bennett, J. 8
Bhalla, A. 84
Bharatiya Agro-Industries Foundation (BAIF) 133
bhoodan 136–7
Bielefeld, W. 183
Biggs, S. 71, 83, 134, 156–7, 164, 167
bilateral donors 2, 22, 48, 74–6; capacity building 206; relationships 182, 184; service delivery 142, 150, 159
Billis, D. 28, 107, 110, 124, 181, 194, 196, 217, 222
biotechnology 152
Black, J.K. 26
Blackburn, J. 51
Black Panthers 69
Blair, H. 57–8, 61
block grants 81
blueprint management 18, 21, 25, 31; culture 104, 115; development 94, 100; relationships 186; understanding 222, 227
boards 29, 47, 179, 187; internal management 193, 195, 199, 203–4, 206; understanding 225
Body Shop 125, 181
Bolivia 172
Booth, D. 25, 39
Bordt, R.L. 222
bottom-up approaches 26, 30–1, 138; ambiguity 223; future trends 228; relationships 183
Brandt Commission 51
Bratton, M. 54, 56, 145–7, 176, 188
Brazil 43, 51, 134, 136, 164, 176–8, 229

Brett, E.A. 90, 99, 141
Bretton Woods institutions 48
bridging role 56, 89, 92, 109, 116, 132–3,
    183, 225
Britain *see* United Kingdom
Britton, B. 117
Brock, K. 138
Brodhead, T. 39
Brown, L.D. 56, 61, 89, 93, 113, 116, 141,
    152, 183, 225
Bruno, S. 154
Bryant, C. 145, 158
Bryman, A. 111
Bryson, J. 33, 241
Bucharest World Population Conference 50
budgets 31–2, 41, 58, 79–81; culture 118;
    development 83, 85; internal management
    210; relationships 166, 179; service delivery
    134, 143
bureaucracy 13, 19, 23, 32, 39; accountability
    169; advocacy 148, 152; ambiguity 124,
    222–3; anthropology 122, 125; business 182;
    complexity 225, 229; contexts 44, 48, 52,
    69; culture 103, 106–7, 113; development
    77; empowerment 136, 138; future trends
    227, 229; government 173; internal
    management 190, 194, 196, 199, 201;
    international agencies 183; organizational
    change 209; relationships 167, 174
Bunch, R. 157
Burkino Faso 76
Bush, G.W. 40
business 1–3, 9, 11–14, 20; accountability 169;
    advocacy 144, 146; ambiguity 125;
    anthropology 125; capacity building 206;
    complexity 224, 227; contexts 40, 44, 46–8,
    50, 57, 68–70; culture 104–5, 112, 114,
    121; debate 23, 28, 31–2; development 88;
    innovation 154–5; management 123, 192–5,
    198, 215, 217–18, 220, 223; organization
    theory 105; organizational change 209;
    partnership 185; relationships 177–82;
    service delivery 134, 142

CAFOD 81, 207
calculative involvement 68
Campbell, P. 78, 105, 198, 218–19
Canada 75, 144
capability approach 26
capacity building 3, 22, 85–6, 88–9; culture
    105, 123; internal management 192, 198,
    200, 205–9, 215; relationships 171

capitalism 12, 40, 54–5, 64, 68, 151, 180, 191
CARE USA 12, 39, 44, 82, 179
careers 44, 51
Caribbean 1
Caritas Internationalis (CI) 85
Caritas Sri Lanka (CSL) 85
Carroll, T.F. 52, 75, 88–90, 125, 133–5, 141,
    143, 172, 184, 203–4
case studies 3, 16, 91, 118, 141, 146–9, 154,
    205, 209
cash crops 89
Castells, M. 214
catalysts 88, 90–3, 95, 100, 116, 130, 134–5
Catholic Church 51
Catholic Relief Services 44
cattle 133
Caucasus 64
Central America 63, 66, 207
Central Asia 64, 82
Cernea, M. 96, 98
certification 169
Chambers, R. 18, 20, 26, 30, 42, 104, 157,
    159, 173
change management 114
chaos theory 17, 211, 215
chapter map 1–2
charismatic leaders 110–11, 113, 117, 150,
    195, 199, 203–4
charities 43, 52, 137, 193, 195, 223
Charnovitz, S. 40, 50–1
Chhetri, R. 52, 172
child labour 12, 180
Chile 61, 174
China 109, 164
Christian Aid 81, 207
Christians 43, 51–2, 61, 193
churches 59, 61, 66, 68–9, 81, 132, 150, 228
citizen organizations 130
citizenship 56, 79, 139–40
CIVICUS 22, 62, 204
Civil Coordination Centre 87
civil society 7, 11, 14, 19, 22; advocacy
    149–50, 152–3; capacity building 206, 209;
    complexity 229; contexts 40, 42–3, 46,
    53–67; dark side 71; development 78–80,
    82–3, 86–7, 90, 93; innovation 156; internal
    management 200, 202; organizational change
    211; relationships 164, 176; service delivery
    146–7; third sector 67–70
Civil Society Challenge Fund (CSCF) 81
civil society organizations (CSOs) 57
clans 63

Clark, J. 42, 55, 67, 145, 150, 154, 156–7, 173, 221, 225
Clarke, G. 63
class 59, 111, 113, 159, 173, 203
clientelism 63, 96, 209
climate change 8, 144
clothing industry 12
co-optation 176, 208
Coalition for Environmentally Responsible Economies (CERES) 144
codes of conduct 144, 169
coffee 179
cold money 200
Cold War 40–1, 50, 53, 58, 61, 144, 229
Coleman, J. 171–2
collectivism 23, 120
collegiality 150
Colombia 61, 204
colonialism 26, 56, 61–2, 123, 142, 203
colonization 25, 38, 61
Comaroff, J.L. 61
command and control 18, 22, 27
Commission on Global Governance 51
Commonwealth Foundation 77
communication skills 121
communism 53, 64, 109
communities 3, 7, 9, 11, 18; accountability 168; advocacy 146–7, 152; ambiguity 222; anthropology 122, 125; business 177–8, 181; catalysts 90; complexity 225; contexts 38, 41, 44, 48–53, 58, 60, 70–1; culture 103, 108–9, 112, 119, 126; debate 28, 30, 32; development 74, 78–9, 84–6, 89, 91, 95–6; empowerment 136, 138; evaluation 159–61; government 176; information management 214; innovation 154; internal management 201–4; life cycles 109; organizational development 123; participation 138; relationships 170–2, 174; service delivery 131, 133–5, 141–2, 162; trade 125
community-based organizations (CBOs) 48
comparative advantage 14, 94, 96, 134, 141, 185, 206
Compassion Capital 40
compassion fatigue 76
complaints procedures 169–70
complaints and redress (C&R) 170
complementary provision 141
Complexity and Mangement Centre (CMC) 211
complexity theory 17, 42, 106, 193–4, 211–12, 214–15, 220, 224–7

compliance 67–8, 152
composite model 2, 218–21
conditionality 55, 79, 200
conflict resolution 16, 49, 57, 132, 206
Congo 61
conscientization 91, 135–6, 143, 172
conservation 75, 150
conservatives 40, 66, 184
Constantino-David, K. 161
consultancy 83, 197, 207
consumer choice 141
contingencies 111, 121, 190
contract payments 77
contracting 76–7, 80–1, 88, 94; internal management 211; service delivery 132, 134, 139–41, 143, 156; understanding 218, 222, 227
Cooke, B. 138, 206
cooperatives 54, 104, 171
coordination 103, 184–5, 191
Cornell University 10
Cornwall, A. 138
corporate responsibility 69
corporations 10–11, 13, 61, 120; internal management 193, 210; relationships 169, 177, 179–80; service delivery 143–4, 149, 151–2; understanding 228
corruption 39, 61, 63, 77, 104; internal management 199; relationships 168, 174–5; service delivery 138, 141, 152
Costa Rica 141
counselling 90, 135
Covey, J. 55, 92–3, 113, 116, 145, 147–8, 152, 183
credit 52, 85, 100, 130, 139; internal management 201, 215; relationships 172, 179, 181; service delivery 161; understanding 222
critical management studies 18
critics 10–12
cross-cultural management 124, 126
cultural anthropology 121
culture 102–26, 131, 149, 167; internal management 196, 200, 204, 206, 214; management approaches 218–19, 221; national 120–1; relationships 178, 186
curious corporations 210
Curtis, D. 124
Czech Republic 64

dark side 61, 172
Dartington, T. 191

data gathering 213
Davis Smith, J. 193, 196
Dawson, E. 162
De Graaf, M. 143, 145, 164–6, 173, 188, 212, 227
De Tocqueville, A. 54, 63
de-naturalization 18
de-radicalization 143
Deacon, B. 8, 41
debt 93, 130, 151–2
Dechalert, P. 107
decision making 11, 24, 26, 40, 57; ambiguity 223; capacity building 207; culture 107, 111–13, 116, 118, 123; development 91–2, 96–8; evaluation 159; innovation 154; internal management 190, 200, 204; management approaches 219; service delivery 135–8, 145–7, 149
defensive routines 115
demand pull 133
DeMars, W.E. 40
democracy 40–3, 46, 51, 53–5; advocacy 144; capacity building 208; contexts 57–8, 61–5, 67, 71; culture 123; development 78, 90, 93; future trends 229; government 176; internal management 193, 202–3; relationships 173–4; service delivery 135, 139–40, 150, 152
demonstrations 147
Denmark 182
Department of Agrarian Reform (DAR) 148
Department for International Development (DFID) 2, 58, 74–5, 79, 81–3, 177, 182, 229
depreciation 96
developees 119–20
development 2, 30, 48, 53, 119; administration 25; changes 78–83; definition 25, 84; management 24–7, 218–19; relief 84–7; role 73–101
Development Assistance Committee (DAC) 76, 82, 97, 182
Development Emergency Committee (DEC) 76
development organization development (DOD) 206
de Waal, A. 10, 97, 99
dhikuri 52
diamond industry 12
Diaz-Albertini, J. 47, 56, 152
DiBella, A. 113, 212
Dichter, T.W. 19, 24, 31–2, 104–5, 161, 180, 217, 228

dictatorship 53, 66, 123, 165
digital divide 214
digital-era governance 33, 42
Dignard, L. 180
DiMaggio, P. 210
diplomacy 80
Direct Budget Support (DBS) 79
directors 47, 114, 201, 203
disabilities 115
disciplines 115
discretionary management 107
discrimination 219
disease 149
distinctive management 217–18
diversion potential 76
do no harm principle 86
donors 2, 10–13, 19–23, 28; accountability 168–9; advocacy 146–7, 150; ambiguity 223; business 177, 179; capacity building 206; catalysts 93; communities 172; complexity 225, 229; consortium 183; contexts 38, 40–1, 43, 48–9, 51, 54–61, 63–6, 71; culture 105, 108; development 74–83, 85, 97; evaluation 97–8, 158–9; government 173; implementation 88, 90; information management 118; innovation 157; internal management 192, 200, 202–3; international agencies 183–4; management approaches 218; organizational change 211; partnership 94, 187; relationships 165, 167, 182; scaling up 161; service delivery 134, 139–40, 142–3
dotcauses 67, 225
double-headed strategy 223
Downing, J. 180
down-sizing 32
Drucker, P. 193
drugs 92
Dunleavy, P. 42
Dunn, E. 61
Dutch 215

Eade, D. 207
earthquakes 8, 76, 84, 86–7, 143
East Africa 142, 207
Eastern Europe 53, 55, 64
Ebrahim, A. 118
ecology 186
economicide 41
economics 41, 43, 47–8, 54–5; advocacy 146; ambiguity 223; business 180–1; capacity building 207; complexity 224; contexts 59,

61, 63–4, 66, 70; culture 120–1; development 74, 79, 84, 90–3, 96–7; empowerment 137; evaluation 160; future trends 227; government 173; information management 213–14; internal management 199; participation 139; partnership 186; relationships 165, 167, 176, 180; service delivery 133, 140, 142, 152
ecotourism 177
Ecuador 140
education 38, 46, 51–3, 55, 58; advocacy 148; anthropology 122; business 181; contexts 64, 69; culture 113, 116; development 75, 77, 79, 81, 86, 90–1; empowerment 135; internal management 201; international agencies 184; leadership 111; life cycles 109; relationships 171, 179; service delivery 130, 132, 140, 142
Edwards, M. 10–11, 31, 84, 92–3, 99, 111, 143, 150–1, 161, 167, 169, 201, 214, 223–4, 229
effectiveness 95–100, 109, 112–13; culture 116; future trends 228; government 173; internal management 193–4, 197, 200, 205–6, 213; relationships 165, 167, 169, 174, 184, 188; service delivery 131, 134, 146–8, 152, 158–60
efficiency 99, 116, 141, 143, 167–8, 185, 197, 213
Egeland, J. 205
Egypt 179
elections 55, 60, 65, 137, 208
elites 51, 55–6, 61, 90–2, 96–8, 115, 145, 171, 211
Ellis, G. 99
emergency work 10, 32, 75–6, 78, 84–5, 88, 183
employees 63, 120, 181, 192
employers 50
employment 29, 92
empowerment 13, 26–7, 30, 38, 44; ambiguity 222–3; contexts 50–2, 56; culture 114, 116; development 84, 86, 88, 90–2, 95; internal management 192; international agencies 183; management approaches 219; relationships 170; service delivery 135–9, 147
enabling management 18, 103, 105, 108, 117, 125, 183, 205, 224
engineering model 112
enlightenment 54
Enron 169

entrepreneurship 3, 48, 116, 130; internal management 192, 196–7, 213; relationships 186; service delivery 140, 143; understanding 223
environment 4, 7–8, 16, 26, 29; advocacy 149; ambiguity 221; business 177, 181–2; communities 171; complexity 229; contexts 39, 42, 46, 49, 58, 63; culture 107–8; development 75, 78, 83, 85, 90, 93; future trends 227; innovation 154; life cycles 110; management approaches 219; organizational change 209–10, 212; participation 162; relationships 164–7; service delivery 144, 147, 151
environmentalists 69, 109, 144, 151–2
equal opportunities 114, 219
Escobar, A. 26, 238
Escobar, J.S. 51
Ethical Trading Initiative 177
ethics 94, 180
Ethiopia 80, 83, 179
ethnicity 56, 58, 63, 113, 141, 173
ethnographic data 121–3
Etzioni, A. 67–70, 190
Europe 2, 15, 28, 38–9, 47, 51; contexts 51, 54, 61–2; culture 119, 122, 124; development 75, 82; future trends 220; service delivery 152
European Community 118
European Union 64, 77, 82, 93, 152
evaluation 97–8, 131, 148, 156; internal management 198, 200, 208; relationships 168, 170; role 158–62
Evans, P. 89, 176
Evers, A. 70
evolutionary model 108–10
exceptionalism 62
exclusion 61, 64, 84, 91, 94, 106, 131, 142, 214
external control 107
Exxon Valdez 144

facilitators 103, 160, 191
failed states 86, 224
failure 117, 131, 142–3, 158, 185, 191, 205
fair trade 12–14, 177, 179–82, 199, 209, 223
faith-based organizations 11, 40
familism 58, 120
famine 39, 76, 84
farming *see* agriculture
Farrington, J. xii, 7, 93, 95, 154, 240
Fayol, H. 17

feminism 171, 222
Ferguson, A. 54
Ferguson, J. 173
Ferlie, E. 9
Fernando, J. L. 38
fieldwork 122
The Fifth Discipline 115
First World War 39
Fisher, J. 39, 99–100, 206, 229
floods 8, 29, 85
food 7, 39, 60, 85–6, 89, 108, 152, 175
for-profit sector 86, 125, 169, 181–2
Forbes, D. 63
Ford Foundation 177, 182
Ford, J. 180
foreign policy 10, 55, 66, 75, 168
Foreman, K. 227
forestry 152
formality 47–8, 58
Fortune 500 12
Forum of Civil Society 51
Fowler, A. 8, 41, 47, 114, 131, 160, 164, 167,
    176, 198–202, 205–6, 217, 229
Fox, J. 152, 168
France 55, 120
franchise state 142
Frank, A.G. 190
fraud 174
free market 10
free trade 50
free-riding 150
Freeman, J. 23
Freire, P. 40, 51, 90, 135–6, 138, 143, 172, 193
Friedmann, A. 70
Friedmann, J. 18, 91–2, 136
Friendly Societies 48
Friends of the Earth 152
functional accountability 167
fundamentalists 60
funding 10–13, 20–1, 24, 29; accountability
    168–9; advocacy 145–7, 152; business
    177–8, 180–1; capacity building 206, 208;
    competition 117; complexity 229; contexts
    40–1, 43–4, 46–7, 52, 59, 61, 71;
    development 74–8, 80–2, 85, 94–5, 97, 99;
    direct 184; evaluation 158–60; information
    management 118; internal management 191,
    193, 199, 202–4; international agencies
    182–4; life cycles 109; management
    approaches 219; organizational change 211;
    partnership 187; relationships 165; service
    delivery 134, 139, 141–3

funerals 60
future trends 227–8

G8 countries 8, 93
Gandhi, M. 51, 90–1, 135–7, 199
Gardner, K. 25, 40, 122, 237
Gaventa, J. 29–30, 84
Geertz, C. 106
gender 8, 19, 39, 49, 59, 63; culture 113;
    development 78, 81, 83, 91, 93, 97;
    empowerment 137; future trends 219, 222;
    internal management 200, 203;
    organizational culture 114; relationships 171,
    173, 180; service delivery 141, 144, 151
Gender Quality Action-Learning (GQAL) 114
generations theory 49, 100, 104, 108–10, 112,
    145
generic management 217, 219
genetically-modified (GM) food 7, 61, 152
genocide 40
Georgia 64
Ghana 94
Giddens, A. 26
Gioia, D.A. 124, 181
glasnost 64
Gledhill, J. 122
Gleneagles summit 8
Global Accountability Framework 170
global civil society 61–2, 66–7
global governance agenda 10–11
Global Partnership Program for NGO Studies,
    Education and Training 22
globalization 8, 18, 67, 84, 121, 126, 173
goal deflection 139, 142, 168, 183
Goetz, A.M. 114
Gosling, L. 158
governance 53, 194, 196, 199, 202–3, 215
government 1, 8–13, 15, 23, 25; accountability
    168–70; advocacy 143, 146–7, 149, 151–2;
    aid industry 74–8; ambiguity 222–3; capacity
    building 205–6, 208; change 78–80;
    communities 171; complexity 224, 227,
    229; contexts 38–40, 42–3, 46–8, 50–1,
    53–4, 58, 60–1, 64–5, 68–70; culture 113;
    debate 28, 32; development 78; effectiveness
    95–9; empowerment 137–8; evaluation
    158–9; future trends 227–8; innovation
    153–4, 156–7; internal management 195,
    198–200; international agencies 184; life
    cycle 108, 111; management approaches
    217–18, 220; organization theory 105;
    participation 138, 162; partnership 93–5,

185–6; policies 55; relationships 164–5, 167, 172–6; relief 84–5, 87–9; scaling up 161; service delivery 130–4, 140–3
government-organized NGOs (GONGOs) 46, 176–7
governors 29, 167, 194–6, 198
Goyder, G. 220, 240
Grameen Bank 44, 92, 154, 161, 172, 180
Gramsci, A. 54, 59, 66
grants 77, 118
grassroots 10, 26, 46, 56, 66; development 77, 85, 88, 91–3; future trends 229; relationships 172, 184; service delivery 132, 141, 147–9, 152, 161
grassroots support organizations (GSOs) 49
Greek Civil War 39
Greenpeace 66, 152
Greiner, L. 108, 111
grey literature 3
gridlock 61
Grint, K. 17
Groves, L. 78, 224
Guatemala 179
GuideStar 169
Guijt, I. 160, 171
Gulf states 82
Gupta, A. 173
gurus 9, 22, 115, 193

Hailey, J. 111, 192, 198, 205
handicrafts 13
Handy, C. 29, 112, 193
Hanlon, J. 10, 97
Hann, C. 61
Hansmann, H. 142
Hamada, T. 124
harambee movement 52, 132
Harding, P. 160
Harmer, A. 86
Harris, M. 28–9, 194–6
Harvard Business School 67
Harzing, A.-W. 224
Hashemi, S.M. 137, 143
Hassan, M. 143
Hatch, M.J. 105, 107–8, 112–13
Havet, J. 180
headquarters 204, 212
health 38, 50, 55, 57, 60; anthropology 122; business 177; contexts 64; culture 108; development 75, 77, 79, 86, 88,

91; empowerment 136; innovation 154; partnership 94; public 50; service delivery 130–2, 134, 139, 142
Hegel, G.W.F. 54
hegemony 54, 59, 61, 66, 125
Hellinger, S. 168
Heston, A. 38
Hickey, S. 139
hidden agendas 96
high salience policy 93, 151
Highlander Institute 30
Hinton, R. 78, 224
Hirschmann, A. 143–5
historical perspective 4
HIV/AIDS 60, 81, 134, 181
hobby groups 7
Hofstede, G. 119–21
Holcombe, S. 92, 136, 162, 238
hometown associations 52
Honey, R. 52
Homer, L. 114
Hood, C. 117
Horn of Africa 41
hot money 200
housing 48, 64, 132
Howell, J. 63, 222, 229
Howes, M. 172
Hoyer, H. J. 221
Hudock, A. 107
Hudson, M. 155, 193
Hulme, D. 40, 52, 143, 161, 167, 169, 223
human development 25
human resources 119, 141, 179, 200, 208
human rights 4, 7–8, 16, 27; contexts 46, 48, 55, 63, 66; development 79, 82–3, 93, 97; future trends 225, 229; relationships 165; service delivery 140, 144, 151
humanitarian work 8, 10–12, 16; contexts 38, 41, 67; culture 111; development 76–7, 79, 81–2, 86, 98; future trends 229; relationships 169, 183; service delivery 144
Hume, D. 54
hurricanes 29
hybridity 221–4, 229

IBM 119–20
ideology 10–11, 19–22, 27, 29; contexts 39, 52, 67; culture 113–14, 119, 122; debate 32; hybridity 222–3; internal management 191, 193, 206, 211; relationships 176; service delivery 136, 142, 152
Ilchman, W.F. 38

illiteracy 51
impact 99, 118, 131, 140, 146, 149, 152–3, 158–62, 168
impasse 39
impeachment 61
implementation 77, 83, 85, 88–90; culture 104; development 92, 100; internal management 191, 197, 202, 212; relationships 166, 174, 184–5; service delivery 130, 132–3, 135, 138, 143, 145–6, 155, 161
improvisation 218, 223
INDESOL 208
India 44, 46, 51, 55, 84; culture 121; development 93, 99; internal management 199, 202, 205, 215; relationships 164, 174, 177; service delivery 134–6, 144, 155, 157
indicators 81, 118, 159–60, 197, 225
indigenous management 119, 125
individualism 120
Indonesia 179
industrialization 7, 14, 42, 49, 82, 122, 180, 220
information management 118, 213–15
information technology 14, 42, 188, 208, 222, 225, 227
informational economy 214
infrastructure 42, 52, 86, 132, 140, 173
inner-directedness 223
innovation 130–3, 153–8, 162; complexity 225, 229; management approaches 217, 221; relationships 164, 169, 174, 181, 185
innovators 130
Institute of Cultural Affairs 149
Institute of Development Research (IDR) 21
institutional development (ID) 57, 206, 209
institutionalization 109, 134, 146, 148, 157
institutions, definition 206
instrumental participation 138
intellectual property rights 50
Inter-American Foundation 203
interest groups 11, 50, 61
internal management 3, 189–215, 225
International Association for Volunteer Efforts (IAVE) 204
International Campaign to Ban Landmines 144
International Council for Voluntary Agencies (ICVA) 21, 30, 198–9
international development agencies 182–4
International Development Enterprises (IDE) 155

International Federation of Tobacco Workers 50
International Institute for Environment and Development (IIED) 209–10
International Labour Organization (ILO) 50
International Monetary Fund (IMF) 42, 93
International NGO Training and Research Centre (INTRAC) 21, 206, 230
international NGOs (INGOs) 204
International Physicians for the Prevention of Nuclear War 149
international relations 8, 46, 74
internationalization 203–4
Internet 14, 67
involvement 68–9, 135, 138, 143
Iran 8
Iraq 8, 10, 12, 41, 86
Islam 61, 86
isomorphism 210, 227, 229
Italy 58

Jaeger, A.M. 119–20
James, R. 123
jan sunvai 175
Japan 84, 86, 120, 199
Jebb, E. 39
Jenkins, J.C. 92, 145–6, 151
Jenkins, R. 174, 224
job descriptions 194, 196
job security 139
John Hopkins University Nonprofit Research Project 46, 124
Joint Funding Scheme 76
Jones, F.E. 103
Jubilee 2000 campaign 150
Jute Works 13–14

Kaldor, M. 67
Kaimonwitz, D. 89, 156
Kanji, xi, xii, 52, 58, 60, 131, 147, 210, 213, 240
Kanter, R.M. 154
Kanungo, R.N. 119–20
Kaplan, A. 214, 227, 229
Kardam, N. 151
Karim, xii, 60
Kashmir 76
Katalysis 207
Kawashima, N. 86
Kay, R. 194–5, 203
Keane, J. 53
Keck, M. 8
Kelleher, D. 114, 224

Kendall, J. 142
Kenya 52, 61, 63, 65, 131–2, 146–7, 173,179, 187
Kenyan National NGO Council 65
Kenyatta, J. 52, 132
Kerbs, T. 205
Key Terms 3, 6, 37, 73, 102, 129, 163, 189, 216
kingship 62
kinship 52, 58, 63, 111, 180, 203
Knapp, M. 142
Knight, B. 49, 143
knowledge 213–14, 229
Kobe earthquake 84
Koenig, B. 204
Korten, D.C. 20–1, 26, 30, 39, 46, 49, 88–90, 92, 100, 103, 108–9, 112, 115, 120, 134, 139, 141, 145, 159, 184, 217
Korten, F.F. 125
Kothari, U. 138
Kramer, R. 28, 237
Kramsjo, B. 133
Ku Klux Klan 60
Kyoto Protocol 144

labelling 43, 210
labour 50, 52, 69, 137–8, 177–80, 182
land gift movement 91, 136
land rights 147–8
landmines 144, 151
Landry, C. 191
language 123, 149, 192, 204, 223, 229
Lapeyre, F. 84
Laquihon, W. 89, 133
Latin America 1–2, 15–16, 49; contexts 51–3, 61; development 82, 84; internal management 198, 221; relationships 172; service delivery 133, 152
law and order 142
Lawrence of Arabia syndrome 203
Leach, E. 124, 181
leadership 107–14, 116–17, 121; definition 194–5; internal management 199–201, 203–5, 209, 213, 215; relationships 166, 168; service delivery 146, 150
League of Arab States 82
League of Nations 46, 50
learning 3, 105, 115–18, 121; culture 125; internal management 192, 200, 205, 210, 212; organizations 116, 159, 210; relationships 185–6; service delivery 133, 155, 160; understanding 222, 225

Learning Objectives 3, 6, 37, 73, 102, 129, 163, 189, 216
Leat, D. 168
legal systems 80, 132
legitimacy 152
Lehmann, D. 52
leisure 7, 47, 59
Levitt, T. 49, 67–70, 190
Lewis, D. 114, 152, 202
liberal democracy 152
liberalization 41, 75
liberals 40, 54, 59–61, 63, 66, 71, 114, 146
liberation management 197–8
liberation theology 51
life cycles 107–12, 121, 125
Light, P.C. 197
Lindblom, C. 212
Lindenberg, M. 145, 158
linkages 94–5, 99, 116, 119, 156, 167, 185–6, 188, 213
Lipsky, M. 28
listening 136
literacy 64, 109, 179, 181
literature 3, 8–10, 14–17, 28; business 177, 181; capacity building 205; contexts 38, 46–8, 70; culture 107, 113–14, 119, 121; debate 32; development 96, 98; evaluation 158; innovation 154; internal management 196, 198, 202, 215; organizational change 209; organizational development 123; partnership 185; scaling up 161; service delivery 133–4, 139, 143; third sector 195
Little, D. 74–5
lobbying 46, 52, 56, 66, 78; culture 113; development 88, 93, 98; internal management 199; relationships 165, 167, 187; service delivery 144–6, 148, 151, 161
local government 28
Lofredo, G. 237
logging 149
logistics 108
Long, A. 26
Long, N. 26
Lovell, C. 162
low salience policy 93, 151
'Lula', President 43

McClelland, D.C. 120
MacDonald, L. 59, 66
McDonalization 227
McGill, M.E. 191–2
MacKeith, J. 217

Mackintosh, M. 172
McLaren, K. 224
Macrae, J. 86
macro-economics 55, 142, 152, 165
McSweeney, B. 120
Madon, S. 152
Make Poverty History 92–3, 143, 151
Malawi 123, 184
management approaches 217–18; capacity 9;
    concept 17–20; cross-cultural 124, 126;
    culture 103–5; debate 6–33; definitions 18;
    development 24–7; indigenous 119, 125;
    information 118; internal 189–215;
    liberation 197–8; public 9; relationships
    165–70; resource dependency 107; role
    20–4; scientific 106, 124, 181, 197–8;
    strategic 164–6; theory 17; third sector 28–9
management by objectives (MBO) 120, 190,
    192
managerialism 18–19, 21–2, 24, 104, 159,
    193, 196, 215, 224
managerialist organization development (MOD)
    206
Manusher Jonno (MJ) 82, 92, 140
marches 147
Marcos, F. 59, 66, 165
market 7, 10, 14, 29, 40–1; advocacy 146;
    ambiguity 221; anthropology 125; capacity
    building 206; complexity 224; contexts 43,
    46, 54–5, 57, 64, 70–1; culture 117, 119;
    development 75, 92; future trends 229;
    information management 213; innovation
    155; internal management 193, 199–200,
    215; organizational change 211; relationships
    164, 175, 177, 179–80; service delivery
    134, 139, 142–3
marketing 14, 53, 67, 92, 150, 179
Marmara Sea 87
Marsden, D. 159
Martens, K. 51
Martin, J. 124, 181
masculinity 120, 173
Maseko, G. 97
Mass Education movement 109
Mawdsley, E. 186
Maxwell, S. 41
Mazdoor Kisan Shakti Sangathan (MKSS)
    174
McCarthy, J.D. 146, 238
McClelland, D.C. 120
McGill, M.E. 190, 191, 192
McGregor, J.A. xii, 97, 98

McLaren, K. 224
media 11–12, 14, 40, 54; contexts 59;
    development 76, 87; internal management
    208; relationships 165; service delivery 146
mental models 115
mergers 197
Mexico 84, 92, 107, 147, 149, 152, 208
Meyerson, D. 124, 181
Michels, R. 229
Micklethwait, I. 9, 235
Midgley, J. 138
micro-credit 85, 130, 143, 161, 172, 179–80,
    215, 222, 227
middle class 47, 51, 56, 119, 171, 173
military 53, 58, 93
Millenium Development Goals (MDGs) 41,
    81
Mindanao Baptist Rural Life Centre (MBRLC)
    89, 132
mines 12, 61
Minogue, M. 9
Mintzberg, H. 104, 211
mission statements 197
missionaries 38, 40, 44, 51–2, 184, 193
Mitlin, D. 157, 223
modernism 17, 105–6
modernization 25, 39, 44, 52, 120
Mohan, G. 139
monitoring 130, 152, 158, 160, 166, 176, 185,
    193, 207
monitors 130
Monsanto 61, 152, 180
morale 197
Morgan, G. 210
Morgan, T. 114, 210
Morris, S. 48
Morris-Suzuki, T. 15
Moser, C.O. 91, 137
Mozambique 131, 147, 213
Mulhare, E.M. 104
multilateral donors 2, 77, 142, 150, 159, 182,
    206
multinationals 119, 149
multiple perspectives approach 105
munno mukabi 60
music 69
Muslims 229
Mysore Relief and Development Agency
    (MYRADA) 157

Najam, A. 44, 60, 68, 70–1, 130, 143, 174
Narayana, E.A. 199

narcotics control 50
Narmada Dam 93, 144
National Campaign for People's Right to
    Information 175
National Farmers' Association of Zimbabwe
    (NFAZ) 146
National Rifle Association 144
Natsios, A. 10
natural disasters 8, 32, 46, 82, 84–5, 87, 143,
    162
nature 50
Nature Conservancy 149
Neame, A. 71, 83, 134, 156–7, 164, 167
neo-colonialism 10, 98
neo-conservatives 10
neo-liberals 10, 40, 43, 142, 173, 229
Nepal 52, 181
nepotism 111
Nerfin, M. 70
Nestlé 180
The Net 171
Netherlands 182
New Labour 142
New Left 69
New Orleans 8, 29
new policy agenda 40–1, 75, 93, 168, 206
New Poverty Agenda 41
new public management (NPM) 9, 32–3, 42,
    94, 211
New Right 18
Newsweek 11
NGO Guidelines 77
NGO Management 30
NGO Management Newsletter 198
NGO Resource Centre 208
NGOs in Action 3
Nicaragua 66, 83
Nigeria 52, 61, 109, 177
Nike 180
non-distribution constraint 47, 142
non-governmental development organizations
    (NGDOs) 4–5, 7
non-governmental organizations (NGOs)
    advocacy 143–53; business 177–82; civil
    society 53–67; communities 170–2;
    conceptual framework 15–17;
    critics/supporters 10–12; culture 102–26;
    debate 6–33; definitions 46–9, 71;
    development 38–41, 73–101; effectiveness
    95–100; examples 13–15; government
    172–6; histories 49–53; information
    management 213–15; innovation 153–8;

management 20–4, 30–3, 217–18; media
    12; official development 76; organizational
    15, 164, 190, 192, 212

Orange revolution 64
Organization for Economic Cooperation and
    Development (OECD) 42, 75–6, 182
Organization of Rural Associations for Progress
    (ORAP) 22
organizational development (OD) 123, 190,
    206
organizations 3, 105, 115–17, 121; change
    209–13, 215, 221–2; culture 106, 112–15,
    117–21, 157, 181, 200–1, 214; ethnography
    122; learning 125, 133, 155, 160, 192,
    200, 212; theory 103, 105–21, 124–6, 164,
    181, 183
organizers 103
orphans 60
Osborne, S.P. 211
outer-directedness 223
Overseas Development Institute (ODI) 76, 182
Owusu, C. 125
Oxfam 12, 38–9, 66, 81, 83; culture 111;
    development 93; internal management
    207–9; relationships 179, 182; service
    delivery 143, 145

packaging 155
Pakistan 29, 205, 208
Palestine 49, 173
parent-teacher associations 132
Parker, B. 117–19, 121, 192, 229
Parry-Williams, J. 161
participation 130, 135–9, 147; ambiguity 221;
    business 178; complexity 225; evaluation
    159; innovation 155; internal management
    192, 195, 200, 203–4; international agencies
    183; management approaches 219–20;
    nominal 138; observation 122; organizational
    change 209, 211; relationships 170; service
    delivery 150, 162
participatory learning and action (PLA) 32
participatory monitoring and evaluation
    (PM&E) 160
participatory rural appraisal (PRA) 154, 157
partnership 3, 9, 11, 22, 24; advocacy 146–8,
    150; business 177, 179, 182; capacity
    building 205–7; contexts 41–3, 70; culture
    114; debate 28; development 74, 77–81, 83,
    85–6, 88, 93–5, 100; discourse 185–8;
    innovation 154; internal management 200;

international agencies 183–4; management approaches 221; organizational change 210; passive 94–5, 185–6, 188; service delivery 140

paternalism 13, 43, 204, 206

Paton, R. 19, 193

peace 7, 50, 66–7, 109, 150

Pearce, J. 63

peasants 51, 148

Pennertz, P. 180

people-centred development 18, 26, 32, 39, 96

people's organizations (POs) 46, 48, 54, 148

Perera, J. 183

perestroika 64

performance-based partnership 94

Perri 6 154

Perrow, C. 190

person culture 112–13

personnel 31, 43, 137

Peru 47, 56, 61, 133, 152, 162, 215

pesticides 131

Peters, T.J. 210

Petras, J.F. 172

Pettigrew, A.M. 210

Pfeffer, J. 183

philanthropy 38, 170, 177, 179

Philippines 59, 63, 66, 89, 92, 132–3, 147–8, 154, 165

Philippines Caucus of Development NGO Networks (CODE-NGO) 169

Philippines Irrigation Authority (PIA) 125

philosophy 53–4, 90, 92, 96, 99

pilot projects 94, 137, 179

pluralism 40, 53–4, 90, 99, 228–9

Poland 64

Polanyi, K. 180

police 91

policy making 41–3, 67, 109, 151, 171, 190–1

policy process 3, 130, 145, 151, 208

Polidano, C. 32, 205

political economy 59, 121

political parties 57, 59–60, 63, 66, 68, 157

political scientists 53

politics 7–11, 13, 15, 17–19; advocacy 144, 146–7, 149, 152; ambiguity 221, 223; analysis 80; capacity building 207–8; complexity 224, 229; contexts 40–1, 43–4, 49, 51–3, 55–6, 59–63, 66, 69; debate 22, 26–7; development 74, 79, 84, 86, 91–2, 96–7; empowerment 136–8; future trends 227; information management 118; internal management 193, 199, 203; international

agencies 183; life cycle 110; management approaches 219; organizational change 211; organizational development 123; participation 139, 162; relationships 165, 167, 173, 176; service delivery 139–40, 142

Pollitt, C. 19

pollution 149

Poole, N. 140

Portugal 107

positivism 18

postgraduates 15

postmodernism 17, 26, 105–7, 113, 124, 181, 212

poverty 1, 7–9, 11, 14–15; advocacy 143–4, 147–9, 151; ambiguity 223; anthropology 125; business 177, 179; communities 172; complexity 224; contexts 39–41, 44, 47, 51–2, 56, 64; culture 108–9, 126; debate 24, 29; development 74–5, 79–81, 84, 86, 92–4, 96–8; evaluation 158, 161; future trends 228; information management 214; innovation 154, 156–7; internal management 193, 199, 201–2; partnership 187; psychosocial 136; service delivery 130, 140

poverty reduction strategy papers (PRSPs) 41, 58, 79–80, 150

Powell, M. 213–14

Powell, W.W. 210

power 67–8, 80, 90–2, 114, 122; coercive 68; culture 112–13; definition 136; distance 120; empowerment 138; government 176; information management 214; internal management 200; international agencies 184; normative 68; organizational change 209–10, 212; participation 139; partnership 186–7; relationships 171; remunerative 68; service delivery 136, 138, 147, 151, 159

Prem Kumar, N. 134

pressure groups 7, 28

Prison Notebooks 54

private contractors 10, 12

private sector 1, 9, 12–15, 19; advocacy 143; ambiguity 222; complexity 229; contexts 40, 69–70; culture 104–5, 114; debates 23–4, 27, 29, 32; development 80, 88–90, 99; evaluation 158; innovation 155; internal management 190–3; management approaches 218; organizational learning 115; partnership 186; relationships 164, 176–7, 180–1; service delivery 140–2 privatization 10, 32, 40, 55; development 75, 93–4; internal management 213; service delivery 140, 142, 152, 156

privileged members 150

process management 222

process/product data 118

professionalism 29–30, 32, 40; capacity building 208; contexts 44, 49, 51, 56, 69; culture 104–5; future trends 220, 222, 227–8; internal management 196, 198–9, 204; normal 20–1

profit 13, 25, 28–9, 47–8; contexts 57; culture 125; development 86; internal management 223; relationships 177, 179–82; service delivery 136, 140

programme partnership agreements (PPAs) 81

Project Development Institute (PDI) 133, 147–8

project tyranny 78, 138

Projeto Bagagem 178

Pronk, J. 168

Proshika 91, 131, 133

protection rackets 11

PROTERRA 133

protest movements 68

Protestantism 51

psychology 91, 119, 136, 222

public administration 9, 25, 32

Public Administration Review 190

public goods 54, 140–2

public interest 172

public opinion 20

public sector 1–2, 9, 12, 14; capacity building 205; complexity 229; contexts 39, 69; culture 114; debates 19–20, 27, 29, 32; development 79, 83; empowerment 137; evaluation 158; innovation 155; internal management 190–1, 193; management approaches 218–19; partnership 186; relationships 176; service delivery 134, 141

public service contractors (PSCs) 42, 46

Putnam, R.D. 58

Putzel, J. 60

quality control 14

Quinn, J.B. 211

Rabkin, J. 10

race 203, 219

racism 21, 60, 113

radicals 40, 51–2, 54, 59–61; ambiguity 222–3; contexts 63, 66, 70–1; culture 106, 114; development 83, 90, 98; internal management 191, 215; service delivery 135–8

radio 87

Rahnema, M. 138

Rao, A. 114

rational change models 211

rations 175

reciprocity 41, 58, 171, 180

reconstruction 8, 10–11

recreation 4

recycling 181

Red Cross 7, 76, 144, 169

reflexivity 15, 18, 106, 198, 205, 209

regovernmentalization 41

rehabilitation 84–5

Reifner, U. 180

relationships 163–88, 194, 196, 202, 206

relativists 61

religion 28, 38, 44, 52, 58, 60–1, 144

reluctant partners 95, 154

remittances 74

replication 97, 99, 116, 161, 178, 186–8

representative participation 138

Republicans 10

research 14–15, 17, 28, 38; advocacy 146, 149; ambiguity 124; anthropology 122, 124, 126; communities 171; complexity 229; contexts 43, 46–7, 49, 69, 71; culture 114, 120–1; development 83, 88–9, 91; evaluation 158; future trends 229; innovation 154–5, 157; internal management 190, 198–9, 203, 205; international agencies 184; leadership 111–12; life cycles 110; management approaches 218, 221; organizational change 210, 212; partnership 185; service delivery 132, 140; third sector 192–8; traditions 105–7

resistance 59, 61–2, 210, 212

resource brokers 97

Resource Centre for the Social Dimensions of Business Practice 177

resource dependence 107, 125, 183–4

responsive management 107

results-based management 192

reversals 26

reverse agenda 83, 183

Review Questions 3, 33, 72, 101, 126, 162, 188, 215, 229

revolutions 64
Riddell, R.C. 23, 158–60, 183
Rieff, D. 67
Right to Information movement 55, 174–5
rights-based approach 79–80, 83–4, 139
Rio Earth Summit 144, 151
Robbins, S.P. 209
Robinson, M. 41, 89, 158–60
role culture 112
Rose revolution 64
Rowlands, J. 90, 136
rural areas 13–14, 58, 60, 91; culture 119; relationships 171, 174–5; service delivery 132, 140, 148, 154–5
Rural Empowerment through Agrarian/Asset Development (READ) 148
Russia 43, 64, 140, 165
Russian Human Rights Research Centre 165
Rwanda 40

Sahley, C. 24, 206–7
Salamon, L. 7, 47, 142
Salancik, G. 183
sanctions 152, 168–9
Sandinistas 66
Sanyal, B. 143
Sarbanes-Oxley Act 169
Sarvodaya 183, 204
Satark Nagrik Sangathan (SNS) 175
Satish, S.134
Sattar, M.G. 161
Satterthwaite, D. 74
Save the Children Fund (SCF) 39, 81
Savings Development Movement (SDM) 146
scaling up 131, 158–62
scandals 169, 197
scanning 107
Schmidt, R.H. 183
Schon, D. 115
School for International Training (SIT) 22
schools 59–60, 178, 184
scientific management 18, 106, 124, 181, 197–8
Scott Morton, M.S. 225
scrutiny 197
Seattle demonstrations 61, 152
Seckinelgin, H. 134
Second World War 2, 7, 44, 47, 50, 74
sector-wide approaches (SWA) 79
securitization 42, 86
Self-Employed Women's Association (SEWA) 46

self-help 7, 26, 28, 38, 44; contexts 46, 52–3, 57, 60, 71; development 90, 96; internal management 201; relationships 172; service delivery 132
self-organization 17
Selznick, P. 137, 220
Semboja, J. 90, 142
Sen, A. 26
Sen, B. 160
Sen, S. 51
Senge, P.M. 115, 210–11
Senillosa, I. 109–10
September 11 2001 41, 86, 168, 224
service delivery 3, 7, 13; advocacy 130–1, 148–9, 162; ambiguity 222; capacity building 205–7; contexts 41–2, 49, 53, 57, 59, 68, 70; debate 19, 28; development 75, 78, 87–90, 92–3, 95, 99–100; dilemmas 139–43; evaluation 158; government 172; innovation 156; internal management 194, 198, 201, 203; life cycles 109; management approaches 219; means/end 131–43; organizational change 211; partnership 186; relationships 164–5; role 129–62; scaling up 161
service providers 130
service provision 22, 38, 44; ambiguity 223–4; complexity 229; contexts 49, 52, 56, 64; culture 108; development 78, 87–90; internal management 196; international agencies 183; role 140, 142
sex tourism 151
sexual harassment 114
shadow summits 151
Shah, M.K. 171
sharp thinking 117
Shaw, M. 59
shock therapy 64
Shon, D. 115
Sidel, M. 169–70
Sikkink, K. 8
Silveira House 56
Simbi, M. 21, 52
Simukonda, H.P.M. 184
Singapore 120
Siy, R.Y. 125
slavery 46, 49–50, 144
sloping agricultural land technology (SALT) 89, 132, 154
Slovakia 64
slums 175
small is beautiful 161

Smillie, I. 20, 78, 117, 158, 192, 198, 205, 227
Smith, B. 96
Smith, C. 70
Smith, G. 40
Smith, S.R. 28
Smith, W.E. 164
Sobhan, B. 184
social anthropology 121–2
social capital 26, 58–61, 88, 116, 171–2, 202
social construction 106, 114
social contract 56, 142
Social and Economic Development Center (SEDEC) 85
social economy 180
social movement organizations 146
social responsibility 179–80
social sciences 122, 171
social services 28, 59–60, 132, 134
social work theory 135
socialism 64
socially-orientated business 125
Society of Participatory Research in India (PRIA) 22
Sogge, D. 74, 98
Solomon, B.B. 136
soil fertility 89
solar energy 178
Somalia 8, 29, 32, 63, 84, 98
soup kitchens 41
South 7, 14, 16, 21–2, 25; capacity building 207, 209; complexity 225; contexts 38–40, 42, 44, 47, 52, 55; culture 114, 119, 124; debate 28, 31–2; development 75, 77–8, 83, 92, 100; future trends 227, 229; internal management 196, 205; management approaches 221; organizational change 210; partnership 186–7; relationships 180, 182; service delivery 144, 150, 158
South Africa 19, 49, 82, 94, 173, 199, 225
South Asia 1, 16, 32, 51–2; culture 111, 115, 125; development 76, 81, 99; internal management 198, 201, 203, 205; service delivery 154
South East Asia 76
Southern NGOs (SNGOs) 48, 74; ambiguity 223; capacity building 205–7; culture 107, 116, 119; development 78, 92–3, 96; future trends 227, 229; internal management 198, 200, 204–5, 215; international agencies 184; management approaches 221; partnership 185, 187; relationships 168; service delivery 144, 148, 160

sovereignty 98
Soviet bloc 1, 61, 63, 165
special interests 151
Sphere Project 169
sports 4, 47, 69
squatters 53
Sri Lanka 32, 85–6, 183, 204
Sri Lanka Bishop's Task Force 85
Sri Lankan Conference of Catholic Bishops 85
Stacey, R. 17
stakeholders 152, 158–61, 167; future trends 220, 227; internal management 190, 193–4, 198, 200, 214; relationships 170
Starbucks 177, 179–80
Stark Biddle, C. 18–19, 23, 103, 198–9
state 3, 7, 10, 14–15, 19; advocacy 146, 152; ambiguity 125, 223; building 86; contexts 39–40, 42–3, 53–7, 59, 61–2, 64–6, 68, 70–1; debate 24, 28; development 74–5, 79, 86–8, 90, 94, 97–8; empowerment 138; innovation 156; international agencies 182; relationships 164, 167, 172–4, 176; service delivery 130, 132, 134, 140–3
State Food and Civil Supplies Department 175
State Government of Delhi 175
Staudt, K. 26
stereotypes 115
Stern, E. 156
Stewart, S. 9, 30, 220
Stichele, M.V. 180
Stockholm Environment Conference 50
Stocking, B. 12
story-telling 123
strategic accountability 168
strategic management 31, 164–6
strategic planning 104, 116, 192, 200, 207, 211–12, 220
strengthening role 56–7, 63; capacity building 208; culture 104, 126; development 83, 93, 96; internal management 201, 203, 205; relationships 171; service delivery 132, 148
structural adjustment 10, 66, 83, 88, 90, 132, 138, 142
structural change 143–53
structural/operational definition 47–8
student groups 69
sub-Saharan Africa 119
subcontracting see contracting
subcultures 113
Sudan 8, 14, 41, 98
Summers, D. 154
superpowers 40, 53

supporters 10–12
Supreme Court on Food Security 175
sustainability 56, 64, 75, 78; advocacy 144–5;
    business 178, 180–2; capacity building
    205–6; communities 172; culture 108, 114;
    development 84, 89–90, 93, 97–100;
    empowerment 137; future trends 227;
    innovation 155, 157; internal management
    194, 200, 202; international agencies 184;
    partnership 185–6; relationships 170, 174;
    service delivery 131, 134–5, 141
Suzuki, N. 199, 202, 205
Sweden 75, 184
Swedish Agency for International Development
    (SIDA) 76, 184
Switzerland 182
symbolic management 107
symbolic-interpretative tradition 105–6, 113
synergy 9, 14, 89, 134, 167, 176, 185
Szabo, S. 204

El Taller 22
Tandon, R. 56, 202–3
Tandon, Y. 10, 49
Tanzania 173
targets 41–2, 81, 88, 118, 151, 185, 197, 224
tariffs 50
task culture 112–13
Tassie, B. 211–13
Tata Foundation 177
tax offices 112
taxation 142, 200
Tayeb, M.H. 121
Taylor, F.W. 17, 106, 197
technical assistance 207
technological change 213
technology transfer 58, 123
Technoserve 213
Tembo, T. 8
Temple, D. 40
Tendler, J. 23, 97–8, 134, 176, 229
Tennessee Valley Authority 137, 220
tent-cities 87
terminology 4–5, 43–6
terrorism 12, 42, 86
textiles 92
Thailand 94, 107, 184
Thatcher, M. 142
Themudo, N. 67, 107, 225
There Is No Alternative (TINA) 18
Therkildsen, O. 90, 142
Thiele, G. 174

think tanks 10
third sector 1, 3–4, 7, 14; accountability
    168–9; advocacy 149; ambiguity 124–5,
    222, 224; anthropology 121–2; business
    177; civil society 67–70; complexity 227;
    contexts 38, 43–4, 46–9, 52–3, 61, 63, 71;
    culture 103, 107, 112–13, 119; debates
    19–20, 22–3, 25–7, 30; development 74,
    83, 86; future trends 229; innovation 156;
    internal management 191–2, 194–8, 202,
    215; international agencies 182; learning
    117; management 28–9, 190, 218–20;
    organizational change 209, 211–12;
    organizational development 124;
    organizational theory 105; relationships 167;
    research 192–8; service delivery 132, 134–5,
    142–3
Third World 29, 98, 100, 151
Thom, G. xii, 21, 52
Thomas, A. 26–7, 91, 136–7
tokenism 138
top-down approach 18, 25, 27; accountability
    169; advocacy 148; ambiguity 222; contexts
    64; culture 103–5, 116; debate 30–1;
    development 93, 97–8; evaluation 159;
    management 125; organizational change
    211, 213; planning 52; service delivery
    137–8
total quality management (TQM) 192
tourism 85, 151, 177–8
trade 8, 25, 50, 84, 92–3; culture 125; internal
    management 199, 208, 218, 221, 223–4;
    relationships 177, 179–82; service delivery
    144, 150, 152
trade unions 19, 28, 59, 61; contexts 63, 66;
    culture 112; development 81; relationships
    177; service delivery 150
traditionalism 120
training 19, 22, 56, 80, 85; culture 121, 123;
    development 88–9; future trends 217;
    internal management 191, 196, 205–8;
    relationships 172, 179; service delivery
    132–3, 137, 141, 157
transaction costs 80–2, 94, 96
Transform Africa 208
Transform Programme 208
transformative participation 138
transparency 80, 93, 169–70, 174, 197, 208,
    210
transportation 50, 85, 149
tropics 123
trustees 114, 145, 167

tsunami 76, 85–6
Tunisia 22
Turkey 86–7
Turner, M. 40
Tvedt, T. 100
tyranny 138

Udoh James, V. 9
Uganda 19, 58–60, 80, 117, 132, 199, 214, 225
Uggla, F. 7, 53
Ukraine 43, 64
Umeh, O.J. 205
uncertainty-avoidance 120
uncivil society 61
underdevelopment 25
unemployment 53
UNESCO 50
United Kingdom (UK) 2, 12, 15; advocacy 149; business 177, 180–1; capacity building 207; complexity 229; contexts 40, 43, 46, 48–50, 52, 55; culture 107, 110, 120–2, 125; debates 19, 21–2, 28–9; development 74–6, 81, 93; innovation 155–6; internal management 191, 194–6; international agencies 182; organizational change 211; partnership 185; service delivery 134, 142–3
United Nations Conference on Environment and Development (UNCED) 51
United Nations Development Programme (UNDP) 26
United Nations Economic and Social Council (ECOSOC) 50
United Nations (UN) 7, 44; Charter 46, 50; contexts 48, 51; Convention on the Rights of the Child 51, 144; development 74, 81–2, 93; future trends 229; internal management 204; relationships 165; service delivery 144, 151; World Conference on Human Rights 79
United States Agency for International Development (USAID) 2, 10, 44, 55, 58, 74, 97
United States (US) 10, 12, 15; advocacy 144–5, 149, 151–2; ambiguity 222; business 177; capacity building 207; complexity 224, 229; contexts 39–40, 43–4, 50, 54, 58, 60–1, 63, 66–9; culture 103–4, 109, 113, 116, 119–22; debates 21–3, 28, 30, 33; development 76, 84, 86, 90, 92; future trends 227;

innovation 154, 157; internal management 190, 192, 197, 199, 204; management approaches 220; scandals 169; service delivery 136, 139, 142–3; third sector 193, 195
universalism 61–2
universities 59, 81, 157, 167, 178
urbanization 13, 61, 64, 119
user fees 94
Uvin, P. 161
Uzbekistan 61

Vakil, A. 46–8, 71
Valdez principles 144
value judgements 25
values 18–20, 27, 29, 40–1; ambiguity 221, 223; anthropology 124–6; complexity 229; contexts 43, 46, 54, 57, 63–5, 68, 70; culture 103, 107, 113–14, 119–21; development 80, 88–90; empowerment 136; future trends 227, 229; internal management 193–4, 200, 204, 215; learning 116; management approaches 218; organizational change 210–13; organizational development 124; service delivery 134
Van Rooy, A. 54, 63, 151–2, 182
Velloso de Santisteban, A. 41
vested interests 97–8, 137
Vetwork UK 14
Victorians 48
violence 11, 32, 63, 133, 137, 224
virtual organizations 14
Vivian, J. 97, 157
voluntarism 29, 32, 47–9; ambiguity 221; contexts 51–3, 70; development 74; internal management 193, 198; life cycles 109; service delivery 134, 154, 156
Voluntary Agencies Development Assistance (VADA) 146
voluntary organizations (VOs) contexts 38, 43–4, 46, 59, 68; culture 122; debate 14–15; internal management 193, 195; service delivery 134
voluntary sector contexts 52; culture 107; debates 19, 22–3, 28; future trends 220; innovation 155–6; internal management 194; service delivery 142–3
Voluntary Service Overseas (VSO) 81
volunteering 76, 85, 96, 109, 178, 182, 194, 196, 215
voters 55, 140

Wallace, T. 19, 114, 199, 214, 221, 229
'war on terror' 12, 86, 168, 224, 229
war on waste 197
wars 8
waste 197
watchdogs 10
watchful eye 197–8
water 86, 125, 177
Waterman, R.H. 111, 124, 181
Watson, H. 89, 133
Weber, M. 70, 106–7, 124, 190–1, 199
websites 4, 10, 22, 62, 169, 178, 208, 230–1
Weick, K.E. 211
Weisbrod, B. 142
welfare 7, 27–8, 30, 38, 40; advocacy 152;
    contexts 44, 49, 53, 56, 59–60, 64, 70;
    culture 108; development 86, 100;
    innovation 156; internal management 200–1;
    service delivery 134
West Africa 31, 38, 107
whistleblowers 169
White, G. 89
White Paper on International Development 40
White, S. 138
Williams, S. 158, 241
women 23, 52, 54, 60, 66; contexts 69;
    culture 109, 114; development 74, 85,
    91–2; hybridity 222; relationships 171, 175,
    180; service delivery 133, 136, 144, 151
Wood, G.D. 63, 111, 133, 142

Wooldridge, A. 9, 235
Wooton, L.M. 191–2
workers see labour
World Bank 2, 26, 42, 59, 74; culture 114;
    development 77, 79, 83, 87–8, 93–4, 96;
    relationships 182; service delivery 151–2
World Congress of International Associations
    50
World Development Movement 46
World Food Conference 151
World Health Organization (WHO) 50
World Neighbors 157
world theory 194
World Trade Organization (WTO) 61, 152
World University Service 208
World War Two see Second World War
Wright, D. 183
Wright, S. 124
Wuthnow, R. 70

Yen, J. 109
Young, D. 149
Yugoslavia 41

Zadek, S. 180, 204
Zald, M.N. 146, 238
Zambia 61, 132
Zeitinger, C.P. 183
Zimbabwe 22, 56, 132, 146, 156, 165, 173
Zwi, A. 67